THERE IS NOTHING FOR YOU HERE

FIONA HILL

THERE IS NOTHING FOR YOU HERE

FINDING OPPORTUNITY IN THE TWENTY-FIRST CENTURY

MARINER BOOKS

An Imprint of HarperCollins*Publishers*

Boston   New York

Library of Congress Cataloging-in-Publication Data is available.
ISBN 978-0-358-57431-6
ISBN 978-0-358-57424-8 (ebook)

Portions of Chapter 13 were originally published in slightly different form in *Politico*.

Book design by Emily Snyder

Printed in the United States of America
2 2021
4500839454

For Alf and June

CONTENTS

Prologue: The "Improbable" Fiona Hill   1

Introduction: From the Coal House to the White House   7

PART ONE: THE COAL HOUSE

1. "Call the United Nations"   17

2. Grasping at the Future   36

3. Out of Your League   45

4. Common Northerner   69

PART TWO: A DIVIDED HOUSE

5. The Land of Opportunity   93

6. Shock Therapy   117

7. Women's Work   135

8. Unlucky Generations   148

PART THREE: THE WHITE HOUSE

9. Me the People   169

10. "Russia Bitch"   191

11. The Price of Populism   218

12. Off with Their Heads   239

13. The Horrible Year   264

PART FOUR: OUR HOUSE

14. The Great Reckoning   285

15. No More Forgotten People   305

16. No More Forgotten Places   329

Conclusion   352

Afterword: Creating Opportunity in the
Twenty-First Century   357

Acknowledgments   362

Notes   371

Index   401

THERE IS NOTHING FOR YOU HERE

PROLOGUE

The "Improbable" Fiona Hill

On November 21, 2019, I walked through the door of Room 1100 of the Longworth Office Building in Washington, D.C., to appear before the House Intelligence Committee. I was there to give public testimony to the United States Congress as one of the two final fact witnesses in the hearings that preceded the first Senate impeachment trial of President Donald Trump in January 2020. I did not know it yet, but my personal and professional lives were about to collide in front of millions of TV viewers around the world.

I had spent the previous few days huddled with my longtime friend and more recent legal counsel, Lee Wolosky, and two of his colleagues, Molly Levinson and Sam Ungar, preparing for my appearance — reviewing all the other witness depositions and the format so I would know what to expect. Lee and Molly knew the congressional hearing room well. It was cavernous and notoriously chilled. The air conditioning was cranked up and the temperature set low to accommodate congress*men* in their layers of undershirts, dress shirts, and suit jackets so there would be no risk of sweaty armpits and brows beaded with perspiration.

Molly warned me that, as a more lightly dressed woman, I risked freezing. She described the phalanx of photographers and the TV cameras that would track my every move and facial expression and stressed that I would be scrutinized for the signals these inadvertently sent. I would be judged by my appearance: "You will be in the fashion section of the *Washington Post*," she predicted. "You need to minimize the distractions — you want everyone to listen to what you are saying and not fixate on what you're wearing or what you're doing with your hands and face." She had me practice pushing the balls of my feet into the floor to stop myself from shivering from the cold — or a combination of the cold and inevitable nerves. "This will help channel the energy out," she said, "*and* keep your teeth from chattering."

Molly told me that she would set me up with a stylist to fix my hair and face in place before the testimony, and she sent me on an expedition into my wardrobe to find an appropriate suit and accessories (if I had them). In some ways this was a familiar exercise for me. As a graduate student at Harvard University, I had traded in my ripped jeans and Doc Martens for simple business attire, after being counseled by older women that certain opportunities would be closed to me until I began to dress the part that I wanted to play in life. I thought about that advice, and about the road I had taken since, as I embarked upon this very different sartorial exercise.

I was given a list of items and instructed to lay out whatever I had in those categories on the floor and send Molly pictures. She settled on a dark blue suit and white top that I had fortuitously purchased in a sale, killing time shopping with my elderly mother while my daughter had braces fitted in October. (My mother had suddenly yelled across the store, which was next door to the orthodontist's, "Hey, Fiona, there are some suits on sale over here — might you need one for that impeachment thingy you're doing?" I had sprinted over to hush her up, but as it happened, I did.) Molly also selected a pair of innocuous black pumps that I almost never wore and a simple gold-plated chain and bracelet and watch that would not draw attention. She reminded me to wear a pair of panty hose to cover up the goose bumps.

This all seemed a bit over the top, and as someone who barely owned any makeup beyond some face powder and an eye pencil, I was initially taken aback and somewhat awed by the extreme prime-time makeover that came at the skilled hands of former American First Lady Michelle Obama's one-time stylist. But Molly was right! For a woman in the spotlight, the self-presentation was ultimately as important as the substantive preparation of reading all the other depositions and watching the witnesses' testimony as Sam took notes on the key points.

At the end of the day, as I wrapped up my testimony alongside David Holmes from the U.S. embassy in Ukraine, the *Washington Post*'s fashion critic gave us her verdict: "Their testimony was pointed. Their clothes were reassuringly dull." Friends complimented me on my hair and makeup.

Molly's mission, at least, was accomplished. I had struggled against sexism throughout my professional life, in a seemingly unending effort to realize my potential and do my job effectively despite the difficulties that somehow seemed intrinsic to being female. Nonetheless, I would never have thought that I would need to worry about my gender being a liability for me — and for the country — at such a critical moment. Yet there I was.

My moment in the global spotlight came almost exactly thirty years after I left my home in Bishop Auckland, County Durham, in the North East of England to embark on a scholarship to Harvard. Since first setting foot in the U.S., in 1989, I had spent three decades establishing myself as a policy expert on Russia. This led to two stints in the U.S. government under three different presidents: George W. Bush, Barack Obama, and Donald Trump.

The congressional hearings and the impeachment trial of 2019–2020 marked the culmination of decades of political polarization in the United States and several years of bitter partisan battles triggered by the contentious 2016 presidential race. They also represented a triumph for Russian president Vladimir Putin, who unleashed the Russian security services to intervene in the 2016 election.

I came into the government in early 2017 to deal with the national security consequences of this intervention. I anticipated a job behind the scenes at the National Security Council (NSC), mitigating the damage Russian operatives had done and heading off future interference. By the end of 2019, I was center stage, embroiled in partisan politics. This first impeachment trial focused on a July 25, 2019, telephone conversation between President Trump and President Zelensky of Ukraine. In the call, President Trump asked his Ukrainian counterpart to investigate former U.S. vice president Joe Biden, who would run against Trump in the 2020 presidential election. Ukraine was in my official portfolio. For the first time in my professional life, I became "the story." I had to prepare an opening statement for the members of Congress to explain who I was and why I was there to answer their questions.

The impeachment of a president was a historic moment. This meant that whether I liked it or not, I was part of history. Several friends texted me to point this out. As an academically trained historian, I found the personal aspect unsettling, but history is written from the raw material of moments like this. Today's media headlines telegraphing the significance of a current event become tomorrow's footnotes in formal historical analysis. The life experiences of individuals who find themselves in the spotlight, by choice or by chance, shape their country's written history. It is based on the stories we tell ourselves about what just happened, who we are, and where we come from. Life experience influences the choices people make and the actions they take. This is why so many personal stories inspire biographies. I wrote a quasi-biography of Vladimir Putin — more of a psychological portrait — to try to explain how key aspects of his life story shaped his worldview and motivated his actions as Russian president. I wrote *this* book, in part, because I was acutely aware of how my own early life laid the path for everything I did subsequently — even my decision to appear before Congress and my earlier choice to enter public service.

In some respects my personal story is an improbable one. I started life in the North East of England as a coal miner's daughter. In the United States, I became a White House adviser on Russia and Europe. I was the first person in my immediate family to go to college. Thanks to a combination of timing, chance encounters, and larger events, I found my way to a career in think tanks and the corridors of power. I came from a distinct economic and political geography in my homeland. My family was neither affluent nor intellectually accomplished. I came to the United States to escape poverty and class discrimination. My life experiences, long before I ended up in the Trump White House, had opened my eyes to the dangerous consequences of economic disruption and social dislocation. In the United Kingdom, my family experienced the overwhelming sense of economic precariousness and political disenfranchisement that also beset millions of people in the U.S. over the generations stretching from the 1960s to 2020. As a result, I had a story to tell.

For a policy professional like me, telling personal stories is an essential way of connecting the vast majority of people, who don't spend their time fixated on foreign affairs, to bigger issues. Stories help explain the complex dynamics behind national security dilemmas and political developments. If people can personally relate to the story, if what you have to say resonates with them, they take away some of the facts and ideas you have conveyed. You provide authenticity, not abstraction.

I learned this intellectually during my university studies, but I only really, truly appreciated it when I applied this technique to my congressional testimony and put myself and my family in the opening statement. Indeed, the personal part of my November 2019 congressional testimony generated particular interest in the United Kingdom as well as the United States. The attention took me entirely by surprise. Long-lost relatives and friends, not quite recovered from the shock of seeing "our Fiona" being interrogated by Congress, got in touch. My face was all over the nightly news and the front page of every major international newspaper.

In the United States, I trended on Twitter. I was the subject of memes on the internet. I even featured in a series of *Bloom County* comic strips by the celebrated American cartoonist Berkeley Breathed, wielding an ax to enforce the return of long-overdue library books. Enterprising people put my image on T-shirts and, most weirdly, on a collection of semi-religious votive candles. Over the next several weeks and months, I received hundreds of postcards and letters from across America in reaction to my statement. Some writers wanted to know how I had done it — both my congressional testimony and my career journey. Others wanted to share their own hardscrabble success stories. Many American writers bemoaned the bitter and fractured politics that paved the way to impeaching President Trump. Some thanked me and my fellow witnesses for our public service. Several letters were deeply thoughtful. They offered ideas on how America might overcome its political divisions and the pervasive sense of political alienation. A few contained small gifts — pictures and mementos. Most writers urged me to share more of my life story publicly.

Across the Atlantic, British newspaper columnists homed in on the assertion in my opening statement that my working-class background and northern English accent limited my professional prospects in the United Kingdom. They pondered the persistence of class and accent discrimination in England and the barriers they posed to career advancement. Somewhat bizarrely, they compared my unlikely professional trajectory to that of British prime minister Boris Johnson, the privileged and plummy-accented product of Eton and Oxford.

I was suddenly the "improbable" Fiona Hill (as the *Financial Times* put it six months later in a June 2020 feature). The newspaper articles, the comments that accompanied them online, subsequent letters to the editor, and personal letters sent directly to me posed a series of questions: Was it true that my background had held me back in the UK in the 1980s? Would it still hold me back four decades later? What did my accent say about who I was, where I was from, and what I should be? If my trajectory was so improbable, then how on earth had I made it from my obscure hometown, Bishop Auckland, to work in the White House? If I had managed to do something like this, could others have similar opportunities? Or was I just a fluke?

This book is a response to those letters and questions. They provided the impetus to interlink my personal storyline with larger political events to explain the origins and nature of America's current crisis and try to offer solutions. Above all else, the book clarifies just how improbable my journey is today — or rather, *why* it is so improbable. Because in hindsight, I *am* a fluke. My story is the exception that proves the rule of class or socioeconomic *im*mobility in the early twenty-first century.

This is a rule that we desperately need to change. The constraints on mobility in America today form the core of our country's ongoing crisis, as do a similar set of problems in the United Kingdom. They mirror challenges that have dogged our historic adversary, Russia, for decades. And unless we figure out a way to solve them, Russia's fate and its slide into authoritarianism since 2000 could well be our own.

INTRODUCTION

From the Coal House to the White House

I was born in 1965 and grew up poor as the daughter of a former coal miner in the United Kingdom's equivalent of America's Rust Belt, the North East of England. In the 1980s, during the period when Margaret Thatcher was Britain's prime minister, we were the pioneers for a unique form of social and economic malaise — a decline from the heyday of the industrial era that would come to define the entire developed world. The local mines closed, along with associated manufacturing industries. Businesses were shuttered, communities gutted. Family and friends lost their way of life. Bishop Auckland, my once-prosperous hometown, was a forgotten place.

In 1984, the year I completed school, the North East of England was in a state of terminal decay. It was wracked by brutal unemployment and poverty. Almost 20 percent of the local population was registered unemployed. Others were in poorly paid jobs, barely making ends meet. Real unemployment was far higher than the recorded rate. In the North East, many women were in fact never formally in the workforce, so they weren't captured in the statistics. As is usually the case, macro-level aggregate figures masked individuals' daily realities at the micro level. The data concealed the impact of the economic changes on actual people.

The prospects for school leavers (high school graduates) like myself were especially grim. All the jobs had moved somewhere else in the country. There were few local opportunities for further education. In the mid-1980s, only 10 percent of people had something lined up when they left school. Youth unemployment was a full-blown national crisis.

8   THERE IS NOTHING FOR YOU HERE

Faced with the prospect that his daughter might end up even worse off than he was, my father told me to get out — to go to London, or Europe, or America. "There's nothing for you here, pet," he said.

Through hard work, luck, and government support, I managed to go farther than my dad could ever have imagined. I studied at St. Andrews University in Scotland, then in Moscow in the late 1980s. I made it across the Atlantic, to America's northeast corridor and Harvard University, in 1989, just as the Cold War ended, and eventually became an American citizen. Education was my route out of poverty and the door to opportunity.

My personal story is a testament to the power of social, economic, and geographic mobility. My journey through different time periods and countries also helps to explain how we got to our current moment. When I began my career as a historian at St. Andrews, I realized that my family were active participants in British and European socioeconomic history. At Harvard, when I took additional courses in political economy and began to familiarize myself with America's postindustrial plight, I discovered that I was a real-time study in mobility — both downward and upward. What was abstract in the lectures and textbooks was my family's actual life. We were living data points.

In the 1970s and 1980s, when I was growing up in Bishop Auckland, we faced the consequences of multigenerational poverty engendered by the rise and fall of the British coal industry and the fallout from the "modernization" of the British manufacturing sector. Over a thirty-year period, as the result of government fiat, industrial manufacturing in the United Kingdom shrank by more than two thirds. This amounted to the largest deindustrialization of any advanced Western country. The deliberate destruction of the UK's heavy industry in the 1980s cast a shadow over British politics for the next four decades.

In the 1990s and early 2000s, I spent years traveling on extended research trips to Russia. I became a long-standing fellow at the Brookings Institution in Washington, D.C., in its foreign policy program. I served in the U.S. government as the top intelligence officer for Russia on the National Intelligence Council (NIC) under George W. Bush and Barack Obama. Then I joined the National Security Council at the White House in the aftermath of Russia's attempts to interfere in the 2016 U.S. presidential election. I served as deputy assistant to the president and senior director for European and Russian affairs under Donald Trump from 2017 to 2019.

All along the way, from the late 1980s to the 2020s, in the heartlands of both Russia and the United States, I saw grim reflections of the decline of my hometown and my family's experiences in the United Kingdom, and I watched similar populist impulses emerge in the politics of all three countries. The opportunities that enabled me, literally as well as metaphorically, to go "from the coal house to the White House" seemed to vanish for later generations. In recent decades America and Britain, two close allies, have offered a depressing reflection of each other's struggles and failings.

In the United States, the gap between those on the lower rungs of the economic ladder and those on the top, in terms of their economic and social circumstances and life opportunities, widened dramatically between 2000 and 2020. Nowhere is this more apparent than in unequal access to education. Manufacturing jobs that were once widely available for Americans without a two- or four-year college degree were decimated over the course of twenty years. This intensified the United States' political divides. Educational attainment is now a significant predictor of whether someone will have the opportunity to secure stable full-time employment and, crucially, how that person will vote. Geography has become a similar determinant. The places people live, either in a major, more affluent, and densely populated urban area or in a rural region or small town, affect their life prospects and political preferences.

But increasingly, even getting a higher education or moving to a place with more opportunity isn't enough. In a fast-changing economy with diminished government support for the education system, it is all too easy for college graduates to find themselves out of a job, burdened by debt, and off the clear path to a brighter future. College graduates in the twenty-first century can feel just as forgotten as everyone else. And as the sense of hopelessness spreads, so does the anger — and the potential for people's fears and frustrations to explode into the political arena, with disastrous consequences.

The United States today, like many other countries around the world, is beset by an ongoing democratic crisis — one preceded and precipitated by this decades-long series of hidden-in-plain-sight events. Like other ailing polities, America is marred by low societal cohesion, political fragmentation, loss of public trust in government, weakened national institutions, and reduced civic engagement. It is also geographically polarized into areas of haves and have-nots. "Forgotten places" blighted by postindustrial decline, like the "flyover states" of the Midwest and Pennsylvania's Lehigh Valley, offer a stark contrast to hubs of innovation and opportunity like the northeast corridor and the Bay Area. Even within cities the uneven allocation of opportunity is becoming more pronounced.

Our health and politics show the effects of this profound imbalance. America is a rich country where millions of people have become so desperate and starved of opportunity, and others so disillusioned with the existing system of government, that they cling to whatever populist messages political leaders serve them, no matter how absurd or harmful.

Postindustrial decline in the United States began with global economic and technological shifts away from large-scale heavy and extractive industry in the 1980s under the presidency of Ronald Reagan. Over the next four decades, this affected some localities far more than others. It hollowed out towns and communities in specific regions through the steady loss of employment and educational and other opportunities. Economic or spatial inequality (the term economists and geographers use for geographic economic disparities) in the United States was further exacerbated by the Great Recession of 2008–2010. In combination with demographic, social, and cultural shifts, the economic downturn facilitated an upsurge of populism in America's politics, culminating in the contentious 2016 election campaign and the selection of Donald Trump, an outsider, "wild card" candidate, as president. Trump's presidency took a dark turn, resulting in two congressional impeachment trials, in 2019 and 2021. The second followed the unprecedented events of January 6, 2021, when a mob of Trump's supporters stormed the Capitol Building as he attempted to stay in power despite having lost the November 2020 election.

The cause and effect of the decline of industry, the crisis of opportunity, and the rise of populist politics across the decades are reflected in the chronology and events of my personal story, which I relate throughout this book. I was a participant in the social history of the period and a witness to its political history. My life and career were directly shaped by the defining challenges of our time.

The example of modern Russia, which I have spent most of my career closely studying, offers a cautionary tale for the United States at this juncture. Russia is America's Ghost of Christmas Future, a harbinger of things to come if we can't adjust course and heal our political polarization. In the late 1980s and 1990s, Russia entered a promising period of democratization that was ultimately weakened by political upheavals and attempted coups, overwhelmed by economic crisis, and undermined by declining opportunity. Vladimir Putin was the first populist president of a major country in the twenty-first century. He came into the presidency at the end of 1999 promising to make Russia a great power again, blazing a restorationist political trail at home and abroad. Putin set a personalized, bravura style of leadership that others, including Donald Trump, sought to emulate. And over the next two decades Putin rolled back Russia's democratic gains to firmly entrench himself in the Kremlin. First he served as president, then as prime minister, and then as president again. Each time he made adjustments to Russia's political system, until finally, in 2020, he amended the constitution. In theory, Vladimir Putin can now stay in power until 2036. Under the guise of Putin strengthening the state and restoring its global position, Russia slowly succumbed to authoritarianism.

Russia's fate over a twenty-year period shows how a country's political path can turn away from democracy toward autocracy. No state, no matter how advanced, is immune from flawed leadership, the erosion of political checks and balances, and the degradation of its institutions. Democracy is not self-repairing. It requires constant attention and renewal, especially during periods of rapid technological and social change and economic uncertainty.

I have seen firsthand just how vulnerable America is to the political afflictions that have befallen Russia. In the second half of this book I offer an account of my own experiences of populist politics in action inside the Trump administration. I share what I learned from this and my observations of how Donald Trump began to follow "the authoritarians' playbook" scripted by Vladimir Putin and other "strongman" leaders. By November 2019, when I was subpoenaed as a fact witness in the first impeachment trial of President Trump and found myself in the international spotlight, I knew that America had embarked on an authoritarian swing of its own. When the global coronavirus pandemic hit, the U.S. teetered on the verge of a system failure. We needed to address our opportunity crisis and pull ourselves back from the brink.

I cover a lot of ground in this book, and a great many interrelated topics. But if there is one message that I hope to convey more forcefully than any other, it is that opportunity does not materialize from thin air and no one does anything alone. Barriers to opportunity and social mobility are personal and universal. Any individual success is a team or collective effort. Delivering greater opportunity for America in the future will be the product of hard work on multiple levels. The federal government, states, local communities, schools, colleges, companies, families, and personal and professional networks all help form the infrastructure of opportunity. When opportunity vanishes, it is because this infrastructure has eroded or even failed.

Back in my personal dystopia of the North East of England in the 1980s, the main obstacles to opportunity were spatial and structural. They were the product of geographically concentrated postindustrial decline, deep-rooted multigenerational poverty, and regional biases and social discrimination based on class and accent. When I moved to the United States, I encountered the classic glass-ceiling issues of sexism and gender and wage discrimination. On the other hand, I discovered that being white in America canceled out some of the impediments to educational and employment opportunity posed by being low-income working class in the North East of England. Race is a deeply embedded, all-pervasive structural barrier to opportunity in the United States. The class distinctions I navigated in the United Kingdom were subsumed, if not completely erased, by race in America. In this case, I was an active observer of how racial discrimination played out in the U.S. for friends and colleagues. I was not on the receiving end of this type of prejudice.

In the North East of England, I overcame the inherent impediments to opportunity with help from national and regional government assistance programs that were initiated after World War II. The people who formed my network of contacts in my local community played an important part in my social mobility. Family members, friends, schoolteachers, university professors and administrators, and professional mentors helped me find scholarships and jobs and generally pointed me in the right direction. It was the same once I came to the United States. I benefited from educational scholarships at Harvard University, and people went out of their way to advise and assist me. I learned that everyone can play a role in eliminating the barriers that hold people back by volunteering, mentoring, and donating time and money wherever and however they can.

The disintegration of the Soviet Union is certainly the specter of a grim future that could lie ahead for the United States, but it also provides some ideas of how to address our opportunity crisis. After I came to America, I spent the decades after 1989 looking at Russia's attempts to rebuild its economy and regenerate its cities after the collapse of the USSR. At Harvard University and the Brookings Institution, I studied what worked, or did not, in Russia and several countries of the former Eastern bloc as they tried to move from central planning to a market economy. For many years I helped the Eurasia Foundation and other U.S.-based and international technical assistance projects scope out programs to redevelop regions in the former USSR. These programs helped populations acquire new skills and create local job opportunities through training workshops, small business development schemes, and venture capital investment funds that were specifically tailored to local conditions. The lessons from all these programs were that individual, group, grassroots, philanthropic, and private-sector actions were just as critical in putting communities on a new path as any top-down government intervention or large-scale transfer of funds.

Even before the COVID-19 pandemic, it was clear to many of the economists I worked with that the United States faced its own reconstruction challenge. Thanks to rapid deindustrialization, poor-quality education, and other indices of poverty and inequality, parts of the United States were in the same need of regeneration and redevelopment as low- and middle-income countries in the former Eastern bloc. Like Russia, the United States is a vast continent-sized power. Individual states are the size of most European countries. For anyone traveling across America, the socioeconomic as well as the geographic and demographic diversity is inescapable. What all this means is that, on the national level, it will require a major policy effort to create the kind of comprehensive antipoverty, education reform, and jobs-creation programs for the United States to succeed in creating a new infrastructure of opportunity for all Americans in the twenty-first century. One-off initiatives and temporary interventions are insufficient. The problems the U.S. faces in the 2020s have festered since the 1980s, so whatever we do will take time — certainly a generation or more to achieve measurable outcomes. Yet there are things that each of us can do today to ensure that the America of the future delivers better outcomes for its people than the America of the present.

In many respects the United States has wasted human capital on an enormous scale over the last forty years by constraining social mobility for millions of people. Ultimately, the United States is only as good as the quality of its population, in terms of its general health and well-being and educational attainment. People, individually and collectively, form the core of America's institutions and drive innovation, yet too often they are an afterthought in our national conversations and our leaders' policy decisions.

Absent sustained individual commitment alongside large-scale intervention, America's crisis of opportunity will continue. It will keep on empowering the political extremes and reinforcing the polarizing appeal of populist politicians. It will make the traumas of the four years from 2016 to 2020 seem like a preface, rather than a postscript, to the United States' democratic demise.

Donald Trump's presidency was both a product and a symptom of the set of complex problems intertwined beneath the surface of our polity. If we fail to fix our ailing society by not addressing them and providing opportunity for all, another American president, just like Vladimir Putin, might decide to stay in power indefinitely. And the next insurrectionary force that invades the U.S. Capitol Building might be better prepared than the January 6, 2021, mob. They might just manage to hold it.

PART I
THE COAL HOUSE

1

"Call the United Nations"

It wasn't until the late 1970s, when I was thirteen, that I became aware that there was a working class and that I was in it.

I was on a school exchange to Tübingen, Germany, sponsored by the education authority of my regional government, Durham County Council. With only one exception, the other students were not from my school or town. In our first encounters, many of them grilled me with a set of three questions that would follow me from childhood to adulthood, all in the following order:

1. "So, where are you from, then?"
2. "What does your father do?" (there was no follow-up about my mother), and
3. "What school do you go to?"

The questions seemed innocent at first, yet I quickly realized that they were anything but. They were not the opener for a "let's get to know each other" conversation. This was a highly determinative trifecta of questions —the beginning of a socioeconomic class sorting exercise. Depending on how you answered, you could be either accepted or written off. And indeed, some of the kids on the exchange decided not to bother talking to me any further after learning where I was from, what my dad did, and where I went to school:

1. Bishop Auckland.
2. Coal miner, then a hospital porter.
3. Bishop Barrington Comprehensive School.

The kids who wrote me off surely assumed that our interactions would be fleeting. Based on the information I provided, we presumably would never meet again after that one trip to Germany. Why take the time to get to know me? I wasn't "their sort."

My first answer — Bishop Auckland, in County Durham, in the North East of England — demarcated my geographic place in the United Kingdom. The second and third answers delineated my place in society and the parameters of the social networks and opportunities available to me. All three of my answers, including my hometown, put me definitively in the blue-collar, working class.

The United Kingdom was, and still is in the twenty-first century, an acutely class-based society. My father's career, or really his job — the people I grew up with in Bishop Auckland had jobs, not careers — as well as the kind of school I went to were supposed to chart the limits of what I might do with my life and how people would regard or judge me.

In the UK, the middle class — at least as I came to understand it growing up — was the category accorded to white-collar workers, accountants, lawyers/solicitors, teachers, and those in similar professions. People in the middle class were the products of different schools — what used to be called grammar schools — as well as private schools and universities. (This is what masquerades as the upper middle class in the United States, although class distinctions in the U.S. are not so defined or rigid. In the United States, race blurs similar distinctions, but class is still a feature of American life. It is not just defined by individual or household income and wealth, it is shaped by the kind of place you live in, your zip or postal code, your educational attainment, and the type of school and college you attended, along with your family structure, your overall health and well-being and projected lifespan, and your leisure pursuits. It also determines whether you even have time for leisure in the first place. Most workers in the lowest income brackets do not. They are too busy surviving.)

The UK is in a league of its own when it comes to mapping, cataloguing, and identifying the particulars of class. The upper classes in the UK always knew exactly who they were. They needed no categorization. They were the hereditary aristocracy, the landed gentry, people who were born into an exulted status. You could move in and out of the working and middle classes with some effort on the one hand or some misfortune on the other. Being propelled into the upper classes was an anomaly—perhaps the result of a lucky marriage. Even if your family fortunes took a turn for the worst, the most impecunious earl or duke or his offspring remained firmly part of the upper class.

The questions the kids first posed to me in Tübingen were generally on the mark in terms of predicting my prospects. Three of the most critical factors in shaping opportunity and determining socioeconomic mobility in the United Kingdom as well as the United States were, and remain, geographic origin (whether you hail from a poor region or a prosperous area), your parents' educational attainment and professions (no college/college, blue-/white-collar), and the kind of school you attend (state/private, under-resourced/well-funded).

Both my parents were also born in the North East of England: my mother, June, in Billingham, an industrial town farther south in Teesside; my father Alfred, Alf, on the edge of Roddymoor, a tiny coal-mining or "pit" village a few miles north of Bishop Auckland. June left school at age sixteen and immediately started nursing training, finding great satisfaction as a midwife. Alf became a coal miner at fourteen. He missed out on any kind of further education apart from on-the-job training because of poverty and family challenges. His working life was scarred by frequent unemployment. He constantly had to start again. When the last of the several local mines he worked in closed, he briefly labored in a brickworks and a steelworks. In the end he became an auxiliary (or ancillary) worker in the National Health Service, or NHS. He met June there, in Bishop Auckland General Hospital, but as a hospital porter, he found himself on the lowest rung of the system. He was in his thirties and never went any further.

Wrong Place, Wrong Time

The nature of the place that I came from, the shift in my father's work from the coal mines to the hospital, my mother's profession as a nurse, my overall family circumstances, and life lessons from my experiences in and outside of school did play important roles in shaping my educational and job opportunities. But ultimately they ended up assisting more than constraining my prospects. And, as I discovered later, in my professional life, they gave me a unique set of insights, offering me an entirely different perspective on global affairs from those of the majority of national security experts.

My family's experiences and the events of my youth from 1965 until I came to America in 1989 were echoed in the lives of millions of others who mostly lived far beyond the political spotlight. In the decades after I arrived in the United States, the fate of my home area in the United Kingdom was that of every major mining community in the Appalachia region, stretching from Mississippi, Alabama, and Georgia in the south up to West Virginia, Ohio, and Pennsylvania in the north. America's coal country too lost the mainstay of its economy and opportunity. It was also emblematic of industrial regions across Russia and the former Soviet Union, and indeed in other parts of Europe. This fact was a significant revelation once I moved beyond the narrow confines of the blighted world that I was from and finally began to understand the forces shaping our lives in the twentieth century.

Structurally, the United Kingdom and the United States — like Russia and other advanced economies — cycled through a rapid buildup of extractive industry and mass manufacturing in the 1920s and 1930s and again at the end of the Second World War. Our nations began the descent into what became known as the postindustrial era in the 1960s, and especially after the 1970s, when they were hit by successive oil shocks. Major oil producers in the Middle East, members of the Organization of Petroleum Exporting Countries (OPEC), imposed an embargo on countries such as the UK and the U.S. for supporting Israel in its Yom Kippur War with Arab states. Both the United Kingdom and the United States had their own sources of oil and gas, but they remained dependent on Middle East imports. Domestic coal — no matter how much you had (and both the UK and the U.S. had a lot) — could not substitute for everything, especially in transportation. The embargo forced a period of harsh adjustment to sudden energy scarcity and soaring prices, including gasoline rationing and utility cuts to curb demand. It also led to a substantial restructuring of the automotive industry to favor smaller, more fuel-efficient cars.

The United Kingdom and its huge coal, steel, shipbuilding, and manufacturing industries were especially hard pressed by the oil shocks and related developments. The 1970s saw stagnant growth and soaring inflation. Alongside the oil embargo, the global economy began to change rapidly, with technological breakthroughs that enabled the automation of manufacturing and put more emphasis on the movement of capital and finance than on raw materials and goods. When I was growing up, the UK, the U.S., and other advanced countries had to figure out how to move their economies from reliance on energy-intensive heavy industry to high-tech manufacturing, finance, and services. These latter sectors had a much smaller manual labor footprint and greater demand for educated, skilled workers.

Breakthroughs in transportation after the Second World War also played a role in changing the economic geography of both the United Kingdom and the United States. From the late nineteenth to the early twentieth centuries, industrial production was essentially rooted in specific places — constrained by distance and the high costs of transportation for raw materials and energy supplies, like iron ore and coal, as well the difficulties of shipping goods to consumers in other parts of the country. Regions in both the UK and the U.S. became specialized in large-scale production if they were close to sources of raw materials and had easy access to transportation routes, including major inland waterways (large rivers and canals in both countries and the Great Lakes system in the U.S.) or coastlines. These regions became freight railway and shipping hubs until new technology — long-haul trucking and heavy-lift aircraft, for example — revolutionized transportation. Advances in power generation and long-distance electricity transmission, alongside other innovations in technology and infrastructure, called for new raw materials (such as rare metals) that had to be sourced globally, and also meant that manufacturing industry no longer had to be tethered to a particular location close to all its inputs. In the postindustrial world, in a highly integrated and complex economy, everything and everyone could theoretically be on the move. The biggest challenge for governments and societies was how to deal with the human costs of modernization and technological change. What would happen to all the places and people that were products of the old, fixed economy but might not be needed in the new?

Regions like mine in the UK North East were the specialized places of a more geographically limited past. The industries that dominated them were no longer competitive at the same scale in the new technologically advanced and globalized economy. Nor were the manual workers, like my father, who had been employed in extractive industry and mass manufacturing for several generations. Workers' education and skills were specifically tailored to thrive in their twentieth-century industrial workplaces. Now they were obsolete. In the nineteenth and early twentieth centuries, people didn't choose what they wanted to do or where they wanted to live. They moved to where the work was. If the jobs were dependable, they stayed. Local educational systems developed alongside the industrial economy, with a specific purpose and job pipeline in mind. Workers' children were being prepared to hew coal or manage a mine, not create computer code or set up their own business. Families went to the same schools and headed toward the same professions — down the mines, into the steelworks, to a shipyard, or onto a factory assembly line. Children learned the same things from the same teachers, textbooks, and classes as their parents, and sometimes their grandparents, had (given the fact that many people married and had children straight out of school).

Places like Bishop Auckland were in the right place for the creation of large-scale extractive and heavy industries in the nineteenth century, but in the wrong place for the new technology and innovation that came along at the end of the twentieth century. They quickly became forgotten backwaters. What had made them attractive as a location for heavy industry made them unattractive for the information economy, which clustered around places without unsightly mine shafts and factory smokestacks but with "locational amenities" more conducive to creating a new density of advanced technology — amenities such as colleges and universities. People who lived in the old, specialized towns and regions suddenly found themselves stuck in place. They were not equipped for the knowledge economy, which was developing in other locations. They didn't have the educational background or the qualifications to move somewhere else — nor did they have the financial means.

The 1980s were the critical turning point. Margaret Thatcher and Ronald Reagan helped to drive the nail into the coffin of twentieth-century industry while ensuring that those trapped inside the casket would find it practically impossible to pry the lid off. Margaret Thatcher came into office in May 1979, right around the time I realized I was part of the working class. Ronald Reagan followed soon after, in January 1981. Together, Thatcher and Reagan dominated the 1980s, my teenage years and early adulthood and my transition to university. They forged an era of increasing consensus on stimulating growth through free-market economic policy, enhanced competition, free trade, and lower taxes. Their policies were shaped by the celebrated University of Chicago economist Milton Friedman, who became an adviser to both. Inspired by Friedman and others from the Chicago school, Thatcher and Reagan broke with post–World War II economic and industrial principles. They espoused minimal state intervention, market liberalization, deregulation, and the privatization of public services.

In the UK, Margaret Thatcher was a trailblazer and a revolutionary. She reprivatized the so-called commanding heights of British industry, pushed unprofitable coal mines, steelworks, and factories to close, broke the backs of trade unions that had paralyzed the country with labor disputes in the 1970s, and liberated or tore individuals (depending on your perspective) from the confines of their traditional workplace-oriented communities. For his part, Reagan even had a term — "Reaganomics" — named after him to sum up his administration's particular policy mix of pulling back government regulations, cutting taxes, reducing social-sector spending, and greatly enhancing military spending.

Thatcher's and Reagan's respective domestic policy choices helped pave the way for economic growth in the 1990s and early 2000s. But they also created deep societal and spatial inequalities in the United Kingdom and United States between the places and people that could adapt to all the changes and those that couldn't. This sparked and then fueled the partisan divides that would produce crippling political rifts decades later, in 2016 through 2020. In some respects the crises of 2020 would mark the final reckoning with the revolutionary reforms of Thatcher and Reagan in the 1980s.

Dying Villages

Up until the 1980s, coal mining defined County Durham. But by the time I was born, in 1965, County Durham's mines were on the verge of closing, as my father had already discovered. Even if I had been a boy, I could not have followed Dad down the pit and maintained a family tradition stretching back generations. That opportunity was gone. The jobs in the mines were not coming back, no matter what desperate action was taken. Demand for coal and coal miners dropped alongside the rise of the new high-tech and financial sectors and automation. Durham miners soon became more famous for initiating big strikes or "industrial actions" than for producing coal. The last pit in County Durham closed for good in 1994, and the last shipment of open-cast-mined County Durham coal out of the North East's world-famous port in Newcastle was in February 2021, as I was working on this book. In just over half a century, everything was gone.

The closure of the coal mines was a colossal blow, depriving the miners

not only of their jobs but also of their entire worlds. In the nineteenth century, the rise of coal brought the North East prosperity. Investors opened
mines, large and small, across the region. Mine owners pulled men in from
local farms and from elsewhere in England, the Scottish borders, Wales,
and Ireland. There were dramatic changes to regional maps and County
Durham's demography between 1801 and 1885. Villages centered around a
mine became towns. The British censuses beginning in 1841 (which was the
first to record the names of individuals in households) captured my relatives driving those demographic changes as they moved about in search of
work, having children along the way. Mining and the pits that spread across
the region were the foundation for every other industry, including the steel
industry (locally called the ironworks) and shipbuilding in coastal cities
such as Newcastle, Sunderland, and Middlesbrough. Each of these three
big cities sat at the mouth of one of the region's principal rivers that flowed
into the North Sea: the Tyne, the Wear, and the Tees. Newcastle-on-Tyne
was the magnet for industry, goods, jobs, and people for a large hinterland
extending north into Scotland as well as south into the English Midlands.
Newcastle became a major financial center, renowned for its fine architecture and gracefully curving city streets.

In this period, County Durham and the rest of the North East of England
were at the center of industrial innovation. It was the industrial forerunner
of America's Silicon Valley. The people of the North East extracted the resources as well as invented and made the technology and manufactured the
goods that people used all around the world. You didn't "take coals to Newcastle," because Newcastle shipped coal across the globe. In Sunderland on
the River Wear, the locals were nicknamed "Mackems." They were the people who "mack 'em," or "make them." They made the steel, ships, trains,
massive machines, and bridges that everyone else needed. Sunderland was
so rich and renowned that American president Ulysses S. Grant came to
preside over the laying of the foundation stone for the city's combined library, museum, and art gallery in September 1877. It was the first UK public
library and museum outside London.

But things turned sour for the region and its inhabitants, including the
Durham miners, in the twentieth century. During World War I, my paternal grandfather, William "Billy" Thompson Hill, and other miners went
from the pits to the trenches in Europe. At the end of the war, mines and
factories scaled back production. Men came back from the front to find
fewer jobs than they expected. The UK spiraled into economic crisis, sad-

dled by high government wartime debt. Trade and consumption patterns shifted.

Then came the 1929 financial crash. The 1930s were a tough time for the North East. Grandad Billy got blacklisted for taking part in strike action. He was in work, but mostly out of it, during the 1920s and 1930s. When Dad was born, in 1932, Grandad was unemployed. The family was homeless. They lived in a condemned building for several years, in a couple of rooms where the rain didn't pour through the roof. Dad slept in the bottom of an old chest of drawers until he was a toddler and then with his parents. The family was dependent on handouts from local charities, including miners' self-help funds, and relatives who still had jobs. Grandad did menial work for local farmers in return for food. Dad's older brother (named Billy after his father) was sent to live with a succession of less-impoverished relatives who could feed and clothe him, leading to a lifetime of estrangement from his parents. Uncle Billy went off as soon as he could to train as a mining engineer elsewhere in the country. The family rarely saw him again.

Thousands in the North East were in the same situation as my grandparents. No one wanted to be on the dole. In October 1936, two hundred unemployed men from County Durham, including some of Grandad's friends and relatives, went on the Jarrow March, one of England's most famous organized labor protests. They walked three hundred miles to London to petition Parliament to bring jobs back to the North East.

It took a few more years, until the eve of the Second World War, for the mines to open again. The war and local labor activism helped propel social and industrial reforms that led to the nationalization of the coal industry, welfare provisions, and a brief golden age for Durham miners in the 1950s. Not coincidentally, this was also the high point for my coal-mining family: the period between 1947, when Dad went down the mines, and the early 1960s, when Grandad retired and Dad's pit closed.

In the 1950s the Durham miners thought they had it made. They were thriving after all the deprivations before and during the war. Miners worked hard down the pit together for several generations. The local community was their safety net and source of contacts for new opportunities. Men working in the pits made sure all the families in the village had coal to heat their homes as well as food from the local Co-op (the Co-operative or community store) if a miner was laid low by work-related injuries. If a pit closed, miners would alert friends and relatives to vacancies and vouch for their work record with new mine managers.

Miners and their families were part of a vibrant social network of welfare clubs and societies stretching across County Durham, funded by the dues they paid to the Durham Miners' Association and community contributions. There were UK amateur cup-winning football teams as well as writing and art societies (George Orwell had links to them, as did some famous Soviet writers from the 1920s). There were pigeon fanciers and whippet and greyhound breeders and trainers. Grandad indulged in these pastimes at various points. Like every other miner, Grandad had an allotment — a share in a communal garden — where he and others grew prizewinning vegetables that went on to be eaten.

To be sure, there was nothing romantic about working down a pit. Dad worked on the so-called Ballarat seam in his pit near Roddymoor. It was a little over three feet at its peak height — a claustrophobic squeeze for even the smallest miners, which Dad was not. It was backbreaking work, and Dad was plagued by a slipped and herniated disk and spinal stenosis later in life.

The mines that gave the men their jobs cast a long shadow over their health in other ways as well. Coal dust and lung damage finally caught up with both my grandfather and my father. Grandad died in the winter of 1979 from pneumonia. Dad passed away in January 2012 from the sudden onset of congestive heart failure, also after a bout of pneumonia. They both made it past their seventies, which wasn't bad for a Durham coal miner. Most miners never made it to retirement at sixty-five. Grandad's younger brother Jonathon, Uncle Jonty, died at ninety-seven, which was way beyond the normal expiration date. Dad always marveled at that. Dad himself had retired from his job at the hospital before pneumoconiosis, or black lung disease, was recognized as an occupational disease by the UK government in the late 1990s. There were not a lot of retired miners still alive to seek compensation by then. Dad had chronic asthma and bronchitis every winter, but because he wasn't, as he put it, "on his last legs" when he applied for compensation, he got the minimal amount. The men who really needed the money, who had been brought down by the dust and the emphysema that came with it, were long dead.

The hard working conditions and the rich communal life came hand in hand — but when one went away, so did the other. The pit closures devastated places like Roddymoor. Unemployed and retired miners were abandoned in dying villages, stripped of their jobs, social networks, and former amenities. Young folk left in droves because they had to, not because they wanted to. There was no work to hold them at home anymore and no opportunity to find something else. There was nothing for them there.

Granny's Death Box

Not everyone could escape the gutted remains of communities like Roddymoor. Dad had lived with and looked after his parents until he married Mam — as many of us called our mothers — and moved permanently to Bishop Auckland in 1964. Granny and Grandad could not make ends meet on Grandad's miner's pension. Granny suffered from crippling arthritis, and Grandad had Parkinson's, which got steadily worse. Until the local government's housing authority did renovations in the early 1970s, their row house, part of a subsidized development that had originally been built for local workers and their families, had no "mod cons" (modern conveniences), including indoor plumbing. They needed help physically as well as economically.

When I was old enough, Dad took me on the bus to stay with my grandparents or sent me on my bike to fill in for him. It was eight miles or so, depending on the route you took, but even covering that short distance up narrow back roads could be an adventure. Everyone knew each other in Roddymoor. When I went up to stay as a child, I was always "Alfie's lass" or "Billy's bairn" when I encountered the neighbors or other relatives. Granny called me "little Alfie." I would collect coal in a scuttle from the coal house in the passageway between their house and the next section of houses to put on the fire in the blackened old range in the main room. This doubled as a stovetop and an oven where they did some of their cooking. The kitchen was basic, with a tiny fridge that used to be chilled with ice blocks, a couple of cupboards, a sink, and a bare floor.

Roddymoor was dimly lit. The electricity, when it was installed, was always flickering and going out. It seemed to have lost its power in transmission. The streetlights were few and far between, which made for fantastic starry nights but unpleasant encounters with potholes in the streets and rats as well as the occasional fox in the back garden on the way to the "nettie," as we called the outhouse. The foxes were after the hens, which Grandad and his neighbors kept in a coop at the bottom of their gardens where they backed onto a field. There were only a few hens, so their loss was a potential disaster. Grandad used to have more hens and a pig on his allotment, but as he got older, he couldn't keep it up anymore. Everything was confined to the tiny back garden.

Dad once told me a story from his early childhood in the condemned building, when a local farmer had given him some eggs to take home. He noticed they were cracked and threw them away. Granny cried. They had nothing at all to eat that day. Mindful of that story, I was always careful when I collected Grandad's eggs.

Beyond what Grandad could grow and whatever Dad could spare from our garden, Granny and Grandad had no fresh produce. The village itself was a "food desert." It had one small shop for basic goods. There was a fish and chip shop and a couple of other shops less than a mile away in the next village, Billy Row, and a whole town full of shops a bit farther away in Crook, where Granny had grown up. But Granny and Grandad couldn't get there. The bus no longer came into Roddymoor and they couldn't walk as far as the next bus stop. Granny was largely immobile because of her arthritis and old injuries from an accident when she had worked in Crook's leather factory. Stuck in the house, she sat in the same chair all day and subsisted on cheap canned food. She became obese. Grandad said there was nothing wrong with being poor, but there was plenty of difficulty in poverty when your life spiraled down.

My grandparents had endured a lifetime bookended by adversity and deprivation. Granny and Grandad had contended with World War I, World War II, and mining and other industrial accidents on top of poverty, poor health, and infectious disease. Granny Hill had a "death box" in her bedroom — an old hatbox filled with death notices, funeral cards, and mementos of her classmates and friends who had died in World War I or down the mines, or "just died." She called it "the box." I called it the death box, because that's what it was — an old battered box filled with death. There were stacks of yellow-stained, mildewed pictures of dead relatives and friends, most of them nameless, tied up with pieces of string. Nothing was scribbled on the back of the pictures to say who they were or who they had once been — someone's sister, brother, mother, father, child, or special friend.

There was a formal school picture in the box, from Granny's school in Crook, taken sometime before World War I. Almost all the boys had been crossed off in black ink across their chests. And judging by the pencil-written postcards in the box, including a couple from the front, Grandad was not Granny's first choice as husband. But he was one of the few who had come back from Flanders. According to relatives, Grandad had been shot ten times or hit with shrapnel from exploding shells, gassed with chlorine and mustard gas, and bayoneted along with his horse after they got trapped in the mud. He seemed invincible. Grandad never gave me any details — I was just a child — but he was certainly covered in plenty of scars. He had narrowly escaped a couple of rockfalls and accidents down the mine, including one just before his retirement when the "windy pick" (pneumatic drill) had pierced his pelvis, forcing him to wear a truss to keep his battered insides in for the rest of his life. Going down the pit never filled Grandad with terror, but he described World War I as hell on earth.

Every County Durham mining town had a cenotaph commemorating the Great War (as well as the conflagrations that came along later and swept off the local men again — World War II, Korea). There was usually a plaque on the stone with the names of the men whose remains were never recovered. Other corners of the town cemetery marked one catastrophe or another down the mines. The men in all those towns and villages were decimated by war and work. There were no cenotaphs or special corners of the graveyard for those who died later from poverty or despair, or both, when the mines had gone, but there should have been.

My grandmother had certainly earned herself a place on a memorial plaque. In her old age, Granny was stuck with Grandad in a rundown row house in Roddymoor with nothing to do, apart from looking through that box, and nowhere to go. Her life was reduced to a couple of rooms and whatever she might see when she dragged herself up to go to the toilet and shuffled past the back window: a sliver of sky and the patch of garden with its broken-down fences, cinder path, and a couple of chickens.

In all the time I spent in Roddymoor, I never really had a proper conversation with Granny. There was little to talk about when you never left the house and every day unfolded and ended in the same way, with no opportunity for something new. She would ask me a few questions about school or what I'd done if I went out to play, but that was about it. She would not reciprocate if I asked her anything about her childhood.

It took me a while to realize how lonely and depressed Granny was. When I was younger, I just figured she was the quiet sort and didn't want to talk. She would sit and sit, and occasionally read some magazines that Mam sent her. So I would also sit quietly and read, or go out to walk about Roddymoor. It was hard to stay upbeat in her situation. Almost no one came to visit apart from us. After Grandad died, Granny came to live with us while she waited for a slot to open up in a government-subsidized nursing home in Bishop Auckland. Dad requested this so we could walk to see her every day. She wasn't a resident of the town, so she had to wait.

This was the most stressful period of my childhood and adolescence, with all of us crammed into our house 24/7 — although the hospital loaned Dad a wheelchair so we could take Granny outside on nice days. Nonetheless, she couldn't get up the stairs to go to the one bathroom we had, and we did not have a spare bedroom for her. In Roddymoor the toilet had been downstairs, in the space where a pantry had been; to go up to bed, Granny would sit on the stairs and push herself up while I or Grandad braced and held on to her. (Coming down was a bit of a nightmare and left her with huge purple bruises on her back, legs, and arms if she slipped.) The stairs in our house were far too narrow to carry out the same maneuver, so Granny spent two years living in our front room, sleeping on the sofa, with a commode so she could go to the toilet at the back of the dining area, in a little wooden addition that Dad built with the help of neighbors. Mam gave her sponge baths.

Eventually Granny got assigned a nursing home place just a few blocks away. She lasted only another year. She wasn't sick, but she was in chronic despair. A week before she died, Granny told Dad she had simply had enough.

Viva Bish Vegas

Bishop Auckland was a metropolis in comparison with Roddymoor when Dad first went to work there, but within the decade it was also spiraling down. In the early 1980s in County Durham, as Margaret Thatcher's reforms kicked into gear, thousands of jobs disappeared at once. In one County Durham town, Consett, which was around the same size as Bishop Auckland and only twenty miles away, the steelworks closed in 1980. British Steel Corporation, the parent entity, declared Consett no longer commercially viable. Its technology was obsolete. At one point in the late 1880s, Consett had housed the largest steel plate factory in the world. When I was born, in the 1960s, about six thousand people worked there. When the steelworks closed, there were around forty-five hundred workers. Everybody's dad, brother, and husband lost their jobs at once. Consett's official unemployment rate was 35 percent, twice the national average in the UK in the 1980s. This had a serious knock-on effect. Numerous regional suppliers and retailers in Bishop Auckland and County Durham were tied to the works at Consett.

In 1984, Shildon Wagon (Railway) Works, one of the last remaining large industrial employers near Bishop Auckland, with 2,600 people on its books, also closed. Jobs in the plant accounted for 86 percent of Shildon's male workforce in manufacturing as well as a sizable percentage of men in Bishop Auckland, who also worked in the forges and foundries that supplied the factory. Even at this juncture, it was one of the largest construction plants for British Railways, having opened in 1833 to serve the Stockton and Darlington Railway, the world's first major rail company. But the orders for new railway wagons and also the contracts for repairs were slowly drying up. The works were no longer profitable.

In Bishop Auckland in the 1980s, the question "What does your father do?" was now "What *did* your father do?" Everyone seemed to be out of work and looking for something. Somehow, my dad actually had a job. In that respect we were extremely lucky. Bishop Auckland and the local hospital were his source of opportunity.

Although it was never as world-famous as Newcastle or Sunderland in its heyday in the nineteenth century, Bishop Auckland had once offered all kinds of opportunity and attractions. The bishop of Durham — a powerful prince, not just a clergyman, who was charged by the king or queen with raising his own army to fend off the Scots — had his county residence in Bishop Auckland, next to the ruins of a Roman fort. The town was a hub for the North East railway network, on the route of the Stockton and Darlington Railway. It was well known for its industry, its large number of churches, and its strong retail sector.

Bishop Auckland's main street, Newgate Street, was the "golden mile." It ran in a straight line along the route of an old Roman road that terminated farther north, at Hadrian's Wall. Newgate Street's portion of this byway stretched from the railway station to the marketplace in front of the Bishop's Palace gates, crowned by a Victorian Gothic town hall. The street was lined with family grocers and butchers, clothing and department stores, several theaters, pubs, and a few fancy tearooms. The celebrated children's writer Lewis Carroll and the comedian Stan Laurel both went to Bishop Auckland's King James I Boys' Grammar School. Stan Laurel's father, Arthur Jefferson, ran the town's music hall, the Eden Theatre, for a while. Great-Grandad Thompson Hill briefly performed there in a vaudeville act with his famous older cousin, Jenny Hill (Elizabeth Thompson), whose other stage name was the "Vital Spark," when she was on a regional tour. The twice-weekly market by the Bishop's Palace attracted shoppers and sellers from around the region, including Travellers (both Gypsy Roma Travellers and Travellers of Irish heritage), who came with their caravans, including traditional vardos and distinctive Vanner horses.

Travellers still came to Bishop Auckland when I was a kid, but by this point the town had changed. They would set up camp at a place down by the River Wear, as well as on vacant land around town, and tether their horses to graze on any available patch of grass. Sometimes this was at the end of my street or in the recreation grounds in the town park near my elementary school. Bishop Auckland was a place with fewer cars than most in the 1970s and 1980s. Most people, like us, couldn't afford one. A common sight on the main streets was a boy, or sometimes several people packed close together, sitting on a two-wheel trap or buggy with a black-and-white Vanner horse trotting out front. Touring the town by buggy or on foot was the main form of entertainment.

When I was a teenager, Bishop Auckland was affectionately known as Bishop or Bish. The big event of the week was "going down Bish" on Saturday afternoon to "look at the shops." We never had any money to buy anything beyond a cup of tea or a soft drink. The real agenda was to walk up and down Newgate Street, hoping to run into someone you knew. We didn't have a phone, so unless my sister, Angela, and I agreed to something on Friday at school or went to knock on someone's door, meeting friends happened on the fly down in the town. At some point "Bish" morphed into "Bish Vegas."

By then Bishop Auckland was the exact opposite of the local entertainment mecca it had been a century before. This clearly started as a joke on a Saturday night in one of the town's pubs. But the moniker fits. Because life in Bish was a bit of a gamble.

"Bish Vegas" became a way for people to make fun of themselves and boost flagging spirits in a place that had once been somewhere and was suddenly nowhere when all the mines and the industry disappeared. Humor reconciled the disconnect between your experience and everything that people, and library books, told you had been there in Bishop Auckland in the not-so-distant past. For forty or fifty years Bishop Auckland was stuck, a hollowed-out husk of its former self.

In summer 2013, a self-styled "Bish Elvis" posted a video on the internet. Titled "Viva Bish Vegas," its soundtrack was a sendup of Elvis Presley's famous song about Las Vegas. Bish Elvis, with some backup from friends, provided a singing commentary as the camera toured up and down Newgate Street and around the marketplace, taking in the boarded-up buildings and FOR SALE and TO LET signs. The historic part of the old King James I Grammar School building had been burned down to its bones in an arson attack. Empty buildings were daubed with graffiti. The video began with a rip-off from the opening moments of the 1977 movie *Star Wars,* offering a wry and quickly retreating textual overview of the town's history. The video was affectionate but damning in its depiction of decades of decay, deprivation, and the loss of opportunity.

Bulldozing the Past

Between the mid-1960s and the 1980s, much of the North East's rich industrial heritage was not only lost, it was actively destroyed. Centuries of economic development and innovation were bulldozed in the name of "reclamation." As coal mining was a centuries-old occupation, the landscape didn't go back exactly to what it had been before. Tiny villages, farms, and patches of woodland, long lost to make pit props and scaffolding, were not restored. Vast new grassy fields, housing developments, and "light industrial estates" covered the old mine workings.

Clearly the past was haunted, its memories too painful to deal with. It was a stain on the present, better to be erased. The disappearance of coal mining, all the other industries, the jobs, and the way of life associated with the pit villages was a major trauma. The industrial remains — the slag heaps and rusted metal of the old pit-head machinery, the empty factories, the abandoned furnaces — meant people were constantly reminded of everything they had lost. No matter that these remnants were monuments to considerable human achievement. They were testaments to the things our grandparents and parents had made and once took pride in.

For my entire childhood, something was being pulled down in Bishop Auckland. On shopping days, when Mam and Dad dragged us downtown to buy food rather than window-shop, every corner was an opportunity for nostalgia. They would pause to look at something: "I remember when this was . . ."; then they'd taper off, leaving the memory hanging and Angela and me asking, "What? What are you talking about? What was here? Where did it go?" The main part of the train station went, erasing all the lines radiating out to places we wanted to get to. Only two lines were left. One went to the town of Darlington and from there to Middlesbrough and Saltburn-by-the-Sea. Taking the train to Darlington was now the only way to get to Durham and Newcastle as well as London and Scotland. The other line went "up the dale," or further up the River Wear toward its source in the Pennine Hills, where there was a big cement works. We didn't really know anyone up there in "woolly back" or "the back of beyond," where there were more sheep than people. Without the train station, the opportunity to visit friends and relatives, including Mam's family, who still lived farther south in Teesside, was confined to bus trips.

Stan Laurel's father's Eden Theatre was demolished. For a while there was nothing on the spot. Then a small bed of flowers and a bench were placed there with a tiny plaque. The site was eventually marked, many years later and only after a public appeal, with a very small statue of Stan. The town cinema closed while I was a teenager. *Star Wars* was the first and last blockbuster movie to come to town. Half the town lined up to get tickets, but generally going to the cinema was another luxury a lot of Bishop Auckland residents couldn't afford in the 1970s and 1980s. There weren't enough revenues to keep the movies coming in and the cinema open. Doggarts department store and its tearoom closed. No more birthday treats of cream teas with Mam's mother, Grandma Vi, when she came to visit. Doggarts' once-grand building was cannibalized into a series of smaller shops. Eventually some of those shops went out of business too. They were just boarded up. And so went the rest of Bishop Auckland's main street.

For kids in Bishop Auckland in the 1970s and 1980s, opportunities for entertainment or out-of-school activities were limited. There was a distinct lack of somewhere, anywhere, to go and something to do if you didn't have a car and were restricted by how far you could walk or cycle. There was a town swimming pool, "the Baths," but limited space and times for taking a plunge. A few of the churches had youth clubs. Most of the public space in the town parks was vandalized, except for the bowling greens and tennis courts, which you had to pay to use and were fenced off. Many families, like ours, couldn't afford the fees.

We found ways to entertain ourselves all the same, but even these were sometimes tinged with despair. In Bishop Auckland we were steeped in alternative and rock music. It was what kept us going: saving up to buy singles for our cheap record player, listening to the radio and taping cassettes of our favorite bands. Our favored songs and lyrics were a response to all the decay around us. Angela and I would sing them out loud in our tiny shared bedroom until Mam and Dad begged us to shut up. In the UK, bands like the Specials and their anthem, "Ghost Town," captured the emptiness of everyone's hometown "as all the shops [were] being closed down." Other bands called out political injustices, urging change through social activism or by somehow getting rid of Margaret Thatcher, as if that would miraculously make a difference.

The downturn in the town's fortunes seemed to have brought out the worst in some people — certainly in terms of exacerbating things and feeding into pernicious stereotypes about the slovenly behavior of the working class and the parlous state of low-income neighborhoods. Dad said that a small number of people did all the damage because they had no pride in themselves or their surroundings. They had lost their self-esteem along with their livelihoods. When he was growing up in Roddymoor and the mines were open and everyone was in work, there was plenty of personal and civic pride and community pressure to pitch in and clean things up. He never saw litter or dogs fouling the streets when he was growing up.

It was different when the decline set in. The park closest to my house, in the neighborhood of Cockton Hill, was grim enough to be dubbed a "wreck-reation" ground by me and my friends, but we went there anyway. The area around the swings, seesaw, and roundabout was covered in glass from broken bottles and smeared with dog dirt. The local council had few resources for regular repairs, so actually trying to use the playground could be both unpleasant and dangerous. A lot of time was spent, as a result, hanging around with friends near the Cockton Hill "wreck," on a white metal barrier that divided the older part of town from the newer housing.

The view of our individual and collective futures from sitting on top of the white barrier wasn't particularly edifying or encouraging. In the 1980s, Dad used to say that parts of Bishop Auckland, and certainly Roddymoor, might as well be in a war zone. We were refugees in our own land, but there was no one there to help. "Perhaps we should call the United Nations," he'd joke. "You could do that one day, Fiona."

For a while I fantasized about becoming the UN secretary-general so I might be able to fix things. I had no idea, of course, how anybody would go about doing that. Just how did you get a job with the United Nations? My friends told me I was mad to even contemplate it. No one from Bishop Auckland was ever likely to get a job like that.

2

Grasping at the Future

There were in fact some jobs to be had in the midst of all the decline in County Durham from the 1960s to the 1980s, but they weren't likely to put anyone on a career ladder headed toward a position in a major international organization. Nonetheless, the region and my town still had some infrastructure of opportunity. It was not as extensive as before, but there were systems and mechanisms and even networks for finding a way forward. The situation was bleak, but not hopeless.

After the mines, foundries, and factories closed in Bishop Auckland, the biggest employer outside the retail sector was Bishop Auckland General Hospital (BAGH). Part of Britain's National Health Service — the much-beloved public health-care system that was set up at the end of the Second World War — the hospital became the main source of reliable full-time and part-time work, the locus of opportunity. In addition to Mam and Dad, some of my friends' parents worked there. I later took a cleaning job at the hospital to cover for regular workers during holidays.

When Dad started at Bishop Auckland hospital, he found that most of the porters were also ex-miners. But whatever their backgrounds, none of the men had chosen their porter job as a profession. They had rolled with the punches and taken whatever work was locally available, even if it was poor compensation for the loss of work down at the coal face. Overtime in the mines got you decent extra pay; overtime in the hospital might get you the minimum living wage, if you were lucky. Everyone knew what a coal miner did. People respected you. What did a hospital porter do, exactly?

Push people around in a wheelchair? It was telling that although Dad eventually worked in the hospital for more than thirty years, he was once and for all a miner. It was his basic identity. He was proud of it. He always said there was dignity in his work in the coal mines of County Durham. You belonged to something bigger than yourself.

For her part, Mam went to BAGH after working in other large hospitals across the North East. Her rise as a nurse had tracked the development of the NHS itself. In 1950, when June started her training as a nurse aide at the Carter Bequest Hospital in Middlesbrough, the hospital was in the process of transitioning from an entirely private hospital to creating public facilities. In 1952 she became a general nurse at Sunderland Royal Infirmary, before beginning her career as a midwife. For several years she was a district midwife, moving between Middlesbrough and Sunderland, delivering babies in working-class areas, slums, and Travellers' camps. She came to Bishop Auckland as a ward sister and lived in the nurses' hostel attached to the hospital.

The NHS was a great social leveler in the UK after World War II. In theory everyone had equal access to health care; anyone could call a midwife like my mam. In fact the UK health-care sector remained a quasi-private public system, and treatment was difficult to obtain if no NHS doctor or hospital was nearby, as was the case for Granny and Grandad in Roddymoor. But at least access to a doctor and a hospital was no longer tied to a person's capacity to pay.

For Mam and Dad, the creation of the NHS provided significant opportunity in many ways. It contributed to their health and well-being, and it gave them both jobs and brought them to Bishop Auckland. Ultimately, it also gave them the chance to buy a house: a small, semidetached home at the open end of a tiny cul-de-sac in a new neighborhood on the edge of Bishop Auckland, built over the remains of a colliery. At the end of our street, beyond a patch of grass and another row of houses, were what was left of the old mine workings — piles of bricks originally from a cable house for pulling coal tubs and some mine tailings or slag, mounds of discarded pieces of coal and other materials. Until this too was "reclaimed," we played hide-and-seek among the rubble and the tall weeds. Now and then a couple of horses would be tethered there to eat dandelions and nettles.

Buying a house was a big deal for all of us. In addition to providing a source of security as a permanent place to live, it put more opportunity within our grasp. In the United Kingdom, just as in the United States, home-

ownership was directly connected to the prospect of building up generational wealth. Both Mam and Dad had grown up or lived in rented workers'
housing and council houses. No one in their direct lines of descent had ever
owned a house. They knew from experience — given the fact that Dad had
been homeless, lived in a condemned building, and frequently had to miss
school — that living in your own house improved children's life chances. In
this sense, my parents' purchase of a home was a critical factor in putting
me on a different path from theirs.

Alf did not actually make enough in his new NHS job to qualify for a
mortgage, but marrying June was the ticket to buying the house. No one
ever seemed to ask what your mother did when they interrogated you with
the three questions that put you in your little social-class box — everyone
assumed that your mam was staying home to look after the kids; perhaps
she might have a small job on the side. My mam had a full-time job when
she met Dad. June was thirty when they married, and Alf was thirty-two.
June had done well in nursing school. She rose up the ranks as a district
midwife, becoming a Queen's Nurse and a senior sister in charge of a maternity ward. She had the better-paying job and built up a small nest egg. As a
district nurse, she had also owned a car, which she sold when they got married. Mam and Dad used her savings and the money from the car to make
the down payment on our home.

Our house was Mam and Dad's investment in the future — our future
— and they put everything into making the mortgage payments. Often this
came at the cost of meeting our other expenses.

Lights Out

Mam and Dad purchased our home in 1964. I was born the following year,
and my sister, Angela, was born in 1968. It became too difficult for Mam to
work and look after us at the same time. There was no state-provided child
care and not much flexibility in her work hours at the hospital. Most of her
shifts were night shifts, which Dad worked too. They could hardly leave us
at home alone at night.

So for a time Mam left her job. Without her income, we immediately
descended into the precarious stratum of the working class. Dad's meager
salary was barely enough to support us; in the 1970s, the wages for hospital
ancillary workers — porters, cleaners, cooks, and laundry workers — were

among the lowest in the country, lower than those of the average unskilled worker as well as the average manual worker. How much you earned depended on the shift you were assigned. You got time and a half for Saturdays and double time for Sundays and major holidays. Dad might make £20 ($25–$26) some weeks and £30 if he worked overtime, which he did if he could. He always worked weekends and holidays. At times we barely saw him. Adjusted for inflation and factoring in overtime, Dad made around $17,500 a year in 2021 dollars. For comparison, the official 2021 U.S. federal government poverty level for a family of four is an annual income of $26,500.

It soon got worse. Between 1975 and 1978, under Prime Minister James Callaghan, the Labour government held down wages for hospital and council workers to curb runaway inflation. Real wages dropped by 21 percent. We were hovering on the edge of absolute poverty — what was called the breadline, where you might find yourself dependent on donated food. In 1977 this proved to be an ironic term when the country's bakery workers went out on strike. Everyone was suddenly in a breadline, queuing outside shops to buy scarce loaves or flour, which had to be rationed. Mam decided to make her own bread in response. Dad had to contend with bricklike loaves that defied cutting and toasting for his work sandwiches. Angela and I declared that we no longer ate bread.

Paying the mortgage meant that we frequently had to turn off the electricity when Dad's paycheck didn't carry us to the end of the month. Admittedly, in the 1970s all the industrial strikes usually ended up in a power cut when the workers at the power plants eventually went out on strike and the plants shut down. The so-called Winter of Discontent of 1978–1979 — the biggest strike action since the General Strike of 1926, which brought out Dad and the other hospital workers alongside what was left of Durham's miners — was a particularly dark period. Picket lines, protests, and power cuts brought the country to a standstill. Everyone's electricity was off. We did our homework by candlelight. In the 1970s we didn't always notice the difference between the "pay cut" and the "power cut" (one of Dad's jokes), which was an odd sort of bonus. The electricity didn't matter so much, as we had a gas fire in the living room and natural gas for cooking and heating the water. We usually scraped up some money to pay the gas bill, and we didn't have a washing machine or any other major electrical appliance (except eventually a TV). We washed everything in the kitchen sink or the bath and dried clothes on an outside line or a clotheshorse beside the gas fire. If we had enough change, Dad would load big bulky items like sheets in a backpack to take down to the town's sole laundromat.

We had no car, no telephone, and at first no TV. These were far too expensive and entailed all kinds of hidden taxes and licensing fees. A TV was a luxury item, but its lack caused practical difficulties. The royal wedding of Queen Elizabeth II's daughter, Princess Anne, to Captain Mark Phillips in 1973 was a personal and family watershed, because it was the event that precipitated our rental of a black-and-white TV. I was in primary school. We were assigned to watch the wedding "on telly" as a school project and then draw a picture and write about what we saw. Mam and some other parents complained to the teacher. How could children watch the wedding if their family didn't have a TV? The teacher stood firm. "If they can't watch it, then I suppose they'll fail."

I did not want to fail. So I took Dad's little radio to listen to the commentary and the music, stood on a piece of grass, and watched the wedding on telly through a neighbor's window. I was too embarrassed to ask them if I could come inside and mortified at the thought that they might spot me. They had a color TV, one of the first in the neighborhood. They'd once seen me and Angela standing on the grass mesmerized by an obviously silent episode of the original *Star Trek* series. "Who is the man with pointed ears? Is that Mr. Spock?" The neighbors closed the curtains. They later yelled at us to go away when we tried to see what the famous British sci-fi series *Dr. Who* was like and why everyone at school was pretending to be Daleks at playtime. In my teens we got a color TV of our own from neighbors who were upgrading. But by then I could only guess at what I'd missed.

Home Economics

My maternal grandmother, Grandma Vi, had plenty of tips to share and sometimes some extra money she had saved to help out. Her husband died early from cancer, and Grandma had long mastered the miraculous art of getting by and keeping up appearances on less than a shoestring. We always joked that she looked like the Queen in her few smartly kept hats and scarves. Her life trajectory had taken her from surviving the German navy's shelling of her coastal hometown, Hartlepool, in 1914, through "downstairs" maid service in a "big house," to helping in a dairy and delivering milk and working in a grocery store managing the food rations during World War

II. Grandma had grown up on a farm and knew how to forage for berries, mushrooms, and edible plants in the local countryside. She grew all kinds of herbs. Her house smelled of lavender, from little sachets that she made from the flowers on the bushes in her tiny garden to place in drawers and behind pillows. Grandma also kept up with a dwindling network of farming families from the old days, who would give her some eggs, a snared field rabbit, or the odd chicken on special occasions. We once came home to Grandma's house in Billingham on the bus from a visit to our Great-Aunt Florrie, who still ran a small farm nearby, with a live chicken trussed and stuffed in Grandma's bag. Back at her house, Grandma dashed into the kitchen, took out the chicken, and chopped its head off before Angela and I had even taken our coats off. The chicken was as shocked as we were. Not realizing that it was dead, it ran around the kitchen without its head for a few seconds, sending Angela and me squealing back toward the front door.

Grandma Vi encouraged Mam to make all our clothes that didn't come from thrift stores, relatives, or neighbors with older girls. Mam had taken a tailoring course at a local technical college, and Grandma gave her a hand-cranked Singer sewing machine. At some point she got a secondhand electric machine. Mam often economized by using the same bolt of fabric for clothes and household accessories. After one mammoth batch of sewing that produced some new kitchen and front-room curtains, she had just enough left to make me a pair of trousers. Sadly, the fabric was strangely textured and a peculiar dark shade of blue — a sale remnant from Doggarts. Mam distinguished the trousers from the curtains with a tasseled fringe (it was the 1970s, after all). The fringe caught on the buckle of my shoes as I walked to school and unraveled. I was always having to trim off the threads so Mam wouldn't see and accuse me of trying to pull it off. I hated the fringe. It looked silly. As a disguise, it fooled no one. The twin girls who lived across the road (in the house with the TV) immediately spotted the similarity with the front-room curtains. I was "Curtain Legs" for a whole year at school.

Grandma Vi taught us to overcome adversity and "just get on with it." And getting on with it in County Durham meant grappling with questions of physical mobility. The operative question was, if you didn't have a car, how far could you go to find a job? Would the bus get you where you needed to be? Would you be on time if it ran only once or twice a day and stopped every half mile? How many times did you have to change buses to get somewhere? What if you missed the bus back? An updated bus schedule was a much-prized possession. Grandma took the bus everywhere. She had a pensioner's pass but always made sure we had a schedule in our pocket along with some bus money in case of emergency. The posted times on the bus stops were always vandalized and illegible. If there was no bus for the route you needed, how far could you cycle or walk every day?

Norman Tebbit, who was one of Margaret Thatcher's ministers in the 1980s, purportedly once commented that the unemployed should get on their bikes and look for work instead of striking or rioting. Dad got on his bike for work when the mines around Roddymoor closed. First he cycled to the brickworks, then to the steelworks, then to Bishop Auckland General Hospital. It was a quick ride from Roddymoor — pretty much downhill most of the way — but that meant a strenuous ride back up lots of steep hills after a tiring shift. Later, when he finally lived in Bishop Auckland, Dad's bike was stolen from our garden shed. He was devastated. He had bought it at his peak earning capacity in the mines in the 1950s. It was a vintage bike, kept in mint condition. Dad couldn't afford a new one. After the theft, he resorted to shank's pony: he walked to work and back. I was always on the red bike I got for my ninth birthday, even when it was too small for me and the white plastic seat and the handlebars were pulled up to their fullest extent, hurtling along narrow back roads, dodging foxes and pheasants darting out of hedgerows, trying to get to Granny and Grandad's or to a part-time job.

Part-time jobs became the norm for everyone, if you could get one. In our case, Mam needed the government's family allowance and child benefit to cover our food and other basic necessities. This was the weekly stipend for each child under sixteen that low-income mothers could claim beginning in the 1970s. It saved many families from the breadline. If Angela and I wanted any clothes other than those Mam made — including underwear and socks (thank god she didn't try to make those) — toiletries, and pretty much anything else, we were on our own. So from age eleven I had part-time jobs to help out the family budget and earn some pocket money.

I started washing people's cars in our street at weekends, then working in a sweet shop at nearby Witton Castle, and briefly as a serving wench for the castle's medieval banquets. I didn't last long at the banquets. We were given ridiculous period costumes to look the part of "buxom lasses." I was tall and skinny, anything but buxom. Angela and some of our friends called me "Treasure," the girl with the sunken chest. With nothing to keep it in place, the ruffled front of the dress kept falling down. Mam made me a pair of boobs from some old pantyhose stuffed with tissue paper. I could push them down the front of the dress and pull the ruffles over. This worked well enough until I slipped on some wayward mashed potato on the stone floor as I transported a giant platter of meringues and cream for dessert. I fell backward onto the floor, dislodging the boobs, which ended up under my chin. The platter of meringues careened toward an unsuspecting banqueter, splattering her head and back with cream. I was relegated to washing the dishes.

Angela and I also worked in another local hotel restaurant, Binchester Hall, at weekends, and eventually I was a barmaid in a couple of different pubs, wherever and whenever there were openings. Dad was always filled with trepidation when I set out for the pub jobs. He knew that things could quickly go wrong for a young person in County Durham after dark — particularly a woman, and especially when substances were involved, as they so often were.

In the North East of England, the closure of major industries and the loss of low-skilled but guaranteed work had immediate social and health effects on both the old (like Granny) and the young. The UK had a heroin epidemic in the 1980s and 1990s. Most people in Bishop Auckland couldn't afford hard drugs. In the 1980s we had glue-sniffers in the Bishop's Palace Park, behind the school bike sheds, and on the wooded paths alongside the River Wear. Glue was a very cheap high. In the hospital, Dad was always taking people to the emergency room from overdoses of solvent and even liquid paper. One kid in school broke into the supply closet and sniffed so much liquid paper one day that he completely blocked up his nose and had to be taken to hospital. We weren't allowed to use liquid paper in our classwork after that.

For the most part, alcohol was the drug of choice in Bishop Auckland. Some people were heavy drinkers. Very heavy drinkers. Drunks smashed up the town marketplace on a Saturday night when the pubs closed. Dad would try to calm them down as the nurses tried to sober and stitch them up. He didn't like Angela and me going downtown on a Saturday night in case we got caught up in a fight, and when I worked in the pubs, he would walk to meet me if he was off work at closing time.

On our walks home, we would talk about my school and his work. Even if it was highly unlikely that I would make it to the lofty career heights of the UN's headquarters in New York, Dad was pretty sure I could make something of myself. Although he was certain that this would mean I would have to leave home, not just Bishop Auckland but also the North East. And, as he kept stressing, even getting out of poverty — the economic side of the social mobility equation — let alone getting somewhere else, meant obtaining a further education of some kind. This in itself was not so easy, because access to higher education in the United Kingdom was anything but equal in the 1980s.

3

Out of Your League

Education was the key to changing my circumstances, but the kind, quality, and affordability of the education would be critical factors. Based on my background, as a schoolgirl in Bishop Auckland I could consider becoming a nurse like my mother. I could aspire to be a teacher like some of our relatives. All this would require hard work and also some good fortune. If the stars aligned and I really excelled at school, I might leave town for a regional university. I might reach higher to acquire other qualifications and become a white-collar professional, a doctor or maybe even a college lecturer. In this way I might attain a place in the British middle class.

I had distant relatives who had pulled off those feats. Dad and Mam would talk of them admiringly. But no one, myself included, could possibly have anticipated that I would end up with a Harvard PhD, become a Russia expert, and work in the American White House. Indeed, when I first arrived at St. Andrews University and then at Harvard, whoever posed the three critical British class questions would always ask a follow-up: "Well, how did you get *here* then?"

I was an obvious outsider, an interloper in a small set of privileged circles where access was strictly limited by who you were and where you were from. How had I overcome the UK's economic and social barriers to an elite education? Was I the exception that proved the rule? Or could I be a sign that things were changing in some fundamental way? If things were changing, would there suddenly be more competition for limited opportunities from people like me from the working class?

Some things, in fact, *were* changing in British society in the 1970s and 1980s in ways that created a new infrastructure of opportunity — the set of structures, systems, and support mechanisms that enable people to improve their educational, employment, economic, and social circumstances. These changes would allow me to overcome impediments to an education that had thwarted the progress of my parents and grandparents.

Similar changes in the infrastructure of opportunity had taken place in the United States, but decades before. One of the most significant pieces of American legislation after World War II was the GI Bill, which opened access to further education for millions of young servicemen who had just left the armed forces. In 1947, almost 50 percent of students admitted to college were veterans. Similarly, in 1965, the year I was born, the U.S. Congress passed a bill as part of the Higher Education Act that created what became known as the Basic Educational Opportunity and, later, Pell Grants. These provided federal funding to the families of low-income American students who were admitted to college — often as the first in their family. Although the amounts of money and conditions of both bills changed over time, they were revolutionary in expanding access to education for millions of Americans. My husband and most of his siblings had federal grants underpinning their bachelor's degrees. In all cases, including in the United Kingdom, these changes and government grants gave people the opportunity to obtain an education without going into debt.

Education in all its forms — from elementary to secondary to further education and professional training — is the beating heart of the infrastructure of opportunity. It has the potential to define and redefine who you are and who you will be. For me, it was everything.

"Cream of the Crop"

Prior to the 1970s, the British school system was highly stratified and selective. In my parents' day, it served to reinforce the UK's class divisions. This was not simply because of the obvious differences between a well-funded private and a more impecunious state school system. In the UK, private schools are in any case known as public schools, open to the fee-paying public, not just the offspring of aristocrats, which makes for a great deal of confusion. In the British state school system, at the end of their time at elementary school, children would sit the eleven-plus exam. This immediately sorted them according to academic attainment. After the eleven-plus, children were rank-ordered, based on their results, and directed by the state onto different educational and life paths. A small number of children who passed the eleven-plus in the top bracket, the "cream of the crop," would secure a free place at a local boys' or girls' grammar school. This would uproot the select few from their working-class origins and prepare them for a white-collar, middle-class job or possibly university. Fewer than 10 percent of British students went on to a university education at this point. The others, who might have narrowly missed the eleven-plus cutoff and could not afford to pay for anything else, would be directed toward larger secondary modern schools. In some cases they might be dispatched to technical and vocational schools that would prepare them for blue-collar trade jobs and eventual industry apprenticeships. Children from the same family would find themselves on divergent paths to opportunity that might lead to a lifetime of separation, all because of one exam, taken at a time when they had barely figured anything out.

If you were a late bloomer educationally, it was difficult to make up down the line for missing the cut at the eleven-plus. And life and family circumstances played a major role in educational attainment then and now. June took the eleven-plus at the end of the Second World War. She was ranked near the top of the girls in her class, in the fourth spot. Only three free places were allotted to girls at her elementary school for the local grammar school. June went to the secondary modern and, encouraged by her parents, quickly directed herself toward government-subsidized courses that would lead to a career in nursing.

For his part, Alf entirely missed taking the eleven-plus. Granny was sick, and Grandad worked multiple shifts down the mine, coming home only to sleep for a few hours. There was no possibility of an exam redo for Alf. In any case, Grandad said, "Who needs the eleven-plus?" Alf was going down the mine; what did it matter? Grandad and Granny didn't want Alf to go to grammar school. Indeed, they didn't want him to stay in school any longer than he legally had to. They needed him to get to work as soon as possible to help put food on the table.

Twenty years after Mam's and Dad's respective experiences with the eleven-plus, successive Labour Party governments engaged in an overhaul of the British education system. The reform was intended to address the inequalities of the rigid early selection process and expand access beyond the bifurcated grammar and secondary modern schools. Experiments with a different, "comprehensive" approach, combining technology and vocational training with the standard academic subjects, were also attempted in the 1940s and 1950s in a few school districts.

Between 1965 and 1975, the British government phased in a new nation-wide comprehensive school system to raise the quality of education and improve the life chances for all children aged eleven to sixteen, not just the select few. This meant that most children in a town or village would end up at the same set of local or neighborhood schools, unless their parents could afford a private option. Those schools remained unchanged. The government also allowed parochial schools to operate separately. Some local authorities in England, including in the North East, petitioned to retain their selective grammar schools, sometimes as (modest) fee-paying entities. In some places, as a result, the inequalities persisted. Place along with class became a key determinant of who got access to a "good" education.

Bishop Auckland steadily progressed toward the comprehensive school system as I moved through my early education. My elementary school, Etherley Lane, which I began in 1970, had a good reputation in town. It had a long history, especially under then-headmaster Mr. Noble-Eddy, of preparing children to take the eleven-plus and move on to the town's boys' and girls' grammar schools. Etherley Lane retained the exam for several years. Some of the children used their exam scores to apply for scholarships at nearby private schools. Mr. Noble-Eddy shared the results automatically with the schools.

I took the eleven-plus in 1976. This was the year the British government fully moved to the new system. We were the last group at Etherley Lane to take it. I was first in my class and ranked in the top cohort in the country. The local private girls' school, Durham High, extended me an offer via Mr. Noble-Eddy. They would waive the fees if I wanted to enroll.

It was a generous proposition, but Mam and Dad would still have to cover the costs of the uniform, as well as books and equipment, bus fares to Durham, and extras like school trips. One of my close friends at Etherley Lane, Heather Dixon, was also offered a place. Mr. Dixon, who had a car, offered to drive me every day. It wasn't enough. Dad balked; we would never be able to afford it, even if additional bursaries were available and I could get uniforms and materials secondhand.

Heather went to Durham High; I never really saw her again. Even when opportunity presented itself, I was learning, it took resources to seize it. I would have to find another way to get the education I needed and desired.

Running from Success

In 1977, I ended up at Bishop Barrington, the newly created comprehensive school closest to our house. So close in fact that we could see it from the bathroom window. In 1979, Angela started there too. We would practically roll out of bed in the morning when we heard the first bell and run through the school gate by the second.

In the time I was there, from 1977 to 1984, Bishop Barrington Comprehensive was a struggling school. It was an amalgamation of two previously existing secondary schools, one of which was technical and vocational. There was a rudimentary gym, some sports fields, and a basic library containing an odd smattering of classic English novels (by authors like Charles Dickens and the Brontë sisters) and poetry anthologies, all donated by a local benefactor. The sports field at the lower school was above an old ventilation shaft for a now-defunct coal mine. Part of it caved in one day during a football game, fortunately to the side of the goal where no one was playing. It took weeks to fill in and the goalposts had to be moved. Inside the classrooms, there were not enough textbooks or equipment to go around. Angela volunteered to work in the library, checking out books for extracurricular reading. Hardly anyone ever came. If you wanted a book, you usually went to the old town library, or a new one at a nearby community center, which had much-sought-after new copies of horror novels by Stephen King and others.

With more poetry anthologies than textbooks in the library, everyone had to take turns to copy by hand from the teacher's edition and take copious notes in class. Otherwise there was nothing to refer to. There was no school photocopying machine at this juncture. Sometimes the town library might have an older version of a textbook that someone had donated, or the librarian would try an intralibrary loan. Occasionally a neighbor who had gone to grammar school might have kept a copy and would lend or give it to you.

In general, finding out basic information for a class assignment was an ordeal. The library was never open when you needed it, or someone had checked out the reference books when you got there. Mam and Dad saved up for a whole year to put the down payment on a discounted set of the

Encyclopedia Britannica, which they paid off in monthly installments. Dad built a special shelf to store the tomes on the upstairs landing near the bathroom, partly blocking the door. Space in our house was always very tight. Angela and I spent hours sitting on the stairs with the encyclopedia, looking up things that otherwise would never be explained.

The proverbial nightmare of taking an exam you hadn't studied for was real life. Many of the teachers at Bishop Barrington were not well prepared for the new courses. Sometimes they didn't even have the latest curriculum. Either the county education authority neglected to send it out or the teacher forgot to check whether there was an update with the school secretary. All too often the council failed to allocate a formal substitute teacher when someone was sick or away on maternity leave.

Bishop Barrington was not exactly the most desirable teaching assignment. A series of temporary teachers might come from one day to the next, or, more likely, the poor physical education or art teacher was sent to struggle through someone else's class in their break time. Teachers and students alike were sometimes terrorized by local bullies in the upper school. The German teacher got locked in a classroom closet overnight. The French teacher was stabbed with a compass. Both left the school.

Windows were always getting smashed and equipment vandalized. Something was forever being set on fire. Exam results were a time of dread, not just because of the revelation of the grades. The full results were posted on the school office window so that everyone could see everything. There was no hiding. The bullies would try to "knack" (hit) you for doing well. You had to learn to navigate the perils and avoid the physical fights as best you could. I was fortunate, living so close to the school. I could check the grades on the window and then be home before anyone had much time to react.

No Great Expectations

Even with the new comprehensive schools, the postindustrial economic downturn made it difficult for working-class kids to succeed in the British education system in the 1970s and 1980s. Local councils and their education authorities were strapped for cash. Students had no family resources to fill in. Many friends qualified for free school meals. Angela and I did too, but Mam had us come home to eat with her and Dad if he was not on a shift — usually some kind of stew and dumplings or the local stalwart of Yorkshire pudding along with vegetables from the garden. We lived so close to the school that this was not an issue, and for us lunch was dinner, the main meal of the day. Leftovers would get served up again in some mystery meal the next day and in Dad's sandwiches. Although school now formally extended to age sixteen, there was a lot of pressure to leave early and get a job. Most of my friends wanted to stay on at school. We all had parents who wanted us to take advantage of the educational opportunities they never had. But life didn't track with the academic timetable.

Students who did well at school could sit the requisite Ordinary examinations, or O-levels, at sixteen (later replaced by the GCSEs — General Certificates of Secondary Education) and then leave. Or they could stay on for two more years, until they were eighteen, to do Advanced exams, or A-levels, in what was called the sixth form. These qualifications could then be used to apply for a white-collar job. Some good local entry-level positions were available in banks and solicitors' offices in Bishop Auckland, for example. You also needed the advanced exams at specific grades to apply for one of the limited places at university or a polytechnic college, which was more focused on applied subjects related to science, technology, engineering, and mathematics (STEM) and professional vocational degrees in business, journalism, and architecture. The local education authority would pay for the course fees and provide a stipend for living expenses on the basis of a means test. Bishop Barrington set up a fledgling two-class sixth form for a small number of aspiring A-level students. Others could apply to go to the town's former boys' grammar school, King James I, which was now a coed comprehensive but retained its grammar-school-era sixth form. There was another sixth-form college in Darlington. The timetable for moving through the various classes and taking the exams was rigid. The local education authority did not have extra resources for students to skip or retake grades. If you failed your exams one year, there were not many second chances. The schools preferred you to be up and out, even under extenuating circumstances.

Bishop Barrington had only a few years of experience with A-levels under its belt by the time I got into the sixth form, which was housed in a set of wooden huts that had once been the vocational college's shorthand and typing classrooms. There was only a handful of students in each of the two years, a fraction of those who had started out in the lower school. Although we were in the sixth form, great things were not expected of A-level students from Bishop Barrington Comprehensive School, or any UK comprehensive school, for that matter, in the 1980s. You usually needed exams in three distinct subjects to apply to university. At Bishop Barrington this was essentially determined by which teachers were qualified as well as available to teach A-level courses. Some subjects were simply off-limits because there was no one to teach them.

I had been on several Durham County–sponsored school exchanges to Germany and France. I knew I wanted to spend some time living or working abroad, so I decided in favor of languages and subjects I was most interested in. There was also the chance to study with an inspiring teacher. Dr. Marshall, the school English teacher, had a PhD from Durham University. He had decided to come to teach in the benighted comprehensive school system, where he thought he could be most useful, instead of at a private school or university. Education was a calling for Dr. Marshall, not a job. He was the best-qualified teacher at school. His classes were well prepared and compelling. The rest was sometimes a roll of the dice.

No one had much advice to give. Not really knowing what combination would work best, I took four A-level courses instead of three in a misguided attempt to maximize my opportunities. The history teacher was in the process of retiring, but we had a good art teacher and some world-class art museums nearby that were free for students. I opted for art and art history instead of history. The German teacher had long gone, so I selected French. In the end I had to complete the French curriculum and exam preparation on my own after the initial teacher (who was stabbed with the compass) left the school. The other girl studying A-level French dropped out after that. I had a dizzying succession of temporary and often eccentric supply teachers, whom I eventually gave up on. One spent his entire time "meditating" at the back of the classroom with his tie around his head, after complaining of a migraine. He instructed me to flick through a *Michelin Guide to France* that he had brought from home for inspiration.

Finally, I studied geography, which was as much economic history as anything else. I had to write a research paper. I decided to apply the theories on industrial location of two German economists, Alfred Weber and August Losch, to the case of Witton Park ironworks. The blast furnaces in Witton Park, opened in 1845, were for a while the world's largest producer of pig iron. They were closed by 1900, and iron and steel production moved elsewhere. All that was left were the ruins of two massive furnaces. Witton Park had an "environmental center" — basically a wooden hut containing artifacts, memorabilia, and documents that had been left behind from the old ironworks' offices. Our neighbor Sidney Lockey, who had grown up there, told me about them. No one else was especially interested in these archives. I could ride my bike from home and access the material easily without the risk of anyone having got there first. Geography classes and my research paper helped explain why Bishop Auckland and the surrounding towns and villages had built up in the nineteenth century and declined in the twentieth.

The experience of A-levels was less edifying than enervating. Like the eleven-plus, A-levels were a onetime set of exams that were supposed to open the door to university and a lifetime of opportunity. There was a major quirk in the application system — you had to apply to university *before* you sat the exam. You would then either be rejected or receive an offer based on your predicted grades from teachers' assessments, coursework, and mock exams.

Most students applied for about five universities and polytechnics in a combined package, listing the applications in descending order of preference. They were then assigned grade requirements — conditions — by each of the institutions. A university might ask for a certain combination of A-level grades. If a university really wanted you to enroll, it might ask for a lower set of grades — or it might even offer a place outright, with no conditions at all. This was an extremely rare occurrence for a working-class kid in a comprehensive school, where expectations for students' performance were considerably lower than in a private school.

In short, the stakes were high and the timeline was tight. You sat the A-levels in the spring, got the results in the summer, and headed to university in the fall. If something went wrong, game over. You might lose your top-choice place and have to work down your contingency list — or you might not go to university at all.

Clever Lasses and Lecherous Lads

Right from the very beginning, Mam and Dad talked about the possibility that both Angela and I could go to university or a polytechnical college after school. Their encouragement was an important factor in charting our path to opportunity. So were the examples of extended family members who had come before us.

Some of Mam's cousins who had gone to grammar school had gone on to degree or teacher-training programs. So had some of the grandchildren of Grandad Hill's siblings. Dad was especially proud of one cousin, Elizabeth Lacey, the granddaughter of Grandad Hill's older sister. Her mother was widowed young and raised two daughters on a tiny salary working as a "lollipop lady," or school crossing guard. Cousin Elizabeth and her sister passed the eleven-plus in the 1950s. Elizabeth went to Wolsingham Secondary School, initially a girls' grammar school, and then studied theology at Durham University in the 1960s. She married a classmate, Peter Fisher, the great-nephew of the archbishop of Canterbury who crowned Queen Elizabeth II in 1953. Peter's father was a canon at St. George's Chapel in Windsor Castle. Now Elizabeth Fisher, our cousin, had become a lecturer in theology in Nottingham, a canon herself, and a member of the General Synod of the Church of England, as well as the moderator of the Churches in Dialogue Commission of the Conference of European Churches (an extremely impressive title as far as we were concerned). Dad dangled Cousin Elizabeth the theologian before me and Angela as the achievable example of academic excellence and lifetime attainment. Her studies and her marriage, Dad noted, had put Cousin Elizabeth just two degrees of separation away from Queen Elizabeth at her literal crowning moment. She was a family trailblazer.

Cousin Elizabeth and most of the other examples Mam and Dad offered were women. They were "clever lasses," all the family said. Everyone was proud of them. Their educational achievements, as I realized later, were even more remarkable for their generation, given the gender barriers to opportunity as well as the class impediments they faced in the 1950s and 1960s. I never realized that gender could combine with class discrimination to become a powerful hindrance to individual advancement until I began to experience it for myself. No one told me in Bishop Auckland that I couldn't or shouldn't study this or that because I was a girl; nor did they warn me that various career options might be closed off to me. I assumed, in listening to Mam and Dad's stories of the clever lasses, that if you made it to university and got a degree, then doors to even more opportunity would open up — as they seemed to have done for Cousin Elizabeth. Education, I thought, would be the great leveler. I just had to study and work hard and take advantage of whatever educational opportunities were available to get ahead.

Gender, my gender, proved to be something more than a speed bump on the road forward once I moved to the United States and began my professional career. Gender was a significant issue in shaping and constraining my opportunity and, at critical times (especially at the Trump White House), an actual obstacle to doing my job. In the United Kingdom, being working-class and living in the North East of England was the primary challenge I faced. The infrastructure of opportunity was skewed toward more privileged people in more desirable places. In the United States, that held true too, but the infrastructure of opportunity was different for women and men. Being a woman in the think tank and the national security arena brought additional layers of unanticipated and unpleasant discrimination of the kind that often pushes women out of the very places and careers that they have struggled and trained to get access to.

Of course, the infrastructure of opportunity for women and men was also different in the UK, I just didn't really see it. I figured that class was what would hold me back. For most of my early life, my gender was just a fact. As a child I didn't dwell on it much. It was the basic descriptor of what I happened to be: female. I didn't see it as a core identity, just as I was unaware that I was working-class until I ended up on the school exchange in Tübingen. I did, obviously, realize early on that my gender had some distinct disadvantages. Being a girl seemed to imply for some men that you were fair game for them to mess with whenever they felt like it. Harassment was normalized by everyone around you. It was presented like a rite of passage: you would have to go through many feats of endurance. There was rarely much social outrage about girls or women getting flashed at, groped, or molested, unless it was on some large, hard-to-ignore scale or you were subjected to a particularly brutal violent attack. In the 1970s and 1980s, as well as through into the 2000s, these and similar encounters were something a girl or a woman just had to deal with.

Having no money created all kinds of unique vulnerabilities for women as well. You needed to get out there and find a job. And as a young girl and woman in the workplace, there was the constant risk of being preyed on by "lecherous lads" and "dirty old men," as our older woman friend Mary Hartnett used to call them when we worked together with Angela at Binchester Hall Hotel.

Mary would advise us younger colleagues on how to rebuff advances with humor to defuse the inevitably tense situation and keep the job when customers and the men we worked with made a move. I didn't always manage to do that successfully. Two of the three chefs at Binchester Hall, Stewart and Anthony, took a literal perverse delight in making vulgar comments about the way we looked and in forcefully groping anyone walking past with her hands full of plates. A trip to the supply closet was an invitation for them to push in behind and grope some more. No one wanted to go in there alone, but banding together didn't seem to help all that much either. The third chef was visibly uncomfortable with all of this but never interceded. They intimidated him as well. His family was originally from Malta. As one of the very few immigrants in Bishop Auckland, he didn't want to draw attention to himself and lose his own opportunity for a steady job. The restaurant owner and manager, Alan and Gilbert, saw it all but laughed it off. The lads were just messing around — just being "stupid buggers." All a bit of fun. No need to get upset. Don't pay attention. Lots of people want these waitressing jobs. If you don't like it, leave.

Everyone seemed to think it was somehow your fault, as a girl, if you were harassed, or didn't laugh it off. Boys could get a job and go out and about in Bishop Auckland, anywhere, anytime, no repercussions or recriminations, but in your case, if something happened, well, what were you doing there? What were you thinking? Why were you, a girl, walking alone by the riverbank or down an empty street, or anywhere around town, at night on your own? You were just asking for it: trouble of some kind.

Even with every precaution, there were countless affronts inside and outside school — pinned down by boys, just messing around at parties or on school trips. Shirt pulled up; hands stuck into your underwear; body shamed. Every one of our friends seemed to go through it at some point or other. Angela and I didn't tell Mam or Dad about most of these episodes in case Dad went berserk, hunted down the offender, and tore him limb from limb. No one wanted their dad in jail for giving someone a thrashing. You learned to keep things to yourself, band together with other girls to repel the personal space invaders, stick to your trusted circle of male friends for protection, and get away or fight back if necessary. It certainly made you nervous and hypervigilant. And it often *did* stop you from taking the opportunity to go somewhere or do something, if you had to walk there alone or ran the risk of someone messing with you. Angela and I spent a lot of time running through what we would do if . . .

Against this backdrop, Angela and I also spent some time considering role models beyond the clever lasses in the extended family. What could women do with themselves, what opportunities and careers were out there given the toxic atmosphere that seemed to prevail at times? After my school exchanges to Germany and France, and all the musing with Dad about the United Nations, I was always glued to the latest world developments on the

Nine O'Clock News. I was sure that I wanted to do something in politics or international relations. But that's where the role models thinned out.

One of the Boys

Sure, there were women who made it onto local councils, but few women at the very top of UK politics — especially from the working class. Margaret Thatcher had theoretically broken through the gender barrier, and yet, after serving as Conservative Party leader and prime minister for almost my entire adolescence and early adulthood, she largely stood alone. Indeed, Margaret Thatcher didn't actively promote other women into prominent positions in her cabinet in the 1980s or improve their chances to follow her path with policy interventions. The exception was Edwina Curry, the beleaguered agriculture minister, who became famous for two things: first, for having to take responsibility for a major outbreak of salmonella in the national egg stocks, and second, much later in life, for having once had an affair with the man who would become Thatcher's successor, John Major. That summed things up. National politics was the realm of men. Women were a rarity or a novelty.

Margaret Thatcher seemed to relish being the only woman and one of the boys. One story in particular made an impression on me as a young woman. Traditionally, Conservative British ministers and members of Parliament join the Carlton Club in London, founded by the Duke of Wellington, who defeated Napoleon at Waterloo. Only men could be full members of the club, which didn't admit women until the 1970s and then only as "associate," or nonvoting, members. The boys' club persisted, even for the Iron Lady, as she was dubbed (Wellington was the Iron Duke). When Thatcher became Conservative Party leader in 1975, she was made an *honorary* full voting member. The rules did not change, and Thatcher didn't push to change them. She enjoyed being the exception that proved the rule: the woman who made it along the man's path. No other woman got her privilege at the Carlton Club until 2008.

From incidents like these, I understood that it wasn't so easy to be accepted as a woman, although a woman like Margaret Thatcher could use the rarity of her position to her advantage in some circumstances. At St. Andrews University, several of my classmates were the children of Thatcher's male ministers. They would pass on gossip from their fathers about how Thatcher manipulated the senior men around her through a formidable combination of keen intelligence, sharp political acumen, feminine charm, and sheer intimidation. Most of the Conservative Party men had been raised by nannies or governesses before being sent off to boarding school and then Oxford and Cambridge universities (Oxbridge). Thatcher was a "clever lass" herself. She had gone to a girls' grammar school and then Oxford on a scholarship to study chemistry. She knew the men she was dealing with. From what I could glean from the St. Andrews gossip — and later read in biographies — Thatcher cleverly played upon their vulnerabilities. She was essentially the nanny supreme, wielding authority over small boys.

While she might have played the role of nanny or governess in power games, Thatcher was nonetheless the arch foe of the UK's "nanny state." She was forged by the patriotism and sense of duty of World War II, not the travails of the Great Depression like my dad. As the daughter of Alfred Roberts, a grocery store owner and small businessman, she believed in the importance of hard work, thriftiness, self-reliance, and personal achievement. The family lived in a flat attached to her father's shop. Although the Robertses were not wealthy, they had assets. Her father worked for himself, not for someone else or an anonymous company. He was also active in local politics, pushing his own agenda. Growing up in this self-sufficient and highly opinionated environment, Margaret Thatcher thought everyone should live as her family did. For her, England was not a society but a country of individuals. She sought to reduce the "coddling" of the cradle-to-grave welfare state that had been introduced after World War II to address the wartime deprivation and give everyone a hand up out of the rubble. Hard work, self-reliance, and personal achievement were all admirable qualities that my family and everyone I grew up with espoused as well, but it was difficult to live up to them when the local opportunities for advancement had disappeared.

Despite her intellectual and political skill and her evident accomplishments, Margaret Thatcher was not a role model for young women in the North of England. How could she be, given her singular role in closing the coal mines, the shipyards, the steelworks, and all the associated industry, or, at the very least, in presiding over all these losses as prime minister? Thatcher's working career as a research chemist and then as a barrister (attorney) had been fairly brief. She launched herself into politics not long after graduating from Oxford and was financially supported by her businessman husband. As far as we could tell, she had little insight into or empathy for the travails of the working class, women or men.

Red Dot and Uncle Charlie

Several factors in the 1980s — not gender — shaped my decision to try to study Russian at university: my local member of Parliament (MP), major world events, and two close family connections. Bishop Auckland's MP, Derek Foster, who became the chief whip of the Labour Party under Prime Minister Tony Blair, and later Lord Foster as a life peer in the House of Lords, played a seminal role in offering encouragement to apply to university in the first place. After he was elected in 1979, Lord Foster visited Bishop Barrington School on numerous occasions. He relayed, then reinforced, the same general message: "You don't have to be defined or held back by where you are now. Work hard and you can do something with your lives."

Derek Foster had started off life in Sunderland. His father was a fitter in the shipyards and was frequently out of work and on the dole, much like Grandad Hill. Lord Foster joined the Salvation Army at age eleven and passed the eleven-plus, securing a free place at Bede Grammar School. From there he won a place at Oxford University. He eventually pursued a passion for youth and adult education and joined the local council in Sunderland as assistant director for education before running for election as MP for Bishop Auckland. Despite his childhood brushes with poverty, Derek Foster told us that education was not just about acquiring information but about doing something with it. If you were lucky enough to get a good education in a place like the North East of England, you needed to give something back to people who were not so fortunate. You needed to guide others to the same opportunity. Getting an education was a right, but it was also a privilege.

Lord Foster made a big impression in those visits to the school. He also made a point of following up with our families, through his parliamentary office in Bishop Auckland or the local Labour Party offices, to see how we were getting on. He saw a key part of his role as MP as strengthening the infrastructure of opportunity for his constituents.

The MP's work in trying to bring new opportunity to Bishop Auckland was greatly complicated in the 1980s by geopolitics. Larger forces and developments exacerbated the social and economic upheaval, and diverted attention as well as government funding from addressing the consequences of postindustrial decline. The travails of places like County Durham seemed to pale in comparison with the exigences of national security and the perils of the Cold War.

My time at Bishop Barrington was dominated by the so-called Euromissile crises and periodic war scares. For an entire decade, essentially from 1977 to 1987, the Soviet Union and the United States confronted each other over their respective decisions to station new SS-20 and Pershing ballistic missile systems in Eastern and Western Europe. In my last year at school, in 1983–1984, the United States and the USSR teetered on the brink of a nuclear confrontation after both misread the intent of a series of respective military exercises.

As I later learned from declassified archives during my work in the U.S. National Intelligence Council, the 1983 "war scare" was real. But even without any formal validation, the international tension was palpable. Popular culture in the UK and Europe, as well as in the United States, was filled with rock songs like Nena's "99 Red Balloons," about the beginning of a missile strike in a divided Germany, and films like *The Day After* in the U.S. and *Threads* in the UK, about ordinary Americans and Brits trying to deal with the aftermath of nuclear Armageddon. Bishop Auckland was close to a couple of airbases and the UK's ballistic missile early warning radar station in Fylingdales in North Yorkshire. Discussions at school would frequently touch on the prospect that we might not even be around to take our A-levels, let alone apply to university. We could be ground zero for a missile strike.

When we were at Etherley Lane sometime in the 1970s, Angela and I had both sat through a public service announcement about the risk of a nuclear missile strike. It was sent around on a film reel from school to school in County Durham to be projected onto a screen during assembly. The announcer, in classically clipped BBC tones, helpfully ran through the various warning and all-clear sirens. He advised where we should take cover if we were at home — preferably in an inner room without windows. Given how tiny most homes were in Bishop Auckland, there weren't many rooms in the first place, and none without windows in our house. We wondered if we would all fit into the cupboard beneath the stairs where Mam stored the vacuum cleaner and ironing board, or if we'd be okay if we pulled the curtains tightly shut. The announcer told us that if we were caught outside far from shelter in a missile strike, then we should lie down in a ditch. For years after this, until well into our teens, while we were out on a walk in the fields, Angela and I would scope out somewhere to throw ourselves in case we heard a siren.

Right in the middle of this major international crisis — at least at the local level — was Mam's cousin, Dorothy, who had been the bridesmaid at her wedding. Dorothy was active in both the Labour Party and the anti-nuclear-weapons and war movement, the Campaign for Nuclear Disarmament (CND). She was a town councilor and the mayor of Darlington as well as a "Greenham Common woman," part of a group of women antinuclear protesters who set up a long-standing peace camp to demand the removal of U.S. cruise missiles from the British air force base, RAF Greenham Common, in Berkshire. We would sometimes see her on the TV news, chained to other women (some of whom were topless) and the fence of the airbase in the South of England. I later found out that Dorothy's nom de guerre was "Red Dot."

Before Red Dot, Dad's older cousin Charles Crabtree, Uncle Charlie, had lived an unlikely life that had taken him into the thick of things. In his teens, he (albeit briefly) fought in the Spanish Civil War. During the Second World War, Uncle Charlie served in the merchant marine. One ship, *HMS Eagle,* was sunk in the Mediterranean by a German submarine in 1942. He went down with the ship but was then blasted to the surface by depth charges. Battered and barely alive, Uncle Charlie floated on his back until he was rescued. Later in the war, he was on a minesweeper, *HMS Lyme Regis,* escorting Russian convoys through the mountainous seas of the Arctic during battles with the Germans. In his middle age, back at home, he was blacklisted by British business for being a union agitator. In his old age, he mellowed and turned to writing copious self-published poetry and letters to the local newspaper. When I was on an exchange program in Moscow in 1987–1988, Uncle Charlie had also started writing poems for Mikhail Gorbachev. He received a commemorative medal from the Soviet embassy in London in honor of his wartime service. I almost had a heart attack when I saw him referenced in an article in a Soviet English-language newspaper along with one of his poems.

During the war scare in the mid-1980s, Uncle Charlie became obsessed with trying to figure out how the USSR had gone from wartime ally to mortal enemy. Running into Dad one day down Bish, he told him that he had heard there were scholarships for the children of former miners: "Your Fiona's good at languages, Alf, she should get one and go and study Russian and figure out why the bloody hell they're trying to blow us up!"

Red Dot's activism and Uncle Charlie's question helped to inspire and launch me off on my educational odyssey. Sadly, Uncle Charlie died just as I moved to the United States. I was never able to give him a detailed answer to his question. And I also almost went in another direction and didn't study Russian at all.

Many of the universities I looked at didn't accept students who hadn't studied Russian at O-level or A-level. St. Andrews was one of the few that did. It had a set of requirements for supplemental summer language courses that I would have to factor in. As it turned out, I had selected an eclectic set of A-levels, which did not easily set me up for other programs. I had inadvertently made things harder for myself. Again, thinking of how I might be able to maximize my opportunities, I thought I should now consider joint degree programs — a language plus something else. I applied to study French and geography at a couple of places, but St. Andrews didn't have a Russian and geography option, so I opted for history.

At Bishop Barrington Comprehensive School in the 1980s, there were all kinds of impediments to applying to university. It was hard to access even basic information about the various colleges, their courses and requirements. We were not well versed in the names and locations of all the UK universities and polytechnical colleges, nor did we have much insight into other options like specialized colleges of art or journalism or apprenticeships and industry training programs. There were no online resources. Most of the teachers had been to local teaching colleges, starting there straight out of school themselves. They could not offer any insight. Dr. Marshall, the English teacher, was the exception. Although he had studied at Durham University, he advised me to apply further away from home. Given the short distance and shrinking budgets, the local Durham County education authority might not pay for me to live in campus accommodation. I might have to stay with my parents if I went to Durham University and commute in on the bus. I would certainly miss out on the full college experience.

Dr. Marshall and the sixth-form head, Mr. Everett, collected some university and polytechnic brochures. There were others in the local library. It was all quite random. I put together my long list to whittle down for the centralized university application form based entirely on the availability of brochures. St. Andrews looked beautiful in the brochure. The others . . . not so much. Partly this was because St. Andrews had printed its material in color (a clever marketing move). Everything else was black-and-white with tiny, daunting print. I put St. Andrews at the top of my list. Mam's godson, Jeff Goodman, my *de facto* older brother, who had been partially raised by Grandma Vi in Billingham, offered to drive me around to some of the places on the list in his beat-up Mini to help me figure it out.

Without Jeff and his Mini, I would not have gone anywhere. Which is ironic, as Jeff himself had left school for an apprenticeship with British Ship-builders in Middlesbrough. As I was figuring out the application forms, he was working in Cammell Laird shipyards in Liverpool and also Appledore in Devon, filling in for labor shortages and fitting out new vessels.

Schopenhauer's Theory of the Will

As I was touring around in Jeff's Mini scoping out my opportunities, Mr. Davidson, Bishop Barrington's headmaster, decided that someone should apply to Oxford. His motivation seemed to be competition with King James I School, which was still benefiting from its former grammar-school status. King James was able to send the occasional student to Oxbridge even as a comprehensive school. Mr. Davidson wanted to make his mark, at least with one. He turned to me and a couple of other students with a "nothing ventured, nothing gained" proposition. The others refused. Oxford required a general entrance exam, and there were a whole host of individual colleges to contend with. How would we select one? After some consultation with Mam and Dad, who were also of the opinion *Why not?*, I agreed to try.

Apart from Derek Foster, we didn't know anyone who had been to Oxford. He had studied philosophy, politics, and economics (PPE), which seemed to be the thing to do for members of Parliament. Not knowing any better, I made a note of that as a possibility for studying there, as well as French and English. Again, taking Russian from scratch did not seem to be an option. There was, however, the problem of the entrance exam. From what we understood, most schools had special preparatory classes for this. No one had seen a sample of the exam before, but Mr. Davidson and Mr. Everett got hold of an old general exam, so we knew that it came in a little booklet form and involved a series of essay questions. I ended up taking the exam at a table in the library surrounded by the poetry anthologies, with no preparation whatsoever and Mr. Everett supervising me.

It was indeed the exam nightmare come to life. I still dream about it.

The first question was something to do with "Schopenhauer's theory of the will." At the time I had no idea who Schopenhauer was. I had never come across him in my perusals of the encyclopedia. I figured he was a German. At first I thought he might be a composer. I have no idea what I actually wrote or what the rest of the questions were. The ideas are long gone, but I have never forgotten the physical feeling of humiliation and panic, and the realization that this exam was not designed for someone like me. It was utterly mortifying.

The fact that I failed the entrance exam did not come as a surprise when the letter arrived in the mail — but I was completely shocked to get an invitation instead of an outright rejection. I was asked to come to Oxford to Hertford College for a "matriculation offer" interview outside of the regular process. Either someone had taken pity on me or they had seen a glimmer of hope in my exam attempt. In any case, here it was, an entirely unexpected second chance — another opportunity.

I was given a date and time to present myself for interview. If I needed to stay the night, I could stay in a college room for free, but I had to buy a train ticket and get myself to Oxford. This was not straightforward from Bishop Auckland. It required several changes. It was also expensive. The ticket took up all the money I had saved from my part-time jobs at this point. And I had to find something to wear. What exactly did you wear for an interview at Oxford? Mam whipped me up a dress from a bolt of fabric with a heraldic pattern — Dad joked I could probably blend into the wallpaper in one of the paneled rooms if I needed to. Grandma Vi bought me a "nice" (if you were eighty) cardigan to wear on top of it from Marks & Spencer, which was having a sale. It wasn't completely terrible, although my little black ankle boots looked a bit out of place with the outfit. I just didn't have any money left for anything else, so I would have to make do.

I managed to make it to Oxford on time for the interview. Hertford College was near the Bodleian Library. Its buildings were joined together by the famous and iconic Bridge of Sighs. It was beautiful, but so clearly out of my league.

A college porter at the gates directed me to the interview, which would take place in one of the professor's studies, up a narrow, paneled flight of stairs. At the top of the stairs was a landing with a long wooden bench built into the wall, facing the professor's door. Three girls were already sitting on the bench. They looked me up and down, eyes taking in the heraldic pattern but fortunately not lingering on the boots. I recognized one of them, although I blanked on her name in the moment (and it has never come back to me). She had been on my German school exchange program. She was from one of County Durham's remaining grammar schools and already sounded more like she worked for the BBC than someone from the North East of England. And she was one of the kids who had decided not to speak to me again after we ran through the three questions about place, father, and school. Nonetheless, she recognized me too and was shocked — seemingly not in a good way. Oddly, she had remembered my name.

"Fiona Hill! What are you doing here?"

I stated the obvious answer and asked her how she was, noticing that the other two girls winced and smirked slightly when I spoke. I squeezed on the end of the bench and tried to make conversation with them to smooth over the evident awkwardness, prattling on about the weather and how beautiful Oxford was and asking where they had traveled from. One girl looked at me quizzically: "I'm so sorry, I have no idea what you just said." My "friend" from Germany immediately jumped in: "Oh don't worry, I can translate for you. North East accents are impenetrable!" That was me put in my place — and by someone else from County Durham at that.

At this very moment the professor's door opened. A girl came out, said goodbye to the others, and went down the stairs. I heard him call my name. By now I was feeling flustered and out of sorts. I stood up to lunge toward the door. One of the girls had her foot out. Either it had been stuck out there all along and I hadn't noticed, or she stuck it out just as I rose to go. Whatever the case, it didn't really matter, because I went flying over her foot and struck my face and nose on the doorframe.

My nose started to bleed. I fumbled for the handkerchief Grandma Vi always made me stick up a cardigan sleeve, just in case. One of the girls snickered. No one asked if I was okay. Holding the handkerchief to my nose, I went into the room, apologizing to the professor for having tripped and the nosebleed.

My interviewer turned out to be very kind. He had some materials in front of him in addition to my application. Instead of asking me academic questions, the professor probed what I wanted to do and where else I had applied. He asked about my school. I got the impression he might have heard some of the exchange outside. It was more like a life counseling session than an interview. I was a bit surprised.

After a period of conversation, the professor reviewed the situation. My A-level choices didn't give me many options. I could probably study PPE, like Derek Foster, and most likely English or French, but not in combination. And it didn't sound as if that's what I really wanted to do. He gently suggested that Oxford might not be the best place for me, although I was "clearly a clever girl." University was what you made of it, he said, not just what it made of you. I could make something better somewhere else. I should study something I would enjoy and felt passionate about. He advised me to go to St. Andrews and study Russian and history. It turned out to be the right advice.

The Gates of Oxbridge

I wasn't the only person who had this kind of "out of my league" experience at Oxford in the 1980s. The stories were manifold. And they spoke to the fundamentally exclusionary nature of Britain's most elite schools — and of the particularly steep barriers to opportunity that disadvantaged applicants found when they tried to get a foot in the door.

In the late 1920s, just 9 percent of Oxford students came from state-funded schools, and they were all men. Oxford did not become coed until the 1960s, and before 1974 only 16 percent of students were women. The 1960s saw the introduction of the standard entrance exam, ostensibly to level the playing field for everyone for entry to the individual colleges; but outside the private school system, no one was fully prepared for either the exam or the interview.

Prior to 1987 — so in the period that I applied — many private schools had special preparatory courses for entry to Oxbridge. Students could opt to spend an additional year at school beyond their A-levels doing advanced coursework tailored toward sitting the exam and performing to the best of their abilities in the interview. It was clearly worth it for such a life-changing opportunity. As a result, private school pupils dominated student admissions for decades.

Even academically well-prepared students from grammar schools could find themselves in trouble if they worked up the courage to apply to these elite institutions. No one informed them about the social and cultural codes at Oxbridge. They had no idea what to expect.

One of my clever-lass working-class cousins, Julia Magill, for example, missed her Cambridge interview dinner in the late 1970s. No one told her when she showed up at the Cambridge college that she should attend dinner that night. The college porter simply told her that dinner was at 6:30

p.m. when he showed her to her room. Thinking this was optional, Julia went out to dinner with relatives who lived nearby. When she showed up on time for her individual interview the next morning, the first observation was "You didn't come to dinner yesterday." Julia immediately realized she had missed a critical social part of the test that she had had no idea existed. Feeling humiliated and inadequate, she knew that even with her best performance, she had already hurt her chances for a successful outcome. There had been no instructions of any kind in her letter — Julia was just supposed to know.

Fiona Anderson, my St. Andrews roommate, also had no coaching before her Oxford interview. Her school had not even advised her to apply to Oxbridge, as it did not offer any of the special preparatory courses. Like Julia, she had done it on her own. She passed the entrance exam — and later aced her A-levels, as did Julia. Fiona and Julia were academically qualified but socially deficient. When we swapped stories, Fiona related to me that her Oxford interview had been a surreal out-of-body experience. She had felt like she was looking at herself through a mirror. Nothing really made sense. She knew she was academically prepared and had every right to be there, but the interview questions were suffused with technical words and college terms she had never heard before.

For girls like me, Julia, and Fiona applying to Oxbridge, there was no path to follow and no one to guide or offer advice. Fiona chose to go to St. Andrews. Julia opted for Durham, as Cousin Elizabeth had several years before. Neither had any regrets, but they did have plenty of criticism about how exclusionary the Oxbridge system was, even for some of the brightest students outside the privileged sphere of private schools.

A Chance Encounter

After my Oxford debacle, Mam, Angela, and I made a weekend trip on the train (three trains, with changes in Darlington and Edinburgh) and bus (from the nearest rail station in Leuchars) to see St. Andrews for ourselves. We had found a cheap B&B at the edge of town near the bus station where we could all share a room (this meant Angela and me squeezing into a single bed together while Mam was in the other). We didn't expect any of the university buildings to be open, but we thought we could at least peer through some windows and get a feel for the town.

The weather was glorious — not a cloud in the sky, a complete rarity for most of the UK. As we stepped off the bus, the whole town seemed to sparkle. It was more beautiful than the brochure. We didn't know where to start. We couldn't check into our B&B yet. Should we find somewhere to leave our bags and go down to walk on the beach or seafront (St. Andrews is by the sea) or should we go into town? As we were standing around conferring, an older man walked up to us. He had heard our North East accents. He himself was from Yorkshire — could he help us? He was a lecturer in the Russian Department and lived nearby.

This was Mr. Sullivan, who proved to be one of my most important teachers and mentors at St. Andrews. A chance encounter on the street outside the bus station. He invited us to tea, took his keys and opened the Russian Department so we could look inside, and filled us in on the courses and requirements. He demystified the process. For me, this completely sealed the deal. I would go to St. Andrews.

4

Common Northerner

As it is for most poor kids anywhere in the world, not only in the UK and the United States, university was a sudden, wrenching, and exhilarating life change. I was propelled up the social ladder with little practical preparation for confronting Britain's class divides. In my case, this improbable personal ascent coincided with a general feeling of descent in society at large.

I entered St. Andrews against the backdrop of a troubled juncture in UK politics that included the national miners' strike. It was also the height of the Cold War and the very year of George Orwell's famously prophetic book *1984*. It was a period when everything seemed to be spiraling down. At times the whole country literally seemed to be on fire or pulling itself apart.

In the mid-1980s, Britain continued to be racked by "the Troubles" — the intracommunal conflict in Northern Ireland that had come to be defined by the Provisional Irish Republican Army's (IRA) widespread mainland bombing campaign, which had been under way since the 1970s. Violence dominated the daily news on TV. Everyone across the UK was vigilant for abandoned bags in shops or on the street, and for parked cars that might conceal a bomb. In 1982 and 1983, bombs in London's royal parks and Harrods department store had killed and maimed scores of people.

In October 1984, just as I began at St. Andrews, the IRA tried to take out Margaret Thatcher and her entire cabinet at a hotel in the seaside town of Brighton during the Conservative Party's annual conference. The IRA used a remote-controlled timer and detonator for the first time, marking a significant technological advance in their capabilities. Thatcher escaped with her life, but five people were killed and others seriously wounded, including the wife of Norman Tebbit, the man who had told unemployed British workers to get on their bikes.

The attack on Thatcher was a major shock. Confidence in the future of the British state took a sharp nosedive. The United Kingdom seemed on the verge of unraveling. Identity conflicts were on the rise and the center was failing to hold. The Troubles in Northern Ireland had been matched by the growth of Scottish and Welsh nationalism and reflected the final fraying of broader British ties with its erstwhile empire. When times were hard and the central government had few resources and opportunities to offer, people turned away from London and inward toward their core identities.

The upheaval was also the product of social changes that came on top of the broader economic processes that had moved the UK away from heavy industry and mass manufacturing in the twentieth century. People such as my grandparents and parents, who had been born before World War II, had their views shaped by the conservative social attitudes and tight bonds of their working-class communities as well as the patriotism of the 1940s and 1950s. In the 1970s they were being displaced by new generations with no memory of the deprivations of the 1920s and 1930s or of everyone rallying around the Union Jack in World War II and during the postwar efforts to rebuild the country. The new generations were facing their own economic crisis, but they no longer had these traditional communities and their attitudes to anchor and influence them.

In the early 1980s, the intra-British communal violence and identity conflicts assumed other dimensions as well. Although there were constant simmering tensions among the English, Irish, Scots, and Welsh, there were now so-called race riots involving immigrant communities in the big cities. These were primarily clashes between residents and the police after heavy-handed arrests and stop-and-search operations that disproportionately targeted the Black and Afro-Caribbean communities. They erupted in large cities like London, Liverpool, and Bristol, which had once been tied to the Atlantic slave trade.

The civic fabric of these British metropolises was shaped by the fortunes that prominent men and a wide range of investors made from centuries of trafficking in people. Private British companies, often under royal license, exported more than three million slaves from Africa (and initially poor white British men and women as indentured servants) to British colonies between 1640 and 1807. The slave trade was not formally abolished and prohibited until January 1, 1808, thanks to a parliamentary bill passed after two decades of bitter political debate in March 1807. During the final years of the slave trade alone, an estimated 767,000 Africans were shipped by British traders to the Caribbean islands of the West Indies and the Americas.

Although slavery did not take root in the British mainland, the UK's role in its export and development in the colonies came back to haunt the country in the modern era as immigrants from the West Indies, Africa, and elsewhere in the old empire came to work in British shipyards and factories, hoping to find their own opportunities. When I was a small child, in April 1968, the Conservative member of Parliament and shadow secretary of defense Enoch Powell encapsulated a growing backlash to the UK's diversification in an infamous speech on immigration. In blunt and racist language, Powell declared that immigrants and their children could never assimilate. They would never be British, even though they had once been subjects of the empire. Powell's speech set the tone for a contentious decade ahead. The 1980s clashes were a major jolt to UK politics, similar to the paroxysms that sparked the movement against racial injustice in the United States in 2020. They highlighted mounting frustration with the legacy of the Atlantic slave trade and decades of entrenched racist attitudes in British society on top of the sharp uptick in national unemployment and the decline in public services.

Everyone seemed to be competing for the UK's ever-diminishing returns and taking it out on those perceived to be lower in the social pecking order. The Irish, Scottish, and Welsh nationalist movements were now matched by an ugly *white* English nationalism, something that would have been a complete anomaly in earlier periods. The British National Party (BNP) and similar far-right groups brought "skinhead" violence to Bishop Auckland and the North East. We had other "tribal" convulsions, with members of different subcultures literally fighting it out over opposing musical tastes, dress styles, and perceptions of social attitudes. And we had rampant football hooliganism — bloody pitched battles among the supporters of opposing teams in the national game. Rampaging and pillaging by one group or another seemed the norm every time we headed out on a family day trip or quick vacation.

The rise of white nationalism in my home region was especially jarring, given that in the 1970s and 1980s, the population in Bishop Auckland and most of County Durham was distinct in its homogeneity. With the few exceptions of the occasional family from Pakistan or Sri Lanka, some shopkeepers and restaurant owners, and doctors and nurses in local hospitals, most of the region's residents were from one of the British indigenous groups. Their English, Irish, Scottish, Welsh, or Traveller ancestors had settled down when the mines and factories were expanding. There was not much to attract new immigrants up north to deindustrializing small towns with no opportunity. Race riots and racial discrimination were something we watched from afar on TV or read about in the papers. It was working-class protests and riots over lost jobs and livelihoods that roiled the region. We were in our own bubble of disadvantage. When I got to St. Andrews, it too was a bubble — of advantage and privilege. But it was equally homogenous.

Coal Not Dole

The 1984–1985 miners' strike dominated my first year at university. Initially intended to pressure the Thatcher government to stop what had become a cascade of pit closures across the country by the National Coal Board, the strike became one of the largest and bitterest labor disputes in UK history. It was a dramatic and wrenching event: a clash of the titans between Arthur Scargill, the head of the National Union of Mineworkers (NUM), and Prime Minister Thatcher, neither of whom wanted to back down. Scargill made it clear that he wanted to destabilize Thatcher's government and force her to capitulate.

The NUM was bitterly divided over the merits of militancy and industrial action. Competing factions within the NUM declared the strike illegal, as there had been no national members' vote ahead of time. Many miners continued to work, fearing that their pits would not open again when the dust had settled. Every community was hard hit. Striking miners and their families were dependent on food parcels and donations, including monies raised by international miners' unions from unlikely places such as the Donbas region in the Soviet Union (now in Ukraine but mired in a conflict provoked by Russia at the time of this writing). Those miners who chose to keep working pushed through picket lines manned by friends and relatives. Families were fractured. There was frequent violence, including in Easington in County Durham. Three people were killed in clashes, and more than eleven thousand were arrested across the country. Riot police were deployed to the streets of every major mining town. Uniformed and undercover policemen kept watch over union leaders' houses and infiltrated picket lines to spy on and pick off activists.

Margaret Thatcher, the Iron Lady, was unwavering, and Arthur Scargill refused to seek any accommodation, but in the end the NUM's resolve withered at the grassroots level. Too many men wanted to get back to work to put food on the table. The strike killed coal mining and weakened the British trade union movement. In the following year, forty thousand miners left the industry, taking redundancy payments in the hope of finding new opportunity. Pit closures continued unabated. The mining towns of the north were changed beyond recognition. They had been built by coal mining, and coal mining was no more.

The miners' strike was a constant refrain when I got to university, kept in mind not just by the headlines but also by some of the people around me. My one contact at St. Andrews from the local and family network was Bill Irving from Hett — a hamlet of nothing, on the way from Bishop Auckland to Durham. Bill was a former coal-mine foreman's son from nearby Tudhoe Colliery. His aunt was a cleaner at the hospital and a friend of my parents. He was a couple of years ahead of me at St. Andrews. He worked in several of the student bars to support himself and wore a COAL NOT DOLE badge on every outfit in solidarity with the miners.

There were other working-class kids at St. Andrews from Scotland, but only a few from North East England. Bill was my lifeline, one friendly face; Angela Bartle was another. Her family lived in South Stanley, outside of Consett. Her father and brothers had lost their jobs when the Consett Steel Works closed in 1980. They were still unemployed. Angela lived near me in the first-year hall of residence. She was trying to stretch her student grant to send money back to her family. Then there was Louise Brown in my Russian class, who turned out to be the granddaughter of the Gillespies who ran the shop in Billingham where Grandma Vi had worked in World War II. This was quite a coincidence.

Bill, Angela, and Louise were the only connections to my past life and my family in that first year. Once I got to St. Andrews, I was *originally* from the North East but no longer *actually* from there. I was now somewhere else entirely, and I would never go back to live in County Durham. I had not yet changed my social class, but I had already changed my geographic place by moving to university.

La Porte Étroite

Back home in Bishop Auckland, everyone had been working-class. Some kids at school had thought that my sister and I were posh because we lived in our own house, not a council house. They had made fun of us because we wanted to do things in our spare time like visit local museums and castles and read the poetry anthologies from the library. Having aspirations wasn't normal — or perhaps it just seemed pointless when you were unlikely to escape poverty or ever leave County Durham. But owning your own home was certainly something. They were right about that — apart from the fact that Mam and Dad didn't really own it for decades and were struggling to pay the mortgage.

At St. Andrews, some of my classmates were seriously, genuinely posh. They were from the uppermost upper reaches of the upper classes — members of the British aristocracy and landed gentry, even relatives of the Queen, as well as the children of prominent members of Parliament and government ministers. A few had castles, real ones in the Scottish countryside that had been in their families for generations. For some of my classmates I was a working-class kid from the lowest rung of the British class system, who had seemingly ended up there by accident.

One of the most memorable incidents in my first year at St. Andrews was an unpleasant exchange with a girl from Cheltenham Ladies' College in my French class. Cheltenham Ladies' College was the antithesis of Bishop Barrington Comprehensive School. I had read about it in novels. It was founded in the South, in Gloucestershire, in the 1850s to give well-bred girls the same educational advantages and opportunities as their counterparts in an all-boys school. It had impressively ornate ivy-clad buildings, first-class facilities, and an entrance exam. It was one of the best schools in the UK, with a roster of graduates including the country's first female diplomat, poets, novelists, doctors, scientists, and its fair share of aristocrats and princesses.

Somehow or other, without the benefit of this illustrious education, I had managed to turn in the best essay on André Gide's *La Porte Étroite* (a book about, appropriately enough, the horrors of adolescence), the week's assignment for my French class. The professor, Mr. Hunt, was called out for an urgent phone call just after he handed back our graded papers. He commended me in front of the class. Ms. Cheltenham Ladies' College turned to me the instant he left: "Did you sleep with Mr. Hunt? How could you have done so well? You're just a common northerner." She had a stern, harsh look on her face. She was completely serious. She clearly couldn't fathom it.

I too was shocked. And not just because of my classmate's disparaging comment. Like most people who find themselves well outside their social and cultural comfort zone, I had an acute case of imposter syndrome. At any moment I expected failing grades and expulsion. I felt exposed in *all* my classes, knowing that except for my forays into the *Encyclopedia Britannica,* I had very little experience with the material other students had covered in their private schools. For a significant number of students, St. Andrews had been their second, safety choice after Oxbridge. Many had done the extra year of advanced preparatory work, which seemed to have included much of the first-year university syllabus. They were coasting along. They seemed to know everything. They exuded confidence. I was filled with self-doubt every time they spoke in class and I had to follow. They knew things that I didn't even know I should know. They sounded intelligent. I sounded hesitant. In an effort to make up for what seemed like the lost time of my entire secondary school education, I spent long hours in the library in a permanent panic attack, reading everything I could get my hands on and taking furious notes.

French was one of those anxiety-inducing courses. My spoken and written French were okay thanks to County Durham's school exchanges and a lot of listening to French-language tapes and reading grammar books at home. But I was well aware of the deficiencies in my grasp of French literature. It was hard enough to get books in English, let alone foreign languages, at Bishop Barrington. My reading had been minimal and tightly circumscribed by the A-level syllabus, which I had obtained from the school secretary and worked through on my own. I had gone on the bus to the Durham University bookshop and a secondhand textbook seller in Durham marketplace to get copies of the books I needed. I had done nothing less, but nothing more.

The accusation landed like an open palm across my face. I'd hardly had any sleep at all working on that essay about Gide's book, let alone time for a dalliance with the professor. I wanted to hit her right back. I didn't know what to say. No one had ever accused me of anything like this.

I got up and walked out. I headed back to my dorm room, my cheeks burning. Now what? Well, at least I didn't slap her or say something rude, which would only have confirmed her view of my "common" nature.

A male classmate came to find me. He had told Mr. Hunt what had happened. Mr. Hunt asked to see me, and when I sat down in his office, I requested a transfer to another tutorial group. I avoided Ms. Cheltenham Ladies' College for the rest of my time at St. Andrews. It wasn't especially hard; there were a few snobs who would never deign to talk to the likes of me. She probably never gave it a second thought. But she scorched herself in my memory. She also spurred me to keep on doing better. I didn't want people like her to take any pleasure in my failure.

On the other hand, for some of my well-heeled classmates and their parents, I was a curiosity — a bit like a performing seal. There was a small seal colony in the Eden River Estuary at the end of St. Andrews' West Sands beach. I used to walk along to watch them pull themselves out of the water and bask in the sun. I felt like a seal out of water most of the time, without the basking. No time for that.

One fellow student asked me to come to tea with his visiting parents a few weeks into term. It was a bit of a surprise, especially when they turned up in a vintage Jaguar, a car I had never seen before, and drove us along the coast a while. I realized they were amused by me and the novelty of chatting with a representative of the lower classes. It was a novelty for me too, especially given the fact that Grandma Vi used to be a servant — probably in a house like theirs, from what I could glean from the conversation.

One girl, during a discussion after class of the virtues of private versus comprehensive schools, when several people had suggested that there was no difference in aptitude between the two cohorts, told me that mediocre students from the middle and upper classes needed private schools to get ahead. If they did not have this advantage, they would get overrun by clever kids from the lower classes, who would then get in everywhere, upsetting the social and political order. People like me, she said, would still do well without unnecessary preferential treatment. It was a weird kind of compliment. There were not enough opportunities, it seemed, to go around; better to limit the class competition in some fundamental and permanent way.

A Hand Up . . . the Skirt

Getting into university was difficult enough for working-class students, but once they got there, things didn't get any easier, academically or economically. Money remained a significant constraint for me in taking advantage of the opportunities open to other students as a matter of course. Low-income students, when I was at St. Andrews in the 1980s (as well as in the

2020s), had a hard time getting the extracurricular experience that employers expected to see on their résumés when they applied for a position after graduation. No one was encouraged to put menial jobs on a résumé, even if these highlighted the practical economic necessity of how to put yourself through college while demonstrating a capacity for hard work as well as the grit and determination to get ahead.

In the United States in particular, employers look for travel and foreign languages as well as prowess at sports and interesting hobbies — which I know only too well after decades of working in universities, think tanks, and the government. These are the markers of the well-rounded, highly accomplished student whom you would like to hire as an intern or entry-level employee. Interesting hobbies tend to be expensive, and it's hard to have one when you have to work long hours to make a living.

When I got to university, even with the maintenance grant, which was supposed to include living costs, I still needed part-time jobs in bars and restaurants to deal with shortfalls for housing, food, and travel costs. As a famous international golf center in addition to a tourist and university town, St. Andrews was expensive. My organized sports from school went straight out the window. They were replaced by cycling to class or work or running for a bus. Between my long hours in the library and maintaining a paid job, there was no time to be well-rounded. Like other low-income students, I needed to be resourceful and enterprising in figuring out how to expand the basic horizons and pursue the college experiences other students took for granted.

Immediately after the conclusion of my first year, in 1985, I had to participate in a mandatory intensive Russian course at the University of East Anglia in Norwich, England. This was one of the conditions for starting Russian from scratch at St. Andrews. My student grant did not extend to summer programs. Although the course organizers waived the fees, I would still need to cover food, lodging, and travel.

Thankfully, I got money from both the Durham Miners' Association (DMA) and the Bishop Auckland Rotary Club to help me. Uncle Charlie Crabtree told Dad about the DMA opportunity. He had heard from one of his friends in Crook that some of the money donated during the national miners' strike — including from the miners of the Donbas — had been put in an educational fund for the children of ex-miners. We had no way of calling ahead to find out if this was the case, so Dad, Angela, and I took the bus to Durham on the off chance. We had a lucky break. The man handling the paperwork for the grant applications at the DMA office had worked with several of Dad's relatives. He knew Grandad and Great-Grandad Hill by repute, and he quickly found Dad's former employment information on file. It turned out I was eligible for a small travel stipend and I could fill out the paperwork there. Our neighbor Sidney Lockey, who worked in a local solicitor's office, was a member of the Bishop Auckland Rotary Club. He recommended me to their educational charity fund for the remainder of the course money. I had to present myself for a short interview with some of the senior members over sandwiches to tell them about my Russian studies and what I hoped to do next.

I was fortunate to have a network of family and neighbors who could help me find opportunities, but at St. Andrews, I never shook off the constant sense of financial insecurity despite having my fees covered. There was no one and nothing to bail me out in a fiscal emergency. Unfortunately, when some people knew you were desperate for a job or a career-enhancing experience, they thought they could take liberties rather than just help you out.

I learned this the hard way when a coveted waitressing job at the bar and restaurant in the St. Andrews Royal and Ancient Golf Club, which was reputed to bring big tips, turned into a one-day stint. One old golfer stuck his hand up the back of my skirt and into my underwear as I bent down with his glass of single malt. I reflexively elbowed him in the face and was ordered out. When I complained about what he had done, the bar manager offered to speak to the other places I worked in St. Andrews to make sure I wouldn't have another job in town. He would also deny it if I reported it to the university, which had no official connection to the golf club apart from proximity.

Back home in Bishop Auckland, I worked multiple jobs for at least some portion of the time from June to September every year. For a couple of weeks here and there as my Russian improved, I assisted Durham County Council's educational exchange office — the same people who had sent me to Germany and France in school — with some newly launched programs with the USSR. But the hospital cleaning job was the best-paid and most reliable. It could be combined with everything else, since I worked the early shifts to cover for full-time cleaning staff on vacation. I often ran into Dad on the wards, and occasionally Mam if I cleaned the floors near the hospital labs.

But even in this comfortably familiar environment, I found myself in uncomfortable situations where I was reminded that my gender and class were drags on my upward mobility. Partway through my first stint back after starting at St. Andrews, I developed contact dermatitis from a new cleaning solution. It got infected and I had to see one of the doctors. He asked if I was a new full-time employee or on a job placement scheme — the latter being a Durham County Council–sponsored program for unemployed youth. I said I was a student. This was my summer job. He then asked if I was at the Bishop Auckland technical (community) college. No. I was not. He obviously didn't expect me to be at university, but he eventually asked where and what I was studying.

I explained that I was at St. Andrews reading (studying) Russian and modern history. The doctor looked completely shocked and blurted that he had started his medical studies at St. Andrews. Then he frowned. Why was I working in the hospital as a cleaner for the summer? Wasn't there something else I could be doing, like an internship? I said that I needed a job. My parents also worked at the hospital. By now the doctor seemed completely uncomfortable with his own questions. Who was my father? Did he know him? Was he another doctor? And my mother? I clearly did not fit into any of his social boxes.

In this situation and others like it, it got tiring explaining that sometimes low-income students got into elite universities, but that even when we did, we still had to work to get ourselves through. As I had discovered when I had been forced to turn down the offer to Durham High, getting accepted into a new sphere of opportunity frequently wasn't enough. Often it opened up a whole new set of challenges to deal with.

A Helping Hand

My most important life- and career-enhancing opportunity at St. Andrews came in 1987–1988, with a formal year of study abroad at Moscow's Maurice Thorez Institute of Foreign Languages, entirely funded by the British government. The late 1980s was a pivotal period in both the UK and the USSR. While the UK was navigating its way through the most acute stage of Thatcherism, the Soviet Union was opening up, just as it was falling apart. I was among the first foreigners forcibly tested for HIV at Moscow's main airport immediately on entry in September 1987, as the authorities fretted about the implications of letting in decadent and deviant capitalists. It was a strange and unnerving start to my year as an exchange student, and only one of many eye-opening experiences that would set me off on the path to becoming a "Russia expert."

It was an unlikely beginning. Not long before, I had almost dropped out of my Russian course. Things weren't going well back at home. The Thatcher government was cutting the NHS budget, and Dad's hours had been reduced. Mam was still working part-time, but I started to worry that they might be in financial trouble again and I wouldn't get a job with a degree in Russian and modern history. I had considered applying to the British Foreign Service or seeking work as a translator, but what if that didn't work out? What else could I do with this education?

I sought out advice at the St. Andrews career service. They weren't particularly helpful, but they did suggest that I could write to an alumnus from their files who might have ideas. The person they offered was George Robertson, who had studied at Queen's College in Dundee, which was part of St. Andrews until it broke away in the late 1960s to become Dundee University.

At that time Mr. Robertson was a member of Parliament for Hamilton South in Scotland. I wrote a letter to him — by hand. In those days all my St. Andrews work was produced by hand, or occasionally typed. I didn't know anyone at university who had a computer; it was still early days in the world of information technology. I was surprised when he wrote back — it was a typewritten letter, possibly dictated to a secretary, but it was a real letter, with a real signature, and real insight and advice.

Robertson encouraged me to keep going with my Russian studies. Noting the potential of Mikhail Gorbachev to make significant change in the USSR, he assured me that I would certainly get a job if I kept on expanding my horizons. He also suggested that I consider studying abroad if there was an opportunity to do so.

A decade later George Robertson became UK secretary of state for defense and then secretary general of NATO, and ultimately Lord Robertson, a British life peer. In October 2002 he visited the Brookings Institution for a public address. We reconnected. I was able to thank him in person for taking the time to write and keeping me on track.

The Electric Seagull

At the time of my first visit to Moscow, the Soviet capital seemed to me more like a giant Roddymoor than the epicenter of a colossal state. On one of my many strolls through the city after class, I was startled to see hens running around in the back garden of an old wooden house, just like at Grandad's. This was only a couple of streets away from the imposing building of the Soviet Foreign Ministry. In fact, most people's families had an *uchastok*, or allotment, although they were usually on the outskirts of Moscow, not right in the center. As in Roddymoor, denizens of the Soviet capital needed a plot of land to see them through hard times.

This was the so-called deficit period when the centralized production of consumer goods, including food, could not keep up with demand. The USSR had become a major producer of oil and gas in the 1960s, which was (and remains) the state's major source of foreign currency earnings. Unfortunately, oil production was beginning to decline by the 1980s, and the Soviet Union exported a significant proportion to the rest of the Eastern bloc at heavily discounted prices. Energy consumption was rising across the bloc, leaving less oil for the hard-currency exports that enabled the state to pay for specialized imported goods for the manufacturing, technology, and consumer sectors. The Soviet state was starting to borrow money to cover shortfalls — a desperate measure that foreshadowed the onrushing collapse of the Soviet economy, and with it the Soviet state.

The student and worker canteens, the *stolovayas* (cafeterias) and Moscow's small restaurants, were often short of food. You would run hopefully down the menu from one item to another, only to learn "No, we don't have it," all the while wishing that the server had just told you in the first place what they *did* have. Usually the items actually on the menu involved some form of sausage, fried or boiled eggs, pickled vegetables, grilled mushrooms in *smetana* (sour cream), borscht, black or white bread, cheese, and packets of ketchup, along with instant Nescafé or black tea. Sometimes there was cake, which seemed to have sat around desiccating for a while. Growing up in the North East of England, I was not much of a food connoisseur in any case and was mostly glad for a chance to eat. I was particularly fond of the cake, even if it was dry.

We didn't have a kitchen in our accommodation, which was a student hotel intended for short stays, not a yearlong exchange program. There was a small fridge in the room. We were allowed to buy a hot plate and an electric kettle from our stipends. But we had to be careful not to overtax the fraying electrical wiring and start a fire. There was also a TV in the room — a real luxury, but also a serious danger. We were warned that exploding televisions were a genuine hazard and had purportedly led to a deadly fire in Moscow's massive Rossiya Hotel in 1977.

Small appliances were preferable, but not so easy to find. And we had a leg up in terms of our purchasing potential and capacity: as foreigners with access to hard currency (pounds sterling or dollars), exchange students in Moscow were allowed to use the specialty Beriozka (Birch Tree) retail stores, which were off-limits for the average Russian. The stores were run by the state and filled with luxury items unobtainable in regular shops and markets. They also sold high-end souvenirs for foreign tourist groups — intricately carved wooden ornaments and lacquer boxes with exquisitely detailed miniature paintings of Russian fairy tales. We had to show our passports as well as our student identification to enter. There was another set of stores for the Communist Party elite and senior Russian officials, who might have been partly paid in foreign currency if they served abroad. They received special coupons to shop there. The contrast between the Beriozkas and the rest of the shops and markets underscored the glaring inequalities that develop in fading states. We treated friends from our institute to something special from the Beriozka around the corner if someone was having a birthday.

But even with this privileged access, I spent several fruitless days looking for the electric kettle that we were allowed to have in our student hotel room. In the course of my search, I was literally chased out of the famous GUM department store on Red Square by an irate saleswoman. I couldn't figure out what the problem was until I checked my earnestly rehearsed request in the dictionary. I had somehow mixed up the word for teapot or kettle, *chaynik,* with *chayka,* seagull, and had been on a futile quest for an electric seagull. The woman had clearly thought that I was yet another brazen foreigner making fun of the Soviet Union and its deficiencies . . . but honestly, why on earth would "seagull" sound like the word for tea?

"We Have Gasoline on Tap!"

Outside the special stores, Moscow's physical infrastructure was crumbling. No one had repaired anything significant for decades. The city council's money had run out, just as in Bishop Auckland. Amenities could hardly be described as "conveniences." Public toilets were virtually impossible to find and alarming when finally discovered (even for people like me who were used to outhouses). The big outdoor markets, where I went with my fellow exchange students, Katy and Tessa, to buy fresh food, had huge pits in the ground. Tessa fell into one in Novye Cheryomushki market after losing her footing on some sodden cardboard around the edge. It was the depth of winter. Katy and I extracted her with the help of an old lady and her cane. Tessa was in a sorry state, and unpleasantly smelly despite the frigid temperature. The trolley driver on our return journey took one look and whiff and wouldn't let us board. We had a very long, icy trudge home with our shopping bags.

There were other, more frightening hazards. Bits of buildings frequently fell off, leaving debris and worse on the sidewalks. In one shocking incident, an old lady was crushed by a balcony in the next block to our institute. Her legs in their felt boots were sticking out from beneath the rubble when my friend Alla and I walked by, clutching each other in horror.

Some of the decaying infrastructure was invisible — until you felt its effects. There were frequent power outages and burst pipes. Gasoline contaminated the water across our section of Moscow for at least a week after a spillage from a storage tank, but nobody warned us. You could smell it when you turned on the tap, and the bathwater ran brown. This made it hard to do our laundry as well as shower. When we mentioned it to the custodian, he quipped, "See how amazing the USSR is? We have gasoline on tap!" Just as in Bish Vegas, humor was the way people kept themselves sane in the Soviet Union when the present no longer lived up to the promises of the past.

Physical mobility could be a huge challenge for poor people in Russia too. In Moscow as well as Bishop Auckland, few people had cars, and there were plenty of horses and carts in the rural villages on the outskirts. In the USSR, cars were a scarce luxury item in limited production. They were virtually inaccessible to the average person. Families without connections were put on a waiting list that stretched for years.

My friend Misha's family was finally told that their long wait was over just as they had given up on the Soviet Union and were about to emigrate to Israel in search of new opportunity (and to escape years of anti-Jewish discrimination). After all this time, they were still determined to get the car. They resolved to sell it (which was permissible in the late 1980s) to help defray some of the costs of moving abroad. A few days after taking possession of the car, Misha's father parked it outside another market, Rizhsky, near their apartment, to buy flowers for his wife. When he came out, a huge sinkhole had opened up where one of Moscow's ubiquitous potholes had been in the road. It had literally swallowed the car.

It was late in the day. Misha's father could not find anyone with a truck to help him retrieve the vehicle until the following afternoon. When they got to the edge of the yawning sinkhole, which was now filling with water, the car was nothing but a carcass. It had been stripped of everything that could be removed — windscreen wipers, mirrors, interior fixtures, all the things that were in short supply when people needed to fix their own cars. Misha's father sold the new car for scrap. And then he left the country.

Working-Class Standard-Bearer

For me, the year abroad in Moscow was a surprisingly easy transition despite the language and cultural differences and learning to navigate a big city for the first time. The dreaded determinative questions of "Where are you from?" and "What does your father do?" met with instant approval. I was from a world-famous coal-mining area and my dad had been a miner. I was a standard-bearer of the working class. This gave me cachet in the Soviet Union. People could relate to me and my family story.

Social mobility through education was the norm in the USSR. Most of the Russian students from my institute, including those from the Communist Party elite, were only one or two generations away from a factory or collective farm or were the first in their families to pursue higher education. Many of my friends' parents were factory workers in the outer reaches of Moscow. They commuted in on the Metro with a student pass. Students were encouraged at weekends to go on *subbotniks* (Saturday work brigades) to pick vegetables or perform some manual task to fill in for labor shortages, which helped retain the old connections. We used to have the same arrangement in the North East of England in October to help farmers with "potato-picking week," and I helped Dad and Grandad with their allotments, so I signed up. An old man from one collective farm was so impressed that "capitalist" kids did this too that he gave me his prized framed picture of Stalin. It was cut from a newspaper and yellowed from sitting on the windowsill in the farm's storage hut.

Another common thread with my fellow Russian students was music. With a student card you could get subsidized entry to the ballet, the opera, cinemas, art galleries, and concerts. I made the most of all those opportunities. Moscow was, as it still is, a world-class cultural center. I had never had any of those experiences before — going to the ballet and the opera. But the late 1980s was the time when Russia's alternative music scene took off.

In Moscow, music offered a vehicle for protest and political engagement as well as entertainment.

I recognized this strain of revolutionary music immediately. In the UK in the 1960s and 1970s, the Beatles had led the charge of working-class youth to shake up the British and global music scene. In the Soviet Union, everyone knew and loved the Beatles. Russian friends studying at our institute took me to see their crumbling family villages or apartment blocks on the outskirts of Moscow, where there was always someone strumming a Beatles song on a guitar or playing a bootleg cassette of a Western band on a beat-up player.

In the USSR in the 1980s, music became revolutionary. New music came out of the decaying industrial might of the Soviet Union's forgotten cities. Forming a band, listening to bands, and going to concerts were ways of assembling, mobilizing, channeling frustration, making yourself heard, and belonging to a new generational movement. British singer Billy Bragg, who sang in 1988 about "Waiting for the Great Leap Forwards" and mixed pop with politics, fit right in when he came to Moscow as part of a wave of Western bands touring the USSR in this period. I traveled across the city to see a group called Nautilus Pompilius, from the Urals industrial city of Sverdlovsk (Yekaterinburg), whose song "Goodbye America" was one of the great anthems of the year, perform in the concert hall of an enormous factory on the outskirts. In keeping with tradition, I surreptitiously taped the concert to play and replay later in my room.

In Moscow it was much easier to get to concerts on the fringes of the city than at home. The Metro ran late into the night like clockwork. Back home I had taken the bus to concerts in Newcastle with Angela and our friends. At St. Andrews, I took the bus to the Dundee Dance Factory. We were often stranded. In Moscow, the Metro, the trains, and the buses always got you where you wanted to be, even when everything else was unreliable.

Coffee for Maria Shriver

It was my exchange year in Russia that brought me directly to America and helped to demystify the application process for Harvard, in stark contrast to my experience with Oxford a few years before. In each case the infrastructure of new opportunity was laid out for me in an accessible way. During the 1988 Moscow summit between Ronald Reagan and Mikhail Gorbachev, I got another lucky break and my most exciting job to date: a translating and stringer gig with America's *NBC News.*

The major U.S. networks were offering $100 a day for a week of 24/7 work. That in itself was an opportunity I could not pass up. The networks advertised for native English-speakers in the U.S., UK, Australian, and Canadian embassies, all of which had small student groups on exchange programs. They pretty much hired everyone who showed up. First day on the job, I was informed that my spoken English was a bit hard to understand — just where was that accent from? — but not to worry, there were plenty of things I could do.

At the time I thought that the highlight of my stint at *NBC News* was seeing the American president. I found Reagan's speech at Moscow State University exhilarating, and I accompanied the NBC camera crew onto Red Square as "Ronnie and Nancy" executed a nighttime walkabout with Gorbachev and his wife, Raisa. I have a lingering image of that moment — one of those sights and impressions that is so distinctive it literally sears itself into your mind's eye. From where we stood, First Lady Nancy Reagan's tiny frame was silhouetted against St. Basil's Cathedral by a powerful, dazzling spotlight, beamed from the top of a Kremlin tower. It backlit her head in such a way that from one angle she appeared to be wearing a giant glowing helmet; from another her head seemed enormous and translucent. The camera crew was worried about the shot and how they wouldn't be able to use the footage because of the stark, blinding light. They wanted to move to a spot away from the light, but the stringent Soviet security on Red Square wouldn't let us, no matter how much I tried out my Russian-language powers of persuasion. The producer kept complaining that Nancy Reagan looked like a giant tadpole, or one of the aliens from *Close Encounters of the Third Kind.*

Most of my other assignments were much more mundane, or at least seemed to be. I was dispatched to pick up dignitaries from the airport and delegated to run around with a Russian film crew taking clips of ordinary Russians doing things that Americans could relate to, like playing baseball and basketball. I sprayed *Nightly News* anchor Tom Brokaw's hair to keep it from blowing around during filming on the rooftop of the Rossiya Hotel across from the Kremlin. And, most consequentially, I made coffee for *Today* host Maria Shriver.

Thanks to this unremarkable assignment, I learned about scholarships to American graduate schools from the Columbia professor Robert Legvold, who was there as an adviser to one of the networks. He helped me clean up a mess I had made in the communal kitchen in my inept first attempt at using a drip filter coffee machine. In our brief encounter, during which Professor Legvold showed me where to put the water, filter, and coffee, he also showed a passing interest in who I was and what I was doing in Moscow. Moving into full-on mentor mode when I mentioned that I would be graduating after I returned to Scotland, he suggested I consider applying for a master's degree in the U.S. and advised me to talk to the cultural attachés at the American and British embassies.

Mike Bird, the deputy attaché at the British embassy, was early in his career with the British Council, the UK's international organization for cultural relations and educational opportunities. The British Council administered the Russian-language undergraduate study program that had placed me and other UK students for a year at the Maurice Thorez Institute. He was the liaison to the students. This was his first posting. Before joining the British Council, Mike himself had had a scholarship to study Russian at Harvard's Russian Research Center — another fortuitous coincidence. He offered to provide me with all the information that would help me apply for this and related scholarships, including getting in touch with St. Andrews University to find out who would be the right people to connect with on my return. This turned out to be one of the St. Andrews staff members, Frank Quinault, who had helped me secure the year abroad in Moscow in the first place. Mike Bird also learned that one of the professors from the Russian Department, Christopher Barnes, a biographer of the Russian author Boris Pasternak, had spent a year as a scholar at Harvard's Russian Research Center. He recommended that I confer with Professor Barnes too on my return to St. Andrews.

This was quite remarkable. It wasn't obvious that I would meet or know people who could guide me through this major life and career step that a chance encounter over a coffee machine in Moscow had set in motion.

In and Out of the Broom Closet

Just as in the case of applying to university in the UK, I was not particularly familiar with American universities. When I first started the application process, Dad hadn't heard of Harvard. At first he was a bit worried. "What about Yale, Fiona?" He'd heard of Yale thanks to reading *The Great Gatsby* and other popular culture references. I had to persuade him that Harvard was okay as far as I could tell. It was America's oldest university. It had come highly recommended by all the people I had spoken to. And, in any case, there did not appear to be any scholarships to Yale that I could apply for.

Nonetheless, the application process for Harvard was daunting, even with advice and assistance. There were several scholarships. I applied to as many as I was eligible for. I ended up being selected for two interviews for the Kennedy Scholarship (which Mike Bird had had) and the Frank Knox Fellowship. The first was established in the UK by public donation after John F. Kennedy's assassination, and the second was bequeathed by Frank Knox, secretary of the navy during World War II. Together the two scholarships were the functional equivalents of the U.S. Rhodes and Marshall fellowships. They were jointly administered by a board of British luminaries, representatives from Harvard and MIT, and the U.S. ambassador to the UK.

The interviews took place in an ancient wood-paneled room in an antique building behind Westminster Abbey, near the Houses of Parliament, over two successive days. The scholarship program miraculously paid for train tickets and somewhere to stay ahead of the interviews. But I blew the first interview, for the Kennedy Scholarship, in a fit of nerves: on the way out of the room, I lurched toward the nearest door handle and walked into the cleaner's closet instead of the hallway. I stayed in the closet just a little too long for everyone's comfort, before sheepishly retreating out and asking where the actual door was. Too many wooden panels.

I soothed myself ahead of the second interview by telling the closet story to the scholarship program secretary, the lovely Miss Marjorie Watson, who was the person I had most related to during the whole process. She had been extremely friendly and helpful throughout. Miss Watson gently advised me to tell it to the selection committee with the same self-deprecating humor I had used with her and turn it to my advantage.

Only after I got the Knox Fellowship did I discover the crucial role Miss Watson had played in the selection process for both of the scholarships. Two other selectees, Sarah Moor and Nigel Gould-Davis, had also talked at length to Miss Watson. Everyone else waiting with them in their particular interview slots had ignored her. The others did not pass "the Miss Watson test." Sarah got a Kennedy Scholarship, and Nigel joined me on the Knox program.

Another critical player in my corner was Margot Gill, the Harvard Graduate School of Arts and Sciences' elegant dean for academic affairs and international programs, who was the constant between the two interviews.

She sought me out after the closet encounter to reassure me that I would have a second chance. It later turned out that the Harvard graduate school was then trying to break free from the Oxbridge stranglehold on its UK fellowships. Harvard overall had embarked on a recruitment drive to bring in more students from low-income and unconventional backgrounds. Again, I had lucky timing.

The North-South Divide

The question posed to all the candidates at the Knox interview was strangely auspicious — there was no other way to describe it. This was January 1989, the peak of Thatcherism. The question was, how would you describe the so-called North-South divide in the United Kingdom and its role in politics? Do you agree that such a social, cultural, and economic divide exists in the first place?

This topic had become one of major public debate in the wake of the miners' strike. The contrast between the mass deindustrialization and high unemployment in the North with the rise of the service and financial sectors in London in the South was fairly inescapable, even though there were clearly pockets of prosperity in the North and poverty in the South. No divisions are ever that neat. The ruling Conservative Party's share of the vote in the North fell dramatically in the 1980s, leaving the region an impenetrable Labour Party stronghold — delineated by what came to be known as the "Red Wall" — that seemed to be in perpetual political conflict with the central government.

It was clearly not an abstract or theoretical question for me. I reviewed some of the salient points in my response but noted that when you were from the North East of England this was a lived experience, not a political issue. I related what working-class life was like in the North, from my family's and community's vantage point, and how the distinctions unfolded as you made a trip south (which I rarely did). London was another world entirely from Bishop Auckland and County Durham.

As I recounted in my Knox interview, in the twentieth century, the long arc of economic development had moved away from small industrial communities and cities to the service and high-tech hubs of large urban areas. By the 1980s, big cities and their immediate hinterlands had become the locus of opportunity — the chance to have a good, stable job and do something with your life beyond eking out an existence. The United States, as

I would soon learn, became "bicoastal" during this same period, with the eastern Atlantic and West Coast regions pulling people and activity away from the center. Similarly, London and the South of England already dominated the United Kingdom in January 1989, when I was taking this interview. The North East of England was an economic wasteland, an opportunity desert. Prosperity was nothing but a mirage: the shimmer of the city of London or even another country somewhere far beyond the horizon.

I told the panel that Moscow was in fact the first big city I had lived in. When I got there on my student exchange program, Moscow was also very much down on its luck. Indeed, everything in the USSR was in a state of decay. In Bishop Auckland many of the shops were boarded up, the direct consequence of mass unemployment and rising poverty, which suppressed demand. In Moscow the shops were open, but there was often nothing in them. There was plenty of demand but no supply. I observed that the Soviet economy and consumer-goods production had run out of steam. The entire population seemed to be in a downward spiral. Although I didn't know it yet, the Soviet Union was headed toward the same devastating levels of unemployment and poverty as the North East once the state collapsed in 1991. For now, in the USSR in 1989, people still had jobs, which was somewhat different from the situation at home.

In any case, the comparisons resonated with the selection committee. They had lots of follow-up questions about my time in the USSR and what I had seen during the Reagan-Gorbachev summit. So now I was on my way to America, thanks in part to my firsthand experience of the North-South divide and a chance encounter over a cup of coffee.

PART II
A DIVIDED HOUSE

5

The Land of Opportunity

When I moved to the United States in 1989, I had not spent any length of time anywhere in England apart from Bishop Auckland and the North East. Having never experienced, except in tantalizingly fleeting visits, the proverbially "sunlit uplands" of England's green and pleasant land, I was finely attuned to industrial decline. I was a product of it. It shaped my entire childhood and adolescence.

I wasn't expecting to see similar patterns and divides when I got to Harvard and the land of opportunity, but parts of the United States were trending in the same direction as County Durham in the 1980s. The American version of England's North East — the Northeast, New England — was also a deindustrializing region. Living in Cambridge, Massachusetts, for the entirety of the next decade, I was struck by the jarring disparities and similar developments to those I had seen in old England and the USSR.

Harvard's campus was a far cry from the other parts of town, including those right on its doorstep. Impecunious graduate students lived in sub-rentals in precariously leaning wooden triple-deckers in "Slummerville," as some students snidely dubbed Somerville, the factory town just north of Cambridge. Their landlords were the former workers in Somerville's once-famous brickworks, Ford Motor assembly, and meatpacking plants. They bought the triple-deckers for their growing families in the boom times. They were forced to rent out rooms or entire floors in the bust when everything closed.

Gentrification and economic revival were still some way off in this period. Harvard's neighbor and sometime rival, MIT, was busy absorbing East Cambridge's old industrial zone. The university was in the process of converting shuttered factory buildings into science laboratories and student housing. Harvard and MIT were major local employers, although of course for administrative and custodial staff positions. The faculty usually came from elsewhere, as did most of the students. There was a lot of town-and-gown tension and evident polarization of political views.

I had to come to Harvard to enroll in a two-year master's program in Soviet studies at the university's Russian Research Center. I ended up tracking the Soviet bloc's free fall in real time over the course of my degree program. The USSR was on the ash heap of history only a few months after I received my degree in June 1991.

Over the course of my studies and based on my personal experiences, it soon dawned on me that the Cold War, the proverbial Iron Curtain, and the ideological veil of the bitter struggle between capitalism and communism had concealed the fact that the United Kingdom, the USSR, and the United States had much in common. Once you lifted the veil, you could see the touch points beneath — especially when you knew what you were looking for.

Stuck in the USSR

For me, born in 1965, and from my vantage point of experiencing life in the North East of England, then the Soviet Union, and then the United States, the big three military and industrial powers of World War II were facing similar postindustrial challenges, albeit on slightly different timescales. Historically, the USSR's trajectory of industrial development was similar to those of the United Kingdom and the United States in the twentieth century, with periods of booms and busts before and after the Second World War. The USSR had been mostly on the sidelines during the oil shocks of the 1970s, as it developed its own oil and gas reserves for domestic consumption, but it could not escape the effects of the technological changes that pushed other economies toward modernization and away from heavy industry. The Soviet Union was the bastion of workers in coal mines and smokestack industries and massive factories. The 1980s were not good times for workers and their enterprises.

When I first got there, in 1987, the Soviet Union was still a centrally planned economy, as it had been since the 1920s. The parts of the economy were closely interlinked. Supply lines stretched across the entire coun-try as well as into neighboring Eastern European countries of the Soviet bloc, such as Poland, Hungary, and East Germany (GDR). Moscow was the hub and the main market for goods. In the USSR, all roads and rail and air routes came into Moscow and out again. Every economic sector and geo-graphic region rose and fell with the others. There was no autonomy, little room for individual innovation, and thus no system flexibility. You pulled on one string and suddenly other parts of the system started to unravel. Ev-eryone knew there was a big, perhaps insurmountable problem by the time Mikhail Gorbachev became the Soviet leader in 1985. Over the next five years, the Soviet state was pulled apart by intra-elite disputes over how to fix the failing economy, with everyone tugging on different strings.

Ordinary people across the Soviet Union's constituent republics had grown disillusioned with a Communist system that never delivered. It was very similar to the situation in the United Kingdom with Ireland, Scotland, and Wales in the same timeframe. By the 1980s, citizens of the USSR no longer fully associated themselves with the overarching Soviet identity the state had promoted. From the Baltic states of Estonia, Latvia, and Lithuania to the Caucasus and republics like Armenia, Azerbaijan, and Georgia, for-mer Soviet "comrades" started to return to older ethnic identities. Even in the Russian republic, ethno-nationalist tensions increased behind the So-viet façade, similar to the rise of English nationalism in the UK. Eventu-ally, in December 1991, the USSR came apart at the seams. The republican heads of Belarus, Ukraine, and Russia met in a hut deep in the Belarussian woods to repudiate Gorbachev's last-ditch efforts to shore up their frac-tured union. They declared the union dead.

In the case of the USSR, its postindustrial difficulties were immediately obvious, even to the outside observer. In the UK and the U.S., postindus-trial decline was more uneven. It was gradual in some places, sudden and brutal in others. It was not even apparent on the surface for most people at the national level, unless you lived in a blighted former industrial neigh-borhood, town, or city — like a Somerville or Bishop Auckland — where the collapse of the local economy was a reality and the rest of the coun-try seemed to move on without you. The United Kingdom and the United States were not centrally planned economies like the Soviet Union. Some might argue that the UK was centrally planned to some extent at the begin-ning of the 1980s. The "commanding heights" of the steel, coal, oil, gas, rail, and shipbuilding industries had been nationalized after World War II, until Margaret Thatcher reprivatized them and pushed them to be profitable or close. There was, however, a great deal of sectoral and regional variation. There was scope for innovation. There was also private capital and government spending to invest in new businesses. Private philanthropy and accumulated family assets (housing, savings) helped smooth things over for some of those who fell on hard times.

Parts of the economy and some regions in both the United States and the United Kingdom adapted relatively quickly to changes in technology. Massachusetts, for example, would turn itself around in the early 2000s, putting some of the travails I first saw in 1989 and in the 1990s behind it. Regions in the Northeast eventually matched the shifts in national and global trade patterns and met the demand for new manufacturing products and services. In the UK, the economy in London and the South of England boomed, driven by new financial and consumer services and an influx of highly qualified migrants and immigrants from around the globe. The mining and manufacturing industries and centers of North East England, and their counterparts in the American Midwest and Appalachia, were not so nimble. Nor were they so fortunate. They also lost everything at once.

In Russia, Moscow mirrored London and some of the individual U.S. cities. It too became a boom town. By the 2010s it was a glitzy megalopolis that eclipsed every other Russian city and region. All the population growth, dynamism, and wealth generation of the new service economy and technology sectors, and all the key connections with global markets, became concentrated in and around Moscow. It became totally different from the city I lived in at the end of the 1980s and during the 1990s. Instead of being the hub for the Soviet bloc, Moscow was now a global city. Everywhere else, even the former Russian imperial capital of St. Petersburg, was a backwater in comparison.

In the UK North East, as its population became economically and demographically depleted, the region's political clout rapidly diminished. There was little effort to cushion the blows or smooth the transition. Successive governments and prime ministers after Margaret Thatcher did not care about the people's plight. Politically, they didn't have to. The North had no means to hold them to account for their losses.

Bishop Auckland's predicament in the 1980s was soon emblematic of hundreds if not thousands of towns across regions of the United States. Left to their own devices, without targeted and sustained state intervention, they simply could not adapt and modernize. They ended up as permanent losers, not winners, in the new economy, and in a state of perpetual decay.

Initially in the United States, after the fall of the Berlin Wall in 1989 and then the collapse of the USSR in 1991, there was no sense that America too was in postindustrial decline. The idea that the West had won the Cold War and capitalism had prevailed over communism deflected attention from the troubles of America's old manufacturing centers and their displaced workers. The Rust Belt seemed an unfortunate anomaly amid an overall picture of steady growth in the U.S. economy and rising prosperity in East and West Coast cities. But at the end of the 1980s, the Rust Belt was far more like the Soviet Union and the North East of England than most Americans realized. The United States' big industries had also developed under a fixed set of technological and economic conditions. They were huge enterprises, centers of mass production, purpose-built for a specific time and place in the first half of the twentieth century. They had been built close to major sources of raw materials, energy, and transportation routes, such as shipping routes across the Great Lakes or down major rivers to the ocean. They had enormous sunken and fixed costs. The enterprises had drawn in hundreds, sometimes thousands of workers, often with central state and local government intervention and direction. Places like Consett, Hartlepool, and Sunderland in my home region of County Durham had their counterparts in Bethlehem, Pennsylvania; Gary, Indiana; and Flint, Michigan; with their steel mills and giant factories. They were in essence the same kind of big company or mono-industry towns as Dnipropetrovsk (now in Ukraine), Stalingrad (now Volgograd), and Magnitogorsk in the USSR. Regardless of the particular circumstances of their individual creation, they were now outmoded and depleted, their big industries shrinking as they modernized and became automated.

Mass industries built the cities, not the other way around. When the industries closed, the place-based economies and societies crumpled in on themselves. The infrastructure of opportunity disappeared. Workers' homes were built right next to the mine or the factory so people could walk or cycle or take a short bus ride to begin their shifts at all hours of the day or night. The towns' civic fabric, every social amenity — the hospitals and health centers, the social clubs, the sports teams, the churches, even holidays and celebrations — was tied to workplaces and jobs. It was the same in the U.S., the UK, and the USSR. When the mine or the factory closed, there was no work, nothing to do, and nowhere to go. Thriving industry-built cities became shattered ghost towns. Everyone was stuck in place, trapped in a time that had passed.

In the 1980s, in the same timeframe as factories closed and demand for labor declined in the United Kingdom and the United States, the USSR faltered. Margaret Thatcher and Ronald Reagan precipitated the end of the Soviet Union as well as the Cold War through the pressures their interactions with Mikhail Gorbachev imposed on him, at a time when he was attempting the reform of the entire Communist system. But in fact, domestically, Margaret Thatcher, Ronald Reagan, and Mikhail Gorbachev were all engaged in the same reform project — out with the old, in with the new. Each adopted a top-down approach notable for its absence of broader social consultation and its politically polarizing effects. Reforms were inflicted or imposed and rarely explained to the population that was most affected by them. But it was only Gorbachev who lost a country.

In the euphoria at the end of the Cold War, the confluence of timing, events, and intent went unnoticed on the western side of the Iron Curtain. The UK and the U.S. could surely not have anything at all in common with the Soviet Union, given the total failure of its system . . . could we?

"Blair's Girls"

My time at Harvard, from 1989 to 1999, was a period of personal and professional transformation and transition, as well as consolidation of knowledge that led me toward these insights into the common patterns among the U.S., U.K., and Russia and the implications of these parallels. The 1990s was the decade in which the connections between my family experiences in the North East of England and developments and events in Russia became clear and I began to see similar reflections in the United States. In my first year at Harvard, I had a few of the same early encounters with class discrimination as I had had at St. Andrews. I could see how it would continue to constrain my opportunities back home. The Oxford philosophy, politics, and economics set that I might have ended up studying with, had things turned out differently at my interview, followed me to Harvard.

PPE, as I had already learned, was the prestigious generalist degree for aspiring politicians and most of the UK ruling class. Graduates of PPE at Oxford had a stranglehold on the UK government for decades, creating a purportedly meritocratic but certainly self-perpetuating dynasty. They dominated the Kennedy Scholarships — the one I missed by walking into the closet. Even Sarah Moor and a couple of others who had graduated from Cambridge felt out of place. The Oxford PPE clique at Harvard exuded confidence and the utter certainty that as part of the UK elite they would make a major impact as political party leaders, journalists, academics, or other public figures back in Britain.

The first social hour, when Harvard brought all the UK fellowship students together, was a rerun of my German school exchange experience a decade earlier. Each new fellow was encouraged to bring "a friend" to mix things up a bit. It was a bit early to have made friends, but Sarah and I were living together in a Harvard dorm, so we invited our immediate neighbors on either side, John Henriksen and Ken Keen (who would later become my husband). They were both from the American Midwest — from Iowa and Illinois, respectively. This was their first introduction to the UK and the vagaries of its class system. They thought it was ridiculous.

Sarah and I, with name tags affixed to our chests, stood around awkwardly clutching drinks, chatting to John and Ken, and waiting to introduce ourselves to the other students if they moved within reach or made eye contact. John and Ken quickly observed that as soon as some of the other Brits heard my answers to the determinative trifecta of questions and took note of my North East accent, they turned away and moved on. One Kennedy Scholar's face puckered up so obviously as I spoke and she sipped her drink that they asked what was going on. John and Ken said it looked like she had taken a swig of pee. They referred to her as "Urine Face" for the rest of the year.

Why was I provoking such unenthusiastic reactions? They didn't get it. So Sarah launched into an explanation of the UK class system, regional accents, and the negative attitudes toward the North East in the rest of England. Sarah had grown up on a farm near Sunderland, but she stressed that it was only because she had gone to a local private girls' school and then to Cambridge that she got a pass for also growing up in the North East. I didn't fit in, even though I had made it to Harvard. She agreed it was ridiculous and unfair.

Accent, the way a person talked, the dialect or language and grammatical constructions they used, were also markers of class in the UK. A distinct regional accent from somewhere like the North East would automatically place you in the working class, even if your family were white-collar professionals. This was a case of guilt by linguistic association with a region once completely dominated by heavy industry and thus by "workers." Scots, Welsh, and Irish also stood out for their accents in England — and were often derided if they were native Gaelic-speakers.

Many of the English dialects came with specific names attached, which often were used in a mocking, demeaning fashion, as if to make a point that you were from a specific, amusing sort of place and didn't fit into regular society. People from Newcastle and Tyneside were Geordies, those from Liverpool and Merseyside were Scousers. In London, the working class from the East End were Cockneys. If you were in the middle or upper classes, by contrast, you usually had "Received Pronunciation" (or RP), the clipped tones sometimes known as the Queen's English (or King's, before Queen Elizabeth II) or Oxford English. This was the accent immortalized by generations of *BBC News* presenters and the UK students who had made it to Harvard.

Aspirational Brits, mockingly dubbed "social climbers," would take elocution lessons to change the tone and pitch of their voice as well as their diction. Margaret Thatcher herself, the middle-class daughter of a small-town grocer who went to Oxford University, famously took voice lessons in the 1970s. This facilitated her ascent up the UK political hierarchy. Others with an ear for the musicality of speech, or a chameleon-like talent, would simply transform themselves as they moved away from their regions or working-class roots and tried to blend in. They took on a new identity with a different accent, becoming something and someone else to avoid drawing undue attention and any risk of discrimination.

I had never considered changing my accent through elocution lessons to acquire Received Pronunciation and pass myself off as something else. I wanted to remain my authentic self. But as the Harvard experience was reinforcing, retaining your true voice was acceptable only within your original geographic and socioeconomic context. It became a problem when you stepped outside, into an arena or profession with different associations and expectations. Other people *did* actually care about your accent, even when you stopped thinking about it or thought it finally might not matter.

At a later Harvard social event, with Sarah and Nigel Gould-Davies in tow, another Kennedy Scholar, Ed Balls, referred to me as "Geordie Fiona," linking me to the distinctive Newcastle accent. It was meant in jest but didn't come off as especially funny. By now it was obvious to me that the UK's class and accent discrimination was not going to go away when I encountered other Brits, no matter what I did and where I was.

My interactions with Harvard's Oxford PPE group that year were part of the reason I stayed on in the United States. I wanted to leave the UK's place- and class-based discrimination behind and move on. As for the Kennedy Scholars, Ed Balls did indeed go on to a high-level political job in the UK. He became the economic secretary to the treasury under Prime Minister Tony Blair and then minister for children, schools, and families under Prime Minister Gordon Brown. Sarah went off to be a barrister in London, while Nigel stayed on at Harvard with me to complete his PhD in the Government Department.

Twenty-five years after my run-in with Ed Balls, I had an unexpected encounter with his boss, by then former British prime minister, Tony Blair, at another social event in the United States. For his part, Blair had been the MP for Sedgefield in County Durham, the next constituency to Bishop Auckland. He had actually grown up in the city of Durham as well as in Edinburgh and had attended prestigious private schools in both cities. Blair had studied law rather than PPE at Oxford but moved in the same social circles as the rest of the Oxford set. We ran into each other at the Aspen Ideas Festival in Colorado in July 2014, where I was presenting a book that I had just written about Russian president Vladimir Putin as well as participating in panels on U.S.-Russian relations.

A close colleague and fellow Russia expert, Angela Stent, was also at Aspen. Angela, like me, was originally British. Her family members were refugees from Germany in the 1930s who rebuilt their lives in London. All too aware of the importance of their children securing a good education, Angela's parents had scrimped and saved to put her through a girls' direct grant school (a form of grammar school that also took fee-paying students). From there she went to Cambridge. Also like me, Angela came to the United States on a graduate scholarship to Harvard, where she completed the same master's degree in Soviet studies and then a PhD in government. Angela had blazed the trail I followed and was a mentor to me throughout my professional career. After forty years in the U.S., however, she sounded more American than British.

One of the Ideas Festival organizers was insistent that we should meet Tony Blair, who was a featured speaker. The organizer spotted Blair in the crowd and called us over. She introduced us as fellow Brits, noting how "exciting" it was to be able to introduce us to "our" former prime minister and remarking that she understood that I was originally from Blair's constituency. I clarified: not quite, but very close.

Blair was taken aback when I gave my quick potted history, the usual rundown through the three determinative questions. "How did you get here?" I feigned ignorance: "On a plane from D.C., Angela and I flew in through Denver and then here. How did you come, directly from London? It's a long trip, isn't it?" "No . . . really . . . come on," he said, "I obviously mean from County Durham to the U.S.; that's also quite a journey, isn't it?" I explained that I was a product of the "Labour Party at work." My local MP, his colleague and former chief whip Derek Foster, had tried to address the local educational deficiencies. He had encouraged me to consider university.

Tony Blair looked more pained than pleased by this revelation. He seemed most perplexed by the fact that I had attended a County Durham comprehensive school *and* retained my northern accent. The two of those together were confounding, while Angela's trajectory, including the family horrors of escaping Nazi Germany, somehow seemed explicable to him. In the UK context, even in the 2010s, moving from the working to the middle class without some divine intervention, in the form perhaps of a scholarship to a private school accompanied by some elocution lessons, appeared more of a feat than Angela's remarkable transformation from refugee to successful citizen. Nevertheless, at the end of our brief encounter, Blair insisted that the three of us take a selfie to commemorate the meeting.

There was an added irony in all this. Several years earlier, from 2006 to 2009, I had served as the national intelligence officer for Russia and Eurasia, in fact succeeding Angela in the position. As part of this assignment, I had to brief President George W. Bush. On our first encounter, he also expressed interest in my accent and where I was from. He was delighted to find out that my hometown was near Blair's home constituency. He had visited Sedgefield on a state visit to the UK in November 2003. He joked that he had waved to my parents. I mentioned that they had actually come out into their back garden to wave to him as he flew over Bishop Auckland in Marine One. They would be pleased to know he had waved back. From then on, President Bush dubbed me "Blair's girl." I didn't tell the former prime minister this. But Angela and I later laughed about our "Blair's girls" commemorative selfie.

The encounter with the former prime minister was a far cry from my much less self-confident interaction with Ed Balls in my first year at Harvard, but the framing was the same. Traditionally, promoting social mobility was one of the key platforms of the Labour Party as well as of the old-style labor unions like the Durham Miners' Association. Tony Blair himself in the late 1990s, when Ed Balls had left Harvard to work in the government, had instituted all kinds of policies to encourage the development of new educational programs for underprivileged kids and raise expectations for what they could achieve. Blair's revamped "New Labour" version of the party, however, was still replete with MPs from middle-class, private school, and Oxbridge backgrounds — and with privileged Kennedy Scholars who had just done a stint at Harvard. The perception, background, and lifestyle gap between Labour Party elites and the working-class grassroots membership widened under Blair's premiership, from 1997 to 2007. It persisted long afterward under subsequent leaders, contributing to the party's downfall in successive local and general elections into the 2020s. Clearly policies promoting societal change took decades to have an impact in the composition of the leadership at the top. And in the meantime the parties that advanced them were apt to reap the whirlwind.

Degrees of Discrimination

Class and accent distinctions and discrimination were one thing in the United Kingdom, but those first years at Harvard opened my eyes to how much worse the situation was for some in the United States. I had thought America was a far more egalitarian society with much less socioeconomic division than I had experienced in the UK. This was not the case. There was plenty of poverty in the former industrial areas of Boston, and the city was evidently segregated into different socioeconomic, ethnic (Portuguese, Italian, Irish), and racial neighborhoods. All I had to do was look around and pay attention on a walk across the invisible line from Cambridge to East Cambridge, or Cambridge to Somerville, or take a stroll from Back Bay and the South End into Roxbury on a trip into Boston itself, to see the divides.

You could also hear the divides as you traveled across Boston. The South Boston Irish accent was particularly distinctive. And I soon learned that there was accent discrimination in the United States, especially for "non-standard English"-speakers. I just wasn't subjected to it once I was transplanted from the UK. Any kind of English accent seemed to fall within acceptable standards. My future husband, Ken, and John Henriksen both claimed that their midwestern accents were the U.S. equivalent of RP — the neutral Middle American tones of the major network newscasters. I wasn't initially convinced, but I did soon discover that there was a geographic reversal in the perception of accents in the United States. Accents from the North seemed to signify that people were somehow smarter and more in command, while southern accents seemed to suggest that the person concerned was "nicer" in some way, albeit a little slow. A complete flipping of the stereotyping in the UK. And then there was the racialization of speech and negative attitudes toward African American dialects that echoed the accent discrimination I experienced at home.

Race, as much as if not more than accent, was an evident impediment to opportunity in America. It was a kind of negative force multiplier for every other obstacle that got in the way of people moving ahead. Back in Bishop Auckland, in our homogenous bubble, race was not something we considered or thought about on a regular basis. I did think about *ethnicity* in the British context. My family had all five of the distinct British ethnic groups in our lineage — English, Irish, Scottish, Welsh, and Traveller. My parents used to describe themselves simply as British, but not English. Our immediate neighbors on either side were Welsh and Irish. They had experienced discrimination as native Welsh- and Irish-language speakers throughout their schooling. But the first time I observed interpersonal racial discrimination close up was when a former classmate who had left school early to join the army brought a friend, Tony, home on leave. Tony was mixed-race: his father was an immigrant from the West Indies; his mother was from Yorkshire. When we all walked downtown together in Bishop Auckland, Tony got sharp stares. Some younger boys loped behind us for a while, making ape noises and rude gestures when we turned around to glare and yell at them. Tony ignored this and shrugged it off more easily than the rest of us did. We hadn't even thought about how nastily some people might react to his presence in an almost all-white town. We were embarrassed and ashamed.

At St. Andrews in the mid-1980s, there were only a handful of Black students, mostly from affluent families from Africa who had been sent to private schools in the UK. A few students were from South Asia — India, Pakistan, Bangladesh, and Sri Lanka — or were second-generation immigrants, and occasionally of mixed racial heritage. The father of one of my closest friends, my roommate from my first year, was originally from Pakistan. Malika came from a working-class area of Billericay in Essex, east of London. She had attended a comprehensive school. We often discussed class and racial issues. She noted that on the surface I fit in . . . until I opened my mouth. She, however, did not fit in. She stood out right away. When people looked at her, all they saw at first was someone "different." In theory, if you worked on it hard enough, you could change your accent and conceal your social origins, Malika said, but you could not change the color of your skin. It would always be a factor drawing additional prejudice on top of class discrimination.

None of these discussions had prepared me in any way for the structural racism I encountered in the United States. I simply didn't expect it. I was starry-eyed about the United States and the obviously life-changing opportunity to study at Harvard. Having only read a few American history books at the time, I assumed that the civil rights movement had relegated racial discrimination to the past. I was sure, at least, that this was the case in Massachusetts, even if things might be different in the American South. In fact, I was more worried at the time about the potential spillover from the Troubles in Northern Ireland in the United States. Boston was a known IRA stronghold, and in my first week at Harvard I had spotted collection boxes for NORAID (the Irish Northern Aid Committee, a charity with purported ties to the militants) on the counters of some of the Irish bars in Cambridge that I went into. On one occasion I had been grilled about my background by one of the bartenders before he would serve me. He clearly wanted to gauge my attitudes toward the Irish republican cause. He eventually seemed satisfied that I was from the North East and not London, and that got me a drink.

With other things preoccupying me, I had not fully processed or factored in how recent the civil rights movement had been. When I got to Harvard in 1989, I was a year younger than the 1964 Civil Rights Act and the same age as the U.S. Voting Rights Act. Black and Native Americans had been recognized as full citizens for only twenty-four years. People of my age or younger in the United States were the first generation who had been born at a time without employment discrimination on the basis of race and enforced segregation in public places. It quickly became apparent, however, that America still had a long way to go before race — like gender, class, and the other social markers that I had experienced to date — would ever be part of someone's personal identity rather than a major impediment to opportunity.

A Crash Course on Race

One of my fellow Harvard graduate students, Tom Stewart, was Black. Tom was pursuing a PhD in political science in the Government Department. Like me, he was from a low-income background. We discussed some of the similar challenges we had faced, but the comparisons stopped there. He had grown up in Washington, D.C., and enrolled in the U.S. Army before going to the University of the District of Columbia. He was older than the rest of us and a compelling advocate for increasing access for students of all backgrounds to a high-quality education. He led student meetings on this issue. He helped open my eyes to the importance of educational reform in the distinctively racist society that was the United States.

The graduate students' dorm association organized a regular pizza night, and on one such evening I volunteered to help Tom, who was a graduate dorm counselor, collect the pizzas in his car while others set things up. We had ordered ahead of time, but when we went in to collect and pay, the pizzeria staff refused to serve him. I was completely appalled and confused. How could they refuse? Why? Tom was clearly angry but holding himself in check. I stepped up closer to the counter. The man asked if we were together. I said of course we were, and then realized from his reaction that he was asking if we were a couple, which was clearly not okay from his point of view. Other people eating in the restaurant were staring at us. We were a spectacle just for walking in together. I said we were both graduate students at Harvard and we had ordered ahead for an official event. What was the problem? We had the payment with us. On hearing my accent, the man softened a bit. I gave him the money and he handed me all the pizzas, averting his gaze from Tom. As we left, he said loudly, "I guess they'll let anyone into Harvard now."

On the way back to campus in the car, Tom offered me my first crash course on race in America. I was clearly clueless. He enlightened me on the specific history of Boston and the desegregation of the city's public schools. Boston had begun to integrate its de facto geographically segregated school system only in 1974, and then only because of a court order after a landmark class-action lawsuit filed by the National Association for the Advancement of Colored People (NAACP). The beginning of forced busing of students from predominantly Black to white neighborhoods had been met with months of violent protests, particularly in the largely Irish Catholic areas of South Boston. Conflicts over school integration continued through the

1970s. As Tom explained, by the time the court-ordered busing ended in 1988, white students had emptied out of Boston's school district. The public schools were now mostly Black. This was the exact opposite outcome to the intent of the original ruling. It was one of the issues that Tom had been looking at in his PhD studies. The scars of desegregation were still raw in Boston. This was literally just yesterday, not the distant past. People like the man in the pizzeria, Tom noted, had probably gone through school during the Boston busing and were still aggrieved.

There were very few Black graduate students like Tom at Harvard in the 1990s. Although the undergraduate student body was rapidly diversifying, racial tensions were rife on and around the campus. A few years later I was a resident tutor in Cabot House, one of the Harvard undergraduate dorms. Two Black students were taking a computer from the dorm to get fixed at Harvard's nearby computer lab. They were stopped by the Harvard police and accused of stealing it. I was one of the people who had to intervene. I got to see at first hand what I had missed in the UK in the 1980s. The United States was not what I had expected when it came to race and equality of opportunity for all Americans. This was a house divided in multiple ways.

In America, as I quickly learned at Harvard, race exacerbates the obstacles to social mobility I had experienced. It functions as an immutable factor in constraining opportunity. Place, class, and accent counted as obstacles to opportunity where I was from — and also gender, which would loom large throughout my career in the U.S. But I had left "place" behind when I moved to St. Andrews. By coming to Harvard, I had also left class behind. Unless I encountered other Brits, like Tony Blair in Aspen, I found that no one had any idea about my accent. Americans were tuned into their own dialects and regional accents, and also to "foreign accents" and unfamiliar speech patterns, but they were clueless about the geographic origins of mine and what it signified in terms of social class, likely income level, and educational attainment. My accent seemed like generic English for most people, although some discerning listeners would notice that it was distinct in some way. They assumed I was Australian, or maybe even from South Africa. Perhaps I might be Irish or Scottish, which has a certain cachet in the United States. At the same time that I was horrified by the new forms of discrimination that I was seeing in the United States, I also reveled in the fact that I no longer automatically came with the "common northerner" label stuck on my forehead.

In the United States, race puts class, place, income status, gender, and everything else that divides and categorizes people in an entirely different frame. As a white British student at Harvard, I was immediately elevated up the social ladder. In contrast to Tom, I got a pass into a whole new realm simply because of the color of my skin. I blended right in without doing anything much at all apart from showing up. This held true for women as well. I faced gender discrimination, but Black women were doubly disadvantaged by gender and race, as I learned though the experience of Black female undergraduates at Harvard and a close colleague in the U.S. government, Danica Starks. Danica was one of the top women experts on Russia, Ukraine, and Eurasia and one of the very few Black and minority women in Russian affairs. She spent two decades building a career in the national security and economic arena at the Department of Commerce and covered every critical policy issue in the region. As she moved through the ranks, Danica had to contend with all kinds of assumptions based entirely on her race, not her résumé. She had grown up in Washington, D.C., in the suburbs, and attended a largely Black public high school before university. Her parents were well educated and solidly middle-class. Yet, she quipped, everyone always presumed that because she was Black, she must be "from the hood" and a low-income background. When people looked at me, because I was white, they thought the opposite.

Danica followed the same path as every other high-performing U.S. national security professional I worked with in government. She learned languages and studied abroad in several European countries, she had internships at prestigious places. Once in the Commerce Department, she acquired additional skills and qualifications, with stints on Capitol Hill, assignments to different agencies, and graduate courses at the National Defense University. But being a Black woman always put her in uncomfortable situations. One meeting at the Department of State summed everything up. It was a large meeting. Men dominated the speaker roster and the participant list. A tiny handful of women ended up seated together at a small table at the back of the room. Danica took in the scene and casually commented on it: "Here we go again, just us." One of the other women at the table looked surprised: "What do you mean? You're not like us. You're Black!" Danica wasn't even allowed to be a woman in that moment. Her Blackness ejected her from the sisterhood.

As Tom's and Danica's experiences underscore, race in the United States creates a hierarchy, a fixed caste system that those within it can never fully escape. Irrespective of their educational and professional achievements and income, they are still seen to belong on the bottom rung.

Opportunity from a Cereal Box

I was at Harvard for the entirety of the 1990s, studying for graduate degrees and working simultaneously as a tutor in the undergraduate residential houses and at Harvard's Kennedy School of Government. Along the way I made the decision to stay in the United States, and in 1995, I also got married. As I progressed through my new American life and was absorbed into my husband's sprawling midwestern family, the United States writ large — not just writ small in Boston — started to look a lot like the United Kingdom that I had left behind. Spatial inequality was an issue in America as well. The United States was not the land of opportunity for everyone in every place. There were plenty of towns and regions that Americans wanted to leave behind.

My American in-laws, Jim and Irma Keen, had never traveled abroad. They did not have passports. Just after we got married, my husband and I thought they should visit my parents in Bishop Auckland and possibly see a bit of the UK — London at least, and some of the more famous parts of the North East, like Hadrian's Wall.

My in-laws and parents were the same age. They were born in the early 1930s, at the height of the Great Depression. They had a lot in common in terms of life experiences and perspectives, despite the obvious distance. They hit it off at our wedding in Cambridge, and it seemed like they might enjoy spending some more time together. We offered to pay for the flights and make all the arrangements, as the Keens didn't have a lot of money. My parents would go down to London to meet them, spend a couple of days there in a B&B, and take them back to Bishop Auckland on the train. They would stay at my parents' house. Mam and Dad still did not have a car, but a family friend offered to drive everyone around. My parents also arranged some bus and train trips, including up to Scotland. Jim and Irma seemed somewhat enthusiastic.

Mr. and Mrs. Keen had grown up in rural South Dakota, in Mr. Keen's case working the family farm. His father had dropped dead of a heart attack in the fields, having already lost an arm trying to fix a piece of rogue machinery. Mr. Keen was the oldest child. He had to support his mother and his younger siblings. After finishing high school, he decided to continue his education. He wanted to help farmers find new markets for their crops. Mr. Keen grew corn and soybeans for a living and had lots of ideas for novel ways of processing them. So, taking advantage of post–World War II educational grants, he hitchhiked during the day to Dakota Wesleyan University in the nearby town of Mitchell (home of the world's one and only Corn Palace) to study chemistry. He came back to manage the farm in the evening and at weekends.

When he had his degree, he got his first job right off the back of a cereal box. He did not have any contacts or networks beyond the immediate farming community. It was the early 1950s. No recruiters, apart from the army, had materialized on campus. Pondering his seemingly limited opportunities over his bowl of Cheerios one morning, Jim noticed an address for the food company on the cereal box. So he wrote to General Mills and sent his résumé. They hired him. Jim's job from the cereal box was his ticket out of South Dakota.

Irma, Mrs. Keen, also wanted to go somewhere other than South Dakota. She met Jim at a local roller rink when she was still in high school and he was already a college student. She was the school valedictorian and the most popular girl in her class, but she was one of six girls. Her father had a hard time keeping steady work. She had no means to go to university. She briefly worked for the telephone company as an operator. Jim had mobility, even if he was of modest means. After they married they packed up and headed east. General Mills moved them to Minneapolis. Jim became a food chemist and found a new job with Corn Products International, which took his growing family to Chicago in the 1960s. Jim and Irma raised twelve children in a small house in the suburbs. Life was more stationary when they got to Chicago. It was hard to travel domestically, let alone abroad, when you had twelve kids in tow, but they had already made a big series of moves.

Dad loved hearing Mr. Keen's story. This was the American Dream. He thought Jim Keen was like a Jimmy Stewart character, right out of an old Hollywood movie. It was "Mr. Keen Goes to Chicago" instead of *Mr. Smith Goes to Washington*. There was even a slight physical resemblance to the famous actor, and a similar understated personality and distinctive drawl. In his discussions with Jim Keen, Dad was struck by the disparity in their circumstances. Unlike Jim, Alf had traveled abroad as a young man. In his twenties, during the 1950s golden age for Durham miners, he earned good money down the pit. He saved up to travel in Europe during his summer vacations with two friends. But in life he had not moved very far. After he married, Alf lived only eight miles from Roddymoor. His professional trajectory was downwardly mobile. He had traded skilled work in the mines for unskilled auxiliary work in Bishop Auckland General Hospital.

Jim suggested that it was probably easier to move and find a new job in the United States than in the United Kingdom. The memory of just packing up and heading off somewhere else was still fresh for the Keens and their extended families. They weren't rooted in centuries of history and generations growing up in the same region. Their grandparents had emigrated from Europe in the late nineteenth century and gone out West to farm, settling alongside people who had gone to the Great Plains as homesteaders in covered wagons and lived in sod huts. Jim's maternal grandfather had moved from Belgium in his sixties with some of his children, leaving several others and his wife back in the home country (the Keens always seemed to have huge families). They started farming from scratch in South Dakota. One grandmother was even a mail-order bride from Sweden! Jim Keen pointed out that when he was growing up in the United States, especially after World War II, there was an expectation of geographic, economic, and social mobility. Even if you grew up on the family farm, you figured you and your children would have the opportunity to go to university or do something else. Not everyone had to stay on the farm.

Dad noted, regretfully, that there was no such expectation in the North East of England — beyond following your father's footsteps down the pit. He recounted how he had considered emigrating to America in the 1960s, when his coal mine closed. It was clear that the writing was on the wall for the other local pits. Former Durham miners who had moved to West Virginia and Pennsylvania's Lehigh Valley after World War II sent recruitment notices back home that the Durham Miners' Association circulated. Dad investigated both options and seriously pursued the Pennsylvania prospects. Some relatives also headed out to Australia and New Zealand under the so-called Ten Pound Poms scheme, when the postwar governments were suffering from labor shortages. They offered subsidized flights and temporary relocation payments for UK industrial workers who could line themselves up with a job and commit to stay for at least two years. Tens of thousands of working-class British families took advantage of these opportunities. Dad wanted to go but discovered he could not take his parents along as dependents. Granny Hill was distraught at the thought of him leaving. There was no one to look after Granny and Grandad in his absence. In contrast, Jim

Keen was from a large family. His younger brother took over for him when he left, looking after both the farm and their mother. Jim moved on. Dad stayed put.

When Jim and Irma came home, I eagerly asked them how the trip had been. Jim said that he thought Bishop Auckland was like his hometown in South Dakota, not somewhere you wanted to stick around. "It's a good place to be *from*," he said. "So did you not like your trip to England then?" I inquired, wondering if this had all been a bad idea. "We had a lovely time with your parents," Irma said tactfully. "We really enjoyed London." In fact, if fate had taken a different turn, there would have been no trip for the Keens to the UK. Dad could have found himself living in small-town USA, which would soon have lost its own primary industries. I could have grown up in Pennsylvania . . . But then again, Dad might not have met Mam without the porter's job in Bishop Auckland General Hospital. I might not have been born at all.

Carbon County

At Harvard, I made friends with Susan Lazorchick, another Russian studies student whose family was from one of those small Pennsylvania coal-mining towns, Nesquehoning. Susan's family were Slavs who emigrated from the Austro-Hungarian empire in the early 1900s. Her paternal grandfather was killed in a mining accident in 1945. Susan's father was drafted into the navy at age eighteen and was then able to go to college, thanks to the GI Bill, at the University of Pittsburgh before studying at Dickinson School of Law in Carlisle, now part of Pennsylvania State University. He was the first generation out of the mines. He had a small law practice in Lansford, just up the hill from Nesquehoning, until he died of cancer when Susan was eleven. We were always surprised by the similarity of our families' experiences, the slight chance that we could have been neighbors, and the fact that we had both ended up at Harvard. Later, when I began work at the Brookings Institution, a colleague, Emily Alinikoff, recounted a similar immigrant experience in a small town between Wilkes-Barre and Scranton, Pennsylvania. Her family also emigrated from the Austro-Hungarian empire in the late 1800s, when coal was king in Pennsylvania. They became part of a small Jewish working-class community in town — one part of her family opened a kosher butcher shop, and another opened a children's clothing store that survived for seventy-five years before it closed in the 1990s. Like Susan,

Emily described the ups and the long down in the town's fortunes and her family's difficult journey. One grandparent initially lived above the town brothel before buying a house. They put all their money into educating the next generations of their children in the hope of ensuring greater mobility. It turned out that it wasn't always so easy making it in America, but Emily and I both made quite a set of moves. We coincidentally ended up working at the White House together, in her case in the Office of Management and Budget.

My husband also lived in Pennsylvania for a while in the early 1990s, just before we got married. Ken worked for a company with industrial operations in both Pennsylvania and New Jersey. He lived in Conshohocken close to one of the plants. One long weekend we took a trip to the nearby Pocono Mountains, with plans to hike in the scenic Lehigh Gorge State Park. We ended up in a bed-and-breakfast in Jim Thorpe — the former Mauch Chunk (a Native American name for "Bear Place"). It was a company town created by the Lehigh Coal and Navigation Company, right next to Nesquehoning. Susan had recommended it, but I had not expected such a shock of familiarity. The strikingly rugged local scenery aside, Jim Thorpe could have been any town in County Durham transplanted to Pennsylvania. Every tourist site in town was linked to coal mining or the railroads or the industrialists who shaped the region's development and grew rich from local seams of anthracite. Anthracite was "hard coal," the most valuable variety for powering industry and heating homes, with low levels of impurities and a high carbon content. Jim Thorpe was the center of Carbon County.

County Durham was the North East of England's equivalent of Carbon County. The exploitation of rich seams of anthracite coal put my home region and Pennsylvania's Lehigh Valley on the map. The timescale of Jim Thorpe's development as an industrial center closely tracked Bishop Auckland's, although Jim Thorpe was far smaller in size and population. Mauch Chunk had been established in the early 1800s and then gone into sharp decline after the Second World War, when the mines began to close. In the 1950s the town presented itself as the resting place and living memorial of the celebrated Native American Olympic athlete Jim Thorpe (who went to school and started running in Carlisle, Pennsylvania). The town took on his name as part of an effort to transform itself into a tourist destination. When I related the trip and what I had seen to Dad, he grew excited. He was sure that Jim Thorpe's number 9 mine, which had closed in 1972 (and much later became a museum), was one of the Pennsylvania mines he had considered in the early 1960s. He remembered the connection with "the Indian run-ner." Dad's American dream, it seemed, was in the Poconos. And his dream wouldn't have lasted all that long; within a decade he would have been look-ing for other opportunities. The Lehigh Valley was another of Mr. Keen's good places to be from when the mines closed down.

The Hard Budget Constraint

In this time period at Harvard, I decided to take some courses in econom-ics to try to put everything I was observing in a larger context. This was a major deficiency in my formal education. I had studied economic history as an undergraduate and plowed through turgid tomes like Karl Marx's *Das Kapital* until late at night in the St. Andrews library, but I had had no op-portunity to study economics as a discipline. To be honest, I wasn't entirely sure what the discipline entailed.

At school we had economics classes that focused on basic finances, and home economics, which tried to set us up to run a household. This was straightforward enough and obviously useful. In terms of financial and monetary issues, I managed to grasp the idea of interest and compound in-terest — in theory, at least. As a child, however, the concept of banks lend-ing out money for anything more than a mortgage was quite alien. Granny and Grandad didn't have a bank account. They kept what little money they had in a biscuit tin in the kitchen cupboard. Everyone else had a basic bank account. As far as we knew (and hoped), our money was just parked there, in the bank where no one could steal it, until we needed to pay the mort-gage and our bills. We did not know anyone who had their own business be-yond a corner shop, a home-care service, or a plumbing, electrical, or con-struction business — and all that on a very small scale. No one in the family had any assets, liquid or otherwise, to be used as collateral for a personal loan. In fact, everyone was terrified of falling into debt. If you needed some money for an emergency, you borrowed from family and close friends and paid it back as quickly as you could.

As I had spent a year in Moscow when Gorbachev was attempting his wholesale reconstruction of the Soviet economic system, I enrolled in a class on reforming socialist economies taught by the celebrated Hungarian economist János Kornai. Professor Kornai had written an influential book on the economics of shortage, outlining the systemic flaws in Communist economies. I had direct experience of the economics of shortage in Moscow, so I had something concrete to relate to. The Berlin Wall came down in November 1989, while Professor Kornai was completing a new book, *The Road to a Free Economy,* which offered ideas for reforming his native Hungary and, by extension, other Eastern bloc countries. One of his lectures delved into soft and hard budget constraints, the effects of inflation, and the respective responses of state-owned companies and private firms. I was assigned to write a paper and found myself completely confused. I went to visit Professor Kornai during his office hours and explained, as well as apologized for, my lack of prior grounding in economics.

Professor Kornai asked a lot of questions about my family life and experiences. Smiling gently, he explained that I should think of my family, my household, as an economic unit. He noted that my family in the UK was like the new private company in Hungary that he had described in his lecture. We had a hard budget constraint. There was no state or anyone else to bail us out of financial trouble. I understood microeconomics reasonably well, Professor Kornai said, I just had to work a bit harder on the macro side of things.

In his book and his lectures, Professor Kornai underscored that poor people and unemployment are the downside of every market economy, including in the United States. He pointed out that the market cannot and does not solve every social problem. And no matter what their aspirations and opportunities may be, not everyone will get rich. Society will always be divided into haves and have-nots; the key question for economists and policymakers to resolve was how to bridge the inevitable income and opportunity gaps. In the case of Eastern Europe, Professor Kornai had recommended the creation of a comprehensive social protection fund and financial aid to cushion the transition to the private sector for laid-off state factory workers. He stressed that this would help boost popular support for free markets and democracy, as well as faith in the government.

Russia and other Eastern European countries did not, however, heed his advice and set up social protection funds in the 1990s. This was hardly a surprise. Neither did the UK in the 1980s, when the big state-dominated heavy industries closed down. In Eastern Europe as well as in the UK, coal miners, steelworkers, and other manufacturing workers had limited assistance from the state as they figured out how to move into private firms and the emerging high-tech and knowledge economies. Most workers ended up —like my dad did when the mines closed—in low-paid, low-skilled manual labor (if they were lucky).

I had seen this transformation up close in England, and I soon would have a chance to see it in the former USSR as well. Right on the eve of the collapse of the Soviet Union, with my master's degree in hand, I got a full-time job working for Professor Graham Allison at the Kennedy School of Government for the Strengthening Democratic Institutions Project, a series of research and technical assistance initiatives focused on the economic and political transition in Russia. With the USSR soon relegated to history and my master's degree in Soviet studies unexpectedly obsolete, I also enrolled in Harvard's History Department to pursue a PhD. I needed to retool. I paid my way through the PhD by working at the Kennedy School and as a resident tutor at Cabot House. The timing proved impeccable for a ringside seat to observe and analyze one of the most consequential geopolitical shifts of the late twentieth century and understand the socioeconomic divisions that would have serious political consequences in the subsequent decades.

6

Shock Therapy

In the 1990s, just like in the North East of England, people in Russia and Eastern Europe suddenly lost their jobs after decades of employment security. Theoretically, at least, in the USSR and the Eastern bloc, everyone had been guaranteed a job as well as a range of social subsidies (for housing, heating, education, health care, etc.) and an eventual pension. Then, in 1992, the Russian government under President Boris Yeltsin, who had displaced Mikhail Gorbachev in December 1991, launched an ambitious economic reform program under the label "shock therapy."

Led by a group of young Russian economists who were working closely with Western counterparts, the program was inspired by the same "radical" free-market policies that had been adopted in the United States and the United Kingdom by Reagan and Thatcher in the 1980s. The young Russian economists thought that the end of communism, the creation of private property, and radical economic change would automatically bring democracy to Russia. It would not take long for them to be proven wrong.

The Kennedy School rented an office in Moscow for several years in the 1990s, and I spent long periods of time there. The precarious situation that I had seen as an exchange student in 1987–1988 went from bad to worse in the 1990s. Even the means of transportation that had impressed me so much a few years before became unreliable or nonexistent in far-flung Russian cities. While I was working for Professor Allison and researching my history PhD, I visited grim places all across Russia and Siberia, including some a few miles outside of Moscow, which had been written off by the national and local governments. My work at Harvard's Strengthening Democratic Institutions Project, and later with the Eurasia Foundation in Washington, D.C., also took me to Central Asia and the South Caucasus. In the course of my travels, on rickety trains and often terrifying plane journeys, I encountered the North East of England on a vast scale.

Both Thatcher and Reagan had been replaced by then, but their ideas cast a long shadow. The driver of the Moscow trolley bus I rode from where I was staying to the Kennedy School's office had a picture of Margaret Thatcher affixed to his windscreen, presumably as a free-market talisman. Her faint Mona Lisa smile and bouffant blond hair radiated in the weak morning sunlight. The economic ideas of the 1980s had by now hardened into what was called the Washington Consensus, a set of policy recommendations touted by the U.S. Treasury, the International Monetary Fund, and the World Bank for countries afflicted by economic and financial crises. Representatives of all these institutions descended on Moscow to oversee the implementation of reforms at the invitation of the Yeltsin government.

Shock therapy was intended to transform Russia from a socialist to a modern market economy overnight — or at least within a short transitional period, perhaps as long as six months to a year. The program proposed not only to get rid of central planning but to privatize industries and property, liberalize prices and trade, free the ruble's fixed exchange rate, and temporarily adopt extreme austerity measures. It was ambitious and brutal. Stringent budget cuts were implemented to rein in long-standing spending deficits and improve the government's fiscal discipline. The cuts completely upended Russia's Soviet-era welfare system and government services. With no social protection fund of the sort that János Kornai had recommended, vulnerable Russian citizens were left to fend for themselves and navigate the transition on their own. The results were ugly.

Like the sudden closure of coal mines, steelworks, and factories in the North East of England in the 1980s, shock therapy was a shock across the board. The Russian state launched the largest privatization program in history — even bigger than Margaret Thatcher's in the UK. They sold off huge state-owned enterprises and heavy industries in the oil, manufacturing, metallurgy, and energy sectors. Blue-collar and white-collar jobs were abruptly eliminated. Prices shot up. Everyone's savings were obliterated by the currency reforms and hyperinflation, including those of the formerly advantaged members of the Communist Party who had frequented the Beriozkas. Wages and pensions were soon in whopping arrears.

Just as in the case of the UK in the 1980s, no large-scale public communications plan had been put in place by the Russian reformers to explain what was happening and why. No one at the top tried to provide any realistic expectations for the population about the inevitability of unemployment and inequality in the new market economy. People's perceptions were negatively shaped by what they saw happening to them and their family and friends. It eroded their faith in both Russia's economic and its political transition.

To make matters worse, the transitional period was not brief. It dragged on for the rest of the decade, culminating in a sudden devaluation of the ruble in August 1998, which wiped everyone out again and left the country pretty much insolvent.

I was there to experience the painful effects of Russia's transition to capitalism firsthand. The Russian economy and its population went into survival mode. Russian enterprises bartered among themselves for supplies to keep production going. Former factory workers found themselves selling black-market cigarettes or household goods on the street. They were joined by factory accountants, as well as scientists and doctors from industrial research labs and health clinics. Friends' fathers and mothers lost their jobs (most women in Russia worked in the Soviet period).

The parallels with the North East of England were even more striking than before — and for many of the same reasons. Both the North East and post-Soviet Russia were on the losing end of 1980s free-market economic reform policies. Like the USSR, with its predominantly nationalized heavy industries and single-industry towns, the North East was a "socialist," state-dependent enclave. The British government had taken control of most of the heavy industry, major utilities, and the railways in the aftermath of World War II, when their private owners were crippled by the exigencies of wartime operations and the effects of being cut off from global commerce and markets for several years. The end of nationalization and government subsidies and the advent of full-blown capitalism put a stake through the hearts of both North East England and post-Soviet Russia.

Russians' health and well-being were casualties of shock therapy too. In the USSR, large enterprises were directed by the government to set up and fund workplace clinics and municipal hospitals as part of their social obligations. When the Soviet-era enterprises shrank or folded in the 1990s, health-care resources eroded too. The Russian state did not step into the breach for many years, prioritizing defense spending over health care until well into the twenty-first century. The result was a humanitarian disaster on a national scale.

In Russia, the biggest killers were alcoholism and acute drug addiction, which were rife in the 1990s. Both were on an even greater scale than anything I had seen at home during the decline in the 1980s. My year in Moscow during college, 1987–1988, had been the so-called dry year, when Gorbachev tried to ban alcohol, despite the fact that vodka sales were a major percentage of Soviet state revenues. With real vodka out of bounds, people resorted to drinking eau de cologne, soaking bread in shoe polish, and making other versions of *samogon* (moonshine). Russians died in droves from ethanol poisoning.

I almost died myself at a classmate's winter birthday party in a faceless block of flats on the outskirts of Moscow. Someone brought some *samogon* that a family member had made. I took one small sip for the ritual birthday toast and ended up dashing outside with my throat burning, then keeling over into a giant snowdrift. If the *samogon* hadn't killed me off, the cold would have. A passing motorist spotted me in the snow, stopped, picked me up, and drove me back to the student hotel.

I was lucky — unlike countless Russians. Even though the prohibition was lifted, Russians continued to improvise alcohol in the 1990s out of desperation. Real vodka was often simply too expensive, and the despair that drove people to drink was simply too pervasive.

Left Out in the Cold

A few well-meaning attempts to create a new infrastructure of opportunity to replace the structures and systems that had disappeared with the Soviet Union did exist. In 1990s Russia, as part of Boris Yeltsin's reforms, a scheme was initiated to put some of the state housing stock directly into the hands of its residents and help them generate some personal wealth. Margaret Thatcher did the same in the UK with the Housing Act of 1980, which allowed five million council house tenants to buy the homes they lived in. In Russia, about 80 percent of the population in cities lived in housing tied directly to state-owned enterprises and housing allocated by the Communist Party. Of the remainder, some lived in communal housing that shared bathrooms and kitchens. Others lived in workers' hostels. As in the UK, the intention was to relieve the state and local governments of the burden of maintaining subsidized properties and to incentivize new owners to take care of things themselves. The Russian government hoped privatization would stimulate the housing and mortgage markets and boost the economy. But while there were successes in Russia as well as in the UK, there were significant downsides. Privatization was not as fair a proposition as it seemed.

Both the UK and the USSR had expanded the state housing stock in the 1970s (of course, it was all state housing in the Soviet Union). They embarked on a spree of building drab, cheaply constructed apartment blocks in large urban areas. To the untrained eye, many of the high- and low-rise blocks of flats in the North East of England and the USSR could have been designed by the same architect, and perhaps they were. The 1970s-era neighborhoods, *mikrorayons,* of big Soviet cities were cookie-cutter identical. Across the country, streets had the same names. Buildings followed the same number patterns. In the UK as well as in Russia, tenants were allocated their housing by local authorities. They had not chosen the house or the street, or perhaps even the neighborhood. They had been given what was available. The house might not have been upgraded in years. Under the new postindustrial economic conditions, there might be few new jobs or existing amenities in the area.

In a desirable region, a house or an apartment was a genuine asset. Somewhere else, turning an undesirable house or flat into personal property was a burden that you might not be able to get rid of — a liability, not an opportunity. It would anchor you to a place you might not want to be if you actually had a choice. An undesirable house was a drag on mobility. Speculators and investors bought up council houses in the UK from tenants who could not afford their mortgages and from similarly disadvantaged new homeowners in Russia. In Moscow and St. Petersburg, where many grand prerevolutionary buildings had been carved up into communal flats in the Soviet period, there were several instances when elderly residents were swindled and even murdered to consolidate and renovate now-lucrative properties. In the UK, few new council houses were built after the Housing Act, pushing those with particularly low incomes, who could not afford to buy under any circumstances, into soaring rental markets and homelessness.

These well-intentioned but often counterproductive efforts were part of a long utopian tradition that inadvertently created unique dystopias in both countries. After World War II, both the USSR and the United Kingdom became pioneers in urban planning. In County Durham we had several towns that were established from scratch under the New Towns Act of 1946, including Peterlee and Newton Aycliffe. They were set up under the auspices of special development corporations to provide new housing for the residents of declining pit villages. Peterlee was named after an actual person — a Durham Miners' Association leader, Peter Lee, whom my Great-Grandad Thompson Hill knew.

The towns in Country Durham were small. The Soviet Union's were huge. Sometimes an originally smaller settlement was renamed after a Soviet leader once it had expanded (Ekaterinburg became Sverdlovsk, Volgograd became Stalingrad, and so on). After World War II, the USSR's central planners built up or created entire cities in the Urals region and Siberia, many of which were economically marooned when the Soviet Union fell apart forty years later. By the late 1980s, the enormous state investment in the cities and Siberia's resources was not paying off. The cost of living was too high in regions thousands of miles from Moscow, where winter temperatures plunged to record-breaking lows and every food and consumer product had to be shipped in. Many of the cities were completely cut off by bad weather in the wintertime, as I found out to my detriment on a couple of research visits in the 1990s. When the USSR collapsed, planned road and rail links that were supposed to connect them to a larger regional hub and the rest of the country were abandoned.

In the UK, urban planners engaged in deliberate creation and also planned destruction. In County Durham, as coal mining faded, development plans between 1951 and 1977 categorized villages as A, B, C, and D settlements to determine how local councils should allocate (or slash) budget money. Category D villages, which had lost their coal mine or mainstay factory, were deemed not worthy of further economic development, or even the maintenance of existing services. They were slated for demolition. Residents of these villages were encouraged to move to the new towns. Villages around Bishop Auckland, including Witton Park, the site of the first ironworks in the North East as well as a mine where Great-Grandad Hill had worked, were given the D grade. Several terraces of housing extending out from Roddymoor were also pulled down by the local council. These included places Granny and Grandad had lived and the condemned building where Dad was born and spent his first years.

In the 1990s, as part of my work on technical assistance projects, I visited towns in Russia, Kazakhstan, and Armenia that the local authorities similarly had declared "without perspective" when factories closed. Bus routes were stopped, shops shuttered, and community centers boarded up. All the infrastructure of opportunity disappeared. Young people delved into their family savings to migrate for work, often without the bureaucratic work permits or travel visas to do so. Their parents and grandparents were left behind, as mine had been in Roddymoor. Russia and other former Soviet republics offered extreme versions of the spatial inequality I experienced in the United Kingdom and saw developing in the United States. Most of the country was a Rust Belt. Having your own home there was of little value. It was not an investment in the future like my parents' purchase of a house had been in Bishop Auckland in the 1960s.

In Russia in the 1990s, some of the most remote cities lost more than 20 percent of their population. Smaller towns lost more than 50 percent. At the beginning of the 2000s, when I joined the Brookings Institution, I worked on a book about the impacts of deindustrialization in Siberia and spatial or geographic inequality in Russia with the Brookings economist Clifford Gaddy. By then more than one million people had simply abandoned their homes and left what Russia called its North. Several thousand more left through a four-year World Bank pilot program launched in 2002. The program provided financial support and transportation as well as housing allowances for some of the poorest Russians from a handful of designated "nonviable" towns close to the Arctic Circle so they could relocate. Others trickled out on their own to "the mainland," which is what the rest of Russia was called when you were cut off in a distant, forgotten town.

Some of the dislocated, or relocated, people went to bigger cities in Siberia that were better connected. But most internal migrants wanted to go to Moscow. The Russian government did not want millions of people trying to move to the capital, where most of the new jobs were being generated. They tried to keep everyone in other places — and prevent them from literally freezing to death — by subsidizing the payrolls of dying industries and gas for home heating. These efforts were expensive and failed to stem the exodus. Moscow's population growth in this period exceeded the government's projections by about two million people, with an estimated additional three million unofficial residents. In both Russia and the UK, postindustrial collapse and the lack of opportunity was hollowing out the North and sending everyone in the direction of the capital city and its monopoly on opportunity and desirable housing.

After the years of my childhood ferrying supplies on my bicycle or trekking with my dad to carry a backpack of groceries from the nearest bus stop to my grandparents, I was particularly drawn to the old people I met in these abandoned places on my travels. Especially in the vastness of Siberia, the situation was far worse than in Roddymoor. Some of the elderly people I met, often veterans of the Second World War, had no one to fetch supplies for them. Their families were often hundreds or thousands of miles away, not a mere eight miles. It was not just a question of making their meager pensions last through the month. If they could not grow enough food in their garden plot in the brief summer, or stock up on canned goods and pickles, they literally starved.

Dorothy Zinberg's Suit

Fortunately, I was not starving myself in this period. I still had a hard budget constraint, but I was finally beginning my career and carving out a portfolio of research on Russia. This was when the issue of being a woman in the workplace came into stark relief in some very specific contexts. In the 1990s, I began to understand that while gender — like place, class, and race — could be an almost insurmountable obstacle to personal mobility and success, women were not necessarily pitted against men in some kind of permanent zero-sum contest. Instead, the professional opportunities for women were there, but the work environment was unequal and always skewed in men's favor in small or large ways.

Gender inequality still persists in academia, for example, especially in certain fields, like science and economics. When I first arrived at university in Scotland in 1984, women were already in the ascendant in terms of overall enrollment but not in the teaching ranks. In fact, there were fewer women at the top levels of academia than in politics at that time. I did not have a single female professor teaching the courses I took at St. Andrews, nor when I got to Harvard, although my Russian-language teachers in my year abroad in Moscow were all women.

I fully grasped the significance of this once I started work at the Kennedy School of Government as a research associate after I completed my master's degree and began work on my PhD. There were women on the faculty at Harvard and at the Kennedy School, but not many relative to the men — and of course almost everyone was white. Female professors were from the same privileged socioeconomic backgrounds and prestigious schools as the men, but they were blocked from moving up the professorial ranks. Women did, however, dominate most of the administrative positions and seemed to keep the university running. In some professional settings at Harvard, I was the only woman as well as the youngest person at the seminar table. I had to learn how to navigate a different situation than before.

I quickly learned that as a woman, appearances, not just being well prepared, mattered — and most things, including the buildings themselves, were set up with the expectation that men would predominate. Sometimes, for example, women's bathrooms were few and far between, uncomfortably reducing the opportunity to pee during breaks. I often deliberately dehydrated myself in important meetings so I wouldn't have to go out and miss something crucial as I searched, and then waited in the inevitable line, to use the tiny ladies' bathroom.

In my first year working at the Kennedy School, I certainly did not look the part of a serious academic or professional woman. I spent most of my time in graduate school in ripped jeans, sweaters or T-shirts, gothic black clothes, the occasional thrift-store vintage dress, and Doc Marten boots, with enormous earrings dangling from my earlobes. Partly this was my late 1980s/early 1990s look, but I also couldn't afford much else. I was genuinely an impecunious graduate student, and I didn't have anything approximating a wardrobe, just whatever I could squeeze into a suitcase when I came to the United States. I still occasionally wore the outfit Mam had made me for my Oxford interview, but the heraldic pattern looked especially ridiculous in the Harvard workplace and I abandoned it after a few too many quizzical stares.

I was barely scraping by when I joined Graham Allison's team in late summer 1991 — literally counting every last cent to make it through the week. My future husband borrowed a quarter one day to make a phone call. I had carefully counted out each one so I could do my laundry at the laundromat at the end of that day. Even if he was "good for the money," as he jokingly put it, if he didn't give me the quarter back, I would have no clean clothes until the next tranche of my stipend. All the other money was spoken for — rent, food, other essentials. I stalked him until he returned it. He never forgot that episode — but neither did I.

One of the prominent women at the Kennedy School in the 1990s was Dorothy Zinberg, a pioneering lecturer in public policy and founding member of the school's Belfer Center for Science and International Affairs, which Graham Allison directed. Dorothy received her PhD from Harvard the year after I was born, in 1966, but never became a full professor. She was an associate of the center rather than a faculty affiliate, but she made sure that no one viewed her as a second-class citizen. Dorothy was active in every meeting, an assertive advocate for gender equality, and a mentor to any young woman (and man) who crossed her path.

Although we did not work directly together on any projects, Dorothy immediately took me under her wing. She perked up when I commented on the implications of the collapse of the USSR during a Kennedy School seminar meeting. We were the only two women there. She liked what I said but immediately noticed my Doc Martens and ripped jeans. She observed that the men in the meeting did too. After the seminar, Dorothy pulled me to one side with some friendly advice. If I was going to get ahead at the Kennedy School, hold my own with the men, and generally get people to listen to me, then I had to present myself differently. Everyone was looking at what I was wearing rather than paying attention to what I was saying — despite my British accent.

"Do you have a suit, or something else you can wear when we have meetings like this?" Dorothy asked. I confessed that I did not, and sadly could not afford to buy one. Next thing we were on our way to TJ Maxx in Dorothy's car. She bought me a suit and some cheap tops to wear underneath: "Consider this my investment in your future!" Now I would blend in and no one would pay too much attention to what I was wearing.

It was a disguise, not a look. Dorothy herself always dressed with flair — long hair sometimes swept up into a towering bun on the top of her head, colorful jackets and scarves, 1960s oversized frame glasses — but she could get away with it, she said. She was "of that age." I, however, could not, so I should play it safe at work. I could make do with that one suit until I had saved some money. In the meantime, she instructed me, I should change my top and earrings on a regular basis and none of the men would ever notice I was wearing the same suit every day. Men did this all the time. As for other women, well, there weren't enough around to comment.

In effect, in the early 1990s, Dorothy Zinberg was the precursor of Molly Levinson, who would prepare me for my congressional testimony in 2019. And Dorothy's suit certainly gave me an initial assist. Not long after I started wearing it, Antonia Handler Chayes, one of the Kennedy School's few female faculty members, a distinguished lawyer and former U.S. undersecretary of the air force, began to invite me to seminars. Toni was the spouse of Abram "Abe" Chayes, a professor at Harvard Law School. They took a keen interest in trying to further the careers of younger women. I had started to work on the ethnopolitical conflicts that erupted after the collapse of the Soviet Union, particularly in the Caucasus region. Abe and Toni recommended me as a participant in a series of workshops that Harvard professor Samuel Huntington was pulling together as background for his famous 1996 book, *The Clash of Civilizations*. My work on the Caucasus and these workshops earned me my first official citation in a proper academic footnote and index, in between Afghan mujahideen leader Gulbuddin Hekmatyar and Adolf Hitler.

Intergirl

Dorothy Zinberg's gift of a suit opened up new professional opportunities for me in the United States, but that same "dressed for success" look was an ironic stumbling block when I had to head out to Russia on research trips. Misogyny and sexism in post-Soviet Russia came roaring back with a vengeance as soon as the USSR was gone and there were no longer quotas for women in political and professional settings. Women melted away from the top levels of government like snowflakes, almost as if they had never been there at all. Only a few lingered on in illustrious positions — like Valentina Matviyenko, a former ambassador, briefly a deputy prime minister under Boris Yeltsin, and later the governor of St. Petersburg, before she was kicked up to an honorary position in the Russian Senate.

The hurdles of gender were far higher than in the UK and the United States. Senior Russian men didn't like Russian women to speak out or speak up in any way. In the 1990s, advertisements for jobs in the newspapers for what were traditionally female professions — secretaries, bookkeepers, press and communications aides, administrators — literally specified that they were looking for "women without complexes." We used to clip and collect these ads and pin them to our bulletin board at the Kennedy School's Moscow office. They were cautionary tales for any future human resources specialist.

In short, most Russia businesses in the 1990s wanted to hire women who "knew their place," were not ambitious and seeking promotion, and — most importantly — wouldn't complain about being groped or harassed or pressed into an affair with the boss. There were also specified dress codes, and not of the kind that most of my friends or colleagues subscribed to.

Makeup, high heels, a certain glamorous look. You need not bother apply-ing if you were trying to camouflage yourself to deflect attention. You were supposed to expect, attract, and then welcome it.

The look might be described as "gentleman's escort lite." At the very end of the Soviet Union, at the height of perestroika, Soviet pollsters had been startled to discover that in a survey of desirable professions, 60 percent of schoolgirls listed hard currency (*valutnaya*) prostitute, servicing foreign businessmen in high-end hotels in Moscow and St. Petersburg, then Len-ingrad. The American correspondent Ted Koppel, making a program in 1990 about sex in the Soviet Union, also learned that this career was ranked eighth out of twenty top professions for young women. This wasn't just a way of making ends meet in desperate times, but also an opportunity — for getting access to luxury goods and potentially, in some cases, to meeting someone who might make you more permanent in his life and whisk you away from the USSR. In 1989 the most popular film in Russia was *Intergirl* (*Interdevochka*), the story of a hard currency prostitute in Leningrad who ends up marrying a client and making an ill-fated move to Sweden.

In the 1990s, being mistaken for an escort or high-end prostitute was an occupational hazard for every reasonably well-dressed woman in her twen-ties and thirties in Moscow. A suit or a nice dress was a liability. The idea that you were a foreign woman on a different kind of business trip as you walked into the lobby of a major hotel was simply inconceivable for the security guards. If I stayed in a hotel instead of one of the flats we rented around Moscow or went for a meeting in a hotel lobby or conference room, I was stopped every time I went through the door. The guard wanted to make sure I paid, or was going to pay, his bribe, fee, or cut right away. I learned eventually not to respond in Russian to the "Where are you going, girl?" question. Nonetheless, the guard would inevitably assume I was pre-tending to be a foreigner. I always had to have my passport at the ready.

The most awkward moment out of the very many was during a project Professor Graham Allison was conducting with Russian and Japanese aca-demics. I was headed into Moscow's Radisson Slavyanskaya Hotel, where we were holding a series of meetings. Graham was staying in the hotel. He asked me to bring the Japanese delegation up to his suite for a quick plan-ning discussion ahead of the full meeting.

I kept my eyes fixed on the elevator and ignored the usual question as we came in through the hotel door. The security guard clearly thought I was destined for an orgy with a group of Japanese businessmen and attempted to head us off at the elevator doors. I pushed past him into the elevator, tailed by the Japanese delegation. They clearly realized something was afoot when the security guard pressed in too. By now he was yelling at me. One of the Japanese professors asked me what was going on. I feigned ignorance.

Graham's room was right opposite the elevator. His door was open. I lunged through to alert him to the situation. The security guard barged in right behind me. I had to explain to Graham in front of the Japanese that the guard thought I was a Russian prostitute and was only pretending to be a foreigner to evade paying him his requisite cut. I pulled my passport out of my bag. Graham assured him that I was British and no, I was not, therefore, a British prostitute moonlighting in Moscow. He, Graham, was not my pimp. All of which I had to translate into Russian.

We eventually persuaded the guard to go away. The Japanese academics were slightly discomfited but also amused — all part of the Moscow experience in the 1990s. A funny anecdote for them to relate when they got home. Not so much for me.

The Notetaker and the Tea Lady

In the 1990s, as my academic career gained steam, mistaken identity became my thing — purely because I was a woman. Gender shifted everyone's assumptions about my role when I was in a professional setting alongside men and reduced my opportunity to participate fully in discussions. In pretty much every meeting where I was taking notes, no matter where it was, most men who didn't know me assumed that I was someone's secretary, a research assistant, or the conference rapporteur. Often in Russia it was assumed that I was all those things and whatever man-I-happened-to-be-with's interpreter.

Early on in my career at the Kennedy School, taking notes and turning them into reports was in fact an integral part of my job. Thanks to my time without sufficient textbooks at Bishop Barrington, I took copious notes as a matter of course. I couldn't really stop myself. Taking notes helped commit things to memory as well as providing material to refer back to later in my finished writing. My notes were an invaluable source. They assisted my career development, even though they seemed to define me. Graham Allison himself had launched his career as the notetaker for a series of seminars at Harvard about the Cuban missile crisis when he was a graduate student working on his PhD in the Government Department. He turned those notes into his dissertation and then a best-selling political science book, *Essence of Decision.* The notetaking and the subsequent book launched his career as a Harvard professor and later as the youngest Harvard dean and founder of the Kennedy School. No one ever thought Graham was a secretary.

Even when it was clear that I wasn't the secretary or notetaker in academic seminars or meetings, my gender would get in the way. I would make a point and wait for a response, only to have some man repeat what I had said a few minutes later in a slightly different formulation. Every time it happened, imposter syndrome would kick in. I wondered, was it my impenetrable North East accent, did no one understand? Was it a stupid or irrelevant point? Was I simply not clear? Does everything a woman say have to be repeated by a man for it to be heard? On occasion I would find myself getting lectured on the very set of issues I worked on directly, sometimes even having to sit and listen as someone cited back something I had written in an article or policy paper, oblivious to where they had read it and whose idea it was. At every stage of my career, at Harvard, at the Brookings Institution, and in the U.S. government, something would happen to remind me of the fact that I was a woman, and not the same as the men around me.

In one incident at Brookings very early in my tenure, when I and the only other young women fellows in the Foreign Policy Program, Meghan O'Sullivan and Suzanne Maloney, found ourselves excluded from an on-site high-level conference, two of our more senior male colleagues told us that we "weren't part of the D.C. policy game." They already had experience in government. We hadn't made our mark on anything yet, so we weren't relevant enough to be invited. We of course noted that similarly junior male think-tank counterparts from across Washington, D.C., were at the meeting. When we asked again why that was, we were told that they had been included for "career advancement purposes." Unsurprisingly, there were no women at all at the meeting, but no one seemed to have noticed the omission. At that point I was the only full-time young female fellow in the Foreign Policy Program. Meghan and Suzanne had doctoral fellowships. There were two senior women, Roberta Cohen and Catharin Dalpino, but it took several years for more women to come on board.

At external conferences where I was invited as a speaker, I was frequently mistaken for the staff. There seemed to be no other explanation for my presence than that I must be on the organizational support team. Sometimes this may have been the result of my relatively young age — in my late thirties and forties, which was of course fairly mature when it came to men — but mostly it was because of my gender. In February 2005, I was invited by the CEO of General Electric, Jeff Immelt, to speak at a Russia-focused session of a meeting of the Business Council in Boca Raton. I was paired with Maurice "Hank" Greenberg, the chairman and chief executive officer of American International Group (AIG). It was, admittedly, quite a step up and a different audience from my usual gig. Immelt had seen me give a presentation at a Brookings event and invited me practically on the spot.

The panel was in the morning, right after a coffee break. I had not met Hank Greenberg before, although his reputation preceded him. A few women were on the Business Council speaking roster, but they were corporate executives and clearly polished and proficient in this environment. In the break before the meeting, I decided to get myself a cup of tea. As I was standing by the hot water urn looking through the array of tea bags, an older man came up to me. We were wearing name tags. I had perused the pictures and bios in the conference materials, so I immediately saw that it was Hank Greenberg. I presumed he was coming over to introduce himself. How gracious . . . But no, he thought I was part of the catering staff. He too was looking for tea. Apparently the container he had just tried to use at the other side of the room had no hot water. Could I do something, please? I was sure he would see my name tag and realize his mistake. Apparently not.

Having been a waitress for all those years back in the UK, my hospitality instincts kicked in. "There's hot water here, Mr. Greenberg, as well as tea bags. What would you like? I'd be happy to pour for you. I am having Earl Grey myself." Still no flicker, no sign that I might be someone other than the tea lady. I guess I looked the part — I made a mental note to no longer wear black suits with a white blouse. This had originally seemed the safest option for the event but was obviously not the right look. The handful of women CEOs wore bold, commanding colors — red, blue, purple — and fancy scarves. Yet again I needed a new wardrobe. I handed Mr. Greenberg his tea and was about to introduce myself as his fellow panelist when he wandered off to greet another CEO. I made my way over to the stage area to get miked up for the session. Jeff Immelt finally came over with Greenberg to introduce us. Greenberg looked slightly embarrassed but more amused than anything else. He probably did this all the time. I smiled and said we had already met in passing over tea and left it at that.

A Decorative Prop

In Russia in the early 2000s, things improved somewhat. In comparison with the 1990s, women became more prevalent in Russian politics, especially in technocratic roles in the Central Bank, financial sector, and research institutes. These were women of my generation who had done advanced economics studies in the West or in new post-Soviet economic institutions. I knew several personally, like Ksenia Yudaeva, the first deputy governor of the Bank of Russia, who received her PhD from MIT. Ksenia crossed over with me while I was in graduate school and was then a fellow at the Carnegie Endowment, next door to Brookings. Despite their prominence, however, Ksenia and her colleagues at the Central Bank were essentially still in traditional Russian "women's professions." They were taking charge of the "national household" and its resources and budget, carefully holding the purse strings in case the men went on an ill-advised spending spree and upended Russia's hard-fought economic recovery since its collapse in the 1990s. There were frequent stories in the press about Ksenia's boss, the Central Bank head, Elvira Nabiullina, taking a firm stand against cabinet members and prominent business figures who were trying to push the bank into lending more money or bailing out key industrial sectors during economic downturns.

Beyond the financial sector, women were prominent in the Russian media and in the government's press departments, including Maria Zakharova, the Foreign Ministry press spokeswoman, and several deputy press spokeswomen for Kremlin officials. One of my contemporaries, Svetlana Mironyuk, was in charge of RIA Novosti, Russia's leading international press agency, for several years, until its abolition in 2013. I had plenty of firsthand interactions with these women in Moscow and considerable opportunity to reach judgments about how they were regarded and treated. Like me, they were appreciated for their technical skills and their ability to interact with global counterparts, but they were also "the staff" and not part of the boys' club.

On a couple of occasions, at meetings of Russia's premier international affairs discussion forum, the Valdai Discussion Club, I sat next to Vladimir Putin — including when I was the national intelligence officer at the National Intelligence Council. Beginning in September 2004, the Valdai meetings were part of an overt Kremlin effort to influence the opinions of Western academics and commentators about Putin's Russia. The Kremlin's press office worked closely with the organizers to shape the meetings and ensure that a set of key messages were transmitted by all the Russian participants to their Western counterparts. They hoped that those of us who attended to be wined and dined and offered access to Russia's top political figures would feel obliged (if not naturally moved) to write positive articles about Russian developments. At one point during a meeting in 2007, Putin himself explicitly stated that he wanted the Western participants to pass on the information and views from the meeting to "combat the strong stereotypes [of Russia] that exist in the West."

My experiences at those meetings highlighted the prevailing attitudes toward *all* women in Russia, even the most prominent at the top of their game. The last time I sat next to Putin was in November 2011, when I was back at Brookings as director of the Center on the U.S. and Europe. I of course took full advantage of the opportunity to observe Putin at very close quarters. I made careful notes on every aspect of the context and situation to analyze and write up later — what he was wearing, how he conducted himself, what he ate and drank, what was on his notecards, what the key messages they wanted us to take away were and why.

Thanks to being right there beside him, I was able to see, for example, that like the rest of us, President Putin suffered from some of the minor aggravations of older age, like presbyopia. He never wore reading glasses — a sign of weakness. I was so close to him that I could see he was not wearing contact lenses, but the super-large font on his notecards was a clear indication. All of this was useful for my subsequent work on the book I wrote about Putin in 2013, but of course I wondered why I was sitting next to him, in a spot that would normally seem significant. Was it, I mused, a Kremlin effort to make a political point, or compromise me in some way because I was or had been the U.S. national intelligence officer covering Russia? Could it be because the Russian security forces had profiled me and decided I was the least likely person to attack Putin with a fork or knife during dinner? All kinds of ideas popped into my head. Naturally, it turned out that it was nothing of the sort.

I was one of the few women in the group, but the Russians did not see me as a real-life version of the celebrated British actress Judi Dench playing the part of M, the first top female spy chief in a James Bond movie. No, I had been selected because of something far more prosaic. Who I was professionally was immaterial. I was a mere decorative prop for the great man. I was a woman who was neither too ugly nor too attractive, neither too young nor too old. I had the elusive Goldilocks factor. No one, apart from the very few people in Russian foreign policy circles who might know who I was, would pay any attention to me. All eyes would be on him. Svetlana Mironyuk from RIA Novosti was sitting on Putin's other side. She enlightened me after the fact, stripping away my fantasies. If a man from the foreign delegation had been sitting there, TV audiences would wonder who this man was. Why was he sitting next to Putin? The man would be a diversion. Similarly, if I was a beautiful or glamorous woman with a plunging neckline, or "too old and overdressed," Svetlana noted, I would draw unwanted attention. So there I was, a nondescript woman, as innocuous as a flower arrangement or potted plant, some tableware framing Mr. Putin. Nothing to look at here.

7

Women's Work

After a while I factored in the indignities of being a woman in Russia as part of the package—another endurance test, but also a source of illuminating experience. It certainly gave me and other women studying the country, like Angela Stent, a different set of insights and perspectives from those of our male counterparts. Sometimes we would glean surprising nuggets of information when the Russian men around us would chat candidly among themselves, entirely forgetting we were there. One issue that I had not factored in at all on the United States' side of the equation, however, was that I would be subjected to another indignity as a woman—gender-based wage discrepancy. This became an additional lesson in the ways that women and disadvantaged groups find themselves locked out of opportunity.

My job at the Kennedy School played a pivotal role in launching my academic career. It also provided a means of earning an income and paying my way through my Harvard graduate education. Ken and I got married in 1995, as he was starting out in his career in the private sector. Neither of us had any savings; I was still an impecunious grad student, and now he was simply impecunious. Because of funding difficulties once I had used up my initial Knox Fellowship, I frequently had to take breaks from pursuing the PhD to work and save money to cover the next phase. Margot Gill, who had recruited me to Harvard, and the university's Graduate School of Arts and Sciences staff helped me identify ways of making ends meet. This included being a resident tutor in Cabot House, an undergraduate dorm, applying for hardship bursaries to cover some of the tuition and other fees, and working for Graham Allison. I did my dissertation research on the side of work trips to Russia for the Kennedy School projects. Harvard provided an infrastructure of opportunity — the mechanisms and support that made things possible.

As I reached the time for completing my PhD, Graham made me a deal to help me move forward. He would give me a three-month unpaid leave, keep my job open, and help me find an office in one of the Harvard libraries where I could work uninterrupted. *But* I had to get the entire dissertation written in that time. This was strict conditionality. And there would be oversight. He would check on me every week to see where I was. I should treat it like my job. Go into the office in the morning, write, take a short lunch break, write some more, then stop in the evening. No time for procrastination. If I failed to finish, I would not get my job back. It was quite the deal — I could not refuse, given the economic consequences. In fact Graham sent a different colleague, or sometimes a random student from one of his classes, every day to check on me in the library. One of them busted me playing hearts on the computer rather than writing and reported back. I got a harsh phone call from Graham that week, even though I tried to argue that it was technically during my lunch break. The fiscal incentive to finish and get back to work along with the frequent check-ins worked. I completed the dissertation in the allotted time.

I had assumed that with the PhD out of the way, the door would now be opened for a significant boost in my compensation. It turned out not to be the case. Instead I was offered a direct insight into the persistent gap between men's and women's compensation, which holds true irrespective of place, class, or race, at all income levels and across blue- and white-collar jobs in the U.S. and also internationally. This gender wage gap, combined with the central role that women play in supporting their families, would in turn help to explain some of the grim political trends that swept the world in the first two decades of the twenty-first century. It was certainly emblematic that in the 2016 American presidential election, almost 40 percent of women voters would opt for Donald Trump and his promise to blow up the existing social system, despite his open and unabashed misogyny during the campaign.

In the United States, the United Kingdom, Russia, and every other country, the obstacles to opportunity — to accessing an education, finding a job, earning sufficient money to thrive, not just survive — no matter what form they come in, contribute to economic hardship. Over time the reality as well as the perception of being unfairly disadvantaged in some way and denied social mobility hardens into political grievance. People want their government to do something to address their difficulties. They want their political system to deliver some relief and to level the playing field. In the early 2000s, all the gaps and discrepancies that had built up in the 1980s and 1990s in advanced societies would push those who were most affected (and thus disaffected) toward politicians who promised to change the situation in some dramatic fashion — even, in the Russian case under Vladimir Putin, at the cost of curtailing their political freedoms.

"Why Do You Need to Be Paid So Much?"

Gender-based salary discrepancies have been well documented and analyzed for decades, including in multiple years of reports from the *Harvard Business Review*. But until I started working at the Kennedy School, I was oblivious to the fact that women spend a good portion of their careers being grossly and unfairly undercompensated. Indeed, most women, like me, have no idea this is the case until some incident shines a spotlight on the yawning gap between their income and those of their male colleagues. In my jobs back in the UK, for example when I was cleaning at Bishop Auckland General Hospital, there was a transparent fixed rate of pay for the position. Even as a temporary worker, I was paid the same rate as everyone else.

When I started working at the Kennedy School, there was no such transparency. The human resource department kept salary information private. I soon learned that wage inequality begins during the initial hiring process, and it persists, with the gap widening, as women advance through their careers. In my first job in the United States, at Harvard, like most women right out of school or university, I didn't have enough information to know what starting salary to ask for when I accepted the job. I was offered a salary. I took it. I had no idea you were supposed to try to negotiate something. Nobody told me I should.

I was equally unaware of the general salary range for the position. I had no previous pay history in the U.S. to fall back on as a guide, and no one to ask what I should expect. Indeed, as I soon learned, employees already on the job — your future colleagues — have no incentive to share their compensation details with you at any point in the process or afterward. They have often negotiated something entirely different for themselves. Salary negotiations, even in universities and think tanks, are competitive and cut-throat — especially if a fixed budget for personnel costs is written into grant applications for research work, and when benefits like health care, life insurance, and retirement all have to be factored on top of the base salary. Academic studies have established that women, unlike men, are in any case frequently denied the salary they ask for in negotiations. And after the fact, when women finally discover that they have been hired at a lower salary than a comparable man, there is often little they can do about it. I had both of these experiences repeatedly, and realized it was the norm.

At the Kennedy School, I had no idea initially what anyone else made but naively assumed I was making the same as anyone else at my level. Senior women I encountered across my career, like Dorothy Zinberg, and later Alice Rivlin, one of the most renowned women scholars at Brookings when I arrived there in 2000, soon disabused me. They had already been there, done that. They often shared their experiences, publicly and privately, and made it clear that wage disparity was a common challenge for all women. It had not necessarily improved with the passage of time.

Dorothy and Alice both came from solidly middle-class and accomplished family backgrounds. Like most of the women I met in academia, they had been high school valedictorians, stellar students at top universities, and pioneers in their fields. But they were women, and still a minority. And, as such, often denied the positions, promotions, and pay of men. Dorothy Zinberg was famous for a quote that she did not want to be sidelined for her entire life as "some brilliant man's bright young assistant." She was honest with me and the other young women she mentored about how hard it was to carve out a path in public policy in the face of overt gender bias. Dorothy frequently criticized the low pay for women academics, the difficulty women had in being appointed to full professorships, and the fact that women were often asked what their husbands did during compensation discussions — as if that should make a difference in the decision. "If your husband has a good job, why do you need to be paid so much?" was the general thrust. Dorothy joined the American Association for the Advancement of Science's first committee on women's issues to try to tackle the discrimination and bridge some of the pay divides.

Similarly, Alice Rivlin, who was the founder of the Congressional Budget Office, head of the Office of Management and Budget at the White House, a vice chair of the Federal Reserve Board, and the recipient of a MacArthur Foundation "genius grant" during her sixty-year career at Brookings, was stuck in a tiny back office in the poorly paid position of research fellow when she first joined in the late 1950s. At an event for the Brookings board of trustees in March 2016, commemorating the institution's hundred-year anniversary, she recalled this inauspicious start. Her male colleagues squirmed with embarrassment at realizing how shabbily *the* Alice Rivlin had been treated in her early days at Brookings, even if it was in line with "the standards of the day" for women, as she put it.

Wage disparity has remained a serious issue for women throughout my career from the 1990s to the 2020s, even though the overall situation has improved over time. At Brookings and elsewhere, pay gaps were eventually documented and put forward for scrutiny. There was more transparency in hiring practices after 2010. Salary ranges for specific positions were published in the nonprofit as well as the private sector. Employers were discouraged from asking about previous salary history and then trying to low-ball a new employee on that basis. The turning point was 2009, the year I turned the ripe old age of forty-four and wrapped up my tenure as national intelligence officer at the National Intelligence Council. That year the U.S. government finally passed legislation enabling women to present an equal-pay lawsuit once they found out they had been consistently underpaid for years on end.

The Lilly Ledbetter Factor

The Lilly Ledbetter Fair Pay Act of 2009 was named after a female supervisor at an Alabama car tire factory who discovered after almost twenty years on the job that she was being paid thousands of dollars less per year than her male counterparts. She received an anonymous note revealing the discrepancy. Ms. Ledbetter was the factory's only woman area manager. She had comparable qualifications and experience to all the men. The only explanation for the stark pay difference was her gender. She filed a lawsuit and won, initially. Her successful suit, however, was challenged by her employer and then overruled by the Supreme Court on a technicality. According to the law, Ms. Ledbetter should have filed her suit within 180 days of the first discriminatory paycheck. Of course, like most women, Lilly Ledbetter found out she was underpaid long after that timeframe and only because of the anonymous tip. The absurdity of the situation was obvious, including to the Supreme Court justices. Celebrated justice Ruth Bader Ginsburg highlighted it in her public commentary on the case in 2007. President Obama signed the congressional legislation designed to rectify the situation as his first official act in office. All the Lilly Ledbetters of the world could now sue their employers as soon as they found out about pay discrimination, irrespective of how long ago or how recently it had started.

Not everyone wants to press a lawsuit, of course, but the existence of the Lilly Ledbetter legislation prior to 2009 might well have helped to rectify some of the issues I faced in my career. It would at least have been something to refer to in discussions with human resource departments. I encountered discrepancies like Lilly Ledbetter's from starting out at Harvard in the 1990s right up until my time at the White House, at what one would assume would be the peak of my career. The bottom line was that no matter where you worked and how senior you were, as a woman you were highly likely to be underpaid — often by tens of thousands of dollars. I learned, literally to my cost, that a salary setback early in a woman's career could set a negative trend virtually for its entirety.

Over a lifetime, this can add up to a significant amount of money, severely limiting women's opportunity to accrue wealth for themselves and their families. At one point I figured out that I was several hundred thousand dollars in arrears over two decades of work owing to salary discrimination. I fretted about it for quite a while, thinking about all the things I could have done with that money and the fact that money is considered a direct signifier of how much you are worth to society and whether your employer values you or not. The overall message of salary discrimination is that women are worth less, even if they have the same or better qualifications and experience than the men they work with.

In my case, working harder and smarter had no impact whatsoever on changing the situation; nor did becoming a U.S. citizen in 2002. The fact that I was either working on a visa or was a U.S. permanent resident for the first decade of my professional life in the United States did not explain or excuse the salary differentiation.

Over the course of my career, I discovered that prestigious universities, think tanks, and nonprofits were just as egregious in their failure to guarantee equal pay for women as Lilly Ledbetter's tire factory in Alabama. When I started my full-time position at the Kennedy School in 1991, I had a master's degree, but I had not yet started work on my PhD. This quickly became a qualification and a financial problem. I was promoted relatively fast from research associate to associate director, taking over this position from two people in that particular role — a woman and a man who left the Kennedy School to join the U.S. government and a consulting company, respectively. I was admittedly junior to them in terms of age and qualifications. They both were recent PhDs, but I was now one person doing the job of two. I also had oversight of the program budget. I soon found out that the man had been paid slightly more than his female counterpart, clearly the outcome of a more successful negotiation, and I was being paid $20,000 less than I should have been, based on the overall responsibilities and performance expectations.

When I raised this discrepancy internally, I was told that the sticking point was the PhD. The salary was based on the qualification. I was capped by my master's degree. When I took care of the initial hurdle by finishing the PhD, I did get a salary bump in my last full year at the Kennedy School — but it was nowhere near $20,000.

My lower salary history for this particular position dogged me for years. Questions about previous pay were part of every other formal interview process. It was hard to figure out how to avoid them and negotiate my way over this opportunity barrier. Later I learned that men did it all the time. My first move from Harvard to Washington, D.C., was particularly painful in this regard. I was recruited by the president of the Eurasia Foundation, Bill Maynes (another important professional mentor), to be the director of strategic planning. The Eurasia Foundation was funded by a congressional line item, and the salary range was publicly available. Based on my qualifications and work experience at that point, I expected something in the mid- to upper level. The problem, of course, was that this would be a significant leap from my Harvard salary.

My first interviews with the foundation's head of human resources went well. The salary discrepancy at Harvard came up. He promised me that he understood the situation. This would not be a decisive issue. I accepted the job based on a verbal salary offer in the upper-middle range and made plans to relocate to Washington. Unfortunately, before I got the formal written offer, the head of human resources abruptly left for another job. Some time passed. I was due to relocate in a couple of weeks and I had still not received anything in writing laying out and confirming all the relocation and compensation details. Bill Maynes was traveling in Russia and then on an extended leave, and when I called, the new human resources director knew next to nothing about me. The former human resources head had not given her any formal notes from our interview and the salary discussion before he left. Nor had he talked to anyone else, other than to confirm that I was coming on board.

When I related the salary agreement, the new director balked. She thought that I was trying to take advantage of the situation to boost my initial offer. I had my own real-time handwritten notes, but they were hardly proof of anything in her mind. There was no official record at the Eurasia Foundation. She told me that it was "inappropriate" for me to expect to double my salary from what I was earning at the Kennedy School. "Why on earth would anyone agree to this?" she retorted. She gave me a counteroffer on the lower end of the scale. It was commensurate with neither my experience and qualifications nor the stated job expectations. I would be paid far less than others at the foundation in comparable director positions.

I was shocked and embarrassed. I was looking forward to working with Bill Maynes. I had already given notice to Graham Allison and lined up somewhere to live. Now things were blowing up at the twelfth hour. Ken was in his final year at business school in the Midwest. We were both living off my salary and he was planning to move to join me afterward. I figured I had little recourse. I managed to retain the small relocation bonus, but the whole thing left an empty and bitter taste in my mouth. By now I was in my mid-thirties and apparently stuck in a pattern. A couple of years later, when I was recruited as a fellow at Brookings, I was similarly unable to overcome my Harvard salary history. When I tried to push up the offer to where it should logically be, based on the position range and what I had expected back at the Eurasia Foundation, the hiring director smirked. It obviously seemed preposterous that I was even trying this.

Each time I got the impression that as a woman, I should consider myself lucky that I was getting a job in the first place. This was exactly what Dorothy Zinberg and Alice Rivlin had encountered decades earlier — the sense that an employer was taking some kind of risk on them because they were women. My fear that I was being systematically underpaid was confirmed in 2005. Brookings gave me an unexpectedly large annual pay raise. It was far in excess of anything I had previously received outside of a promotion or a new job. One of the Brookings human resource staff quietly told me that a new team had been looking through the salaries. I was the only woman senior fellow in the Brookings Foreign Policy Program. They were trying to correct at least some of the discrepancy between my pay and that of the next man on the salary chart. I had no idea, of course, what any of the men were making and how far out of alignment my salary was.

Passing on the Wage Gap

The situation became extremely complicated when I started at the National Intelligence Council (NIC) shortly afterward, in 2006, as the national intelligence officer (NIO) for Russia and Eurasia. The NIC is part of the Office of the Director of National Intelligence (ODNI), which was set up in 2005 to improve coordination among the U.S. government's sixteen intelligence agencies. The NIC was created in 1979 to function partly as an intelligence think tank for U.S. policymakers and a strategic foresight entity producing the government's national intelligence assessments and long-range analyses of global trends. In that regard, it was not that different from the Brookings Institution. It initially proved to be similar to Brookings in other ways as well.

When I joined the NIC, I was on loan from Brookings through something called an intergovernmental personnel agreement (IPA). This was designed for academic institutions and national research institutes like the National Laboratories to send staff into government service on a temporary basis. Brookings would be compensated for my work and would technically continue to pay my salary. I was informed that I would be paid within the official NIO pay grade, which was part of the U.S. government's Senior Executive Service (SES).

The NIC administrative staff assigned me the same salary as my immediate predecessor, who was also a woman on loan from academia. I was pleased with this development, as it amounted to a significant boost in my pay. I did not ask any further questions and figured everything was in order. Brookings added a monthly supplement to my salary for my time at the NIC rather than raising my base pay, as the overall benefits would not be reimbursed.

A year or so into my tenure, the Office of the Director of National Intelligence launched an effort to streamline and reconcile its pay scales. A formal salary grid was circulated to all the subunits, including the NIOs, laying out the parameters for different levels of pay. Although there were several female deputies, I was the only woman NIO. The vice chair of the NIC immediately realized that I was being paid far less than the men and called me in.

We would have to correct this. It was the same situation as at Brookings. He could not compensate me retroactively, but my salary would be adjusted for the next fiscal year. Brookings in turn had to more than double the monthly supplement moving forward. When I returned to Brookings at the end of 2009, I retained the higher pay and was also promoted to director of the Center on the United States and Europe. I felt that my hard work had finally been recognized. After almost twenty years, I was now finally on the salary track I would have been on as a man.

These experiences were part of a common pattern for working women. Men get more pay because they ask. Men are viewed as strong when they ask for money. Women appear grasping or greedy. Men always seem to have more leverage in a negotiation than women. Employers presume men will walk away if they don't get what they want. They have more job options because they are men. Women always fear that they have fewer options and there will be untoward consequences. Somehow, walking away from a bad pay offer or calling out a discrepancy will be held against them. They will earn a reputation for being difficult. As was the case for me, hiring managers push women to take what's offered and ask for a pay raise once they have proved themselves on the job. Women are a risk. Men are a proven quantity. The cumulative opportunity and monetary cost of all this bias against women, individually and collectively, is extremely high.

Looking back on my personal experiences, I realize that I was lucky. I managed to break through some of the gender and pay barriers later in my professional life because of new legislation, government intervention, and my stint at the National Intelligence Council. After my husband finished his MBA in 2000 and moved up in the private sector, our financial circumstances vastly improved, irrespective of my individual wage discrepancies. We were a two-salary family. My husband and I had moved way beyond our initial socioeconomic circumstances. I was also a white-collar professional, so already in a different compensation bracket from most women. The situation remained far worse for single women in other jobs, and especially for single mothers. In their case, the wage discrimination and the consequences of years of forfeited earnings from the gender pay gap were passed on to their children, impinging on the opportunities and life chances of the next generation.

My Brookings colleague Isabel (Belle) Sawhill devoted her long career as an economist to researching the socioeconomic factors shaping the lives of women and children in America. In a 2018 book, *The Forgotten Ameri-*

cans, Belle describes how families and schools become the early determinants of future opportunity for children in the United States. Family structure—whether children have two *working* parents or not—is particularly important in shaping opportunity. As Belle notes in the book, the majority of married couples with children in the United States were both working by the 2010s. Since the 1970s, women's wages have made a critical contribution to the growth in middle-class family incomes and to reducing poverty. In the second decade of this century, although women's participation rates in the labor force had stalled because of child-care demands, more than 40 percent of women were their family's primary breadwinners.

The women's pay gap was particularly significant in this context, because between 1960 and 2016, the proportion of children under the age of eighteen in the United States in a single-parent home increased from 10 percent to more than 27 percent. Seventy-one percent of these single parents were women. Their children depended entirely on their ability to secure and maintain a stable, full-time salaried job.

My husband and I were both shaped by our experiences of growing up in cash-strapped households with family histories of poverty and deprivation. We took conscious, much-discussed decisions about buying a house and having children, remembering our own parents' struggles with their mortgages and raising a family. Ken's parents raised twelve children in a small four-bedroom house on one salary. The Keens never tried to live beyond their means. The four girls shared one room; the boys shared another, crowded room with multiple sets of bunk beds. The parents had their own room. The oldest child got his or her own space in the tiny "spare" or box room. All the children's clothes were passed to the next in line, including the underwear. Ken used to joke that if something was clean and generally fit, then you just took it and wore it. There was no such thing as "yours." If the Keens took a vacation, they drove back to the family farm in South Dakota in a station wagon fitted out with rows of bench seats. Every child had some kind of classic American job—delivering papers, cutting lawns, babysitting—along with a few unusual ones like trapping mosquitoes for the greater Chicago mosquito abatement district.

Ken and I got married in our thirties. I had to help my parents financially back in the UK after Dad was pushed into early retirement by NHS cuts in 1994. Dad's pension was based on the low base rate of his salary. He had no separate retirement or other savings apart from the equity in the house. I was nervous about being stretched too thin by trying to cover our mortgage and the costs of a child and supporting my aging parents for however long that would be. We bought our own home after five years. We waited another six before we had our daughter. I was forty-one.

Matriarchs and Midwives

For a single mother in her twenties or thirties, with fewer working years under her belt and limited time to save money (even with a job immediately after high school or college), a volatile rental market and or demands of a mortgage can simply prove too much. In Bishop Auckland we had felt the pain of covering housing costs on my dad's meager salary; but in the United States in recent years, 84 percent of homeless families were headed by a single mother. Most homeless mothers (53 percent) had not completed their high school diploma. Black families were also overrepresented in the homeless population (given their relatively small proportion of the U.S. population at just over 13 percent), accounting for 43 percent in contrast to 38 percent for white families.

In the United States, the gender wage discrepancy is mirrored by a racial salary gap. Black women are doubly disadvantaged, by gender and race, when it comes to their earning capacity and even further disadvantaged by where they are most likely to live — in postindustrial and impoverished neighborhoods with inadequate affordable day-care facilities, underresourced schools, and limited job opportunities in the immediate vicinity. All of these factors constrain single Black mothers' ability to work and thus limit the prospects for their children.

Another Brookings colleague, Rashawn Ray, a professor of sociology at the University of Maryland, focuses on the role that families play in shaping Americans' lives and how race affects opportunity and social mobility. Rashawn himself was raised by a single mother in Tennessee, whose job opportunities underscored the central themes of his work. His own career success was the result of growing up embedded in a matriarchy of nurses — mother, aunts, and his grandmother — who all worked at the local hospital and formed a mutually reinforcing social network for child-rearing and economic support. Despite the obvious differences, Rashawn's childhood experience was strikingly similar to mine in the way that a woman's nursing career provided a good salary, paid for a house, and opened up all kinds of social connections. Just as it did for my mother in the UK, nursing offered a good, solid, dependable career path with transparent wage scales and benefits for a single Black mother in the United States.

Even before the challenges of work and child care kick in, having a baby creates all kinds of difficulties for working women. When I started out on my career, none of my jobs came with paid maternity leave as part of the benefits. In this respect, the United States is an outlier among advanced countries, including the United Kingdom, in having no national mandate for parental leave. Universities, think tanks, and other nonprofits pushed new mothers to use up accrued sick leave and then vacation time and to return to work as quickly as possible. This was the case even at Brookings.

When I found out that I was pregnant in 2006, I was fortunate that I was working at the National Intelligence Council, not at Brookings, especially because I had to have an emergency C-section. I needed more time off to recover than planned, and the U.S. government had better overall benefits and a more enlightened approach to childbirth and child care than the think-tank world. I was also a "function," not an individual, in my role as NIO. A deputy could step in and fill in for me. Although I was the only pregnant NIO (mainly because I was the only woman), all my colleagues at the NIC, including women in other positions, seemed to have lots of children relative to the general population. The government offered maternity and paternity leave coverage and assistance with child care. This enabled government employees, including single mothers, to have families, still do their jobs, and serve the country.

Brookings introduced maternity leave after I returned in 2010. As the demographics of the institution changed, more women of childbearing age came on board. When I had started in the early 2000s, the Brookings Institution was the bastion of men. Only a handful of older women had managed to make it past all the gender barriers. By the time these women made it to the top as senior fellows, they were often well into their fifties and past the time when paid maternity leave would have made a difference. Even having moved beyond all my early socioeconomic challenges, as a woman of childbearing age I was still an outlier.

8

Unlucky Generations

Despite all the complications of gender, the United States gave me opportunities that I would never have had in the United Kingdom. By coming to America, I changed my geographic place and social class and shed the stigma of my accent. I benefited from an education at Harvard University. I became a citizen; and eventually I had the unique opportunity to work for the government of my adopted country.

But over time I came to understand that the opportunities from which I was benefiting were time- and even generation-specific. Younger generations of Brits and Americans from similar backgrounds could not replicate my success in overcoming the obstacles to socioeconomic mobility in subsequent decades. They were being thwarted both by critical changes in the existing infrastructure of opportunity — especially in education — and by the effects of a serious economic crisis, the so-called Great Recession: the December 2007–June 2009 collapse of the U.S. housing market and subsequent global financial crisis.

Despite the hardships of my childhood, I had managed to overcome adversity thanks to a confluence of factors that played to my advantage. My education in the UK had been subsidized by the government. I had arrived in America just as the country embarked on a run of prosperity in the 1990s, with the Cold War rapidly receding in the rearview mirror. And I had come to Harvard University through the two-year Knox Scholarship: everything was initially paid for, even my transatlantic flight. I was not encumbered by debt when I graduated, and my university education became the key to my professional success in both the UK and the U.S. thanks to a persistent interest in my field of specialization, Russia.

In this regard, I mirrored the experience of millions of young Americans after World War II, who found college to be the door to a job and a better life than their parents'. But in contrast to the prevailing perception in the United States that anyone can go to college if they study hard, when I began work on this book, I found that 72 percent of students (men and women) at the 150 top colleges in the United States, including Harvard, came from the *richest* 25 percent of American families. Only 3 percent came from the poorest, and yet this was the stratum in which I had started out in life in the United Kingdom.

Money was, of course, a major part of the problem. Those in my cohort of Generation X, born in the 1960s and 1970s in both the UK and the U.S., had to contend with the upheavals of deindustrialization and the economic difficulties this created for their parents. But they often found some kind of state support for their education. For those born in the 1980s, in contrast, the opportunities to apply for a student grant when their time for higher education came around were dramatically reduced.

By the end of the 1990s, the expectation in the United States was that young Americans should and would have to pay for their own education because of the personal advancement it promised. In keeping with the post-1980s focus on individual responsibility and attainment, the state would provide neither a handout nor a hand up; instead, students should take out loans that they could pay off later. Armed with their degrees and other qualifications, they would surely find higher-skilled, better-paid jobs in the new knowledge economy than their parents had found in the old industrial sectors.

In short, a college degree and other advanced or technical training were individuals' personal investments in their own future, not part of the state's investment in its population's education or in the country's future. The ethos of Thatcherism and Reaganism had spread from economics to education. Here, perhaps more than anywhere else, their influence would eventually prove disastrous on both a human and a political level.

Vicious Circles

As the generation born in the 1980s and 1990s — Millennials — reached adulthood, they suddenly found their much-anticipated employment opportunities dramatically constrained. This was the case even for those with a college degree (about 47 percent of the cohort). Suddenly the entire premise of the new educational paradigm collapsed: students who had taken out loans to support their educations could no longer afford to pay them off and sank into debt. Rather than a springboard to opportunity, advanced education suddenly seemed like a millstone around this generation's neck.

Given their relatively high level of educational achievement, it is a testament to the toughness of the times that Millennials have been deemed the "unluckiest generation" in American history. In the early 2000s, which was supposedly "their era," Millennials were hit by economic setbacks from which they never recovered. These included the Great Recession, which struck just as they were either entering or trying to establish themselves in the job market. Ten years after that crisis, Millennials had still not recovered. They generally had fewer savings and assets than previous generations. Most of those who identified themselves in this group in social surveys told pollsters in 2018 that they would be unable to cover $1,000 in emergency expenses.

In interviews that I conducted for this book, Millennials described feeling economically and politically insecure and were acutely aware of their inequality. My nieces, nephews, and younger cousins in the United States all fell into this category. In fact, people born in the 1980s and 1990s had only a 50 percent chance of making more money than their parents. Millennials were doing worse than my parents' and in-laws' Silent Generation of 1925–1945, which was held back by the Great Depression of the 1930s and the Second World War.

In his seminal 2015 book, *Our Kids: The American Dream in Crisis,* Harvard professor Bob Putnam, with whom I worked when he was dean of the Kennedy School of Government, lays out in detail the consequences of socioeconomic divisions and inequality for Millennials and Generation Z — the two generational cohorts spanning birth dates from the early 1980s to the early 2010s, which have primarily driven demographic change in the United States. In his work, Putnam drew on extensive interviews with residents of his hometown, Port Clinton, Ohio, at the mouth of the Portage River on Lake Erie, where he grew up in the 1950s. He demonstrated that in this century it was no longer "self-evident" that all children in the United States, irrespective of their family and economic background, could expect to go to college or improve their position in life by finding a well-paid job right out of high school. He described a situation of stark class and generational divides, shaped by economic changes as well as shifts in family structures and parenting and declines in the quality of schools and neighborhoods over a seventy-year period. American youth in the generations that would shape the twenty-first century, Putnam concluded, faced the prospect of low absolute and relative socioeconomic mobility. Unlike their parents and grandparents, they had no assurance of a better life.

I had seen these developments in both the United Kingdom and the United States, and my experiences growing up in the North East of England led me to predict more of the same there in the decades ahead. But when I arrived in the U.S. in 1989, I had assumed that America was the land of opportunity, not a country with places like Port Clinton, Ohio — bigger versions of Bishop Auckland, where people's prospects were in decline and children could not expect to do better than their parents educationally and economically. And even as I began to comprehend the unfortunate parallels between my home country and my adopted one, I could not have predicted where this shortfall of opportunity would lead the United States.

There had been signs that Millennials' enormous gains in education were resting on a shaky foundation in both the U.S. and the UK. In the years after I left St. Andrews, for instance, the UK student body had become more diverse in terms of both class and race, in line with the shifts in the country's demographic profile. The Labour government increased places at university through the Further and Higher Education Act of 1992, which removed the distinction between universities and polytechnic colleges and increased entry for poor and working-class students. These changes were not, however, matched by a significant boost in funding for higher education. Compounding the paucity of new funding was the fact that local education authorities could no longer afford to pay all the fees and provide full maintenance grants for low-income students, as they had in the 1980s. The infrastructure of opportunity had seemingly expanded, but without a critical component. More university places simply meant more student demand for scarce public resources.

Thirty years later, unlike in the 1980s, a university education was no longer the guarantee of a good job — certainly not one that could pay off high levels of accumulated student debt. The expansion of education in both the United Kingdom and the United States increased the competition for jobs and thus employer expectations of higher qualifications for entry-level positions. With more graduates with bachelor's degrees, a master's plus other experience, such as internships and language or other special skills, became the norm for entry-level research assistant positions at places like the Brookings Institution, for instance. But undertaking additional years of study for a master's degree comes with a high opportunity cost.

When students stay in college and out of the workforce longer, they accrue more debt and lengthen the repayment schedule. The prospect of accumulating debt could easily become another barrier to entry into elite universities as well as every other college program for aspiring low-income students. Indeed, a series of reports on higher education in 2020 revealed that student debt in the United States had reached $1.6 trillion in total — more than tripling since 2006 — as increasing numbers of students pursued master's degrees and other qualifications. Although a Brookings Institution analysis in October 2020 demonstrated that most of this debt was held by former students who were now in the highest U.S. income brackets, it also underscored that these students were themselves from higher-income households. In other words, students from more affluent families were more likely to go to college in the first place than those with less affluent family backgrounds.

Brookings colleagues who focused on the differential impacts of student debt across racial groups noted the high negative impact of debt on Black students in particular. Black college graduates owed substantially more on average than whites, and the debt gap tripled in the years following graduation. Student debt had now become another obstacle to wealth creation for Black Americans. High accruing levels of debt were a contributing factor to Black students dropping out of college because of ongoing financial and family issues, further exacerbating inequality in educational attainment and incomes. Data from the U.S. Department of Education in 2016–2017 showed that 60 percent of Black students who started college in 2010 did not finish within six years. Their loans were not forgiven when they dropped out. Those loans became a lost investment and an additional financial burden, limiting their prospects. It was a vicious circle.

In the United Kingdom, unlike the United States, students who take out loans for their education pay them back based on what they earn, not on the sum they owe. In theory, if they are in a low-paid job, they can defer the debt indefinitely. No one hounds them and puts liens on their earnings and property. Nonetheless, the idea of taking on a debt that you may never pay off is a daunting prospect for low-income students, no matter who or where they are, holding them back from enrolling in college. The provision of student grants, in particular for minority and low-income students, would greatly expand their opportunity to enter university as well as the chances to improve their life and material circumstances.

Based on my own family circumstances in the 1980s, I would certainly have thought twice and adjusted my sights to cheaper college options closer to home if I or my parents had had to go into debt. I went to St. Andrews because it was affordable thanks to government funding. Neither I nor my parents had to take out a loan or a second mortgage, as many of my friends' parents did in the United States, to cover costs. It was the same with Harvard, because of the possibility of the Knox and other scholarships. If there had been no grants, I would never have come to America. I never would have found my way into the pipeline that funnels academics into the U.S. government. And I never would have had a front-row seat for what came next.

The Rise of the Populists

The decrease in government grants put higher education out of reach for many Americans. Coming on top of reduced employment opportunities after the Great Recession, this helped create the deep-rooted separation between low-income workers and college-educated elites. This cleavage in turn fueled worsening social divisions and political polarization in the first decade and a half of the twenty-first century. Despite all the purported social progress of the twentieth century, the top of the political hierarchy in both the U.S. and the UK in the new century was as much the bastion of the wealthy and upper classes as it had been in the 1980s and in earlier periods. With a few notable exceptions, it was also still predominantly male and white.

The absence of someone like you at the top completely undercuts the idea, supposedly embedded in modern societies, that everyone has an equal opportunity to succeed. You seem stuck in place, while others — a privileged few — are always moving up and improving their situation. For many women, Black Americans, and members of other marginalized groups, this becomes so discouraging that they abandon the fields that they have worked so hard to break into. Outliers in the lower ranks find the obstacles to moving up simply too daunting, and few want to find themselves as the token representative of their group, thrown into sharp relief at the top, with no one else coming up behind to join them.

My pedigree of a Harvard PhD and decades of work in universities and think tanks certainly made me an unlikely representative of the working class or a disadvantaged minority in America. Academics in the United States, and especially tenured faculty, are predominantly white and rooted in the country's more economically privileged socioeconomic strata. They are rarely the first people in their family to go to college. And although women have made significant inroads over the course of the past twenty years, many academic fields are still dominated by men in the professorial ranks. This is the same in the United Kingdom.

This lack of a direct relationship between ordinary people and prominent intellectual and political elites leaves the playing field open for others to step in and present themselves as advocates for the entire working or middle class or other distinct underrepresented groups. Indeed, politics since 2000 has been marked by the rise of populists — politicians who spurn "out-of-touch experts" and who claim to speak on behalf of millions of people with whom they in fact have no authentic connection, and in whom they have no genuine interest beyond securing votes to support their own often very personal agendas.

In America, the first sign of things to come was during the Great Recession, with the emergence of the Tea Party movement in the Republican Party, inside and outside Congress. The movement formed in reaction to the efforts by the administration of Barack Obama to bail out the U.S. financial sector in the midst of the economic crisis. Its members initially presented themselves as fiscal conservatives, calling for the kind of lower taxes and limited government spending espoused by Ronald Reagan. They quickly moved on to oppose the administration's promotion of universal health care and other social policies, and soon morphed into an activist protest movement supporting new candidates for office with a mixture of conservative, libertarian, and right-wing populist credentials. Many of these Tea Party candidates would later support Donald Trump's election in 2016.

Populist politicians in both the United States and the United Kingdom were given a further boost by large-scale demographic change, which came on top of the long-standing postindustrial economic dislocation and in tandem with the crisis of the Great Recession. The composition of the population began to change just as all the jobs that had previously anchored people to their specific communities seemed to disappear beneath them.

In the United States, migration within the country as well as immigration from outside have tended to be constants throughout the country's history — unlike in the United Kingdom, whose modern demographic diversification only truly began with the Second World War and the postwar dissolution of the British empire. The embrace of mass immigration from the European Union produced further rapid change in both the composition and the size of the population in the 2000s. In America, however, demographic change did take on a new character beginning in the 1960s. Specifically, it began to go hand in hand with generational change.

Consider that baby boomers, the generation of Americans born between World War II and the mid-1960s, are 82 percent white. Now consider the fact that within a century of this generation's starting point, the nation will have undergone a demographic sea change. By 2045, if demographic trends across the subsequent generations adhere to current projections, the United States will be overall "majority minority." But this is not happening for the reason that many people think: according to U.S. Census Bureau data, the Pew Research Center, and my colleagues at the Brookings Institution, the racial shifts of the most diverse recent cohort, Generation Z, born after the mid-1990s, are driven by domestic, internal, and personal factors such as interracial marriage and birthrates; they are not the result of immigration, which has been increasingly restricted by government policy in recent years.

Critically, some regions' populations have been changing more quickly than others. Younger people have tended to leave hollowed-out postindustrial regions if they can, and the people without jobs or with precarious finances who still live there have frequently chosen not to have children, or certainly to have fewer children (as was the case with my own family in North East England).

Thus, generational and racial diversity have become increasingly uneven across the United States. Some people have found themselves in places with little demographic diversity as well as fewer educational opportunities and jobs. Others live in vibrant diverse, multicultural communities with plenty of access to opportunity. They all have different perspectives on what it means to be American and where the country is headed.

In the 2000s, in short, uneven distribution of opportunity in the United States dovetailed with uneven demographic changes. Americans in deindustrialized regions wondered if the rest of the country was leaving them behind. Books like Amy Goldstein's *Janesville* and Jennifer Silva's *We're Still*

Here, among many others, recounted the predicament of distressed towns across the United States and the growing socioeconomic, health, and identity crises of the marginalized postindustrial white American working class.

Those who were attracted to the Tea Party and other populist movements were reacting to, and hoping to counter and even reverse, the effects of economic crises and demographic changes. The populists' supporters were also reacting to and seeking a salve for the intense emotions that these changes and challenges elicited. Major societal changes, especially when they happen rapidly and in combination, help fuel what celebrated scholars of the twentieth century like Fritz Stern called "cultural despair." Cultural despair is the sense of loss, grievance, and anxiety that occurs when people feel dislocated from their communities and broader society as everything and everyone shifts around them. Especially when the sense of identity that develops from working in a particular job or industry, like my father's image of himself as a coal miner, also recedes or is abruptly removed, people lose their grasp of the familiar. They can then easily fall prey to those who promise to put things — including jobs, people, or even entire countries — back in "their rightful place."

Stern was looking at the confluence of economic and social developments that engendered National Socialism in Germany in the 1920s and 1930s, after World War I and during the Great Depression. But his observations are universal and help to explain why the appeal of populists spiked when it did.

Separate and Unequal

Americans at the dawn of the twenty-first century could be excused for feeling a particularly acute despair. By early 2020, inequality in the United States had grown to such an extent that it mirrored the circumstances of the 1930s even more than my experience of the 1980s. The facts were sobering. Every newspaper and book that I picked up described how incomes had stagnated for all but the top 10 percent, which was where I now fell, thanks to my opportunities for higher education and career advancement since 1989. Fewer than 8 percent of American children from the bottom fifth of the income pile could reasonably expect to make their way to the top, as I had.

The United States also had the most persistent and widespread poverty rates among similar countries. Poverty experts noted that almost 60 percent of Americans aged twenty to seventy-five nationally — across all urban, suburban, and rural areas — could expect to spend at least one year below the official poverty line. The negative statistical divergence in individuals' incomes and their life outcomes could even be traced directly on a graph to 1980, around the time when I started my own journey out of poverty in the UK.

Race in the United States added an extra and distinct dimension of disadvantage for poor Americans. In some research, American fathers passed on about 50 percent of their income advantage to their sons. Generational wealth had a major impact on children's prospects, as was the case for me back in the United Kingdom. But in the United States, the average Black family had ten times *less* accumulated wealth than the average white family. And they were far less likely to own a home. This was often due to the legacy and persistence of restrictive zoning laws, tax code biases, and mortgage lending prohibitions dating from before the 1960s and the Civil Rights Act.

Within and across generations, inequality, poverty, and discrimination shape an individual's prospects for wealth and prosperity — and health and well-being. While the United States has the largest health-care spending of any country, life expectancy has fallen for lower-income Americans in the past two decades. In 2019, only the well-insured rich lived seven years longer than they used to. Thirty million people had no health insurance, and many more were classed as underinsured.

Every analysis of health discrepancy further underscored that much of this inequality was rooted in education — or rather the lack of access to a good education or higher education. Those without a college degree were the hardest hit by every negative metric. Americans without a college degree tended to be concentrated in rural areas, traditional Black communities, and urban areas that had lost the previous mainstays of their economies, where the tax base and house values plummeted and educational, health, and other basic services were degraded.

The North East of England had a parallel experience when I was growing up in the 1970s and 1980s and the major industries closed. Just as I had seen drugs and alcohol consume Britain and Russia in the 1980s and 1990s, the United States was engulfed by the opioid crisis after mass closures hit the U.S. coal, steel, and manufacturing sectors. As the basic welfare provisions and safety net — initially enshrined in President Franklin Delano Roosevelt's New Deal to reconstruct the U.S. after the Great Depression of the 1930s — were steadily chipped away, colleagues at the Brookings Institution and leading American economists catalogued the "deaths of despair" from the loss of personal identity tied to meaningful jobs and the death toll from poor access to basic medical care.

In short, the economic geographies of both the United Kingdom and the United States were askew. Wealth and opportunity were concentrated in certain cities and postal codes. They were no longer spread around. And although white American families in aggregate terms had more wealth and assets and better health, this was in large part because their numbers were greater in the population, and because upper-income whites tended to be so much richer and better off on every measure than everyone else.

National statistics masked the plight of poor whites in America's forgotten towns and deindustrialized regions. They had far more in common with Black and other minority group Americans than they might have thought. Inequality was a calamity for *all* the lower income brackets of the U.S. population. Americans were suffering regardless of their race.

The UN Arrives

In the 1980s in Bishop Auckland, we were well aware of the calamity that had befallen us. Dad had joked that we needed to call in the United Nations to take a look at Roddymoor and all the other godforsaken parts of the North East. In fact, thirty years later and a decade after the Great Recession, both the UK and the U.S. governments *did* invite the UN to come in as part of a larger UN investigation into poverty and human rights. By this time conditions in parts of both countries mirrored the deprivation when I was growing up in Bishop Auckland, and in some places were even worse.

In the UK, ten years of austerity policies, imposed by the Conservative Party government to stabilize the macroeconomy after the global financial crisis and the Great Recession, had slashed local council budgets. Government policies had also further eroded the postwar safety nets, already under assault from Margaret Thatcher in the 1980s, in the process exacerbating the North East's by now deeply entrenched economic and social crisis. Can you even *be* in a state of permanent crisis? Dad used to wonder back in the 1980s. When does that just become normal life rather than something that's going to go away or be solved? By the start of the 2020s, the state of crisis was indeed normal life for some people.

The UN named Philip Alston, an Australian independent expert on human rights law and a professor at New York University, as special rapporteur on extreme poverty for the UN high commissioner on human rights. In the UK, Alston was specifically asked to examine the impact of the government's social service cuts since 2010 on the country's most vulnerable populations. He visited the North East of England as well as other deprived regions. And what he found there was brutal — a crisis reminiscent of that of Russia in the 1990s, when the whole country had fallen off a cliff and spiraled into poverty after the dissolution of the Soviet Union.

The budgetary retreat from the UK's postwar welfare system had had the same effect on the country's most vulnerable regions and populations as the USSR's wholesale collapse and ten years of shock therapy. Indeed, the policies of the post–Great Recession British and post-Soviet Russian governments were similar, as were their goals: cut government spending to the bare minimum, restore fiscal discipline, and hopefully, eventually, at some point, boost the country's economic competitiveness.

When Professor Alston showed up in the UK in 2018, austerity policies had left the unlucky generations in Bishop Auckland subsisting on handouts from community crisis centers and food banks, including one in the Woodhouse Close Community Church, where my elderly mother volunteered. Some parts of the neighborhood around the church had been recorded among the most deprived and destitute areas in the UK for decades, certainly since the 1970s and 1980s. Mam would recount weekly stories of desperation that reminded her of some of the worst living conditions she had seen as a midwife in her early days on the district in Teesside in the 1950s, immediately after World War II. At least ninety local families, and at times as many as six hundred people individually, were dependent on the center and its limited resources for some kind of social and economic assistance.

According to Professor Alston's report from his UK visit, 20 percent of the British population — fourteen million people — were living in poverty, with 1.5 million facing absolute destitution (subsisting on less than £10, or about $13, a day). Around 30 percent of the nation's children, in his assessment, were living in relative or absolute poverty. Professor Alston noted that during his interviews he had heard harrowing tales of homelessness and suicide provoked by poverty and despair.

The UN rapporteur commended voluntary organizations like Woodhouse Close Community Church for stepping in to help address this crisis, but he also urged immediate state action. His conclusion was that almost a decade of deliberate government disinvestment in the UK's social safety net had created a colossal social and political crisis. This could not be overcome by existing employment opportunities in places like the North East of England. Something new and drastic would have to be done in order to rescue Britain's neediest from a state of permanent crisis.

Professor Alston conducted a similar visit to the United States and several other countries between 2017 and 2019. In the U.S. he noted the roughly thirty million people living in relative poverty. He observed that, unlike other Western and European countries (including the UK after World War II), the United States did not enshrine citizens' access to health care or housing as a basic right. In an October 2019 interview with the International Bar Association, Professor Alston stated his conclusion that "in terms of social mobility, the sad reality of the 'Great American Dream' . . . is that statistically the U.S. is less [socially] mobile than almost any other developed country." There were so many impediments to moving from a low-income group to another in the U.S. — ranging from poor health and inadequate health care to unequal access to food, limited job opportunities in blighted regions, and the consequences of accidents and sheer bad luck — that it was almost impossible to do it alone.

Professor Alston also drew a direct link, in both the United States and the United Kingdom, between poverty and a poor education. The two were inextricably intertwined — a lesson that I had absorbed firsthand during my upbringing in County Durham, and which I was reminded of each time I returned on a visit to the land of my birth.

Unteachable?

In the early 2000s, wanting to give something back in return for all the educational opportunities that I had benefited from in both the U.S. and the UK, I served as the president of the St. Andrews American Foundation. This is an alumni and donor body, established to raise money to help less privileged American students attend the university in Scotland. But my tenure on the foundation ended up highlighting the disadvantages that students face even after gaining admission to elite universities such as St. Andrews — and the level of intervention required to assist them.

For part of my tenure, beginning in 2009, the principal of St. Andrews was Louise Richardson, an Irish political scientist, former professor at Harvard, and executive dean of the Radcliffe Institute of Advanced Study. Dr.

Richardson left St. Andrews to become the chancellor of Oxford University in 2015. We had overlapped at Harvard in the 1990s, but I had not had much interaction with her until my time on the St. Andrews American Foundation.

One conversation with Dr. Richardson stuck with me. While access to the university had improved for students from comprehensive schools and less economically advantaged backgrounds since I had graduated in 1989, I wondered what the university was doing to recruit more low-income students. I put this question to Dr. Richardson, who was, I thought at the time, surprisingly dismissive of the general endeavor. She noted that St. Andrews had in fact stepped up its recruitment efforts, but in her experience, low-income students struggled when they got to St. Andrews. They often dropped out.

Dr. Richardson went on to explain that the university had had to lower its standards and make extra accommodations because low-income state school students' grades and general grasp of their chosen subject matter often weren't "good enough" in the first instance for them to be admitted. They were simply not prepared for college, she asserted. When I suggested (feeling somewhat affronted, given my own background and experience) that this might be because of deficiencies in their secondary school education, Dr. Richardson countered that it should not be the role of St. Andrews, or universities in general, to fix the problems of the UK secondary school system. This was the responsibility of the central government and local education authorities.

Dr. Richardson in fact made a valid point. She was highlighting a persistent problem in the elementary and secondary school system in the UK, and by extension in the United States: children from disadvantaged backgrounds who make it into elite colleges often struggle because of a lack of preparation and support. I had learned this the hard way as a student in Bishop Auckland: just because an opportunity presented itself didn't mean that I could necessarily seize it (like the chance to apply to Oxford). Dr. Richardson was right too in arguing that individual institutions would have considerable difficulty solving this problem on their own without leadership from the government.

The experience of one of my clever-lass cousins, Julia Magill, further underscores this problem — and also demonstrates the importance of government or some other form of sustained outside intervention to assist students in completing school and positioning themselves for further education. When the government (both local and central) does intervene on behalf of needy students, she showed, the results can be remarkable.

Informed by her own working-class background and the lucky break of the eleven-plus and a local authority scholarship scheme that had sent her on to an independent school and then to Durham University, Julia spent 2012–2015 as the cabinet member for education and skills for Cardiff Council in the capital city of Wales. There she was tasked with turning around the equivalent of the United States' K-12 system, including in one of the poorest school districts, distinguished by a history of unemployment and a sizable population of Traveller children, much like Bishop Auckland.

When Julia started, in some schools fewer than 30 percent of students were achieving the basic requirements to graduate (passing GCSEs in five subjects). A higher-than-average number of students were eligible for free school meals. Low expectations of low-income kids in some of the poorer parts of the city had become hardwired into the educational system. She even heard children being referred to as "feral" and "unteachable."

As Julia surmised, however, the problems were not with the students' inherent abilities but with the simple lack of resources and inadequate facilities that imposed additional burdens on top of family poverty. Students needed extra help to succeed at their basic school lessons even before they could consider preparing themselves for possibly going to university. But Cardiff's education budget was under considerable strain. Some school buildings were literally falling apart and riddled with mold because of limited maintenance funds. Teachers had not received the additional support and training they needed to cope with a challenging classroom environment.

Julia and her team pushed to have the decaying school buildings closed and demolished and the students consolidated in district schools with still-functioning facilities. Meanwhile she worked with Welsh government ministers to identify resources to replace poor school buildings across the city, including constructing a new state-of-the-art district high school. The education authority looked at best national and international practices for education to see what lessons they could learn to improve the system. Welsh elementary schools had adopted a model created in Finland, which was replicable to an extent without a major infusion of resources and had a proven track record of success. The Cardiff team pioneered rapidly improving elementary and secondary education by creating networks of teachers across several local authority areas to share effective procedures and materials as well as offer mutual support.

Thanks to these thoughtful interventions, grades and outcomes across the district gradually and measurably improved. Julia and her team eventually proved that low-income students in Cardiff were, as they always had been, eminently teachable, provided educators had confidence in them and high expectations of them — and if they had the right systems and facilities in place that others took for granted.

By and large, the lack of such systems continues to lock disadvantaged students out of opportunity. In 2020, the UK Parliament's Education Select Committee, which covered England but not Wales and Scotland, held hearings on the state of national education. Several academics who gave evidence to the committee underscored Julia's on-the-job observations in Wales a few years before. They noted that what were formally designated as "White British" working-class kids in England were neglected in national educational discussions and excluded from an "elitist curriculum."

The term "White British" first came into use in the 2011 census as an ethnic classification to distinguish indigenous British groups from white immigrants from the European Union or countries such as Australia and Canada. "White British" certainly wasn't used as a meaningful demographic categorization when I was growing up. As a classification, it encompasses a number of officially recognized ethnicities — English, Irish, Scottish, Welsh, and Traveller — which also have distinct and sometimes conflicting subidentities.

While progress had been made since 2010 in addressing some of the racial barriers for minority students to accessing quality education in the UK, the committee acknowledged that the country's low-income whites faced a "status deficit." They were left behind in terms of educational attainment. There had been no improvement in the metrics for low-income whites between a 2014 select committee report and 2020. Committee witnesses asserted that minority students in the UK had different attitudes toward education from White British students who had been ground down by several generations of living in deindustrialized, forgotten towns with few prospects for employment. In 2020, 59 percent of Black students and 64 percent of Asian students in the UK would make it to university. Moreover, minorities tended to live in London and other larger towns and cities, where there might be more resources available to assist their progress. Committee witnesses stressed that the message low-income children tended to receive from teachers, society, and their families was that higher education was not for them. They shouldn't even bother thinking about it.

The Locus of Opportunity

The struggles of needy white students in the United Kingdom highlight something that is not always evident in the United States. Unlike America, most of the UK is still predominantly white (around 86 percent in the 2011 census) at the national level. Outside London and some other big cities, the rate and extent of demographic change across the equivalent generations are not as dramatic as America's. So this throws into relief the pernicious impacts of poverty, class, and place *in combination* and illustrates how this mixture helps to feed a sense of cultural despair, epitomized (and then exacerbated) by low educational attainment.

It might go without saying, but working-class children who are classified as White British are not disadvantaged because they are white. Their predicament has nothing to do with their race or ethnicity; rather, it has to do with where they live. They are disadvantaged and discriminated against because they are poor, and because they live in economically ravaged areas devoid of opportunity. In some respects, the relatively new concept of White British has become a distraction from these factors in official UK government reports. In 2020 the UK government's watchdog for fair access measured education outcomes across several overlapping factors (poverty, race, gender, and place of residence) to determine which British groups had the lowest educational attainment. Their combined measure underscored that "White teenagers" on free school meals living in towns and cities across the UK's formerly industrial North and Midlands, as well as in coastal towns that had lost their shipyards, ports, or seaside attractions, were at the bottom of the list. Again, most of these places are not demographically diverse. Their demographic profile has changed little since I lived in one of those forgotten towns in the 1980s, so the classification of "White teenagers" in this instance is something of a diversion, what you could call a white rather than a red herring. Anyone, from any ethnic or racial background, would do poorly if they lived in one of these towns — and most likely worse, given the negative effect of race as an additional impediment to opportunity.

Spatial, educational, and employment inequality is an issue not just between urban and rural areas but also within large urban areas. Take London, which on its face offers a stark contrast to the rest of the United Kingdom.

London is the UK's center of educational and employment opportunity. Thanks to immigration, London also has a diverse population that mirrors large cities in the United States but puts it out of step with the rest of the country. According to 2011 census figures, just under 45 percent of the population of London is "White British." Thirty-seven percent of London's population was born outside the UK (including in EU countries); Asians accounted for 18.5 percent of the population and the Black and Caribbean community for just over 13 percent. Inner London is more diverse proportionally than the outer city boroughs.

Because of its sheer size and its political and economic influence within the country, London is the focus of most government and private philanthropic efforts to address inequality. London proves definitively that where you live and what resources are available shape educational and other opportunity. In inner London, 49 percent of the most disadvantaged students on free school meals proceeded to higher education in 2020. In the rest of the country, just over a quarter (26.3 percent) of those who were eligible for free school meals did the same.

Yet within London there is considerable differentiation in educational attainment across the individual boroughs, based on their aggregate wealth and demographic profile. Some boroughs in East London more resemble the rest of the country than the rest of London. Like the North East of England, East London boroughs such as Tower Hamlets lost the industrial mainstays of their local economy in the 1980s to the same forces of modernization as everywhere else. They mirror the deprivation rates of other UK regions, retaining high youth and adult unemployment levels as well as large numbers of children on free school meals. Although theoretically there are far more opportunities on children's doorsteps in these communities than in other parts of the country, their schools also struggle with a lower tax base, and most employment is in low-paid, low-skill jobs — this at a time when demand for low-skilled labor in cities has also diminished. Well-paid jobs in the knowledge economy and financial sector elsewhere in London require specialized skills. Such skills in turn require an educational groundwork that begins at a very young age — something that is out of most people's reach in London's poorest boroughs, in places that are systemically disadvantaged.

Just as I had rarely been to the UK's capital when I grew up in County Durham, kids in East London may have never visited central London. Their lives follow the same pattern as mine did in a small faraway town. And the same phenomenon of comparative deprivation unfolds in big cities across the United States as well. Just as a college education is no longer a dependable way of improving one's prospects, moving to a locus of opportunity like London or New York — and in some cases even living there — is no longer a guarantee of social mobility.

Today students from the richest families have become the sole beneficiaries of this set of circumstances in the UK as well as the U.S. Their parents cover their education. Their networks help them find jobs. They have a different infrastructure of opportunity, one that has proved impervious to the impact of deindustrialization in the 1980s and recession more recently.

The rest of their cohort of Millennials and Generation Z have not been so lucky. And just as female workers, former industrial workers, and other disadvantaged groups were chafing at the beginning of the twenty-first century under a system that was clearly skewed against them, so too would this new wave of younger aspiring workers come to feel an acute and justifiable grievance — one that would soon have a seismic effect on democratic politics on both sides of the Atlantic, but especially in the United States.

PART III

THE WHITE HOUSE

9

Me the People

On June 23, 2016, just before the U.S. presidential election, the United Kingdom held a referendum on what was dubbed "Brexit." British voters were asked to decide whether the UK should remain a member of or leave the European Union. The issue was multifaceted and complicated, and the question had progressively become a divisive issue within the ruling Conservative (Tory) Party. Many Tories believed that EU membership imposed onerous economic, political, and legal constraints on the United Kingdom. Membership drained tax revenues away for EU common funding and prevented the UK from charting its own course on trade and general business issues. Some decried the growing strain on the UK's schools, public services, and NHS budgets caused by the EU's free-movement-of-people directive, which had boosted Britain's population by an estimated 3.6 million after 2004. Others saw benefits from continued formal membership but wanted to push Brussels on institutional and budgetary reforms to increase the UK's room for maneuver. The prime minister at the time, David Cameron, fell into the latter camp. Cameron hoped to resolve the party's internal disputes once and for all by throwing the issue open to the population at large. He gambled that he could use the referendum to improve his negotiating leverage with the EU hierarchy in Brussels.

Prior to 2016, the United Kingdom had held only two national referenda. The first, in 1975, was to confirm the country's 1973 membership in the European Union in the first place. The second referendum focused on changing the British electoral system from "first-past-the-post" to an alternative voting system. This proposal was roundly rejected. The stakes were high for the third, given the daunting prospects of withdrawing from forty years of deeply entrenched formal economic and political relationships and trade networks.

The Brexit, or "Leave," referendum campaign followed a pattern similar to that of the 2016 U.S. presidential election. It dominated UK politics for months. It was well-funded and led by an insurgent figure from outside the political mainstream, Nigel Farage, the charismatic head of the UK Independence Party (UKIP). Farage's UKIP was a movement rather than a party, with little representation outside of the European Parliament and no accountability in British politics. UKIP had only one platform — extracting the United Kingdom from the European Union. Farage had managed to secure a position in the European Parliament as a fringe candidate, even though the EU was his "political enemy." He sought to attack it from the inside even as he drew a salary from the European parliamentary budget. Farage had never actually been elected to a seat in the British Parliament in Westminster. Nonetheless, he claimed to channel the desire of the entire British population to be liberated from Europe.

Several other vocal and flamboyant political activists jumped into the Brexit fray, including future British prime minister Boris Johnson, who tried to out-Farage Farage — to leverage the Brexit campaign for himself and accelerate his political momentum up the echelons of the Conservative Party. The Remain campaign was run by Prime Minister Cameron's government, but with a limited budget and little enthusiasm. The government, and UK pollsters initially presumed the British electorate would continue to see the benefits of EU membership and vote to remain by a small but comfortable margin. They were wrong. They had not factored in the opinions and sentiments of all the people living in the UK's forgotten places, like County Durham.

Referenda attract voters who stay home during normal elections. In the case of the Brexit referendum, 72 percent of the British electorate turned out, including large numbers of people who had not previously participated in national elections — from medium-sized cities, small towns, rural areas, and impoverished districts of major cities, including in the North East of England. These voters had not been captured by earlier exit polls, so they were not featured in pollsters' existing data sets and projections.

Many of these "new" — or rather previously unseen or marginalized voters — tipped the referendum in favor of leaving the European Union.

The outcome shocked the denizens of more populous and prosperous urban areas, who wanted to stay in the EU. In Bishop Auckland, 61 percent of voters opted for Brexit, even though EU structural funds had underpinned some of the town's fitful attempts at regeneration since the 1980s and that money would clearly now be lost.

The eventual winner of the 2016 U.S. election, Donald Trump, was in the United Kingdom during the Brexit referendum. He happened to be playing golf at a resort he owned at Turnberry in Scotland. Trump immediately grasped the British dynamic. His pollsters had been busy at home surveying the American electorate and saw similar patterns. Trump predicted that the U.S. would have its own "Brexit moment" in November — a prediction that proved to be true, again to many people's surprise, and thanks in large part to his campaign's ability to draw out disaffected and low-income voters in similar regions in the United States.

In 2016, Trump and Brexit became lumped together in the popular imagination. In the aftermath of Trump's election, British pundits were so surprised that they even wondered if the Russian intelligence services had anything to do with the shocking outcome. Perhaps Brexit had been a dry run for Russian interference in the American election. Nigel Farage and other Brexiteers had appeared on Russian state TV and were frequently featured in other Russian propaganda outlets. Farage was a self-declared supporter of President Trump and an early endorser of his campaign.

Subsequent efforts by UK parliamentary groups to investigate the possibility of Russian meddling found nothing conclusive. There was, however, a "Russia connection" between the two sets of events on either side of the Atlantic — a connection that was rooted in the populist politics that infused the UK and America in 2016.

In the Populist Mold

Populism is a political approach with no fixed ideology. It can pop up on both the left and the right of political thinking, and pretty much in any setting. The essence of populism is creating a direct link with "the people" or specific groups within a population and either bypassing or eliminating intermediaries like political parties, parliamentary representatives, and established institutions. Referenda, plebiscites, direct appeals, and executive orders form the substance of populism.

Vladimir Putin epitomized the populist approach in Russia in the early

2000s. Unlike his predecessor, Boris Yeltsin (and of course Mikhail Gorbachev as head of the Soviet Communist Party), as Russian president, Putin did not belong to a formal political party, more to a looser movement like Nigel Farage's UKIP. Putin's position as president was solely outlined and circumscribed by the Russian constitution. There was no other intermediation between him and the Russian people, the *narod*. Since 2000, Russian presidential elections had become national referenda on the choice of a stand-alone leader — the one and only Vladimir Putin — versus the occasional obscure or even manufactured opposition candidate. Populism had short-circuited Russian representational democracy, and now it was coming for the UK and the U.S. too.

Nigel Farage in the UK and Donald Trump in the U.S. both fit Putin's populist mold. They were charismatic leaders who dealt in pithy slogans that offered promises, not programs. Populists deal exclusively in "us" versus "them." In their depiction, they are the only political leaders who can possibly fix tough issues. They always present themselves as the champions of "the people."

Populists like Trump and Farage offered quick and simple solutions for complex problems. They promised to take action against a broadly defined and shadowy "elite," or an incumbent political establishment that was corrupt or self-serving and exclusively focused on blocking reforms that would benefit the people. In 2016, Farage and other Brexiteers blamed Brussels-based elites, unelected EU officials, for British voters' social and economic grievances across the country. Trump blamed previous presidents, Democrats, the U.S. federal government writ large, and nameless Washington, D.C.–based bureaucrats for Americans' woes in places like the Rust Belt and other regions left behind by the twenty-first century's knowledge-based economy.

To hear Trump tell it, Washington bureaucrats, like Brussels "Eurocrats," were the denizens of what was practically a foreign country, a city that was out of touch with the rest of America. D.C. bureaucrats were proponents of globalization and decades of U.S. trade policies that had seen American manufacturing jobs move overseas, especially to China after it joined the World Trade Organization (WTO) in 2001. They were also, in Trump's depiction, siphoning off tax resources to ensconce themselves in lifetime public-sector sinecures without any fear of accountability. They were "swamp dwellers," feeding off the American people.

The Brexit and Trump platforms were heavy on fearmongering and blame-shifting and light on the sort of detailed policy agendas that might actually stand a chance of fixing these deep-rooted socioeconomic challenges. Brexiteers promised voters that the UK would "take back control" as well as money. Tax revenues would stay to be spent in the UK and not go to Brussels. Trump promised to put "America first" and "Make America Great Again." In the UK, no one especially knew what Brexit entailed, apart from leaving the European Union and saving money. In the U.S., Trump said he would rein in Washington, D.C. He would "drain the swamp" of the "elite globalists" and unelected bureaucrats who had let American jobs slip away. He would slap tariffs on China and other trading "miscreants," who were flooding the U.S. with cheap goods. Both Brexiteers and the Trump campaign homed in on immigrants — from Europe and its periphery in the case of the UK, from Mexico and the rest of Latin America in the case of the U.S. — as a source of additional pressure on British and American working-class jobs. In fact, Trump's most concrete proposal (literally) was to build a wall along the U.S. southern border to keep those immigrants out.

Throughout history, populists have offered compelling narratives for people who feel they have lost their identities and cultural moorings as well as their jobs in an economic downturn and at times of rapid social change and political uncertainty. Populism was a major feature of European and also U.S. politics at pivotal points in the twentieth century: in the 1920s and 1930s after World War I, the 1918 influenza pandemic and the Great Depression, in the 1960s and again in the 1980s during generational and technological changes. Putin, for example, first came to power in Russia on December 31, 1999, right at the very end of a decade of wrenching economic crisis, political upheaval, and strife, including a war in Chechnya, in Russia's North Caucasus region. Putin promised to fix all this.

Populists like Putin provide straightforward, plain-speaking explanations for people's misfortunes. They offer scapegoats, like corrupt bureaucrats and conniving immigrants, or the West trying to keep Russia down, in Putin's case. They produce memorable catchphrases that encapsulate the ambitious claims that they, and only they, can solve "the people's" problems and ease their cultural despair. "The people" is also who they say it is — not everyone, just a specific group that they define. This group of "their people" (*nashi*, or "ours" in Russian) is then divided against the rest of society.

Labels proliferate. In the case of Brexit, those who opposed the idea of leaving the EU were "Remoaners," not just "Remainers" — cosmopolitan elitists whining and complaining about the loss of their ability to roam around Europe as they pleased. For those in Trump circles, opponents were "globalists" or "liberals" or just "libs" — wealthy coastal elites wrapped up in the bubble of their own alternative cultural circles, who wanted to hold on to their privileges at the expense of everyone else. Much of the rhetoric around Brexit and the rise of Trump focused on the political combat of labeling any dissent or dissenters accordingly and then mobilizing "the people" to try to outwit and marginalize the Remoaners or "make the libs cry."

Populism is as much about a leader's personal style as it is anything approximating a political belief system. In 2016, both Farage and Trump figured out how to make a direct connection with voters through the media. Trump was especially adept at using Twitter and other social media platforms as a direct (and nonstop) means of communication with voters. As president he invented "policy by tweet," bypassing formal press releases and other presidential messaging norms. His tweets were devoid of complicated language and often verifiable facts. Instead they were heavy on assertion and declarative style, with all capitals and lots of exclamation marks.

Both Farage and Trump adopted a "man of the people's" direct, plain, colloquial speech in their personal interactions and at in-person rallies, pitched at those without a college education. Educational attainment became a primary battleground. Neither Farage nor Trump was an authentic representative of the UK working class or American middle class, although Trump had hired plenty of workers (including immigrants) as a businessman. But they knew how to talk the talk of the working class, even though they had certainly never walked the walk of poverty or low-income status. They were sons of privilege.

Farage's father was a London stockbroker. He was educated at a private school, Dulwich College, although he did not go on to study at university. Farage made his lack of a college degree a badge of honor, even though when he graduated from school in the early 1980s it was quite common for young men from private schools to go directly to a job in the City of London. This was not the case for Farage's working-class equivalents — certainly not for my friends and relatives in the North East of England. Before launching his political career, Farage worked as a commodities trader. He honed his "everyman" pitch in pubs, where he would hold court after work. As the head of the UK Independence Party, he was frequently pictured during the Brexit campaign in a pub with a cigarette and beer in hand, even though some of his colleagues confessed to the press that Farage drank beer in public only "to be seen with it." It was purely part of his contrived image.

Trump, a teetotaler, offered a different image of the self-made, "pull yourself up by your bootstraps," successful businessman, even though he had inherited his real estate company and fortune from his father and frequently faced bankruptcy. Trump enhanced his personal and commercial brand through his appearance in the popular reality show *The Apprentice*. He was far more successful playing a businessman on TV than he had actually been in real life. Trump developed his man-of-the-people's speech on the streets of the blue-collar neighborhood in Queens in New York, where he grew up, and on the Trump family construction sites.

For their part, British and American voters found it easier to connect with Farage and Trump than with other politicians, who first touted their educational and professional backgrounds and expertise and then dealt in detailed policy programs. Farage and Trump mostly skipped these stages. They declared themselves inherently smarter than other politicians. Then they moved in directly to speak to and channel "the people's" grievances.

In fact, Farage and Trump seemed aggrieved themselves by some of the same things that riled working- and middle-class voters — especially the lack of respect afforded to them and their lack of acknowledgment by elite society. Trump and Farage both had been dismissed as fringe candidates by mainstream politicians. Their clear anger and frustration made them relatable — and made their threats to upend the system believable. Voters had little to lose, and much to gain, if these populists turned out to be something other than charlatans and made good — or forced other politicians to make good, in the case of Farage (who was not elected to UK public office) — on even a few of their outlandish promises.

"The People's Champion"

Populists play in the gaps created by generational and demographic change, divergent economic circumstances, competing social and cultural identities, and along the seams of inequality. In the first decades of the 2000s, the areas with the greatest socioeconomic distress in the United Kingdom and the United States showed significant support for a range of populist parties and leaders.

Thanks to frequent trips to visit my in-laws in the Midwest, as well as visits back to the North East of England and discussions with extended family, I had seen what one might call the rifts of 2016 coming in both countries. They were hard to miss if you had regular personal contact with people outside elite circles in major urban areas. My roots in Bishop Auckland in particular gave me insights into what was going on behind the scenes in similar impoverished and geographically or spatially disadvantaged towns in the United States.

Bishop Auckland was the kind of forgotten place where voters' choices took big-city elites by surprise in the UK in 2016. My hometown was one of the pivotal constituencies during Brexit, and it would play the same role in the 2019 general election, when Bishop Auckland selected a Conservative member of Parliament for the first time in more than one hundred years. The town served as a bellwether for other small towns in the weeks before the ballot, as journalists flocked from across the UK to interview local voters and gauge the turning of a political tide.

In 2019, Bishop Auckland would help to break the so-called Red Wall in the North, where the Labour Party had previously held sway uncontested. Trump did the same with the Blue Wall in the United States in 2016. In American versions of Bishop Auckland, voters opted for Trump instead of Clinton, the Democratic candidate, who traditionally would have been the defender of the working class, rupturing decades of Democratic Party dominance in America's old manufacturing and heavy-industrial regions.

The millions of people who voted for Donald Trump in 2016 thought they were voting for a "people's champion," as his daughter Ivanka had dubbed him — a big, strong man, a larger-than-life personality, who would work hard, day in and day out, on behalf of the American people (as his press office always said he was doing). Trump's voters expected him to bring jobs back to forgotten places in America and push through policies that would create a new infrastructure of opportunity that would benefit them directly. They did not anticipate that Trump would instead — as he in fact did over the entire four years of his presidency — endlessly obsess about himself and how other people were treating or mistreating him. He was, after all, the president of the United States. He had reached the pinnacle of opportunity and achievement in America. His voters hoped he would help them do the same.

On the campaign trail after he launched his presidential bid in June 2015, Trump reached out directly to the white working class in the postindustrial regions of the United States. He showed up in the American heartland and promised to reopen shuttered coal mines and build new steel mills. Trump promised huge investments in U.S. infrastructure — roads, pipelines, ports, bridges, railways, and so on — which would increase demand for coal and steel products. The over fifty thousand American miners and their families in coal-mining regions in the U.S., and the roughly eighty-five thousand workers in blast furnaces and steel mills, saw Trump as their salvation. He was the president who would reverse the decline of U.S. manufacturing industry and ensure them the trappings of a middle-class life. Indeed, Trump genuinely wanted to create new jobs in the coal and steel industries and other manufacturing sectors. Jobs meant votes. But saying he was going to do something proved easier than actually doing something.

Between 2017 and 2020, Trump made good on some of the policy aspects of these promises to the men of coal and steel — although not the massive infrastructure projects. He pulled out of the Paris Climate Accord in June 2017. He then removed environmental regulations targeted at reducing the use of coal in American power plants and curbing the dumping of wastewater and other pollutants into rivers and streams. In 2018, Trump slapped 25 percent tariffs on Chinese and other international producers exporting cheap steel and aluminum to the United States. Steel prices shot up and production increased. Nonetheless, Trump couldn't reverse decades of industrial automation and new technology development, shifts to natural gas and renewable fuels for generating electricity, and the growing demand for specialized steel products, as well as increased global competition.

In the case of U.S. coal, just as in the UK in the 1980s, there was no turning back the clock. It was déjà vu for me watching things unfold in America's coal country from inside the White House rather than from my perch at St. Andrews during the UK miners' strike. Over the four years that Trump was in office, coal production continued to fall. Coal companies filed for bankruptcy or went out of business; more miners lost their jobs. Metallurgical coal remained important for the steel industry, but the U.S. steel sector's overall demand for coal was considerably reduced in the 2010s. American steel had moved away from blast furnaces to new electric arc furnaces and "mini-mills" rather than the huge plants of the past.

Unlike the coal industry, the U.S. steel sector was generally holding its own, thanks to technological innovation, when President Trump came into office. Nonetheless, in a speech in Pennsylvania in August 2019, Trump claimed that the steel industry had been dead. He bragged that he alone had brought it back to life. This was not the case. He further asserted that no new steel mills had been built in the U.S. for thirty years before he came into office, which was not true. Then he claimed that plans for new steel plants in the U.S. were the direct result of his intervention, even when expansion plans had been under way for years.

I soon would have the opportunity to observe firsthand — over and over again — that Trump was far more interested in seizing the opportunity to claim credit and say he had done "amazing things" for people, things that "nobody had ever done before," than in engaging in the hard work necessary for real accomplishments. Most of the meetings I would attend during my time working in his administration would degenerate into some prolonged criticism of his predecessors — Barack Obama, George W. Bush, Bill Clinton, and occasionally George H. W. Bush — for failing to do something or simply for being "idiots" and then Trump claiming success for himself wherever they had failed. I joked to my colleagues after these meetings that the president's timeframe was divided into AD and BC — "After Donald" and "Before, when everything was Crap!"

Probably because of his background in real estate construction, men in hard hats epitomized Trump's personal image of workers in the U.S. economy. The more men in hard hats in factories than men in suits in offices the better, from his perspective. Building things clearly interested Trump the most. He constantly referred to his success in putting up huge buildings and paying attention to every detail from pouring the concrete to installing the bathroom fixtures. He would use his knowledge of building and construction as a reference point in trade and economic discussions with foreign leaders. Trump did not see financial and other services as part of the real economy, even though he was also in the hospitality and service sector and a significant part of his business was franchising and branding. He was dismissive of capital and investment flows. He thought about things in terms of the "stuff" of his own business that he and others could touch and see — construction materials, steel, concrete, and other manufactured goods, like lifts and elevators, lighting fixtures, furnishings. Everything was self-referential in some way. He wanted the United States to produce more manufacturing goods to sell at home and abroad, not more financial or digital services. In this way, of course, Trump's passions and interests aligned with those of the workers who would, like the men of Sunderland back in the North East of England in the old days, "mack 'em" — make all these things and earn a decent wage and living in doing so. Like them, Trump took genuine pride in the things he had made.

The Billionaires' Club

From my vantage point growing up in the industrial North East, it was easy to see Trump's allure for American workers. He also initially appealed to some of my friends and relatives in the UK, including Mam's godson Jeff, who had voted for Brexit before Trump was elected in 2016. In County Durham, people who had participated in the miners' strike in 1984 or lost their jobs when the Consett steelworks closed down had been staunch supporters of the Labour Party. Twenty-five years later, in the 2019 general election, they voted for the Tories.

On trips to visit my family, I heard plenty of complaints in Bishop Auckland, including from Mam, about the way local voters were taken for granted by Labour politicians who wanted a safe seat in Parliament to satisfy their own ambitions. In their view, the Labour Party had abandoned the working class. They had just stood by and done nothing as jobs in the North East were decimated. The last huge steelworks and massive blast furnace in the North East, in Redcar, where several of Mam's cousins had worked, closed down in 2015. This definitely colored people's views on the eve of the Brexit referendum. During the Brexit campaign, Nigel Farage and also future prime minister Boris Johnson blamed the EU for these closures as well as for the growing strain on the budgets of the NHS, one of the last big regional employers. So people in Bishop Auckland and the North East voted for the Tories to "get Brexit done" and bring money and attention back home.

Similarly, in the United States, workers believed the Democratic Party had abandoned them. They saw Trump as a businessman who could get things done. As far as they were concerned, he had launched big construction projects. He knew how to create jobs. My U.S. relatives in the Midwest complained constantly about "establishment elites" and "professional politicians" who had no idea how to create jobs or run a business and were out of touch with the average American worker. In 2016 they complained about how Hillary Clinton was paid thousands of dollars to give corporate speeches and palled around with celebrities during her campaign, drinking champagne instead of coming to the American heartland to hear what they had to say about the state of the country. It was no matter that Trump was rich and had a lifestyle that could not have been more different from theirs, or that he had inherited his company from his father.

For struggling Americans, the new president was both a relatable and an aspirational figure. Trump personified success. He ran his own company. He was his own man. No one gave him orders. He didn't report to anyone at all — no middle or upper management to tell him what to do. And, most importantly, even though he had lots of money, he seemed like everyone else. He talked like an ordinary American. He liked fast food, not fancy restaurant food that most people couldn't afford. He didn't talk down to people. He was blunt and direct, the same in public and private. As a real estate mogul, Trump also epitomized the aspiration that transcends race and class in the United States. He not only owned a house, he built houses, and many other things besides. Trump put his name on every property. He was the brander of the bricks and mortar of the American dream. Many of the people who voted for Trump would have loved to have as much money as he did, be their own boss, and pass on wealth and property to their children.

Stories about Trump's frequent bankruptcies and unscrupulous business practices were dismissed by his supporters as efforts to defame or discredit him. Trump's outsider status was another major part of his appeal in 2016 — the fact that he was not accepted by the upper classes and political elites, including within the Republican Party. When Trump announced his candidacy, he was mocked and disrespected, especially as he later recounted it in his campaign rallies and in public appearances. "No politician in history [. . .] has been treated worse or more unfairly," he said. He was going to show everyone up by winning. His candidacy and presidency were a giant middle finger directed at all those who doubted him. Trump stiffed the privileged world that excluded him. This gave him crossover appeal for the large swath of middle-class workers in the heartland without a college degree, who felt that they were also judged by East and West Coast elites for taking or wanting a good, stable full-time job rather than going to college.

Throughout history and internationally, populism emerges from the sense of illegitimate and unfair transfers of wealth in society from the bottom to the top. Populists like Trump say they are the people's champion. They will fight corruption ("drain the swamp") and redistribute wealth from the top to the bottom. Trump said he would share America's wealth by creating jobs, but not by giving, in his words, "something for nothing" through increased welfare payments for the poor and unemployed. This was "socialism" and unfair to the American worker. Trump's plan to deliver jobs for voters involved people like himself — other billionaires being freed up to do business — rather than elaborate plans for a new U.S. industrial policy. He saw himself as leading an American billionaires' club that would "bestow" jobs on America.

In Trump's view, as under Reagan and Thatcher in the 1980s, government deregulation and tax breaks would ease the way for billionaires and other businesses to expand their operations. Trump also talked about training schemes linking local community colleges to America's big businesses to prepare workers for jobs requiring new technical skills. The billionaires would help foot the bill. As in the case of his claims about coal and steel, Trump continually bragged about the jobs and training schemes he created or had instructed businesses to create with his top-down approach and executive orders.

It was certainly the case that unemployment dropped during Trump's time in office, including for Black Americans and other minorities, but many of the new jobs created during the first three years of his administration turned out to be ephemeral once the U.S. was put under lockdown conditions in 2020. And the new jobs lacked security. At the same time that Trump focused on "unleashing" billionaires and big business, he also launched efforts to weaken American workers' protections and benefits — just as Margaret Thatcher had targeted the UK "nanny state" in the 1980s. Trump went after trade unions' efforts to deploy collective bargaining for pay raises and the Obama administration's Affordable Care Act, which had expanded access to health insurance for millions of Americans, and he rolled back environmental standards and health and safety codes. His anti-union attitude was well documented. He was always railing against unions in meetings, expressing his opposition to organized labor and employees, rather than shareholders, who wanted stakes in companies.

Donald Trump, like Nigel Farage across the Atlantic, may have been an improbable figurehead for the American working class, yet the grievances that motivated UK and U.S. voters to go to the polls in 2016 in support of both Brexit and Trump were genuine. They were the product of internal fissures that were real and long-standing. There are political costs when places and the people who live in them are effectively written off and their most basic needs neglected. Their unhappiness eventually shows up as dissent at the ballot box — even if in some cases, as in Bishop Auckland, it takes thirty years.

As it turned out, I had not been the only one for whom an outsider's or foreign perspective helped illuminate the dangerous course that the United

States was on. Russian leaders in the Kremlin had seen the grievances too. And they had resolved to take advantage of them.

Back to the Future

As a former intelligence operative, Vladimir Putin had determined over the years that Russia and the United States were really not so different. The two countries were essentially subject to the same larger economic and social forces, and their populations were equally susceptible to political manipulation.

Over the course of successive terms in office as both president and prime minister, Putin had figured out how to channel, if not completely control, the populist forces at home. When he decided to intervene in the 2016 U.S. presidential election, he unleashed the Russian security services to use tactics abroad that they had already successfully deployed to quash Russia's opposition and keep domestic political dissent and social protests in check.

Russia's intervention came right out of a Cold War "active measures" textbook of the kind I had studied since the 1980s. Russian operatives employed propaganda, disinformation, and deception. As later American government public and independent press reports would reveal, the Russians used a sophisticated combination of new cybertools, alongside the state-backed media, to hack the email messages of prominent American political figures, disseminate leaked documents, and amplify inflammatory news items. The Russian government set up "private" proxies to spearhead some of the most brazen operations and distance the Kremlin from direct responsibility.

One of these proxies, the innocuously named Internet Research Agency (IRA), was headed by the former director of a Kremlin catering company, Evgeny Prigozhin — who had, in a strange coincidence, been in charge of the Valdai Discussion Club dinner where I sat beside Putin in November 2011. Since then Mr. Prigozhin had branched out in less savory directions, including setting up the IRA and providing paramilitary forces for clandestine Russian operations in the Middle East and Africa. The IRA analyzed U.S. public opinion and social divisions, scrutinized U.S. polling, and hired droves of young Russians with English-language skills to pose as Americans on internet platforms like Facebook and Twitter. There, these "Americans" opined on contentious issues like race, religion, and gun control. The agency also bought online ads to target American voters on both sides of the ever-growing partisan Democratic and Republican Party divide.

As Putin and the Russian security services had suspected, the United States was vulnerable to its own 1990s Russia-style political upheaval in 2016. Ahead of the election, opinion polls showed that American voters were divided by red/blue, Republican/Democratic affiliations, whether they lived in rural or urban areas and in terms of educational attainment, income, race, religion, and gender as well as a whole range of preferences and perceptions about the extent of state intervention in the economy, globalization, trade, immigration, and social and cultural mores.

The 2016 presidential race was also uniquely vitriolic. Both parties were split in their support of the candidates: First Lady, senator, and secretary of state Hillary Clinton for the Democrats, and insurgent political newcomer, reality TV star, and real estate mogul Donald Trump for the Republicans. Clinton had engaged in a bitter primary competition with a self-declared socialist, Senator Bernie Sanders of Vermont, who usually functioned as an independent in Congress and was something of a populist himself. Donald Trump had never been part of the Republican Party and had once been registered as a Democrat in New York. He was the last man standing from a huge field of seventeen candidates representing the Republican Party's mainstream. They successively knocked each other out over the course of the primaries. Neither the Republicans nor the Democrats imagined Donald Trump would ultimately be the candidate.

The Kremlin anticipated that Hillary Clinton would win the election and seek to constrain Russia's room for maneuver. As secretary of state under President Obama, Clinton was particularly outspoken about Russian foreign and domestic policy and critical of Putin's return to the presidency in 2012 after a four-year term as prime minister. Russia's operation sought to weaken her. Russian propaganda efforts promoted both Bernie Sanders and Donald Trump as well as third-party candidates like Jill Stein of the Green Party. Russian operatives from the military intelligence services, the GRU, were later revealed to be behind efforts to penetrate Clinton's personal emails and the "hack and release" of the Democratic National Committee's (DNC) emails. These operations were particularly damaging to Clinton's campaign. They represented a new level of dirty tricks, even by Cold War standards. In the end Clinton lost to Trump by an extremely narrow margin in the Electoral College. She won the popular vote by almost three million votes. The election turned on 79,646 votes from only three counties in three U.S. states — Wisconsin, Pennsylvania, and Michigan. The 2016 election was both a fluke and a perfect storm in its strange confluence of events.

Russia's efforts to exploit U.S. homegrown resentments, push American political buttons, and interfere in the 2016 presidential campaign provoked a seemingly endless domestic crisis. In 2000 a similar discrepancy between the popular vote and the Electoral College had played out in the election of Republican president George W. Bush, who had been in a tight race with his Democratic opponent, former vice president Al Gore. But in 2016 the votes on the margins were so tight that American politicians and pundits credited the Russian intervention with affecting public opinion. Some commentators went so far as to declare Trump "illegitimate" and assert that President Putin and the Russian security services had "elected" him.

To be sure, Trump had long-standing business interests in Russia, as well as ties to a number of businessmen there who moved in Kremlin circles. There were also Russian investors in some of his U.S. properties. And without a doubt Trump invited the charges of his illegitimacy by openly and not so openly courting Russian assistance in the election that sent him to the White House.

During the campaign, members of Trump's inner circle, including his son Donald Jr. and son-in-law, Jared Kushner, had met with politically connected Russians who promised potentially damaging information on Hillary Clinton. Trump himself had openly welcomed the hack and release of Clinton's and the DNC's emails. Trump's longtime associate Roger Stone had also bragged of contacts with Wikileaks, the internet platform that posted the emails. These actions in themselves stoked plenty of suspicion and public outrage.

In May 2017, Deputy Attorney General Rod Rosenstein authorized an official probe into possible links between the Kremlin and Trump's campaign ahead of the election. He appointed a special prosecutor, former director of the Federal Bureau of Investigation Robert Mueller, to oversee the inquiry, and also to figure out the full extent of Russia's efforts to interfere. True to populist form, Trump dubbed the claims of "collusion" between his campaign and the Russians a "witch hunt" and the Mueller investigation into the Russian security services' election interference "the Russia hoax."

The investigation wrapped up in March 2019, without conclusive evidence of direct collusion. It did, however, highlight the fact that Trump and his campaign team had been willing to use whatever information came their way from whatever source, including Russia, for their own political ends. In seeking to defeat Hillary Clinton, Trump's and the Kremlin's objectives had aligned. The final report from Mueller and his team provided considerable detail about the extent of the Russian intervention, and it made the case for indicting several Russian actors and entities, including Evgeny Prigozhin and the IRA.

With the Mueller investigation ongoing behind the scenes, Democrats and Republicans in Congress constantly fought over the outcome of the election and Russia's role in it. As a result of focusing on the Russians, they generally ignored the genesis of the domestic political divisions that had shaped such a contentious election in the first place and propelled Trump to the presidency. This was a major mistake as far as the country's future was concerned.

Both Vladimir Putin and Donald Trump were a distraction from the real crisis at hand inside the United States — a crisis that mirrored the one sweeping the United Kingdom at the same time, and which shared many of its underlying causes. Donald Trump's insurgent presidential candidacy and election and the UK's decision to hold a referendum on withdrawing from the European Union in 2016 became part of the same phenomenon. In the voting booths of both countries, low-income and working-class voters had lashed out in protest. My family members in the UK and the U.S. voted for Brexit and Trump for similar reasons — establishment political elites weren't paying attention to what was happening to them. In circumstances where millions of people feel marginalized and mainstream political parties have no evident solutions, populists fill the vacuum.

The Big Show

President Trump, who oversaw a family business, not a multinational corporation, was now running a country for the first time. Essentially, he saw this as the same enterprise, at home and abroad, just scaled up. As a businessman Trump had focused on maximizing his family's profits, which meant holding on to as much money as possible and paying others less if he could get away with it. He was infamous for finding ways to avoid reimbursing contractors on his big real estate projects and for not fully compensating his workers. He often called people "losers" for giving things away. When it came to America's European allies, Trump was especially cynical and scathing. He viewed the world just like he viewed his real estate business and simply applied the same approach to foreign policy as he did to everything else.

There were no allies or permanent partners in cutthroat New York business circles. If you were at the head of a family business, you and you alone could protect your interests. You had to be strong and push back against others, who might be trying to "play us like suckers" or "rip us off." This was the way Trump talked about U.S. allies in my presence in meetings — and not just behind their backs. They weren't strong or sovereign if they needed something from the United States and couldn't take care of their own defense, for example. They were more like supplicants. They were weak. Trump also couldn't believe that anyone would genuinely do something out of altruism. From his perspective, postwar European ideas of trying to create a more just and equal society must be rooted in something more pernicious and ideological, like "socialism." In Trump's worldview, everyone was self-serving. People always did something for a reason — power, money, lust, fame. And countries, by extension, operated in the same way. They should put themselves first, like he did.

Of course, when it came to the home front, President Trump was careful to give the impression that he was always putting his voters first and looking out for their interests. Like any politician, he knew he should not take his voter base for granted. They had given their votes to him, and they could just as easily take them somewhere else if he didn't deliver. So he always looked like he was delivering — making good on the surface. In his public speeches, Trump always favored workers, not billionaires or businesses. He spoke directly to workers, not past them. He went to his voters in person, by holding mass rallies all around the country. He invited workers' representatives to the White House. And if there was no opportunity for a face-to-face, then his voters could follow him every day and all day on Twitter or watch him on Fox News, where he would endlessly entertain them. Trump clearly derived personal, not just political, energy from his encounters with workers and the crowds at his rallies. West Wing staff, such as Nick Luna, the president's "body man," and the military staff frequently talked about it when we were all together on presidential trips. They described him as the "Energizer Bunny," always on the go, always wanting to wade in and greet "his people."

Having watched a lot of boxing on TV with Dad back in the UK, I often thought of President Trump as more the pugilist entertainer than politician on those occasions. He spoke to the crowd like a bare-knuckle boxer, revving everyone up before he jumped into the ring for a sparring match. Boxing, wrestling, all forms of fighting, were classic working-class sports. Trump often used the language of a fight, "the big smack-down," in his rallies, most notably and ominously at the January 6, 2021, rally when he told his supporters to go out and "fight like hell" for him. Trump also played up his ties with the U.S. boxing and wrestling entertainment industries throughout his time in office. He highlighted his connections with boxing promoters from his days running casinos and showed up at wrestling matches to solicit political and financial endorsements from industry owners. He even appointed former professional wrestling executive Linda McMahon to his cabinet to head the Small Business Administration in 2017. People generally like someone who will "talk trash" and fight for them and not take them for granted. They respond when someone focuses on them and speaks their language.

As well as the fighting talk, what Trump loved most of all was the big showpiece event that would put everything in motion. As I would see firsthand, his presidency was dominated by the photo op, the staging of events, where people would stand around watching him as he signed some "major deal" or document. Trump loved to play the patron in public, seemingly creating opportunity for the American people with the flourish of his signature black Sharpie rather than a pen. *The Apprentice* reality TV show and franchising and branding were the most successful parts of the Trump business after his early construction projects in New York and Chicago and his phase building casinos. TV was Trump's arena. How things looked on TV, not how they worked per se, was always the most important aspect of any meeting. Almost every meeting involved some kind of public performance, like a press conference, even when there was nothing much to play up or it was patently better do something quietly, without any fanfare.

The episode that summed all this up for me came in March 2018. President Trump invited ten steel and aluminum workers to the White House to watch as he signed a proclamation on tariffs on cheaper imported steel and aluminum coming into the United States, especially from China. The workers were political props — mostly men, one woman, one Black worker. They were in the Roosevelt Room, standing around the president, who was seated at a desk. They were in freshly pressed work clothes and overalls, some clutching hard hats. No suits even for a White House visit. They had been asked to come "in costume." They had to look the part. Trump was always talking about "Central Casting," about how everyone around him should have the right look.

After signing the proclamation, President Trump invited the workers to make some comments for the press. One steelworker from Pennsylvania related how his father had lost his job in a steel mill in the 1980s. His father was "crushed" — no longer able to "go to work, joke around with the guys, tell good stories, and be able to support a wife and six kids." Obviously thinking that all steelworkers must have Hobbesian brutal and short lives, Trump remarked that the steelworker's father must now be very proud, watching him in the White House from up in heaven. Trump's remark fit the tableau he was trying to present — of him, the president, saving American workers from destitution and death by slapping tariffs on Chinese steel imports. The worker, slightly embarrassed, had to correct the president. His father was actually still alive and watching all this on TV. Trump was surprised but made a quick joke of it.

Personally, I cringed watching the scene unfold on the White House TV screens. My dad had often been in the same situation at Bishop Auckland General Hospital when some visiting dignitary would make a speech on the importance of the UK's beloved National Health Service. The NHS was always the flag that British politicians liked to wrap around themselves on the campaign trail. Dad would be pulled away from work and rolled out with the other porters in their uniforms to stand around during the speech for the benefit of the press. Then they would have their picture taken with the dignitary. What might start off well would inevitably degenerate into embarrassment when people failed to play their appointed role in the political pageant. During one rollout, a pompous and self-important visitor had made a point of telling Dad that "I admire you people . . . for the way you are." "What do you mean, the way we are?" Dad had shot back. "Simple?" "Oh no, no, of course not," the startled visitor had replied. "Um, I mean, um, hardworking."

The hardworking part was definitely right. Dad and the steelworkers in the Roosevelt Room wanted to work hard and have the opportunity to do so. They wanted a job that would let them get ahead, not just survive. They were willing to be part of someone else's "big show" if it came to something. They wanted respect *and* results. In that moment in March 2018, the workers who attended the signing *did* feel respected by President Trump. I was the one cringing. I had a different view of how things were unfolding behind the scenes. The steel and aluminum workers were thrilled at the opportunity to be in the White House. This was the American people's house, and they were meeting the American president. But when they got back home and related the story to their colleagues, they clearly underscored what results they expected from President Trump's signature on the tariff proclamation. This wasn't just a performance or a show-and-tell for them.

One of the workers, a United Steelworkers Union representative from Pennsylvania, noted that ultimately the visit and the tariffs were all about saving jobs, "good American jobs," and the aspirations that came with them. He summed it up directly. This was so "people can have the ability to live the American dream. Can I buy a house? How many people at work these days can afford to buy a house? There is not a whole lot anymore. There's not a lot that can buy new cars and help their kids go to college and can save up and actually go on a vacation. If you work hard all of your life, after 30 years you can actually get a pension so you can live and not have to go back to work. I won't have to decide if I'm going to eat or pay for my medicine . . . These are the jobs that make the difference."

The Populist's Playbook

For his political base, President Trump was a ubiquitous presence out in front of the cameras, signing proclamations and executive orders promising jobs. The rest of the government was remote and often invisible, doing nobody knew what apart from spending taxpayers' hard-earned money. That, of course, was the point of the big show, making the president look good. Trump took all the credit for initiatives that might have been devised and would certainly be carried out at lower levels of the government. He was the person working for the American people — not the faceless "deep-state bureaucrats" that he frequently railed against. Fueling long-standing popular distrust in public servants and the U.S. federal government helped to boost Trump's popularity during his campaign and once he was in office. It was a classic populist move that helped keep him in the limelight.

In the White House, Trump continued the style that had made him famous on *The Apprentice*. Reality TV offers the surface verisimilitude of real life, but it's all artifice, playing for the cameras. As president, Trump was always camera-ready in full makeup. White House press conferences, "exclusive" interviews with selected journalists, and public rallies put him at the center of national attention. When any political opponent or sometimes even a cabinet member held an event, Trump arranged a competing event or sent off a flurry of provocative tweets to draw the media's and public's attention away. If he had nothing to talk about, he would manufacture a scandal or a crisis to get everyone talking about him.

As the head of an eponymous family firm — as I observed from the references he made and the way he talked about things — Trump saw the United States of America as "Trump U.S.A." Once he became the president, he set about rebranding America, in a kind of merger and acquisition with Trump family enterprises. He talked about redesigning and "Trumpifying" Air Force One, for example, to make it look more like his own personal luxury aircraft. It was the same with the White House itself. Every president puts his stamp on the American people's house in terms of changing the decor and making additions or upgrades to the grounds or buildings. But Trump, more than anyone, tried to make it his own. He frequently violated the norms of using the building by holding political rallies and campaign events there.

In this way, the people's house — the White House — became Trump's house. "We the people" — the principle of American government, embedded in the Declaration of Independence — was for Trump "Me the people." Trump's 2016 campaign slogan, "Make America Great Again," and its acronym, MAGA, were plastered everywhere and on everything. There was "MAGA world" and then everything and everyone else outside. Trump repeatedly stated that he didn't consider the people or states that had not voted for him in 2016 as part of "his America." There were red Republican states and blue Democratic states. His were red. MAGA was emblazoned on red baseball hats that he threw out at rallies. The others, the blues, could be punished and threatened. It was tribal in the extreme.

I had watched the beginnings of Trump's cult of personality during the campaign, reflecting with concern on what it portended for the country. At the time I would never have guessed that this was a world that I was about to enter.

10

"Russia Bitch"

I did not join Donald Trump's National Security Council for the glamour or thrill of working at the White House. I wanted to serve my country, and I felt that I had something to offer, given my educational training and long experience of dealing with Russia, including during my previous stint in government at the National Intelligence Council. But in retrospect, I was naive about U.S. politics and how much it was possible — or not possible — to get done in such a highly charged environment after the 2016 election.

Given the nature of the threat posed by the Russian security services, I hoped I would be able to cut through the outside noise and focus on national security and foreign policy. This was certainly what most of my colleagues at the NSC and across the government were trying to do. But on the job I spent more than two years essentially fighting home-front fires. Because throughout the Trump presidency, America was at war with itself, including inside the government.

I began to think of my NSC job, with all the endless hits and explosions, like the World War II Blitz that I had heard about as a child in North East England. Grandma Vi and Mam had recounted particularly memorable stories about Billingham, a factory town and home of one of the largest chemical plants in Europe, ICI. It was a constant target during the German air force's nightly bombing campaign against Britain in 1940–1941. Mam's father was an air raid warden for Billingham County Council. During the Blitz, he ran around extinguishing incendiary devices and navigational flares dropped by German advance planes by placing them in buckets of sand before the big bombers could come to take out the ICI chemical works. Some nights he would have to chase little boys through the blackout. They had run off with the flares to use as firecrackers. The war was a game for them until something terrible happened.

It was just as exhausting putting out political incendiary devices at the White House before someone's game blew us up too. At times it would have been dispiriting and pointless if not for the camaraderie and inspiring professionalism of other public servants. In this instance, looking around me, I often felt like I was down at the coalface, as Grandad Hill and Dad described from the good old days. We were stuck together in a confined space just trying to get the job done without losing anyone in a political accident.

More than anything else, however, I ended up dealing with this by treating it as I had treated every life experience outside Bishop Auckland — as a foray into terra incognita. I found myself conducting a social anthropological study of the White House, turning the lens around on the United States and noting the parallels with upheavals I had seen and experienced elsewhere. The political machinations around the Trump White House turned out to be as dirty and filled with intrigue as the Kremlin's, and the atmosphere was as tumultuous as my life in the UK had been in the 1970s and 1980s. In many respects America's populist turn in electing Trump in 2016 was the culmination of the forty-year sweep of time that marked my own life and career trajectory.

The United Kingdom and its relationship with the United States was a major theme of my policy portfolio. It was, of course, strange to have my family's and friends' lives and dilemmas back in the UK and Europe as part of my official responsibilities. When we produced reports on the consequences of Brexit and on the rise of populism and democratic backsliding in Europe and the implications for U.S. foreign policy, it was hard not to dwell on the growing similarities at home in America.

A Tough Assignment

I was first approached to join the Trump administration by K. T. McFarland, a Fox News program host who, like me, was a member of the Council on Foreign Relations (CFR). We had frequently discussed U.S.-Russian relations on the margins of CFR events. After the publication of the first version of the book on Putin I cowrote with my Brookings colleague Cliff

Gaddy in 2013, K. T. invited me onto her show, *Defcon 3*. I appeared several times to talk about Putin and his views on the United States.

The last time I appeared on K. T.'s TV show was in November 2016, just after the presidential election. K. T. wanted to talk to me about Russian interference in the election and the prospects for newly elected President Trump to deal with his Russian counterpart under these circumstances. We chatted a little in the studio after the session. I had only just learned that K. T. had been part of Trump's campaign. I joked that perhaps she would be the next national security adviser, unaware that she was on the transition team.

In fact K. T. was designated as the deputy to Trump's first national security adviser, General Michael Flynn, whom I had worked with when I was national intelligence officer for Russia and Eurasia at the National Intelligence Council from 2006 to 2009. Back then General Flynn was intelligence chief for the Joint Chiefs of Staff (JCS) under its chairman, Admiral Michael Mullen. We had close contacts in that period, dealing with Russia and the 2008 war in Georgia in particular. I frequently briefed Admiral Mullen and the JCS team on the fast-moving developments and took part in strategy sessions. Although I had little contact with General Flynn after I returned to the Brookings Institution at the end of 2009, he remembered me. Flynn also recruited some former close colleagues from the NIC to positions at the National Security Council, who reached out to me.

K. T. and General Flynn thought I could help them sit down with the president to brief him on dealing with Putin, as I had for Presidents Bush and Obama when I was NIO. Another retired general, Keith Kellogg, whom I knew tangentially from my time at the NIC, was the new NSC chief of staff, having also served on the campaign. In late December 2016 and early January 2017, K. T. and General Kellogg sought my advice on how to approach the Russia challenge and offered me the position of senior director for Europe and Russia.

I initially thought I could offer general advice from my perch at the Brookings Institution, but given the scale of the Russian effort to influence the 2016 election, that was clearly not going to be an option. Someone would have to work on this from the inside. It was obvious that joining the administration would be a tough and controversial assignment, but with the encouragement of Brookings colleagues and longtime mentors like Graham Allison, I resolved to see what I could do to help tackle the Russian intelligence services' attack on American democracy.

Sitting with the President

Within my first couple of weeks at the NSC in April 2017, it very quickly became apparent that I was never going to have any kind of sit-down with Donald Trump to talk about Vladimir Putin or Russia, or pretty much anything else in my portfolio. One of the major reasons was that I was a woman, and a completely unknown quantity at that.

These two factors became critical in shaping my time in the NSC. Despite the unexpected opportunity to serve in the White House and decades of hard work and preparation for just this eventuality, the fact that I was an "unknown woman" was detrimental to my ability to step up to meet the Russian challenge. It was an obstacle to doing the job I had been hired for. As far as President Trump was concerned, my academic and professional credentials and expertise were irrelevant. For all intents and purposes, as a woman and an outsider, I was not part of his team.

Only making matters more difficult, General Flynn was ousted from his position before I even got to the White House, having lied to both the FBI and the vice president about the content of a phone call with Russian ambassador Sergey Kislyak in the period before he was officially in office. Flynn was replaced in February 2017 by another general, H. R. McMaster, who was still in active service rather than retired. Like me, General McMaster had no prior relationship with the president. He was in the process of figuring out for himself how to navigate the White House when I came on board. Our mutual lack of familiarity with Trump and his team would prove to be a huge obstacle in the year ahead.

The early months at the NSC were chaotic and fraught, a swirl of rumors inside and outside the building. It soon became apparent that K. T. might also not keep her position for long — and indeed she was nominated to be U.S. ambassador to Singapore in May 2017. Trump had run a bare-bones campaign in terms of personnel, drawing people from his real estate business, immediate family, and close personal associates. He had to rely on the Republican Party apparatus, which he had never been part of, to staff the transition and recruit for key positions. The result was a motley crew of people with few ties to each other and some with no prior government experience whatsoever, all jockeying for influence — and often launching political assaults to oust perceived enemies from their positions. Unsurprisingly, General McMaster and I ended up frequent targets of malicious leaks to the press.

Sneakers in the Oval Office

I did not get off to an auspicious start at the NSC, even though on my first day I ended up in the Oval Office. As in my job at the medieval banquet hall at Witton Castle, or as was nearly the case in my early career at the Kennedy School, my attire proved to be my undoing.

The day before I was to start my new job, my daughter came down with one of those short, sharp stomach bugs that has you gripping the porcelain for twenty-four hours. At one point she had thrown up on me. Late at night I went out to grab some Gatorade and other supplies for her from a local pharmacy. In the dark, I bashed myself in the face with the door to the car trunk, cutting and bruising the side of my right eye. By the time the morning came around, I hadn't had a wink of sleep and was completely exhausted. I consoled myself that I would be in an orientation session and security briefings and wouldn't, hopefully, have to do too much more than endure.

In my befuddlement, I left my work shoes in a bag by the door as I laced up my sneakers to dash to the Metro. Partway through the orientation session, someone came to pull me out. General McMaster needed me to go with him to the Oval Office to brief the president on the terrorist attack on the St. Petersburg Metro. Trump was going to make a condolence call to President Putin.

What terrorist attack? I was completely out of the loop. With everything going on at home, I had not checked the news. I had been locked in a room since I got in the White House. A staffer from General McMaster's office gave me a quick rundown. There was no time for anything more.

I racked my brains for something to say — there had previously been attacks on the Moscow Metro, but this was a first for St. Petersburg. It was Putin's hometown, so he would take the attack personally. I would keep whatever I said simple and straightforward; it wasn't as if I had much more information to impart anyway.

I only fully processed that I was wearing sneakers as I was running over to the West Wing. It was too late to find a pair of shoes. For his part, McMaster was unperturbed. This was a man who had presided over a significant tank battle in Iraq and was now contending with political firefights in the White House. Women in sneakers were the least of his problems. He just told me to stick close to him and make sure, when we sat down, that my feet were out of the president's sightline, either under my chair or pressed against the Resolute Desk.

President Trump didn't even look up when we came in. He was scribbling something with a Sharpie on a piece of paper on the desk. He had his arm around it, so I couldn't see what it was. I presumed some notes to prepare for the call.

General McMaster made a brief introduction and turned to me for my quick summary about the significance of the attack. Still no acknowledgment. Zero interest in who had come in with his national security adviser. As Trump picked up the phone and made the call, his gaze flicked across us for a moment. I barely registered. He relayed his condolences to Putin, noting how personal this must be for him — the first terrorist attack on his home city. Small victory for my point. And that was that.

We were about to get up to go when the president's daughter Ivanka wafted into the room wearing an elaborately lacy two-piece white outfit and alarmingly high stiletto heels, as if she were off to a gala rather than another day at the office. Ivanka sat down right beside me, immediately taking in my black sneakers, which I had failed to conceal under the chair, and flashing me a look of surprise.

I was busted. During a break in the afternoon, I went out to buy a pair of shoes to keep in my office at all times. Yet again my wardrobe was going to be an issue — and a potential impediment to doing my job. By now, at least, I was not completely surprised.

After my failure to imprint on the first day, K. T. made a valiant attempt to reintroduce me to the president a week or so later. Again it fell totally flat.

The president was slated to sign a treaty formally approving the accession of the Balkan country of Montenegro to NATO. I had no role in this achievement and had merely inherited the end result as part of my portfolio. Nonetheless, K. T. and I and the NSC staff who had worked on the accession were to stand beside Trump as he affixed his signature to the official document. There would be a photograph. It was a historic moment for Montenegro and NATO.

K. T. bustled me into the office slightly ahead of the rest of the group. Trump was wrapping up a meeting with some of his cabinet members, who were sitting on the two sofas and a row of chairs in front of the desk. The room felt very full. All eyes were on us. What did we want?

Taking it all in her stride, K. T. drew me to the side of the Resolute Desk. "Mr. President, this is Dr. Fiona Hill, your new Russia adviser. She's written *the* best book on Putin."

Now Trump looked at me, but not with much interest. "Rex is doing

Russia," he said pointedly. Rex Tillerson, the former CEO of ExxonMobil and new secretary of state, gave me a slight smile. We had met in passing at a conference. "He's done billion-dollar energy deals with Putin," said the president. "So what do you think, is he a nice man, Putin? Am I going to like him?" I never got to respond, as the cabinet members got up to leave. The rest of the group was ushered in for the photo.

The absurdity of the situation, and the president's dim view of me, quickly sank in. Just who was I? Who made me an expert on Putin? What could I possibly have to say? I had written a book. "Rex" had been in charge of the world's largest oil company, in action, doing deals in Russia and all around the world. Trump wanted to do a deal with the Russians too — on nuclear weapons and arms control. Who was he going to listen to, Rex or some woman?

It turned out that Trump was genuinely fixated on arms control and the unfinished business of the U.S.-Soviet negotiations conducted by Ronald Reagan and Mikhail Gorbachev in the 1980s after the Euromissile war scare. This was the very issue that had drawn me into studying Russian in 1984, and the 1988 Gorbachev-Reagan summit had started me off on my American journey. K. T., General Kellogg, and I had talked about the president's interest in our early discussions. Trump wanted his moment alone with Putin to work his deal-making magic. They had thought I could help to put things in context, given my direct experiences and insights into both Russia and Putin since the 1980s. But judging from that encounter in the Oval, Trump was not going to be receptive.

Eighties Man

The Trump White House was a man's world — predominantly one man's world — and Trump was a very familiar type for me. In many respects he was not that much of a surprise in the way that he acted and interacted with people, apart from the fact that he was the American president. He was definitely and unabashedly a 1980s man in his approach to life and politics.

Being an eighties man was something that Donald Trump talked about in meetings, as he constantly referred back to the era. Having been born right after the Second World War, in 1946, as part of the baby boomer generation, Trump had been in his thirties and forties in the 1980s. He was hitting both his stride and his peak. The 1980s were the period when he fully emerged into the national and international spotlight as a celebrity businessman with presidential aspirations, drawing attention to himself in magazine interviews and with paid advertisements in major U.S. newspapers that offered his political pronouncements on domestic and foreign affairs.

I might have been in the North East of England and at St. Andrews in that period, but I hadn't been living under a rock. I knew exactly who Donald Trump was. I had read about him for years as well as watched him on TV — in cameos in movies like *Home Alone 2* and later on *The Apprentice*. What did surprise me in real life was that he hadn't really changed his worldview since the 1980s, even after all the things that had happened in the years since.

Nearly two decades into the twenty-first century, Trump remained obsessed with the various challenges to America's power that had begun in the 1980s — the military competition with the Soviet Union and the economic rise of Asian countries, first Japan and now China. He was also steeped in the era's debates over the merits of free markets and global trade versus protectionism. Trump definitely came down on the side of protectionism. In addition to being an eighties man, he referred to himself as "Tariff Man." Trump wanted to slap tariffs on everything from Chinese steel to German cars, theoretically at least, to boost U.S. industry. He often commented in meetings on how long he had been waiting to do this.

Back in the 1980s, Trump had proffered himself as Reagan's arms control negotiator in magazine interviews. He had bragged that he could easily reach a deal if he just got the chance to sit down with Gorbachev. In 1990 he told *Playboy Magazine* that nuclear war was the "ultimate catastrophe" and he personally wanted to do something about it. He had been sixteen during the trauma of the Cuban missile crisis in the 1960s and had then had to contemplate the rerun of a war scare in the 1980s. Trump had an uncle who was a nuclear physicist at MIT, so by some process of family and genetic osmosis, he believed he already fully understood the issue. And he was convinced that his business experience and personal charisma would sway Gorbachev and any subsequent Soviet or Russian leader into agreeing to reduce or even eliminate weapons. During a visit by Mikhail Gorbachev to New York in 1988, Trump made a well-documented but fruitless effort to secure a meeting.

Now that he was president, Trump saw his chance to finish off the 1980s. He would sit down with Putin and finally conclude the elusive big U.S.-Russian arms control deal. Although journalists and other commentators focused more on Trump's ripping up international deals, especially those that former U.S. presidents like Barack Obama had made, Trump really wanted to put his personal stamp on this one. In meetings with other world leaders, he would stress his view that nuclear weapons were *the* critical global security issue, surpassing climate change and everything else on the list of official talking points. This also framed his particular interests in Iran and North Korea during his tenure.

I obviously had some sympathy for President Trump's views on nuclear war and his desire to conclude an arms control deal, given my own preoccupations with the threat in my teenage years. I too was shaped by the events of the 1980s and the policies of its leaders, although more directly, of course, by Margaret Thatcher than by Ronald Reagan.

The shadows of Thatcher and Reagan loomed especially large in the Trump White House. Both had believed in strong executive power and in the authority of the executive, the leader at the top. Donald Trump believed in this too. The 1980s had marked the loss of faith in the state in both the UK and the U.S. and the search for a one-off leader to fill in the gap. The 1980s thus helped set the stage for the style of leadership that Trump embraced for himself when he won the presidential race in 2016. The 1980s were the "me, me, me" era. They were in many respects already verging toward the hyper-personalized. Trump became the extreme example of this three decades later.

As far as I could see, though, in my direct encounters, Trump was weaker in character than Ronald Reagan and Margaret Thatcher. Reagan had had a sunnier, more optimistic, can-do disposition. Thatcher had had an iron will and unwavering principles. Trump was individualistic to the point of being obsessed — first with himself and then with his family, which, of course, is just an extension of self. Trump was selfish to his core and had the most fragile ego of anyone I had encountered to date. Everything and everyone was seen through his eyes in terms of how their interactions reflected on him and what they said about him. I didn't make this harsh assessment ahead of time, but it became glaringly obvious seeing him in action and through discussions with other NSC staff and White House officials.

The Secretary

My next encounter with the president came on May 2, 2017. It was disastrous. Only a month in, it could easily have marked the end of my tenure at the NSC. I fully anticipated being sacked in the aftermath and joining the roster of officials who were removed in those early days and throughout Trump's presidency with increasing alacrity.

The occasion was another scheduled call with Putin. In those days Trump took his calls from the Resolute Desk. Later he would do many alone from his residence in the White House. There was a lot of jostling by cabinet officials as well as other senior directors and West Wing officials to get into the Oval for these early calls, hoping to catch the president afterward to press their personal agendas. It made it challenging for those of us who actually needed to be close to the action.

Syria and its ongoing civil war were the primary focus for this call. On April 7, in my very first week on the job, the president had ordered retaliatory U.S. missile strikes against a Syrian military airbase after the government launched a chemical weapons attack against civilians in opposition-held towns. Russia had intervened in the civil war in 2015 in support of Syrian leader Bashar al-Assad and was clearly not happy with the U.S. action. There had been some tense public exchanges in the interim, but this would be the first direct contact between the American and Russia presidents since the missile strike.

The NSC staff had prepared talking points and a bland prewritten press release referencing the call. One of the Russia directors, Charlie Bergen, was scheduled to accompany me and General McMaster into the Oval, but the two Middle East senior directors, Derek Harvey and Joel Rayburn, pulled rank. They insisted on going and wanted to take the lead. Charlie was pushed off into a listening room elsewhere in the West Wing complex. Only I made it into Trump's presence.

When we got into the office, Rex Tillerson and his chief of staff, Margaret Peterlin, were already there. The secretary of state was sitting in one of two chairs right in front of the Resolute Desk, and Margaret was discreetly off to one side. McMaster took the other chair. Derek and Joel pressed ahead of me to take two other strategically placed chairs behind them. I was left wondering where to place myself when Ivanka Trump and her husband, Jared Kushner, came in and sat down on one of the sofas.

I was surprised, and a bit thrown off. Ivanka and Jared were both senior advisers, but I had had no idea they would be sitting in on the Putin call. It wasn't exactly their remit, but obviously this call was going to be a family affair. I quickly sat on the other sofa, opposite them and alongside Steve Charon, the staffer from the Executive Secretariat who was managing and patching the phone call through the White House Situation Room as well as liaising with the State Department interpreter and the Russians on the other end.

This was generally not a good day for me. Less than a week before the call, I had developed an infection. My doctor put me on a short course of antibiotics. I had a reaction to the medication and was feeling particularly unwell—slightly dizzy and nauseous, with a pounding headache. Again, however, the president took little notice of me, or anyone else for that matter. He was completely uninterested in the meeting preparation. He just wanted to get on with the call and speak to Putin.

I figured I should concentrate on keeping myself together and taking good notes: listening carefully to what Putin had to say and how he was saying it and how the whole conversation was being translated on both sides. After years of observing Putin and studying Russian, I knew how deliberate he was in his speech and the way he presented things. I was the only Russian-speaker in the room. Surely the president and others might be interested in discussing what Putin was emphasizing. Was there something missing in the moment from the translation? And what in particular should I follow up on afterward with General McMaster? I was completely overthinking everything.

The call began. The president was listening on his phone, with the rest of us on speakerphone. The volume was soft. It was hard to hear. I was straining to catch everything, my headache increasing in intensity. I scribbled notes to myself of pertinent things to flag for the others. Then it was over. President Trump professed great satisfaction with the call. It was good—good tone, good vibe. Putin seemed calm, measured, friendly even. Ivanka and Jared concurred. I was not so sure. That might be the impression from the translator and the translation, yes, but I had detected more menace in what Putin had to say. There were some issues that we should pay attention to. I was gathering my thoughts as best I could through my headache to interject, but the president was now busy with the press release. He didn't want to discuss the call, even with Tillerson and McMaster. He had no interest in the substance at all, just the fact that he had a "good" call with Putin and that Ivanka and Jared had agreed. The whole thing was slightly surreal.

Then Trump wanted to rewrite the press release in his own words. He was dictating some changes. I didn't have a copy. My colleague, Charlie, had all the prep materials and he was in the listening room. I didn't know the drill. There had been no prior discussion on how things might unfold in the Oval and who would do what.

There was an exchange between the president and McMaster that I didn't catch. Then the president raised his voice: "Well, can she do it? Can she go type it up and bring it back?" *She?* I thought. *What? What just happened?* Only then did I realize Trump was talking about me. "She" could only be me. There were three shes in the room, and the she in question was certainly not Ivanka and unlikely to be Margaret Peterlin. Suddenly he was practically yelling— "Hey, darlin', are you listening? Are you paying attention?"

I looked up. I actually wasn't. Classic deer-in-the-headlights moment. No one said anything. McMaster and Tillerson were both looking at me directly. Derek and Joel were glaring. Margaret was examining her shoes. I did not make eye contact with Ivanka and Jared, but I could tell they were also staring at me. The president clearly thought I was part of the Executive Secretariat, and in fact I was sitting next to Steve Charon beside the phone, so it was an easy mistake. He wanted me to type up the revised press release.

I hesitated just a little too long. I thought at least someone might tell him who I was, introduce me again, or even help me out a bit with the next steps. McMaster was now holding out the press release with the president's edits all over it. I jumped up, grabbing my notebook and my pens, and took the paper. I hadn't prepared the press release. I had had no idea I would be asked to do this. I was still finding my way around and figuring things out. I didn't have enough information or experience in that moment to be creative. What was I supposed to do? Where was I supposed to type it? Charlie would have known what to do, but he was somewhere else in the building. I could see the president's executive assistant, Madeleine Westerhout, at her desk just outside the Oval. I hadn't met her, but perhaps she could help. I dashed into her office. She was friendly and offered her computer. I didn't know where to find the file. Neither did she. Now what?

McMaster came in and pulled me away toward his office. I wasn't supposed to do this at Madeleine's desk! He would ask his assistant to do the edits and take it back. I apologized profusely. I was caught off-guard. I was so sorry. I confessed that I had a terrible headache and hadn't paid proper attention once the call ended. I should have been taking note of what was going on, not just taking notes. Clearly I could have reacted with a bit more professional composure.

I asked if I could go back in to apologize to the president. Straighten things out. McMaster said no: "The president will think it's a sign of weakness. You won't be able to sit down with him again. He'll only remember that you apologized and there was something negative about you."

It was now obvious that everyone walked on eggshells around the president. He wasn't someone you could engage with in any meaningful way. He was unpredictable and quick to judge. It was literally every man for himself. If you got crosswise with him, you would have to figure things out and stand up for yourself and your team. No one was going to throw you a lifeline.

At this point the Europe and Russia directorate at the NSC, which I now led, was trying to hold its own with the Middle East directorate in a classic bureaucratic turf war. The Middle East senior directors, Derek and Joel, wanted to take the lead on any issue that overlapped with their portfolio. In particular, they tried to drive Russia policy through the prism of Syria. They had both joined the NSC at the very beginning, in January 2017, along with General Flynn. In March, before I came on board, they had tried to transfer Turkey from the Europe and Russia directorate to their office and attempted to fire the Turkey director in my office, who was on loan from the Pentagon. Turkey sat right on the border of Syria as well as our respective areas of responsibility. They also wanted to get rid of several other detailees from across the U.S. government who had started work under the Obama administration. General McMaster had managed to block them until now.

The incident in the Oval became more fodder for the turf battle. Joel made a point of coming to my office later in the day to pile on. The president and Ivanka had thought I was rude. I should have been ready to revise the press release. Did I think I was too important to type something up?

I pointed out that I was very sorry about the situation. I had been on the job for only a few weeks. This was my first full-length call apart from the condolence call. No one had asked me to do anything on a press release then. How could I know what to do if no one told me? He, Joel, had displaced Charlie from the room with all the prep materials. I also noted that neither he nor Derek had tried to help me out, as I would have done for them if the tables were turned. They had a copy in their materials and had written down the revisions on it.

I also stressed that I hadn't been rude, I had just been taken by surprise. I only realized the president was talking to me when he said, "Hey, darlin'!" Joel himself was now surprised. He hadn't noticed that — although McMaster certainly had. I observed that this was because no other man would ever refer to him as "darlin'," so why would he notice? I, in contrast, was called all kinds of things by older men who didn't know my name: "dar-

ling," "sweetie," "honey." And it wasn't the first or the last time that I would
be mistaken for the secretary — it was a long-standing occupational hazard.

Nonplayers in His World

Several months later, someone leaked the story of my misadventure in the
Oval to the *Washington Post* as an "anonymous source." It was obvious that
the culprit must have been someone at the NSC who had learned about the
events from Derek and Joel, based on their repeated snide remarks to me
and others about "the incident." Whoever it was wanted to make both me
and McMaster look bad, as well as marginalize me within the NSC. The
source told the *Post* reporter that the president had mistaken me for the secretary, which was true; that McMaster had yelled at me, which was not; and
that Ivanka had banned me from the Oval Office for being rude, which as
far as I knew was also not true. But if it was true, of course, and I was ban-
ished, then this would be devastating for me as a senior director. I could
not do my job effectively without access to the meetings. A long-term ban
would pave the way for my removal and the installation of a replacement.

After the incident, McMaster came to my defense. As far as he was concerned, I wasn't going anywhere. He thought we should let things cool off a
bit before I went back into the Oval Office. In the interim we would send in
some of the other Europe and Russia directors to take notes.

K. T. also called me in for a strategy session. She was not going to give
up on trying to get me into the Oval for "the Putin talk" before she left
the NSC. Over lunch at the White House Mess, I asked her if I should approach Ivanka to smooth things over. Theoretically, at least, we were counterparts. Like McMaster, K. T. thought this would draw more attention to
my faux pas. The Trumps never apologized for anything, large or small. But
there was so much going on, she said, they would quickly forget about it. If
I stayed out of sight for a while, I could be reintroduced and start afresh. I
had a large portfolio. After a couple of weeks I could sit in on some meetings with European leaders and reacclimatize.

K. T. wasn't at all concerned that I had been mistaken for the secretary.
No big deal. She had first worked in the Nixon White House. Back then,
the only way for professional women to get a job at the White House was
indeed to work as a secretary, or in the press and communications department. She had worked herself up across several administrations, from the
nighttime typing pool under Nixon, to a research assistant in the Ford ad-

ministration, then a speechwriter under Ronald Reagan. Now she was the deputy national security adviser. It had taken her decades to get there.

Anyway, K. T. explained, I had just had a crash course in Trump's psychology. President Trump essentially thought everyone at the National Security Council was a secretary in one form or another. He looked at the NSC as an extension of the Executive Secretariat and the staff as no different from his military aides in the West Wing. He thought we all carried out basic administrative functions. Coming into government from his personally branded family enterprise and the world of reality television, where he was the one and only, exclusive boss who set his own agenda, the whole concept of an autonomous advisory body was entirely alien to him. Why did he even need this? He'd got this far in business and in politics by following his own instincts. He knew everything he needed to know.

Trump was also suspicious of people taking notes, K. T. explained. He thought they were reporting on him. Perhaps they were even spying on him to leak information to the newspapers, rather than maintaining the official presidential record of his meetings for follow-up or the historical archives. He was constantly tearing or scrunching up his own notes and memos and throwing them in the garbage can, and admonishing even his cabinet members when they took notes in the Oval. The White House lawyers regularly explained the need and legal requirement for record-keeping to him. K. T. had two very specific pieces of practical advice: first, I should be less obtrusive and more discreet in my notetaking; second, I should never wear the dress I had had on that day in the Oval again. Trump, she said, always noticed what women were wearing and what they looked like.

K. T.'s points were reinforced much later by the *New Yorker* journalist Adam Entous. He published a lengthy article in late June 2020 about my time in the White House as I tried to navigate the political perils of Russia policy and the events that led to my November 2019 impeachment testimony. Entous had interviewed most of the people I interacted with at the NSC and the White House. He elicited information that I had previously been unaware of for his story. In the course of our final set of interviews, he informed me that after the May 2017 Oval incident, Trump's former chief of staff, Reince Priebus, and some others had started to refer to me as "the Russia bitch."

I couldn't even recall having any one-on-one exchange with Reince Priebus, yet somehow I had merited a nickname. Entous's interviews and this moniker underscored the misogyny rife in the Trump White House. Entous also highlighted this in his piece. Trump fixated on how women looked on TV as well as in person. If they were having an off day or had some physical feature — height, weight, the appearance of their hair or skin — that he didn't like, he would point it out to others and to their face in public. Trump would frequently berate and belittle female aides, including senior women, in front of their male counterparts — none of whom would intercede on their behalf. Just being a woman became an obstacle to getting their job done.

None of this was surprising, given President Trump's documented history with women. I had taken part in the Women's March in January 2017, protesting the way that he had talked about women during the presidential campaign. Ironically, this turned out to be the day before General Kellogg called to ask me to come in for a sit-down in his office and formally offer me a position. I went from being a woman marching around the perimeter of the White House one day to going in through the visitors' gate to the West Wing the next.

Inside the NSC itself, the situation was quite different from the immediate environment around Trump. Neither General McMaster nor his successor, Ambassador John Bolton, nor General Kellogg, nor any of the other men I worked with on the NSC, behaved in anything other than a completely straightforward and professional manner. Some people might have wanted me out of the NSC, but it wasn't because I was a woman. I was simply impinging on their personal policy agendas.

This being the case, I figured after my early encounters with the president that I would focus my efforts elsewhere. I would make sure that my boss, the national security adviser — first General McMaster and then Ambassador Bolton — and all my colleagues at the NSC got the best information, insight, and advice I could offer on Putin, Russia, and everything else in my portfolio. I would concentrate on forging good relations with the other officials working on Europe and Russia across the U.S. government as well as my counterparts in foreign governments.

I did get back into the Oval Office again relatively quickly, always taking care to wear a different dress and look "presentable." After a while, despite my persistent notetaking, I was at so many meetings that I eventually seemed to blend into the background as far as President Trump was concerned. On every occasion I took careful note, not just notes, of what was happening around me.

Ultimately, however, I wasn't just suffering from imposter syndrome in the Trump White House — I was for Trump and his inner circle an actual imposter. I was an interloper. As one former White House official related the situation to Adam Entous, "Forgive me, Fiona's attractive, but he [Trump] doesn't trust women that are kind of nonplayers in his world."

Prom Night

No matter where or who you are, it seems, women can never fully escape from being judged by the way they look and dress. Every new work environment brings its own challenges until you figure out how to camouflage yourself so you can just do your job. In the Trump White House, once you walked across West Executive Drive from the NSC's Old Executive Office Building to the West Wing, you entered a different world entirely. Outside the national security adviser's office and his on-site team, a different species of woman inhabited the place. They operated in a parallel universe. In the Trump White House, Ivanka Trump and Fox News set the dress code for women. Ivanka's staff were usually decked out in something from her personal fashion line. It was high and intimidating glamour.

One of my female NSC colleagues quipped that it was like being at your high school prom night, every day. Having never been to a high school prom — this was not a feature of UK comprehensive schools, which you left without any fanfare whatsoever — I couldn't really say for myself. But many of the young female staffers running around the West Wing had indeed worked at some point at Fox or for other cable news channels and print outlets. I knew that style and it was constantly reinforced.

In fact, if there were women whom Trump *did* consider players, odds were that they were somehow connected to Fox News. The cable news channel was beamed into the workplace 24/7 on the complex's ubiquitous TV screens. It was so intertwined with the day-to-day operations of the White House that President Trump frequently tied his opening remarks with visitors — foreign and domestic — to something he had just seen on a Fox News program. "Did you see that? What did you think of it?" he would say, often thoroughly confusing the person he was talking to, who had been at another meeting or waiting to pass through the White House security checkpoints, not glued to the television.

At one point, during a supposedly serious meeting in the Oval Office with U.S. ambassador to Russia Jon Huntsman to discuss how to approach Putin before their first summit meeting, in Helsinki in 2018, Trump spontaneously called the ambassador's daughter, Abby Huntsman. She was then the cohost of one of the president's favorite Fox News programs, *Fox & Friends Weekend*. I was sitting next to Ambassador Huntsman along with Russia director Joe Wang and presidential chief of staff John Kelly. We had barely got into the discussion when this idea popped into the president's head. It was obvious that he wasn't interested in hearing any advice about Putin, even from someone as distinguished as Ambassador Huntsman, a former governor of Utah, ambassador to China, and presidential candidate. The ambassador, Joe Wang, and I had all huddled with Ambassador Bolton in advance to make the most of the rare opportunity to have Ambassador Huntsman in the Oval. The chance to make some pertinent points was immediately out the window. All President Trump was interested in was schmoozing with Abby Huntsman on the phone to catch up on the latest from Fox News. Ambassador Huntsman could hardly say no to the call. We never got the meeting back on track.

It was readily apparent that for Trump and those around him, it was all about the look, the image, not who you were and what you did. I was never going to suddenly grow the flowing blond or brunette locks or get hair extensions to get the look of a Fox News host. Nor was I going to head off for a Botox session or spend hours on crafting primetime TV makeup before I got on the Metro in the morning. No more attempts at the equivalent of stuffing tights down the front of a dress for a fake boob job, as at Witton Castle in my serving-wench days, trying to be something I wasn't. But I did at least splash out on some colorful new dresses from a recognizable designer so I could get in and out of the West Wing without sticking out too much.

Flattery Will Get You Everywhere

So many episodes illustrated the personalization of Trump's approach to the presidency during my time at the NSC. As president, Trump favored a top-down approach to governance while demanding bottom-up support. Issues were rarely open to consultation outside his inner circle. His family was on the top, including in the White House, as I quickly learned after encountering Jared Kushner and Ivanka Trump in early Oval Office meetings. Everyone else in his cabinet, at the NSC, and across the government was just supporting cast, like the front and back office and custodial staff at one of his hotels or country clubs and the steelworkers in the Roosevelt Room in March 2018. We were there to make the place work as he directed.

From his staff and everyone who came into his orbit, Trump demanded constant attention and adulation. When the press was invited into cabinet sessions, senior officials would compete to see who could outdo the others in praising Trump for the cameras. The president took note of those who didn't, like defense secretary Jim Mattis, who always seemed to find some way of avoiding this exercise in self-debasement. The president's vanity and fragile self-esteem were a point of acute vulnerability. He was a liability to himself and the country — a clear security or counterintelligence risk. It wasn't just a question of the Russians or President Putin being able to manipulate or exploit him, as many commentators feared they would, given the events of 2016. Anyone at all, including the "average American," the Twitter follower "on the street," could influence him by deploying nothing more than basic flattery in public. No one needed something "on him" in terms of compromising information to blackmail Trump, although some former senior officials worried that the Kremlin had secured what the Russians called *kompromat* during his past trips to Moscow.

Indeed, plenty of derogatory material about President Trump was floating around everywhere, including on audio- and videotapes from American media sources, not foreign intelligence services. He was something of an open book. Trump was easily induced into action by someone who first praised him or his policies and then recommended or asked for something. U.S. political commentators would try to get themselves on a Fox News program that was prime Trump viewing to influence him in this way. Several got jobs in the White House because he liked what they said about him before they launched into policy advice. Ambassador Bolton had initially been one of those, as was Anthony Scaramucci, Trump's remarkably short-lived White House head of communications (he lasted just over a week). Many of these individuals soured on President Trump once they had the opportunity to see him in action.

Trump frequently retweeted fawning comments from Twitter followers, no matter who they were and what unsavory associations they might end up having on closer scrutiny. And beyond the Twitter-sphere, Trump seemed to think that any world leader who "said nice things about me" or paid homage to him in some way was his "close friend." This was sometimes irrespective of the long-term nature of that person's country's interactions with the United States and specific policy disagreements.

Foreign counterparts quickly learned to be obsequious with the president. Vladimir Putin took pains to flatter Trump in press comments; we closely tracked all of these, as it was glaringly obvious that Putin was trying to get Trump's attention that way. On one occasion in December 2017, Trump called Putin just to say thank-you for some casual public praise about the U.S. economy's performance.

Others went to greater, formal lengths. King Salman of Saudi Arabia splashed out millions of dollars and pulled out all the stops for Trump's first foreign trip, in May 2017. The trip consisted of an extravagant series of one-off events that combined public flattery with over-the-top luxury and absurdly lavish displays. At one point the Saudis invited the president to commune with a giant glowing golden orb. Trump was thoroughly delighted with all the attention. President Emmanuel Macron of France invited Trump to Bastille Day events in July 2017 and to a special, exclusive, "just for you, Donald" dinner at the top of the Eiffel Tower, which President Trump talked about endlessly afterward. Prime Minister Abe of Japan repeatedly invited President Trump to extra-special occasions that had never been extended to other foreign visitors, like a sumo wrestling tournament with a "Trump Trophy" award in May 2019. Again Trump commented on how pleased he was with the very personal nature of all these events. Leaders were paying tribute to him, not to the country.

Conversely, Trump was so sensitive to slights that we were instructed to scour the pronouncements of world leaders for anything harsh they might have said, at any point in the past or present. But it was impossible to catch everything. I found myself in trouble after an incident with visiting Greek prime minister Alexis Tsipras during an October 2017 press conference in the Rose Garden. At the end of their respective remarks, Fox News reporter John Roberts asked Tsipras if he still stood by his comments from March 2016 that Trump was "evil." A dark cloud came over the president's face. He glared at both Roberts and Tsipras. "I wish I had known that before my remarks!" he said.

I wished I had too. I was sitting near the front of the press conference. Up until this point I had been preoccupied by a bee, which was hovering around both Trump's and Tsipras's heads instead of taking in the flowers. I was hoping it wouldn't sting one of them. Roberts's question immediately got my attention. We had missed these comments entirely. The Fox News team must have thoroughly searched all the Greek-language press for something derogatory, which we had not.

Tsipras looked distinctly uncomfortable — no wonder, at being caught in such an awkward moment — but he managed to dodge the question by praising the United States and Greek-American solidarity. I didn't get off so easily. I got yelled at by one of White House deputy press secretaries. How had we missed this comment?

After the Rose Garden episode, all U.S. embassies and the respective country offices at the State Department were directed to keep tabs on anything "bad" a foreign official said about Trump. We had to compile this material before a visit as part of the briefing package. When someone was caught in the act of making some negative comment, he or she would end up on Trump's "nasty list." We were instructed to exclude them from meetings during foreign trips.

At first I found President Trump's fragility perplexing. Given his highly privileged upbringing, he seemed to have had unbridled access to opportunity. I often questioned why he was perpetually aggrieved when everything had so obviously been handed to him since birth. And I wondered how he would cope if someone dropped him alone on a random street in a faraway town like Bishop Auckland or on the Keen family farm in South Dakota to fend for himself. I concluded, not well at all.

Trump needed to have everything done for him. At times he seemed helpless when little things went wrong. He was thin-skinned and quick to anger, with little hint of self-reflection or consideration of other options. Trump would never take any responsibility for a problem of his own making; someone in his entourage would always have to fix things or take the fall. He was also obsessed with performances of presidential power that would validate his ego. Nowhere was this made clearer to me than in his theatrics surrounding the prospect of a state visit to England, which the British government had dangled in front of his nose from the very start of his administration.

Tea with the Queen

UK prime minister Theresa May was the first world leader to visit the White House, in January 2017, just days after the president's inauguration. She immediately invited President Trump for a state visit to cement the so-called special relationship between the U.S. and the UK. As soon as Prime Minister May arrived home there was a backlash. In December 2015, during his first presidential campaign, Trump and his oldest son, Donald Jr., had initiated an often bitter, long-running Twitter feud with Sadiq Khan, the mayor of London, sparked by Trump Sr.'s pledge to "ban Muslims from the U.S." The mayor made it clear that from his perspective Trump would not be a welcome guest in his city. For the next year or so, the Brits tried to put the visit off — never formally extending the invitation, coming up with various excuses about timing — as the president grew increasingly frustrated with the delay. It was an impressive exercise in exquisitely polite obfuscation.

The Brits benefited in their delaying tactics from the fact that there were very few notes from the earliest meetings with foreign visitors at the White House. The notetaking systems were not fully in place, and some of the original participants on the U.S. side, like national security adviser Mike Flynn, had resigned or been removed in the following weeks. In my first month at the NSC, I was asked to review a bare-bones account of the May-Trump meeting. There was scant detail on what had been discussed and almost nothing on the invitation for Trump to visit the UK. One of the names on the list of attendees was Fiona Hill. The Executive Secretariat wanted to know if I "still had notes and could flesh things out." This was not me. The Fiona Hill mentioned in the transcript was Theresa May's personal adviser. This caused confusion and consternation for some time, until she left her position at Number 10 Downing Street later in 2017. In the meantime, press and online commentators fused us together as one Fiona Hill, simultaneously working for the UK prime minister and the American president.

The absence of detailed notes on our side meant that the UK could interpret what had been offered in different ways. The president, for his part, was very clear that he had been invited for a state visit to the United Kingdom with all the bells and whistles. He was hoping it would be one of his first major visits. When it wasn't, he obsessed about it. Going to Buckingham Palace was supposed to be a highlight of his presidency.

Meeting Queen Elizabeth II was particularly important to President Trump. He often referred in conversation to his mother, Mary Anne MacLeod, who was originally from Scotland, and her admiration for Queen Elizabeth. Trump was clearly an admirer himself and was always slightly awestruck when he talked about her — his voice and his face would soften.

A meeting with the Queen of England was the ultimate sign that he, Trump, had made it in life.

Trump had two golf courses in Scotland, in Aberdeen and Turnberry, which gave him a personal foothold in the UK. Turnberry was one of the international properties he was most proud of owning. He always found a way to bring it into conversation. He rhetorically supported Brexit while golfing there in 2016. Later, when a European leader suggested to him that Brexit might lead to Scottish independence and the breakup of the UK, President Trump was taken aback. He immediately thought about the implications for his golf courses — how could you have the British Open if there was no more Great Britain? What a disaster. The somewhat surprised leader agreed that "they might have to rename it." Trump always said his mother was born in "real Scotland" — in the Outer Hebrides, the remote and windswept islands off the northern coast where people spoke Gaelic — but he saw himself as rooted in the United Kingdom or Queendom.

In every encounter with Theresa May and British officials after January 2017, including at various international summits, Trump would drop not-so-subtle hints about his state visit. In the middle of a meeting or in an obvious tangent at the end, he would, apropos of nothing in particular, suddenly talk about his desire to golf once more at Turnberry. May and her colleagues would pretend not to understand the conversational thrust and change the subject.

Behind the scenes they made it clear to us that the president's visit would be a huge political headache for them. When it became too embarrassing to keep putting it off, they floated the idea of a lesser working visit as a face-saver. It would be part of a larger presidential trip to Europe in 2018 that would also include a NATO summit in Brussels and the president's first stand-alone summit meeting with Vladimir Putin in Helsinki. Ten Downing Street evidently hoped that the UK portion of the visit would somehow get lost in the mix if it was sandwiched in between some inevitable blowup over NATO and an overly anticipated and hyped-up encounter between Trump and Putin. President Trump could visit Queen Elizabeth for tea at Windsor Castle, just outside London; there would be a dinner at Blenheim Palace, the ancestral home of the Dukes of Marlborough and Winston Churchill, to commemorate U.S.-UK relations; and then Trump could have his golf weekend in Turnberry. If Sadiq Khan and others on the president's UK "nasty list" said something negative, or protested — which people did in the tens of thousands, under the shadow of a large balloon effigy depicting the president as an angry orange baby dressed in a diaper and holding a smartphone — then at least the president would be away from the maddened crowd.

A Family Affair

President Trump's "working visit" to the UK took place in July 2018. He was assuaged but not fully satisfied. Eventually the Brits relented on the actual state visit, which they appropriately tied to the seventy-fifth anniversary of the D-Day and Normandy landings, in June 2019. The visit would begin with a presidential program in London. Then the president and the Queen would decamp to Portsmouth and from there over to France to join other leaders in commemorating the events of World War II.

When we finally got to the planning stages, Trump was mostly going through the motions on the political aspects of the trip. Prime Minister May was due to step down, to be replaced by Boris Johnson. The state visit was her last act, fulfilling her original promise from January 2017. Trump evinced no desire to have a formal agenda for discussion at the last meeting in 10 Downing Street. Instead he wanted events that would put his family at the center of attention. All his adult children would travel with him to London.

In our planning sessions, it was apparent that the main purpose of the state visit was to introduce one dynasty (his) to another (the Queen's family), not to celebrate U.S.-UK ties. The West Wing staff was perpetually fearful that Trump was not getting the same treatment as previous American presidents or other world leaders whenever he traveled, so the level of pomp and circumstance in the UK was critical for them. Some leaders had a ceremonial golden carriage ride through London with the Queen; Bill Clinton had attended a joint session of Parliament; George W. Bush had given a public speech and visited Prime Minister Tony Blair in County Durham; Barack Obama had stayed overnight in Buckingham Palace; several leaders had visited the Queen at one of her other residences. Back in the day, the Queen had ridden on horseback with Ronald Reagan around the grounds of Windsor Castle. We had to compile charts.

In this case, the president didn't want to give any speeches, the golden carriage and Buckingham Palace's guest rooms were undergoing repairs, and President Trump had already had tea at Windsor in 2018, so these were not viable options. He was clearly disappointed about missing out on staying at Buckingham Palace, although the state dinner would be held there.

On substance, we organized a meeting for the president at Kensington Palace with a group of top UK and London-based U.S. business leaders, one of his favorite types of meetings. The intent was to showcase the close economic ties between the two countries and areas of innovation and potential future growth in relations, including in the pharmaceutical, financial technology, and large-scale construction sectors. Queen Elizabeth's son Prince Andrew, who at that point was an envoy for British business, was also in attendance. We presumed that the meeting would maintain the president's attention on substantive issues. But instead of engaging with the business leaders, President Trump focused on his daughter Ivanka.

Trump had taken Ivanka along to the meeting. Now he made her the centerpiece, pushing some of the key staff from the table to seats along the wall. Acting like the proverbial proud parent, the president continually brought the discussion back to what Ivanka was doing with her various White House projects. Praising her for signing up businesses for training schemes to bring women into the workplace, he claimed that Ivanka had single-handedly created thousands of jobs and encouraged the others at the table to praise her too. He paid perfunctory attention to the issues the UK and U.S. business leaders wanted to raise. This was a Trump family show.

Me, Me, Me

Most of Trump's meetings with foreign business leaders that I attended were, like the episode in Kensington Palace, more about holding court than holding forth on issues of concern for American workers. Sometimes the president took bizarre turns into rambling monologues completely lacking in substance. It was becoming clear that this was how the man who had ridden into the White House on the grievances of ordinary Americans was going to fritter away his time in office — forcing captive audiences to indulge him as he went off on personal tangents.

During one encounter with Sweden's most prominent business leaders in March 2018, the discussion quickly veered off onto the subject of the Nobel Peace Prize and medal. Although Nobel Peace Prizes are awarded by a Norwegian committee in Oslo, the founder of the prizes, Alfred Nobel, was a Swedish-born industrialist, and the committee for all the other prizes is in Stockholm. The meeting was, like many, in the Roosevelt Room, across from the Oval Office. President Teddy Roosevelt had won the Nobel Peace Prize in 1906 for brokering the Portsmouth Peace Treaty ending the 1905 Russo-Japanese war. President Roosevelt's medal hung on the wall. President Trump stared at it balefully. He was aggrieved that his predecessor, Barack Obama, had been awarded the Nobel Peace Prize at the very beginning of his tenure, "without even doing anything." Trump had frequently complained about this publicly, and now, privately, he was complaining again because of the location in full sight of the offending medal itself and a captive audience of Swedes, who would surely relay his complaint back to the Nobel committee.

Discussions with world leaders similarly became "me, me, me" sessions. Trump rarely talked about U.S. policy, and never really bothered to read the briefing materials that laid out the policy points in the first instance. He would refer to things happening on "my watch," offer his views on topics, which were often based on a conversation he had had with a personal friend (which he would actually say directly), or repeat something he had heard on Fox News. Whenever he could, Trump would turn the discussion around to some of his pet peeves to get them off his chest — windmills and the advent of wind power was one that always came up. The president was not a fan of most renewable energy projects, except for hydropower. He would go on at length about how huge wind turbines marred the view and reduced property values or decimated migratory birds.

During the July 2019 state visit, the Brits had wanted to talk about climate change. They tried to put the issue on the formal agenda for the meeting at Number 10. The president refused. It was not an issue he wanted to talk about after pulling out of the Paris Climate Agreement. He hated Europeans' trying to raise it again and put him on the spot. So the Brits deputized Queen Elizabeth's eldest son and heir, Prince Charles, to discuss the subject at the U.S. ambassador's dinner. That way Trump had to at least listen to the prince's points, even though he was not enthused (and said so to the press after the dinner). Trump's favorite topics were golf or other sporting events and related analogies, and his personal or family's business success. Many times, taking notes and having to write them up again for the record, I would be tempted to summarize rather than relate all the little details. I got to the point where I could have just scripted the dialogue myself. I knew all the stories by heart, including the variations and embellishments.

When cabinet members, ambassadors, or NSC staff would try to interject to offer thoughts on policy issues during prep sessions, Trump would push back: "I know this better than all of you . . . What do you have to tell me? I have been doing deals all my life. I don't need to learn anything from you." He was also always playing hardball on policy issues with counterparts to cajole or intimidate them into doing something. It was rarely a measured discussion. He often set out extreme possibilities, like threatening to leave NATO if Germany, France, and other countries didn't increase their defense spending in line with alliance commitments. If someone around him cautioned about the foreign policy risks of even raising these threats, he would immediately shoot back: "Fellas, you're currying my play . . . You are ruining my leverage." Everything was framed like a hardnosed business deal. Eventually foreign leaders like German chancellor Angela Merkel and French president Emmanuel Macron started to call him out on it in their exchanges. Clearly they had given up trying to work constructively with Trump. And as his presidency wore on, Trump seemed to have given up on doing much substantive work of his own, too. As was becoming clear, he had other plans.

11

The Price of Populism

It was an easy slide from Donald Trump's sometimes perverse machismo and personalization of the presidency into something more malign than benign. His time in office would come to mark not only the contours of the rise of populism in the United States but also the emergence of a definite authoritarian streak in American executive power. Although his behavior sometimes seemed more malevolent than it actually was, his penchant for strongman tactics — and for strongmen themselves — cast a pall over America, diminishing its standing on the world stage and foreclosing the possibility that some good could come out of his administration in addition to all the chaos and strife.

In the United States, the peculiarities of the institution of the presidency, as well as of the political party system, made it remarkably easy for a president like Trump to claim excessive power. The American president is at least three things in one: head of state, commander in chief, and chief executive. And in many respects the presidency has become aggrandized over time, taking on more roles and accruing executive authorities, all the while losing some of the careful calibrations and constraints devised by the Founding Fathers.

Like the office of the presidency, the Democratic and the Republican parties also are open to exploitation. Unlike the parties I grew up with in the UK and elsewhere in Europe, the U.S. parties are both big-tent political movements with weak internal leadership and discipline and no fixed platforms. They provide havens for all kinds of individuals and groups with extreme views on the left and the right — including on the far right in Republican circles, such as white supremacist movements and militias, which Trump increasingly appealed to during his presidency.

In time Trump would prove himself able to turn all these factors to his advantage. And the way in which he did so begged yet another inauspicious comparison between the United States and Russia. In many of his actions there were shades not just of the tyranny of the past, which had propelled the American colonies to seek independence from Great Britain, but also of the authoritarian playbook adopted by Vladimir Putin and other global leaders over the years to subvert democracy. In the course of his presidency, indeed, Trump would come more to resemble Putin in political practice and predilection than he resembled any of his recent American presidential predecessors. Sometimes even I was startled by how glaringly obvious the similarities were.

In the case of both Putin in Russia and Trump in the United States, for example, prominent legal scholars around them were willing to push the idea that they, as president, were the embodiment of the executive branch and the constitution. And as they stood above everyone and anything else, they should be in control of the country almost without limits. President Trump was certainly a great believer in his executive privilege rather than in the powers of the larger executive branch per se. During his first campaign, Trump bragged that he could shoot someone on Fifth Avenue and get away with it. Later, after his first impeachment trial, in January 2020, he seemed to believe that he now had license to commit political murder — usurping power — as well as literal murder, when he set out to retain the presidency at the end of that year.

Trump was completely transparent about his admiration for autocrats and authoritarians and their style of governance. In a wide-ranging series of taped telephone interviews, he told the veteran American journalist Bob Woodward that he much preferred autocratic strongmen to his democratic counterparts: "It's funny, the relationships I have, the tougher and meaner they are, the better I get along with them. You'll explain that to me someday, okay? But maybe it's not a bad thing. The easy ones I maybe don't like as much or don't get along with as much."

Even before the revelations from Woodward's tapes, the president's views were clear to anyone who saw him in action at the White House. In May 2019, for instance, President Trump met with Hungarian prime minister and self-styled populist strongman Viktor Orbán. He was full of praise for

Orbán in press interviews, notwithstanding the frequent European criticisms of Orbán's illiberal turns at home.

Ambassador Bolton had sat in on the private Oval Office meeting between the two while the rest of us waited in the Cabinet Room for an expanded meeting with the Hungarian delegation. Ambassador Bolton rushed out ahead of the president and prime minister, clearly unhappy with the trajectory of the conversation. He turned to me and said, emphatically, "Well, he's [Orbán's] definitely his [Trump's] kind of guy."

The U.S. ambassador to Hungary, David Cornstein, a jeweler from New York who had known Trump for decades, concurred. The ambassador had worked hard to set up this meeting of kindred spirits. In a shockingly frank interview with *The Atlantic* in June 2019, Cornstein told journalist Franklin Foer, "I can tell you, knowing the president for a good twenty-five or thirty years, that he would love to have the situation that Viktor Orbán has, but he doesn't." In my discussions with Ambassador Cornstein, he said the same thing to me, seemingly without any comprehension that his observation might be problematic for the future of democracy in the United States.

President Trump was attracted to "the tougher and meaner" leaders because he literally wanted to be them. In the international arena, Trump saw himself sparring, wrestling with the tough guys, as he had with real estate titans back in New York. But in the U.S., he wanted to govern like them. He wanted raw power without much in the way of constitutional or other checks and balances. In time, the country whose divisions and decay had led to Trump's election would pay an even steeper price for that fateful set of personal political preferences.

Autocrat Envy

Trump was clearly envious of Orbán, but also of a number of other contemporary leaders and international figures. He referred to Turkish president Recep Tayyip Erdoğan as "the Sultan" and often bantered with him about how he, Trump, was jealous of Erdoğan's seemingly boundless ability to get his own way at home. Trump made similar comments about President Xi of China, who had lifted his own term limits on staying in office and had removed the Chinese Communist Party's ten-year collective leadership turnover rule. Trump stated that he would be delighted to do the same — usually in a jocular manner, so that he could say he was joking if anyone commented. But the frequency of the references told a different story. He was deadly serious.

Queen Elizabeth II was another subject of envy as well as admiration, because of the reverence accorded her at home and abroad and her fabulous wealth. In the 1980s the Queen had been one of the world's richest individuals and certainly the richest in the UK. She had been deposed on that front in the new century by all kinds of billionaires at home and abroad, but irrespective of this and the constraints on her actual political power, she was still the Queen of England. She was the symbol of the state. Whenever Trump looked into the Queen's, Orbán's, Erdoğan's, or Xi's eyes, or anyone else's of this vaunted global stature, he was seeking the reflection of himself.

Putin, even more than the others, was the ultimate international populist in style, swagger, and potential wealth. Russia had more than its fair share of billionaires — the emergence of the super-rich in Russia, the so-called oligarchs, as well as in the United States and globally — was a major phenomenon in the 2000s, but Putin was rumored to be the richest man in the world, the billionaire to top all billionaires. Trump seemed to look up to Putin because of his wealth, and he admired the way Putin ran Russia like his own private company. People like Putin, who was simultaneously an autocrat and reputedly super-rich, were an elite of their own. This was the group Trump wanted to see himself in — the internationally very rich, very powerful, and very famous.

This was a troubling aspiration for an American president, to say the least, and it had grim implications for an already struggling United States. In Russia in the 1990s and early 2000s, those with the best political connections (first to President Yeltsin and then to Putin) captured everything. Russia's billionaire oligarchs grabbed the plum assets in key industries during the government's privatization program and then moved money out of Russia to banks and shell companies overseas. As a result, Russia (and other former Soviet states) became kleptocracies, not just market economies, and eventually descended into authoritarianism. Oligarchs used their enormous fortunes to bribe politicians and fight regulations and oversight, thus undermining Russia's nascent democracy. They also evaded taxes and deprived the state of revenues. Cronies — insiders to the Russian system — were always preferred to outsiders in big state contracts and other business deals. They took advantage of those contracts to amass more wealth by padding out contract budgets with "creative billing" and bringing in their family members and personal networks as staff or subcontractors.

Putin, for his part, had perfected the art of populist patronage and the big show that Trump tried to emulate. Putin was frequently featured on Russian TV, summoning the oligarchs and publicly upbraiding them for something they had done or not done. It was obvious when you turned the lens around from Putin and Russia to the United States that Trump was trying to do the same thing: order business leaders around.

When Trump set up his short-lived Business Council, or invited businessmen to one-on-one or small group meetings, or deployed Wilbur Ross, his billionaire commerce secretary, to deal with pet projects, or phoned up the heads of huge American companies to berate them, the U.S. president was doing exactly what Putin did. I once heard Trump telling Wilbur Ross in April 2019 to figure out how to increase U.S. investment in Turkey as a favor to President Erdoğan. I also watched and heard Trump call out U.S. businessmen and -women to cajole them into following some specific set of personal directions. One of these played out publicly in November 2018, when Trump called Mary Barra, the head of General Motors, to insist that she not close four factories in Ohio, a particularly important issue for his voter base. Just as in the case of Putin in Russia, Trump's meetings and calls to account were purely for show — the populist at work in ostentatious displays.

But behind this flashy showmanship there was a darker kind of substance. Under Trump, the United States began to develop its own version of "the people who run the country own it," which was a description applied to Russia by the Carnegie Moscow program head Dmitri Trenin. In populist settings you frequently end up with crony capitalism. Those who have personal ties get preferential treatment and rise to the top of the economy. The grabbing hand of state becomes the grabbing hand of the head of state. Personalized leadership tilts the playing field away from good governance and the true private sector toward corruption and nepotism. In the public realm, the focus is on the political — creating jobs for "your" voters, which is something Trump always said he wanted to do.

Inevitably, cronyism bolsters the desire for authoritarianism, retaining power by any means to keep you and yours in charge of the state and its spoils. In the end, this trend leads to economic stagnation. Democracy and growth are clearly correlated in Europe as well as in the United States. When democracy slides, so does the economy. This is the lesson from Russia and the former Soviet Union and Eastern Europe in the early 2000s. But in the following decade it became clear that Trump had drawn a very different conclusion from his Russian case study.

America's robust and vibrant democracy and vaunted political stability were always the spur for domestic and foreign investment. But after Trump assumed power, he set about undermining that cornerstone of the country's economic foundation. He systematically attempted to appoint his personal friends or cronies to state offices, regardless of their qualifications for the positions. He also sought to privatize some of the U.S. state assets or reduce them in size and repurpose them — like the U.S. Postal Service, as well as federal lands run by the Department of the Interior through the sale of licenses and the deregulation of land use — which would ultimately leach revenues away from the state. Indeed, Trump had a low view of handing money over to the U.S. government. Taxes, he essentially said, were for suckers or losers — or at least the ordinary Americans who weren't billionaires. Not paying them made him "smart."

Under Trump, foreign investors and businesses started to hesitate and pull back when America seemed to go off the rails. In 2019, when I was wrapping up my time at the NSC, several top European businessmen privately told me and other colleagues that despite the U.S. economic performance, they were starting to see Trump's United States as a politically risky investment proposition. Not knowing where it was heading, they were holding off on some of their foreign direct investment commitments. This was the kind of discussion I was more used to having about Russia than about America.

The Real Deal

When you looked more closely, Trump and Putin seemed to have a lot in common in terms of their domestic political tactics as well as their strategy. But a closer inspection also revealed important differences — contrasts that further underscored why Trump's personalized and populist political approach was so detrimental both to America's democracy and to its national security.

In contrast to Trump, Putin, before he became a reputed billionaire head of state, was the real deal of the "average working-class guy" in Russia. Unlike Trump, Putin grew up in a poor family in a poor neighborhood of St. Petersburg — in a communal flat, where multiple families shared a large divided apartment and all its facilities. As president, Putin shared the same political base as Trump in the U.S., with similar grievances — older, more male, less educated than others. In Russia's case, most of Putin's supporters worked in the public sector, given the heavy state influence in the economy. But, also like Trump's, Putin's supporters were more religiously observant and often living in semirural small towns and cities. Putin's support was weak in the big cities, including Moscow and his hometown of St. Petersburg. Putin loved to play the regular guy with factory workers — men in hard hats — and appeal to their strongman instincts.

At one point, during huge demonstrations against his rule in Moscow in 2011, Putin visited a massive tank plant in Nizhny Tagil in the Ural Mountains, a place renowned for its fervent support of his presidency. The factory foreman offered to go to Moscow with "some of the boys" to "sort out" the protesters for Putin. The Russian president declined the offer, but later appointed the factory foreman to be his official presidential representative to the Urals region. It was a spectacular piece of political populism. It was also strikingly reminiscent of President Trump's efforts to solicit support from the far-right Proud Boys militia, who would violently confront Black Lives Matter protesters in the summer of 2020. After public outcry on that occasion, Trump called on the Proud Boys to "stand back and stand by" instead of asking them to cease and desist their activities. They would not stand by for long: on January 6, 2021, in the waning days of Trump's presidency, the Proud Boys would be among the militia groups and other Trump supporters who stormed the U.S. Capitol Building.

There were many other ways in which Putin and Trump resembled each other in playing to their similar crowds. Manipulation and exploitation of the media were one of the more obvious — a Kremlin stock-in-trade — but there were others that were perhaps less evident. Trump tried to prevent the removal of Confederate-era statues and the renaming of American military forts named after Confederate generals. Putin put the statues of Soviet-era figures back on their pedestals and restored Soviet memorials that had been toppled under Gorbachev and Yeltsin. Both created and invoked their own versions of the country's "golden" or "silver" ages and their personal lists of "national heroes" to appeal to their voters' nostalgia or conservatism. Both constantly talked about their direct connection to "the people." They used this constant invocation to draw authority directly from the powers of the presidency, the number of votes in their favor, and opinion polls rather than from their nominal political party. And they always blamed bad bureaucrats for anything that went wrong.

Ironically, however, Putin was much more cautious than Trump in who he blamed and how he whipped up division. Putin would never blame the "deep state," for example. He was a product of the real deep state, having walked the back corridors of the Soviet-era KGB to power. Putin ruled Russia as a state insider, unlike Trump, who wanted to rule America as an outsider. Putin saw the state apparatus as a useful tool for wielding power; Trump saw the state and its structures as an obstacle to his power games.

In part because he was such a consummate deep-stater, Putin was not keen on militias. Independent paramilitary organizations could be dangerous in Russia, where the state always wanted to ensure the complete monopolization of firepower. Putin reined them in at home, although he often allowed them to operate abroad as proxies for the state in conflicts in places such as Ukraine and Syria where he wanted to minimize regular Russian military forces' exposure.

Unlike Trump, Putin also would never incite far-right groups against minorities, many of whom were historically core to the Russia state and his own political support, including Russian Muslims and Jews and immigrants from Central Asia. Russia gave the world the word "pogrom." And in Russia's imperial past, it was potentially explosive to provoke an ethnic or religious riot. These usually got out of hand and resulted in large-scale massacres. In modern times, someone from Putin's internal or external opposition could theoretically whip up a pogrom and turn people against *him* by exploiting divisions.

Thus, when Putin tried to sow or exploit division, he homed in on the smallest and weakest possible groups, which were easy targets. These included Russia's LGBTQ community and tiny political opposition parties or loose opposition movements that he dubbed "pro-Western, fifth-column liberals." And of course Putin played up the United States as an external enemy which was — in his depiction — manipulating internal dissent in Russia to bring the country to its knees.

Putin did not, like Trump, rail against the Russian government and generally play with the country's political, social, racial, and religious divisions to see what he could get out of it. Putin was always stressing unity — one synthetic Russian culture and identity to overcome the conflicts of the past that had destabilized and helped to bring down both the Russian empire and the USSR in the twentieth century. Putin had no desire to emulate Nicholas II or Mikhail Gorbachev, the czar and president who had both lost their countries.

In sum, Putin's approach was a stark contrast to Trump's efforts to emphasize America's divides and pit political parties, politicians, social movements, and racial and religious groups against each other in 2016 and 2020. Putin wanted one Russia. Trump wanted many Americas, not one.

This was a telling difference, and a critical one, because Vladimir Putin was only too happy to unleash the Russian security services to exploit America's divisions, playing up the many Americas and playing them against each other, all with the goal of weakening the United States. In this respect, Trump played right into Putin's hands.

After 2016, Trump was accused of being the "Manchurian candidate" or "Russian candidate" — a puppet run by Vladimir Putin, who had stolen the election for him. But despite the similarities in their approaches and Trump's autocrat envy, I don't believe Trump was intentionally doing something for Putin or for anyone else. Trump was only ever concerned with himself, as would become strikingly clear after the November 2020 election.

Of course, this is not what many people thought for most of his tenure. Outside the White House — perhaps until the revelations from Bob Woodward's tapes — it seemed hard for people to imagine that Trump was fixated on authoritarians in general, not Putin in particular. I saw in multiple settings how deference to the strongman was a persistent pattern across all of Trump's interactions with world leaders. It was only against the backdrop of Russian interference in 2016 that people outside the White House thought it applied solely to Putin.

One episode in Trump's term, his meeting with Putin at Helsinki in July 2018, was broadly seen as the proof of Trump's complicity and collusion with Putin and the Russian security services in 2016. For me, it was instead another example of Trump's autocrat envy, as well as the vulnerabilities inherent in his personal vanity and fragile ego. That distinction, however, did not make the spectacle any easier to watch and endure.

The Big Summit

The Helsinki meeting with Putin was supposed to be Trump's big arms-control summit, like the encounters between Gorbachev and Reagan in places like Geneva, Switzerland, and Reykjavik, Iceland, in the 1980s. George

H. W. Bush had met with Gorbachev for a summit in Helsinki in 1990, and the Finns were glad to oblige again. They quickly got into the spirit of hosting an old-style high-level meeting.

President Sauli Niinistö lent his Presidential Palace in the heart of the city by the Helsinki port for the occasion. Crowds lined the streets from the airport to the city when the Russian and U.S. presidents arrived. It was very different from the "working visit" in London just a few days before. There were fewer insults and protests directed at President Trump, no baby Trump balloon, and more enthusiasm for the possibility of another U.S.-Russian security breakthrough. Images of Ronald Reagan and George H. W. Bush meeting with Gorbachev for arms negotiations were shown on screens in a continuous loop in the state rooms where we sat. The Finnish president gave Trump a few tips on speaking to Putin and things to look out for, in a breakfast meeting just before the summit. It was one of the few times someone managed to penetrate with a bit of useful, objective advice.

When it came to nuclear weapons, Trump always had a pattern break with the norm, which showed that he really cared about the topic. He was genuinely interested and paid attention when nuclear issues came up, be it with Russia, Iran, or North Korea. Here and there, when something like this resonated with him and fit his personal interests and worldview, he would perk up. Countering terrorism, striking back against al-Assad when he used chemical weapons against the civilian population in Syria, trade tariffs, and dealing with China fell into that category.

Trump cared so much about the nuclear issue, indeed, that at times it seemed to take the Russians by surprise. At Helsinki, in his one-on-one meeting with Putin, Trump caught the Russian president making an inaccurate assertion on the terms of extending the 2010 New START agreement. President Trump brought it up at the lunch with cabinet members. Putin was slightly embarrassed and had to walk his comments back and clarify. His foreign minister, Sergey Lavrov, glared at him. The Russians had clearly hoped to trip Trump up. By now everyone knew that Trump never paid attention to his brief.

Even minor victories such as these were few and far between, however. Trump's failure to read his briefs or to stick to the policy plan (even if he had come up with it in the first place) was a major liability in every aspect of national security affairs. Whenever he got to meetings and the conversation started, it seemed like the first time he was hearing things from world leaders. Having skipped the background notes, and sometimes even the bullet-pointed notecards, Trump gave Putin or whoever was with him the opportunity to promote his own version of history and events and seize the policy advantage.

Some leaders, like President Erdoğan of Turkey, would get angry in meetings or on calls when Trump obviously had no idea what they were talking about. Erdoğan would complain on the spot about the "bad American advisers" who weren't giving Trump the "right information," or he would presume that Trump was strategically feigning ignorance. Eventually Erdoğan would bypass the NSC and the White House staff to talk to Trump directly. He would call the president when he knew none of the "bad advisers" were around, as on Thanksgiving, when Trump was golfing with a skeleton staff. Erdoğan and his staff even joked to journalists and others about the appropriateness of calling on "Turkey Day" and bragged that they kept tabs on Trump's schedule.

When Trump was winging it, he could be persuaded of all kinds of things. If his foreign visitor or caller was one of his favored strongmen, he would always give him the benefit of the doubt over his advisers. After meeting Viktor Orbán in May 2018, for example, Trump cut off U.S. defense secretary Patrick Shanahan, who was trying to make a point in the cabinet meeting. Trump told Shanahan in front of everyone else that Orbán had already explained this very issue to him in their Oval Office meeting. Orbán knew everything better than Shanahan did. The autocratic leader simply had more authority than the people who worked for Trump. The leader was his equal, his staff members were not. For Trump, information trickled down from him, not up to him. He would listen only to someone he considered to be at his level, or close to it — like his host, Finnish president Niinistö, and then just for a moment over breakfast.

This tendency of Trump's was lamentable when it played out behind closed doors, but it was inexcusable — and indeed impossible to explain or justify — when it spilled out into public view. For instance in Helsinki, where it played out in spectacular fashion in a mortifying press conference.

Before the press conference, Trump was pleased with how things had gone in his one-on-one meeting with Putin. He had finally had his proper sit-down with the Russian president. The world was watching. It had not only been a big show, but the two presidents had agreed to get arms-control negotiations going. They had also approved meetings between the two national security councils as well as potentially a joint business roundtable.

Of course, Putin had thrown a few curveballs that would complicate these modest achievements. Trump never took notes. He usually was not paying attention as everything was translated. He focused on the overall impression — the mood music rather than the lyrics — as I had seen him do the first time in the May 2, 2017, Oval Office phone call when he thought I was the secretary. Trump habitually threw dealing with the details over to his staff. He would do this by telling the leader in their personal meeting that "your guys should talk to my guys" and then deputizing a cabinet member or the national security adviser as the point person to follow up when he came out. Other times Trump would ask the world leader to repeat what he had said for general discussion and notetaking in an expanded meeting.

This was Trump's tack with Putin at Helsinki. Trump asked "Vladimir" to "repeat what you just told me to my guys" in the lunch with the two delegations after their sit-down.

In between the one-on-one and the lunch, Joe Wang and I, along with one of the NSC lawyers, Michael Ellis, had quickly debriefed the American translator so we could check to make sure everything tracked with expectations and to see if there was something we would have to deal with. This debriefing alerted us to the fact that Putin had tried to pull another fast one.

At this time, Special Counsel Mueller's investigation was still under way. The question of whether Trump's campaign had colluded with Russian agents and Putin had stolen the election for Trump hovered above everything. As a result of the investigation, a U.S. Department of Justice grand jury had just — on the very eve of the summit — indicted twelve Russian intelligence agents for "hacking offenses" during the 2016 election interference operation. It was the FBI's shot across the Russian president's bow.

Putin had been quick to shoot back. In their conversation, Putin suggested to Trump that the U.S. and Russia could invoke an existing bilateral mutual legal assistance treaty (MLAT) to address this development. The treaty would enable U.S. law enforcement to interview the twelve Russian intelligence operatives accused of election interference. The rub was that as the MLAT was mutual, Russia would also like to have its own interviews.

Putin said that "some Americans" had been involved in "corruption" cases in Moscow. He mentioned businessman Bill Browder, the American-born son of the former head of the U.S. Communist Party, who was now a British citizen living in London. In the 1990s, Browder had made millions investing in Russia, but he had lost his fortune when Russian rivals seized his assets. He was accused of tax evasion and deported. Browder's Russian accountant, Sergei Magnitsky, was arrested and died in jail. Browder related all of this in a best-selling book, *Red Notice*. He also lobbied Congress to impose sanctions on the Russian officials involved in the episode. The bill was named the Sergei Magnitsky Act after his Russian associate. Putin had an ax to grind against Browder for the Magnitsky bill.

It was immediately apparent to the translator that President Trump had no idea what the Russian president was talking about, who Browder was, or what the MLAT entailed. Trump did not probe the offer in more detail. The idea that the FBI might get to interview some Russian agents sounded generally promising. It might also draw attention away from the scrutiny of his campaign. So Trump declared it "interesting."

This was an understatement. Putin's offer was a clear effort to distract attention from what Russia had done in 2016 by stirring up outrage at the mere suggestion that Americans could possibly be subject to Russian interrogation. It was glaringly obvious to us that Putin had carefully laid a trap — one that his American counterpart had been only too happy to walk into.

Putin raised the MLAT again during the lunch. Secretary of State Pompeo, already forewarned from the debrief, shut the idea down. President Trump, still not grasping the Russian president's intent, gave Putin another opening to elaborate on it at the press conference. But Putin would not wait that long. He had already seized the initiative. While the Russian leader was dangling the MLAT idea at Helsinki, he had evidently instructed officials back home to announce a full list of the Americans that they would like to interview. Although Putin never mentioned this list to Trump or at the subsequent press conference, it included — in addition to Bill Browder — several U.S. officials, congressional staff members, and the former U.S. ambassador to Russia, Michael McFaul.

This was a classic Putin ploy. I had witnessed him do this repeatedly. He would make people complicit in something nefarious by first introducing it in a deliberately vague and innocuous way. Putin said it. The other person heard it. Putin then created guilt by association when he later added new and damning details.

Putin obviously intended to tie American diplomats up in knots after Helsinki dealing with the fallout from his suggestion. At the end of it all, he no doubt imagined the U.S. government would find its pursuit of Russian agents even more complicated than before. Mission accomplished.

Trump was oblivious to all this. He thought the general atmosphere of the conversation was upbeat. He was visibly thrilled and satisfied at the lunch. But then came the press conference.

Agony in Helsinki

I had questioned the idea of having a press conference in the first place, but it was a summit and Trump loved press conferences. I had instantly been overruled.

This was the first stand-alone summit meeting between Trump and Putin. After Russia's 2016 election interference, the mere idea that Trump would talk to Putin at all — on the phone, on the margins of meetings, anywhere, anytime — sent the U.S. and international press corps into a frenzy. Everyone was convinced that if Trump met with Putin "alone," even at large international meetings, some secret undertakings could easily be made. There was little consideration of the fact that everything had to be interpreted back and forth, which took some time; and with interpreters in the room, the two leaders were hardly alone.

During Putin and Trump's first face-to-face, in Hamburg at the G20 meeting in July 2017, Foreign Minister Lavrov and Secretary of State Tillerson had sat in on the meeting. This was in the period when Trump's lawyers were still harping on him to let people take notes, and a mini-scandal had been generated by Trump taking the U.S. interpreter's notes and stuffing them in his pocket. Never mind that interpreter's notes were usually in shorthand — quick word and phrase prompts to make sure they caught everything accurately in a sentence. They were never intended to be verbatim notes for the record.

Even without his notes, the U.S. interpreter had debriefed me and acting assistant secretary of state John Heffern on the content of the Hamburg meeting. Secretary Tillerson had also made some notes for himself. Tillerson had an excellent recall of the conversation, as one might imagine of the former CEO of ExxonMobil, who had been dealing with Putin and Russia for many years. The secretary gave a readout to me and General McMaster, among others, as well as relating the main points at a press conference.

Nothing that had emerged about the first Trump-Putin meeting implied that Trump was the "Russian candidate" receiving secret instructions from Putin. Nonetheless, the idea persisted. And it returned with a vengeance at the Helsinki press conference.

Things went wrong immediately. As Trump and Putin stood behind their separate podiums in front of a crowd of journalists, it quickly became clear that the press questions would be focused on probing Trump on what Putin might have said or not said regarding 2016 and election interference. U.S. reporters wanted Trump to denounce the Russian interference in front of Putin. For his part, President Trump was still thinking about nuclear weapons and 1980s summitry. He was in an entirely different headspace from the U.S. media. Trump expected their praise for meeting with Putin and tackling the nuclear threat, which he kept referring to, to no avail.

From where I sat, all this was both farcical and tragic. Naturally, when the question was put to him, Putin denied any involvement in the 2016 election. One journalist, Jonathan Lemire from the Associated Press, finally asked Trump outright whom he believed, Putin or the U.S. intelligence agencies, which had concluded that Russia interfered. Lemire pressed Trump hard: "Would you now with the whole world watching tell President Putin — would you denounce what happened in 2016 and would you warn him to never do it again?"

Trump balked. He really didn't want to answer this. Of course he did not want to take on Putin, his fellow strongman, in front of the U.S. and world media. He had hoped to bask in the glory of the two of them doing what U.S. and Russian presidents used to do in the 1980s — hold high-level diplomatic summits. So, as he usually did, he tried to turn the question around. He attempted to fold into his answer a convoluted conspiracy theory that he was particularly fond of but that had repeatedly been debunked by his own White House staff. This centered on a supposedly missing computer server for the DNC, which was purportedly taken by the FBI as part of its 2016 investigation and might even have ended up in Ukraine. The server, according to President Trump, contained thousands of Hillary Clinton's emails.

It was Trump's routine deflection from what the Russians had done. But the conspiracy was so convoluted, even for Trump, that he got tangled up in the narrative threads and ended up with a muddled, rambling, and at times nonsensical answer:

Where is the server? I want to know, where is the server and what is the server saying? With that being said, all I can do is ask the question. My people came to me, [Director of National Intelligence] Dan Coats came to me and some others and said they think it's Russia. I have President Putin. He just said it's not Russia. I will say this. I don't see any reason why it would be, but I really do want to see the server. But I have confidence in both parties . . . I think it's a disgrace that we can't get Hillary Clinton's 33,000 emails. So, I have great confidence in my intelligence people, but I will tell you that President Putin was extremely strong and powerful in his denial today. And what he did is an incredible offer [the MLAT]. He offered to have the people working on the case come and work with their investigators, with respect to the 12 people [indicted Russian operatives]. I think that's an incredible offer. Okay thank you.

This was the kind of head-spinning, incoherent monologue that I had tried on numerous occasions to document for the presidential record as notetaker. It was a word fog, in which you stumbled around looking for meaning. Somewhere in the haze, however, President Trump *had* said that he believed Putin over his intelligence officials. The telling lines for me were that "Putin was extremely strong and powerful in his denial" and "He just said it's not Russia [so] I don't see any reason why it would be."

Putin was Trump's counterpart, which in Trump's mind meant that Putin was therefore more likely to be right than anyone else. But for Trump, answering media questions about Russian interference or siding with the conclusions of U.S. intelligence agencies was also tantamount to admitting that he hadn't won the 2016 election. The questions got right to the heart of his insecurities. If he said, "Yes, they interfered" and "Yes, they interfered on my behalf," then he might as well say, "I am illegitimate." Indeed, he made a point in a further elaboration of his Helsinki response of referencing his "brilliant campaign" in 2016 as proof that he had won on his own, without an assist from Putin.

The reality is that, as those of us who worked with him well knew, President Trump simply could not distinguish between Russia's broad-based attack on the American election and democratic system and his own position and ego. He erupted in anger every single time the issue of Russia's election intervention came up, because he saw it as a personal attack.

Trump also jumped all over any U.S. official who discussed Russia's election interference in public. One of the incidents that had helped to precipitate General McMaster's departure from the NSC several months earlier, in March 2018, was a speech that he had given at the Munich Security Conference in February 2018. During the question-and-answer session with the audience, General McMaster had taken a question from a prominent Russian parliamentarian. He used the opportunity to forcefully push back on

Russia's interference in 2016, calling the evidence of what they had done "incontrovertible."

On the plane back to Washington, D.C., from Munich, we discovered that the president had tweeted his displeasure. It was strikingly similar to his later comments at Helsinki, although clearer because of the 140-character constraint: "General McMaster forgot to say that the results of the 2016 election were not impacted or changed by the Russians and that the only Collusion was between Russia and Crooked H [Hillary Clinton], the DNC and the Dems [Democratic Party]."

After General McMaster had left the White House, others in the president's immediate circle in the West Wing took note of his fate and tried to avoid bringing up the issue with Trump directly. If Ambassador Bolton, in his role as national security adviser, or any other U.S. official took the Russians to task after that, it was done to their faces but behind closed doors so President Trump wouldn't shoot the messenger and contradict the message.

The outcome of the Helsinki press conference was entirely predictable, but it was still agonizing to behold. As far as Trump was concerned, standing there in Helsinki in July 2018, the media had tried to embarrass him and make him look weak. Journalists, American government officials, intelligence analysts — none of these people were his audience, nor were they his peers. Only Putin was. The journalists' questions punctured Trump's image of the rerun of a Reagan-Gorbachev 1980s arms-control summit. It ruined his populist performance, his big show.

As Trump responded that he believed Putin over his own intelligence analysts, I wanted to end the whole thing. I contemplated throwing a fit or faking a seizure and hurling myself backward into the row of journalists behind me. But it would only have added to the humiliating spectacle.

It was obvious to everyone present that the press conference would be a scandal. Although he reveled in the excruciating embarrassment for the U.S. in that moment, even Putin knew that it would provoke a backlash that would undermine the various, completely anodyne commitments made at the meeting. On his way out the door from the conference he told his press secretary, within earshot of our interpreter, that the press conference was "bullshit." Indeed it was.

I got letters and notes from people I hadn't heard from in decades, including a long-lost classmate from my Russian-language lessons at St. Andrews, advising me that I should resign because of what had happened in

Helsinki. But what had happened in Helsinki was nothing more or less than a terrible press conference and Trump's fragile ego compounding the usual difficulties of dealing with Russia.

Perhaps more than anything else, the press conference highlighted — for me, and for the public — just how low America could sink in its own estimation and in the eyes of the world. The country's long-festering domestic crisis had exploded into view with Trump's election, and now we were seeing the consequences on the international stage. This, I felt, was the agony of American populism. But it wasn't over yet.

99 Red Balloons

Because of an uncomfortable press conference, Trump had lost his chance to begin cutting a new arms-control deal with the Russians. Eventually he ran out of presidential runway to finish the mission he had set himself in the 1980s. It wasn't for want of trying, but things kept going wrong and he would never stick to the preapproved plan. This was just one element in what was perhaps the most surreal period in the NSC for me. My own 1980s nuclear preoccupations came full circle, even if Trump's did not.

Three months after Helsinki, in October 2018, Trump short-circuited the negotiation process with the Russians on the potential U.S. withdrawal from the Intermediate-Range Nuclear Forces (INF) Treaty by telling a "press gaggle" that the U.S. was going to pull out. The INF Treaty had up until that point been in place since Reagan and Gorbachev signed it in December 1987 — when I was on my exchange program in Moscow — ending the decade-long Cold War standoff (from 1977–1987) over stationing ballistic missiles in Western and Eastern Europe. The two countries had agreed both to eliminate ground-based weapons and to engage in regular inspections to verify that each was adhering to the various terms of the treaty.

But although it had been hugely consequential at the time of its signing, the INF Treaty had frayed. In the years before Trump's election, the Russians had been violating the missile testing limitations of INF, and bilateral arms talks were bogged down in mutual recriminations. Because of all the back-and-forth on INF, the U.S. and Russia had both been unable to move on to the next phase of arms control to discuss what they would do about extending or revising other treaties on strategic or long-range missiles and dealing with the ongoing proliferation of nuclear weapons. Countries like China had been building up nuclear arsenals since the 1980s, while others, like Iran and North Korea, were fixated on developing their own capabilities. Unlike the Cold War, global arms control was no longer an issue for the U.S. and Russia simply to work out between themselves.

While the president was tipping his hand to the press, I was at that very moment taking off on a plane to Moscow with Ambassador Bolton and a group from the NSC to initiate discussions with the Russians about the future of INF and what might come after it. At that point Trump had been discouraged from meeting with Putin again, to avoid another Helsinki-style public relations debacle. He had to deputize Bolton to move things along. But Trump clearly didn't like the idea that Bolton might somehow steal his nuclear thunder by meeting with Putin. Trump's comments threw everyone on the plane into disarray for a while, scrambling for a new approach to the talks.

This moment was emblematic of another deep-seated problem with Trump's particular style of brash leadership. As president, Trump had, theoretically, every opportunity to accomplish his long-desired and much-vaunted "big deal" with Vladimir Putin. But his populist tendencies and inattention to detail got the better of him. He had successfully ridden into the White House on the crest of a political wave that had first risen and taken shape in the 1980s under Reagan and Thatcher. Their free-market deregulation and hyper-competitive and individualistic policies had both swept away the defunct industrial economy and eroded state support for vulnerable groups at home. Overseas, their military buildup and the forcefulness of their foreign polices helped carry off Mikhail Gorbachev and the already teetering Soviet Union. Now the wave had finally washed back to America's shores, pushing into the political rifts and partisan divides they had helped to create in the first place.

Trump was a success as a populist in exploiting those domestic divisions, but ultimately a failure as policymaker for the same reason. He couldn't pull himself or America together to overcome them and get things done domestically. And internationally, as president, where he in fact had all the executive authority to set the agenda and accomplish objectives, he was mesmerized by autocrats, carried away by his own sense of infallibility, and unwilling to do the homework necessary to follow through on a coherent foreign policy strategy. As far as Trump's nuclear agenda was concerned, this was something of a personal and political tragedy for him. And insofar as nuclear arms control is one of the most consequential and pressing issues facing the world today, the tragedy didn't end with Trump.

For me, the end of the INF Treaty was a culmination (although not a very satisfactory one) of my efforts to resolve Uncle Charlie Crabtree's question about "why the bloody hell [the Russians were] trying to blow us up." I had gone off to St. Andrews to study Russian against the backdrop of the Euromissile war scare in the 1980s. I had been in Moscow when the INF Treaty had been signed. Now I was at the NSC, and part of the U.S. effort to pull out of INF. I accompanied Ambassador Bolton to Moscow to discuss this with Putin. Colleagues fanned out to NATO headquarters in Brussels and other European capitals. I also went solo to Germany in February 2019 to talk to some of the German politicians who wanted the U.S. and Russia to keep the INF Treaty in place and to explain the situation from the American perspective. And in fact, Germany came to play a key role in the INF endgame.

At the very end of 2018 there was a G20 summit in Buenos Aires, Argentina. Initially Trump had hoped for a second chance to meet with Putin to discuss arms control and follow up himself on Bolton's Moscow INF meetings. On the eve of the summit, the Russians detained a Ukrainian ship and its sailors in the Sea of Azov and refused to release them. The Putin meeting was off. INF was, however, still on the agenda for Trump's G20 meeting with German chancellor Angela Merkel. Up until then he had been reluctant to coordinate closely with the Europeans on the INF withdrawal (which eventually came in August 2019). The treaty was between the United States and Russia; Trump didn't really see the point. Angela Merkel and her team had cut their political teeth on this issue in their younger days. As she explained in Buenos Aires, she had taken part in 1980s antinuclear protests in East Germany, while her colleagues in West Germany had launched their political careers through their opposition to stationing U.S. missiles in Europe. She patiently and even humorously laid out all of this and how the risk of a U.S.-Soviet nuclear war had been the all-encompassing topic of her youth. The strains of "99 Red Balloons," Nena's 1980s German antinuclear anthem, practically filled the room.

This was the first time Trump had ever listened to the Europeans' perspective on the 1980s and heard why U.S.-Russian arms-control negotiations were important to them as well. It was clear that none of this had ever occurred to him before. I was sitting next to White House chief of staff John Kelly. He leaned over to me and whispered, "The problem is the president doesn't know any of this. He doesn't know any history at all, even some of the basics on the U.S." As usual, Trump had not bothered to read up on anything ahead of the meeting, but Chancellor Merkel's personal recounting of her experiences, looking at things from the other side of the Berlin Wall, grabbed his attention. We all could have been blown up in both the West and the East, she said, but the INF saved the day. Trump, for once, agreed on closer coordination. Angela Merkel struck a chord by channeling the 1980s for Eighties Man.

The INF episode was one of the bright spots in my time at the NSC — as strange as that may seem, given the fact that this was the withdrawal from what had been such an important arms-control treaty for forty years — and one that assuaged my fears of having to throw myself in a ditch during a ballistic missile strike. But this bright spot was small and lost in the general gloom that followed, in what would be my last year at the NSC.

When I had started out, one of my close colleagues and mentors at Brookings, Martin Indyk, had given me a piece of important advice. He had taken on the thankless and even futile task of stepping into the breach as the U.S. special envoy for Israeli-Palestinian negotiations from July 2013 to June 2014. He had been asked to assume the role unexpectedly. Having also served as NSC senior director for Near East and South Asian affairs, U.S. ambassador to Israel, and assistant secretary for the Near East, Martin knew that the odds of reaching a peace agreement were slim. He put them at around 6 percent. He concluded that it was worth the attempt, so he would take a leave from Brookings but would give himself a limited timeframe. If he got nowhere in six months to a year, he would resign and return. The key, Martin told me, was "to see if you can be part of a solution, not just part of a problem." He advised me to take the same approach. I decided to give myself two years — if I wasn't sacked or pushed out in the meantime. The two years would be up in April 2019.

By the beginning of 2019, not long after the meeting in Argentina, it looked like I was headed toward becoming part of a problem, not a solution. Things began to go off the rails at the NSC. This was when the events leading up to Trump's firing of the U.S. ambassador to Ukraine, Marie (Masha) Yovanovitch, drew my attention. This scandal further highlighted and underscored the problems inherent in personalized populist politics. It revealed the deep and troubling ways in which Trump was susceptible to influence. And eventually it would drag me into the spotlight too.

12

Off with Their Heads

The affair that would lead to the first impeachment of Donald Trump began innocuously enough, at least from my perspective. At first we got a few odd calls from political lobbyists implying that Ambassador Yovanovitch was an "Obama holdover" who was trying to undermine the president. We brushed it off, thinking that it was just more of the same — the usual machinations swirling around the White House as well as political intrigues in Ukraine itself. Someone had it in for her, for sure, but we didn't think it would amount to anything. But the calls turned out to be just one tiny element in something quite pernicious and complicated that would not be fully explained until the first impeachment hearings and trial.

From my perspective, Masha was the victim of a long, drawn-out professional political mugging. It turned out that this had been directed since 2018 by two Ukrainian Americans, Lev Parnas and Igor Fruman, who had business interests in Ukraine that they thought she was blocking. The two were working closely with Rudy Giuliani, the president's personal lawyer, who was perpetrating the myth that the Ukrainian government had interfered in the 2016 election as a diversion from Russia's actual role. They were trying to come up with any kind of material that might help bolster the president's Helsinki diatribe about the DNC server that might have been bizarrely spirited away to Ukraine. And they were looking for compromising information on Joe Biden and his son, Hunter, who had been on the board of a Ukrainian energy company.

On April 30, 2018, Parnas and Fruman, who moved in Republican donor circles, were invited to a private dinner with President Trump in Washington, D.C., at the Trump International Hotel. Fruman recorded a video of the dinner, which Lev Parnas later handed over to the news media. The video captured Parnas and Fruman telling Trump that the U.S. ambassador in Kyiv was badmouthing him. Parnas suggested that Masha had actually been in Kyiv since the Clinton administration, even though her first ambassadorial postings had been under George W. Bush and she was not appointed to Ukraine until August 2016. She was supposedly causing a lot of problems, he said, walking around telling Ukrainians that Trump would be impeached.

Parnas's and Fruman's comments had no basis in fact whatsoever, but they got an instant and chilling response from Trump: "Get rid of her! Get her out tomorrow. I don't care. Get her out tomorrow. Take her out. Okay? Do it." Ambassador Yovanovitch had shamed him — or at least the idea of her saying something negative had shamed him. The fabricated comments made him lose face in front of White House insiders. He didn't question whether or not they were true. Parnas and Fruman were donors, they were in his peer circles, they were instantly believed — just as Putin would be at Helsinki a few months later. The object of offense, the U.S. ambassador in Ukraine, would have to be taken out.

It was clear from listening to the audio — which I did several times — that Trump didn't know who Ambassador Yovanovitch was, but this was the beginning of her professional demise. A straight line led from that dinner at the Trump International Hotel in April 2018 to President Trump's impeachment trial in the U.S. Senate in January 2020.

The video, when it was released, demonstrated just how easy it was for people to hand Trump a piece of bait to get him riled up and then push what they personally wanted — in this case, to get some obstacle (a U.S. ambassador) out of the way. I saw this repeatedly in my time at the NSC. People like Lev Parnas and Igor Fruman were simply manipulating Trump — trying to take some of his power for themselves. Trump was exquisitely vulnerable to this, given his fragile ego. He couldn't see their game.

Alice in Wonderland

If someone told Trump that another person had crossed him, he would immediately believe it. Then he would verbally bludgeon the source of perceived embarrassment to reassert his authority. He did this with world leaders as well. In one publicly captured incident, Trump railed against Canadian prime minister Justin Trudeau after a high-level summit, when it came to his attention that Trudeau had said something negative about him at a press conference. Shortly beforehand Trump had praised the prime minister. It was just like the episode in the Rose Garden with Prime Minister Tsipras.

Anyone who insulted Trump, in a real or perceived way, went on his "nasty list." And that person was headed for some kind of payback. In the July 2019 call with Ukrainian president Zelensky that eventually would precipitate his impeachment, President Trump noted that Ambassador Yovanovitch would "go through some things," even though she had already been fired at this juncture and had gone through plenty.

At times like this I felt like Alice in Wonderland watching the Queen of Hearts constantly calling "Off with his head!" or "Off with her head!" whenever someone displeased her. The children's author Lewis Carroll had family ties to County Durham, and I had been steeped in his books as a kid. Now I felt I was living them.

With all kinds of conspiracy theories swirling around, we constantly found ourselves going down rabbit holes. And the president was forever wanting people "taken out." Lewis Carroll had, as he put it, conceived of the Queen of Hearts as the representative of "ungovernable passion — a blind and aimless Fury." She "had only one way of settling all difficulties, great or small. 'Off with his head!' she said, without even looking around." That was essentially what Trump demanded of Masha Yovanovitch, equally reflexively: "Get rid of her! Off with her head!"

In four years Trump took off lots of heads. He churned through ambassadors, cabinet officials, and advisers, getting rid of anyone who crossed him or was said to have crossed him, installing loyalists in their place. He often bypassed Congress for extended periods to put acting officials in key positions. They would then be beholden to him to carry out what I called at the impeachment hearings "domestic political errands." The most obvious was Richard Grenell, whom Trump plucked from his ambassadorial post in Germany to act as director of national intelligence for a short period, with the assumed purpose of ferreting out information for the president to disprove "the Russia hoax." Acting officials were also installed at various junctures in the Pentagon, the Department of Homeland Security, and the Department of Justice, especially in the late stages of the presidency, on Trump's assumption that he could push them to clean out perceived enemies and do his bidding on overturning the election or blocking the transfer of executive power. Trump had the highest cabinet turnover of any contemporary U.S. president between January 2017 and 2021.

From my studies of the USSR, this turnover reminded me of Joseph Stalin's purges in the 1930s and 1940s, which had caught up figures large and small in their intensity. Stalin famously purged his entire officer class on the eve of World War II, leaving the military headless and reeling as Hitler invaded. Trump frequently called out the U.S. judiciary to go after his political opponents and "lock them all up."

Fortunately, American judges never did Trump's bidding on that score. But like Lev Parnas and Igor Fruman, American lobbyists and foreign governments soon learned that they could take down U.S. diplomats and other public servants whom they disliked for diligently pressing and holding U.S. policy lines, in the hope that they could then push their own replacement candidates. Many of these diplomats, and others who were targeted, were women, like Masha Yovanovitch. It was easier for Trump to dismiss women and see them as problems — women who got in the way. They were, after all, the "nonplayers in his world," as a senior administration official put it to the *New Yorker* journalist Adam Entous. And like these other "nonplayers," I too found myself in the crosshairs.

The Enemies List

In addition to his "nasty list," President Trump had a lengthy roster of political enemies, many of them more imagined than real. He and his political team conjured them to stoke controversy, exacerbate existing societal divisions, and mobilize his base. As in the case of all populists, Trump's politics were framed around "us" against "them." With the help of Fox News and other pro-Trump media outlets, enemies were fabricated in the broadest possible brushstrokes: a mishmash of Democrats, liberals, globalists, radical socialists, Communists, Antifa leftists, the Black Lives Matter movement, the "mainstream media," the billionaire financier and philanthropist George Soros, various other bogeymen and -women, deep-state bureaucrats, and even congressional Republicans who were loyal to their party rather than to Trump personally. Often it was hard to keep up with the list. New enemies were added and new labels applied by those who claimed to support Trump inside and outside his political circles.

I ended up on the list with surprising speed in my first weeks on the job.

At the Trump White House, I learned that anything and anyone could become fodder for someone else's obscure personal or political game or for a complex conspiracy theory of the kind I had often studied in Russia. In the screeds of trolls on Twitter, I was labeled a "Democrat stooge," a "globalist," a "Soros Mole," a deep-state coup-plotting bureaucrat, a Never Trumper, and many other things besides.

My work on Russia had long made me a target for public and personal criticism. I wasn't sure that I was actually on Putin's enemies list, although thanks to the Putin book I might just as well have been. I wrote it after I was seated next to him at the 2011 Valdai dinner and thus rendered myself less of a nondescript woman than I had been. But I certainly popped up in all kinds of weird Russia-related postings on the internet. Even my seating assignment at the Valdai dinner inspired several internet conspiracy theories after I joined the National Security Council in 2017. Just what was it with me and Putin having dinner together?

So at first, when I joined the NSC, I tried to take the opprobrium in my stride. It wasn't that different really from my experiences in school. As adults, some people still seemed to relish bullying, especially if they could safely launch attacks on their targets from a distance by phone, mail, and email—and later Twitter. Since my debut in an American TV interview back at the Kennedy School in the 1990s, I had kept a file of letters and emails from people who took issue with something I said.

Sometimes my appearance itself was enough to cause offense—just the way I looked or sounded. I was out of place as a woman from the North East of England in the U.S. national security space. I once went back to my Brookings office after an appearance on C-Span to find a long diatribe on my answering machine from a woman in Georgia. She was outraged that a woman who looked and sounded like me would dare to appear on American television. After my November 2019 public testimony, a woman from Nevada wrote a similarly long note complaining about how I still talked "like a British person" rather than "an American," and who on earth had "chosen" me to become an American citizen?

All these writers asked the same general thing: What gave me the right to comment on anything? What made me an expert? None of these critics cared at all about qualifications, hard work, expertise, books written, if you were an affront to their views and opinions. Often, judging from the notes, something I said was misconstrued or taken out of context.

Initially I tried to respond, to see if I could correct the record and engage in a proper discussion. But most who wrote didn't want to engage. They were convinced I had some hidden agenda. Random connections would be parsed for meaning. Perhaps I was a British spy? A Russian double agent? As the daughter of a coal miner, surely I must be a Marxist or a Communist playing a long game of subversion?

Over thirty years I could see a pattern emerging: of groups of people latching on to conspiracy theories and refusing to be swayed no matter what contrary evidence was presented to them. The idea that someone might be just what they were on the surface, a nonpartisan national security professional trying to impart information and steer well clear of domestic politics, seemed less believable than a fantastically convoluted tale.

At the White House, the personal attention reached new levels. First someone produced a Wikipedia page for me in my initial month at the White House. I had never previously merited one, nor had I thought about creating one myself. There was plenty of Brookings Institution material on the internet. I was surprised. Who had been so "thoughtful"? Given the curation of the content — Trump calling me a secretary, my reported links with various enemies of the president — it was clear that someone had created it primarily to post derogatory material related to my time at the NSC. Shortly after the *Washington Post* story relating my May 2017 run-in with the president in the Oval Office came out, someone updated the Wikipedia page to highlight this under the title of "details of Hill's interactions with H. R. McMaster and Donald Trump." A couple of tech-savvy friends spotted the page and decided to keep an eye on it. One removed the paragraph and deleted it on the basis that this edit "intentionally presented Ms. Hill in an unfavorable light and was based on anonymous sources." A few months later, my mystery Wikipedia contributor was back, reposting the references as an "important biographical point" that provided information about my relationships inside the White House. Another friend discovered that the same anonymous contributor's username had been active elsewhere on Wikipedia at exactly the same time, adding suspiciously flattering material to the page of another NSC senior director and removing anything disparaging. My Wikipedia page was the digital equivalent of a rude note stuck on your school locker door or offensive graffiti about you inside the school bathroom stall.

Given how petty so much of this was, I tried to ignore it and get on with my work. But it was hard to ignore everything. In keeping with the typical, crudely gendered vitriol that women in public life endure, I received frequent phone messages at work from a woman calling me by name and referring to me with an unprintable term — the notorious c-word. The NSC security team traced the number to Palm Beach, Florida, home of some of President Trump's most ardent supporters. Every time an unknown number popped up at work, I would have to let it go to voicemail. Then the woman called our home. My daughter picked up. I refused to explain to her what the c-word meant, although I eventually had to after Adam Entous retold the story in *The New Yorker*.

As an aside, even in the pantheon of swear words in the North East of England, a place where swearing is routine, using that word will get you into trouble. Grandad Hill, who swore a lot, only ever used it once in my presence. He uttered it as he accidentally sliced a spade into his foot, digging through the hard-packed earth of his allotment. I was probably around seven or eight. I had no idea what it meant. I liked to try out new words whenever they seemed situationally appropriate, so when I cut my hand with a paring knife helping Mam in the kitchen, I went ahead. Mam never swore at all, but the fury of her response shocked me. She grabbed my head and washed my mouth out with the bar of green soap by the sink that we used for scrubbing the clothes. The soap caught in the gap between my front teeth. I was gagging. She was yelling, "Where did you hear that word? Who told you that? Don't you *ever* use that again!" I didn't dare say I'd heard it from Grandad and cause a family rift. I endured the punishment but made a mental note of the word's potentially severe reactions. Later, when I was a student in Scotland, on a visit to Glasgow with my sister, a man in a pub was savagely beaten after he deployed this word against another patron during an argument. This was a fighting term in the UK, so I had no illusions about the intent of those who used it against me in the United States.

"Soros Mole"

At the end of May 2017, I featured on *Infowars*, the website run by the notorious conspiracy theorist Alex Jones that ruined many an ordinary American's life by targeting them, including the grieving families of children killed in school shootings, which Jones declared "government hoaxes." I was excoriated by Jones and Trump's adviser Roger Stone in a lengthy segment in which they "unmasked" me as George Soros's mole in the White House. Apparently I was in cahoots with General McMaster in a plot against the president.

I eventually learned that this attack had originated with a former Republican congressman from Florida, Connie Mack. He was now a lobbyist working for Hungarian prime minister Viktor Orbán. Mack had sold me out to Roger Stone as part of his efforts to secure Orbán his meeting with President Trump in the Oval Office. Mack had even officially filed information on what he planned to do with the U.S. government in accordance with the Foreign Agent Registration Act (FARA). This act was passed in the 1940s to prevent representatives of Nazi Germany from covertly trying to influence members of the U.S. Congress and other public officials.

By the early 2000s, a FARA filing was a pro forma cover-your-ass exercise for U.S. lobbyists. People like Connie Mack could register their activities in a government database without any scrutiny or response, even if they were intending to damage the reputation of a public servant or government official. If a target complained about these activities after the fact, the lobbyist could point to the filing. The lobbyists were transparent. They had done nothing wrong. The filing outlined everything they intended to do. No one had tried to stop them (probably because no one from the government ever seemed to review the database), so therefore there was no problem.

The whole thing was perverse and preposterous and even more reminiscent of the kind of denunciations that Russians used to file against their enemies with the Soviet security services during Stalin's purges. A colleague sent me a link to Connie Mack's FARA filing. Mack had shown up for a meeting with the vice president's national security team shortly before the *Infowars* segment and proceeded to denounce me. He demanded that I be removed from my position. They were surprised and so was I. What had I done so early in my tenure to merit his ire? I had never even met the man.

I later learned that, based on an early congratulatory phone call between Orbán and Trump that Mack had facilitated, the Hungarians believed that Viktor Orbán would be one of the first European leaders to visit the White House. When the promised visit did not materialize, they wanted to know why. Mack thought someone must be blocking it. He presumed the problem must be in the White House, although meeting requests were also channeled through the State Department.

Mack started looking at the backgrounds of some of the staff and spotted me as the senior director for Europe. A quick look on the internet turned up my curriculum vitae on the Brookings website. Mack learned that up until 2006, I had served on advisory boards for Open Society Foundation (OSF) initiatives in the Caucasus and Central Asia. OSF was George Soros's philanthropic enterprise. The fact that this had been ten years ago was irrelevant. George Soros was by now the central feature of a right-wing conspiracy theory that had him orchestrating all kinds of left-wing political activities domestically and internationally. My previous employers — Harvard University, the Eurasia Foundation, and the Brookings Institution — also had various institutional ties to Soros-funded programs.

This was sufficient for Connie Mack. I was the source of the problem, so I had to be neutralized. He made his FARA filing, included my CV as proof, then proceeded to shop my information around town, telling everyone that I was doing Soros's bidding and trying to undermine President Trump *and* the entire country of Hungary.

In the aftermath of my appearance on *Infowars,* my sister, Angela, who tracked social media, counted hundreds of abusive and threatening comments against me and my family on Twitter and YouTube. She called me in alarm and advised me to "get out of the White House." She asked how I had managed to get myself from Bishop Auckland into the middle of all this. It clearly wasn't a normal or safe place to be. Angela also spent hours writing to the platforms' managers asking them to remove the threats and other inflammatory content. By now I kept away from social media, but this was certainly taking things up a notch from previous experiences. The internet had indeed become a perverse version of a perpetual middle or high school in a rough neighborhood where people traded insults and threats at the slightest provocation. In middle school you personally knew who you were dealing with. You could defend yourself one way or another. But here were hundreds of often anonymous strangers, egged on by Alex Jones and Roger Stone, calling for me to be harmed and even killed, with no accountability whatsoever.

Connie Mack was apologetic about the death threats, at least, when asked about them later by a reporter. I also got a card from the Hungarian ambassador, who realized things had gotten out of hand. Roger Stone, for his part, was completely unrepentant.

I now knew at first hand that this was the way that Trump and some (although not all) of the people in his circle pressed their agendas. They traded in disinformation and weaponized it, just like the Soviets had during the Cold War and Putin still did in Russia. "Soros Mole" was a particularly useful label. Once applied, it could bring someone down.

After the *Infowars* episode, I started to pay close attention to how "Soros Mole" was used. Others noticed too. In early 2019, while I was still at the

White House, *BuzzFeed News* published an article laying out the origins of the "Soros conspiracy." It had originated in 2008, when two prominent political consultants in New York, Arthur Finkelstein and George Birnbaum, were recruited by Viktor Orbán to assist his political campaign. They had previously worked for Israeli prime minister Bibi Netanyahu, who was friendly with Orbán. Netanyahu recommended them.

Finkelstein and Birnbaum decided they should create an external political enemy to help Orbán mobilize support for his bid to become Hungarian prime minister. They selected Soros, a prominent Hungarian Jew whose family had fled Budapest during the Holocaust. Soros was both famous and controversial, and still connected to Hungary. He funded a range of nonprofit organizations and educational institutions there and had even provided a scholarship for Orbán early in his career. It was not a complete stretch to suggest that Soros had now turned against Orbán and was trying to pull political strings to control the country from abroad, all for disreputable left-wing purposes.

The Soros ploy was successful. Orbán won the ballot and became prime minister. Soros became his permanent political foil, rolled out at every election. Finkelstein and Birnbaum then refreshed the Soros conspiracy for political figures elsewhere, including in the United States. Finkelstein was a political player in Republican Party circles and connected to Roger Stone. By 2016, Soros was also one of Trump's political enemies.

The Protocols of Conspiracy

No matter who invented the Soros conspiracy myth, its content and propagation followed the pattern of a classic, historical anti-Semitic conspiracy theory that was also specifically devised for political ends, *The Protocols of the Elders of Zion*. *The Protocols* was a fabricated document circulated in the early 1900s, outlining a long-running Jewish plot to subvert European governments. The basic ideas of the plot were pulled from a number of sources, including a pamphlet attacking Napoleon III in France in the 1860s. The document was often used as the basis for anti-Jewish purges and pogroms in czarist Russia. It was still widely in print in the West as well as in Russia. On a trip in the Russian provinces a few years earlier, I had seen copies for sale in church bookstores. I pointed out the parallels in my November 2019 testimony before Congress, explaining how all the accusations against George Soros and the anti-Semitic undertones were obvious to any historian of modern Europe. I had even discussed this directly with David Cornstein. He was a friend not only of Trump but also of Finkelstein from his days as a prominent New York jeweler. Ambassador Cornstein's mother's family, like Soros, were Hungarian Jews. I wondered why he didn't try to push back on the attacks against Soros, given the risks that this might get out of hand.

Ambassador Cornstein knew all about the origins of the Soros conspiracy. In fact, he confirmed the details in the *BuzzFeed* article for me. Soros's political activity in support of left-wing causes was the focus of the fabrication. It was just politics. Not serious, he said. It wasn't even particularly personal. Orbán had no reason to hate Soros. I noted that I had received death threats because of my long-ago association with Soros, which felt pretty personal at the time. There were hundreds, if not thousands, more threats against Soros on the internet, many referring to him as a Jew, and in October 2018 someone sent a pipe bomb to his house. Ambassador Cornstein conceded that this was unfortunate, of course, but Finkelstein and Birnbaum could hardly be to blame for other people's anti-Semitic attitudes. In Viktor Orbán's case, all he wanted was to be elected and reelected. The Soros conspiracy was ingenious, and it worked.

The Soros conspiracy was only one of many that Trump and others around him, like Alex Jones and Roger Stone, deployed for political mobilization. It was a useful tactical weapon against those on the enemies list. Historically, conspiracy theories have proven extremely useful for populists, revolutionaries, autocrats, and dictators in providing justifications for their actions. Any small detail or innocent association, combined with underlying societal grievances (inequality, distrust of government), political partisan divisions, and an economic crisis added in for good measure, can suddenly become part of an elaborate global plot. After World War I, *The Protocols of the Elders of Zion* was woven into Adolf Hitler's anti-Semitic Nazi fantasies and featured in *Mein Kampf* as part of the "big lie" that Jews had "stabbed Germany in the back" during World War I. President Trump was an early exponent of "birtherism," which posited that his predecessor, Barack Obama, had been born in Kenya, not the United States, and was therefore an illegitimate president. Then there was QAnon, a conspiracy with Trump at the center in the sense of the president combating a ring of child-trafficking pedophiles, led by Hillary Clinton, among others, and a shadowy group inside and outside the U.S. government.

The woman who left crude messages on my phone at the NSC gave herself away as a QAnon follower when she asserted, on several occasions, that the U.S. government was run by "deep-state pedophiles" and asked whether I knew I was working for them. Given the reach of the internet, the QAnon conspiracy quickly spread during Trump's term from the United States to Europe, securing thousands of adherents in places like the UK and Germany. Trump assisted the spread by appearing to endorse it, while others in his circle, including former national security adviser Mike Flynn, openly embraced it. Given General Flynn's background in intelligence and psychological operations while he was in the military, it was obvious to me that he saw the political utility of the conspiracy. But as a result of all this eagerness at the top to embrace fictional narratives for purely personal and domestic political purposes, the United States under Trump joined the historical pantheon of states promoting conspiracy theories. America was no different from Hitler's Germany or czarist, Soviet, and modern Russia. George Orwell's *1984* moment — of state manipulation of information to deceive and repress the population — came to fruition in 2016–2020 with the QAnon conspiracy and with Trump's eventual Big Lie — that he had won the presidential election.

Storming the Oval

Viktor Orbán's promotion of the Soros conspiracy and his attempts to get into the White House to see Trump were part of Orbán's personal political game. There was no upside for U.S. foreign policy or even for U.S.-Hungarian relations. It was simply what Orbán could get out of Trump. Like Parnas and Fruman, Orbán wanted to influence and exploit Trump. A meeting and a photo opportunity in the Oval Office alongside a fellow populist, the most powerful man in the world, Donald Trump, would boost Orbán's standing back home in Hungary. If Trump said "nice things" about Orbán and praised him, which he did, then even better. Orbán wanted the May 2019 visit purely for domestic purposes ahead of the European elections. His ambassador in the U.S. accidentally confessed this in an email to the NSC director who covered Hungary, thinking he had sent the message to someone else. Oval Office visits, and the photo ops pursued by Orbán and others, were the bane of our existence at the NSC. They were the stock-in-trade for Trump too. Irrespective of what the other people wanted for themselves, Trump loved schmoozing with world leaders. Having his photo taken with them put him in the center of attention at home and abroad.

One Albanian conservative party politician with aspirations for higher office went to great lengths to get a picture with the president. Having failed to get an audience through diplomatic channels, he showed up with a lobbyist in Wisconsin in June 2017 at a fund-raising event President Trump was attending for the local governor. The Albanian waited along the rope line with everyone else. Then he posted his picture with President Trump everywhere, making it look as if he were in Washington, D.C., on an official visit. At the NSC we received a formal complaint from the Albanian embassy asking why he had been shown preference. How had he gained access to the president at the White House without their knowledge? Other foreign politicians would call in chits with celebrities, not just lobbyists. Our office fielded surprise phone calls, forwarded through the White House switchboard, from random movie stars asking for their favorite prime minister or presidential friend in a certain European country (where they might recently have made a film) to visit President Trump.

We were hounded on all sides. The president's schedule was not in our hands. It was the purview of the chief of staff and the West Wing, although the national security adviser and the secretary of state would weigh in on high-level visits. When the meeting didn't occur or people didn't get what they wanted, we were targeted. There were many "Connie Macks," lobbyists and intermediaries with personal connections to Trump, his family, or someone else in his circle, who would complain about us to whoever they could reach in the West Wing. They were also quick to set an attack dog on us to rile up the internet trolls, because this always seemed to work. Ambassador Yovanovitch's dismissal from her position in early May 2019 became the ultimate proof of the concept. *Stand in the way and we will take you out.*

A handful of U.S. ambassadors who were in the president's inner circle, such as the ambassador to the European Union, Gordon Sondland, and Richard Grenell, the ambassador to Germany, followed the same pattern as Connie Mack and Lev Parnas and Igor Fruman. Their behavior epitomized the dangers of a hyperpersonalized populist presidency, in which U.S. national security interests could be superseded by political opportunists and clever sycophants. They courted the president to pursue their own priorities.

Ambassador Sondland was a hotel mogul and major donor to Trump's campaign. It was his first time in government. Ambassador Grenell had previously served at the State Department and the United Nations and had been a political and media consultant for several Republican campaigns. Both Sondland and Grenell told us that they had been directly tasked by the president to be his man in Europe, directing U.S. policy from Brussels and Berlin, respectively. They were following his explicit direction, they said. They didn't take their cues from the State Department. They were Trump's *personal* plenipotentiaries.

Sondland and Grenell always invoked Trump's name or those of members of his family when pulling rank. In addition to meetings with the president, they would demand that we set up meetings with the national security adviser for European politicians they were trying to impress. When Ambassador Bolton demurred on a meeting, they would play hardball, accusing NSC staff of blocking them. Ambassador Sondland gave some Romanian officials our personal cell-phone numbers and sent them to the White House gates to insist we make an appointment. He would also work his way around us through the chief of staff's office. As a major donor to the president's campaign, Sondland usually got an audience and what he wanted.

In one memorable call — which I had to write down and report in detail to Ambassador Bolton and other senior staff, given the fury, threat level, and pointed references to his personal relationship with the president — Ambassador Grenell came out swinging. He started with accusations and insults: We at the NSC were "not part of the team." We were peons, "nonissues" who were getting in his way. Our role was "low-level." We were supposed to set things up as instructed, not ask questions. He went on to accuse my office of leaking information to the press. Then he threatened to call Donald Trump Jr., a close friend of his, to have me and a colleague "sacked by tweet."

This was all provoked by Ambassador Bolton's initially declining to meet with a German politician favored by Grenell. Bolton wanted first to make sure the request followed diplomatic protocol and also came from the German embassy in Washington. Ambassador Grenell learned from a colleague that the director covering Germany had called the embassy. He didn't care that the director was following instructions from the national security adviser. Nor had he tried to call Ambassador Bolton directly himself to request the meeting.

Given Grenell's stated low opinion of me and my colleague, I wondered at first why he had bothered to call me. But it was abundantly clear that Grenell was simply livid that his personal agenda had been spotlighted and he wasn't immediately getting his own way. President Trump's personalization of the presidency and his hard-charging, no-holds-barred behavior was emulated by many of those around him in MAGA world.

Ambassador Grenell, among others, also suggested that I might be "Anonymous," the Trump administration staffer who wrote a 2018 op-ed criticizing the president and later a book detailing the political machinations in the administration. I was alerted to this by several U.S. ambassadors to Europe after a regional meeting organized by the American embassy in Lisbon a week after the publication of the op-ed. "Anonymous" revealed himself in late October 2020 to be Miles Taylor, the former chief of staff to the secretary of homeland security, Kirstjen Nielsen—a frequent target of Trump's misogyny. Like "Soros Mole," being framed as "Anonymous" was in the meantime used as a device to expel officials from the government and staff from the NSC. The accusations clung to me for the remainder of my time at the NSC. Eventually, during my closed-door deposition in Congress in October 2019, I put them to rest.

Not Part of the Team

Over the course of my more than two years in the White House, the NSC and its staff, along with career public servants across the U.S. government, were steadily reduced in stature by these relentless attacks and denunciations. Their professional roles and responsibilities were appropriated by Trump loyalists carrying out parallel foreign policy efforts behind the scenes, often for purely partisan political purposes or personal gain. It was strikingly reminiscent of the outcomes in populist regimes historically and internationally. And it made it extremely difficult to prevent the kind of privatization of national security that led to Trump's first impeachment, when he tried to use the Ukrainian president to target Joe Biden.

I got many reminders that most of the professional staff on the NSC were not considered part of Trump's team, as Ambassador Grenell had asserted. For instance, in my final week in the office, I learned that one of the women over in the West Wing, who liaised between the NSC and the Chief of Staff's Office, had now also called me the c-word. My crime was trying to push a set of policy issues during my last set of engagements at the G20 summit in Osaka, Japan, in late June 2019. They didn't need anyone acting with autonomy. They just wanted staff to shut up and do whatever the president wanted.

There were other, material ways in which this attitude toward the NSC staff manifested itself. When I had taken the job at the National Security Council in 2017, money certainly had not been a factor in my decision. I knew I would have to take a pay cut by being back in government, but I did not anticipate how severe that would be. Given the rank and responsibilities of the senior director position, I presumed the pay would be in the range of the Senior Executive Service salaries at the National Intelligence Council. I supposed that I might be paid approximately the same as I had been a decade earlier. This turned out not to be the case.

Ultimately, at the Trump White House, politics and personal connections were more important than qualifications, experience, and previous government service. The higher SES-level-equivalent salaries went to President Trump's West Wing staff and political appointees. At the NSC, the incoming salaries for professional staff like myself, who were hired directly but had not been on Trump's presidential campaign, were capped at lower levels. This was not specifically gender-related, as it had been in other settings. Much younger women in Trump's inner circle were awarded higher salaries. The NSC's operating budget was also constrained, and I was told up front that nothing would be open to negotiation. In the spirit of public service, I wondered if it might even be better to consider forgoing a salary entirely. I figured I could manage for the two years I had signed up for, since my husband was working full-time in the private sector, but the NSC wouldn't allow it. The human resources department informed me that this would mean I was essentially giving a gift to the government.

Unexpectedly, in my very last weeks at the NSC, before I departed in July 2019, I got a significant pay raise. This pushed the level up to what I had initially anticipated. I was told that I would be paid at this rate for July and August, while I used up my vacation days. I was surprised. I wondered why the NSC would bother to boost my salary as I was on my way out the door. This was outside the normal readjustment period and the government's fiscal year. Something was afoot.

As with my experience at Brookings in 2005, a contact in the human resources office told me quietly that my male successor had negotiated a higher salary. He had played the usual male hardball. He would not take the job unless he was paid more. He was far more politically connected than I was, but his higher salary would also create a discrepancy for some of the other senior directors, who were NSC direct hires and staying on. This group included at least one woman with seniority and experience similar to mine, who had often complained about the low salary. We had frequently discussed the pay gap between the NSC and the West Wing and the way things like this tended to play out for women in general. The salary change would eventually become public after I left. It would certainly not look good when people spotted the difference. So, thanks to a man's successful negotiation, everyone's pay boat floated higher.

This was not the only way in which the working environment at Trump's White House was unfavorable to professional and government employees, and to "nonplayer" women. When I got to the White House as a working mother, life became very difficult. I juggled long, unpredictable hours and child care. My daughter was ten when I started. My husband traveled for work at least four days a week every week. I was fortunate that we had a longtime babysitter who could step in while I was at work and my daughter was not in school, but there were many times when I found myself scrambling at the last minute to cobble something together. I could afford to cover child care and emergencies, but some of my younger NSC colleagues with small children really struggled. When I was at the NIC, on a couple of occasions just after my daughter was born, I had to take her into the office after I was summoned in the middle of the night or the early hours of the morning. Babies were permitted past security. Colleagues who were parents were only too happy to step in for a moment while I dealt with a crisis. That was not an option at the White House.

The most ironic and jarring aspect of my time as a working mother in the NSC was that the president's daughter Ivanka held the portfolio over at the West Wing covering women's empowerment and issues affecting working families. Ivanka's qualifications for this position as special adviser to the president appeared to be the facts that, first, she was a woman; second, she had children; third, she had worked for her father and set up her own fashion line (drawing on family funds); and finally, she had written a book, *Women Who Work*.

Ivanka's book, which was published in early 2017, just as I joined the NSC, appeared quite frequently in our collective workplace. Guests to the White House, including international visitors, would bring a copy for Ivanka to sign. I used these occasions to flick through it. The book was a glossy self-branding exercise. It was pitched as a self-help or self-actualization book for the well-heeled. It focused on work-life balance from Ivanka's perspective, and featured essays from businesspeople and political figures in her orbit. It was a small portal into the lives of the rich and famous, but not of much help for anyone else. Even for the women working around Ivanka at the

NSC and the White House, her life and work experiences could not have been more different. Ivanka Trump was the most unlikely role model for the average American working mother. No one could reasonably ever aspire to have her opportunities, or her child-care assistance.

Government Steelworkers

Indeed, hidden away at the White House, the NSC staff were less like Ivanka Trump and more like the steelworkers who had clustered around her father in the Roosevelt Room in March 2018 to watch him sign the tariff proclamation against cheap steel and aluminum imports. We shared the same family backgrounds and the same aspirations for a meaningful job; we frequently endured similar struggles. So it was a tragedy that in rallying workers like these around his personal cause, Trump turned them against workers like us.

Many of my NSC colleagues had gone to college on the back of their parents' American dream. They had been inspired to enter public service after participating in a middle or high school civics education trip to Washington, D.C., or by a visit to the office of their local member of Congress on Capitol Hill. The terrorist attacks of September 11, 2001, had spurred several colleagues to pursue a career in national security or join the military. Some had come into the government after being recruited by the army from a main-street office in their hometown right out of high school. Others had joined the military in college or came from families with a tradition of military service. Many had served decades in the armed forces, been deployed overseas, and fought in Iraq and Afghanistan. They still wanted to serve their country as civilians after retirement. There were numerous immigrants like me, and refugees from war-torn countries, all naturalized citizens who wanted to give something back to the country that had offered them the opportunity for a new life.

The backgrounds of those in my office were emblematic: kids of low-income workers who got government grants and other college scholarships, middle-class kids whose fathers had blue-collar trade union jobs and who were the first in their family in a white-collar profession, and one who grew up on a family cattle ranch in Utah, the first in generations to leave the range and go into national security. In every case my colleagues had parents and grandparents like the steelworkers' who were proud of them for their achievements. NSC staff were from all over the United States — they had come to Washington to work. Most of them weren't born in the nation's capital, even though they were now raising their families in the region.

In all of these ways and more, my colleagues at the NSC and elsewhere in the U.S. government were a stark contrast with the First Family. The Trumps were celebrities who claimed the popular touch. Those who worked behind the scenes were the true representatives of "the people" and the diversity and desires of Americans. The government employees and public servants I worked with at the NSC, and earlier at the NIC, were not Trump's so-called swamp. Nor were they part of some geographically concentrated, self-perpetuating bureaucratic caste or faceless elite that was out of touch with the rest of the country, where they had been born and where their relatives still lived.

Americans don't normally see their public servants in action on TV, featured on the front pages of newspapers, or depicted in films unless something has gone wrong—as at the first impeachment hearings in October and November 2019, when so many of us were subpoenaed to testify. Some of my colleagues got letters and emails from their families and friends after the public testimonies telling them that it was now clear what they were doing at work. They had often wondered. The first impeachment process was essentially a big civics exercise for those who watched it unfold and who read through the depositions.

The people I worked with at the NSC, including some of the political appointees, were neither partisan nor ideologically constrained. They were pragmatic and operational, focused on accomplishing the mission. But they had to contend with the fact that since the 1960s, popular appreciation and respect for government service and public servants had steadily declined in the United States. This made them easy targets for populist opprobrium from President Trump and others in MAGA world.

In an April 2019 Pew poll, the vast majority of respondents expressed negative views of public servants, and only 17 percent indicated that they trusted the federal government "to do the right thing." Misconceptions about the federal government and its individual agencies, like the idea that the U.S. government is vast and unwieldly, became deeply entrenched in American society in the early 2000s. Those who described themselves as Republicans in surveys were far more likely than supporters of the Democratic Party to favor shrinking the government. Trump tapped into these sentiments during his political campaign when he launched rhetorical attacks on the government apparatus and called for the "deconstruction of the administrative state." This was a pet issue of Steve Bannon, one of his early policy advisers, but Trump fully embraced it.

In 2018–2019, President Trump forced a government shutdown in a fight with Congress over the budget. It was another of his big shows. He figured that the federal government and its funding were easy political targets that would not elicit much public sympathy. He said he was taking Congress to task on behalf of "the American people," in his depiction of the motivation for the shutdown. But his actions ultimately hurt real American people — government workers on low salaries and Americans across the country dependent on federal government payments and services.

More than 60 percent of affected federal workers reported exhausting their savings during the shutdown, which was the longest in U.S. history. It extended for thirty-five days, from December 22, 2018, to January 25, 2019. Eight hundred thousand employees from nine federal government departments were put on either furlough or compulsory work without pay, along with four million government contractors who had hours cut or projects put on hold. The shutdown stopped the disbursement of federal grants, loans for small businesses, and Internal Revenue Service rebate checks. Small companies dependent on government orders and employee patronage lost daily business. Essential employees from agencies such as the Transportation Security Administration (TSA) and the coast guard — some of whom were detailed to the NSC — had to work without compensation.

I was deemed "essential," so during the shutdown I worked without pay. I was one of the lucky ones with savings as well as a working spouse. Like many other Americans, most federal government workers, including many single mothers, lived from paycheck to paycheck and were the sole breadwinners for their families. Most of my colleagues were deeply distressed by the way they were treated during the shutdown, as well as by the president's constant depiction of government employees as an unaccountable privileged elite feeding off the rest of the country.

"Just Upset About Everything"

By fall 2019 — a year that began with the government shutdown, and for me had initially seemed to culminate with my summer departure from the NSC — I had started to fear that the U.S. was stuck in a period of profound and dangerous disruption. It was not just that Trump was embarrassing our country in press conferences abroad and playing a tin-pot dictator at home. It was that the disaffection, decay, and divisions that had given rise to Trump and the MAGA phenomenon were getting worse. They threatened to corrode the infrastructure of our democracy, affecting not just the oft-maligned government steelworkers but also the support struts themselves.

On October 14, as a prelude to the November 21 public testimony ahead of the first impeachment trial, I participated in a closed-door deposition with a small group of Republican and Democratic members of Congress. Republican congressman Matt Gaetz from Florida, who was not part of the committee holding the hearings, burst in before we got started. He took up a prominent position at the far end of the table from me, the witness. Gaetz was sitting opposite the congressman from my home district in Maryland, Jamie Raskin, who would go on to play a prominent role as one of the managers of Donald Trump's second congressional impeachment trial, in January 2021.

The Democratic members of the committee protested Gaetz's presence. He insisted that he had the right to sit there to observe a "secret political show trial" hidden behind closed doors and to protect the interests of the president. In fact several of President Trump's stalwart congressional supporters were at the table, not least Ohio congressman Jim Jordan, who was leading the grilling of the witnesses. And there was certainly nothing secret about the proceedings. The press was everywhere. Even while we were in session, they seemed on top of what was going on. I never left the room, apart from an escorted bathroom break and then a lunch break, nor did Lee Wolosky and Sam Ungar, on my legal team. But members of Congress from both parties went in and out, evidently filling people in. By the time I got home late that evening, everyone seemed to know what I had said.

The impeachment managers sent someone to consult with Congress's nonpartisan rule-keeper, the Office of the Parliamentarian. It took a long while for them to come back with a procedural note that instructed Gaetz to leave the room. In the meantime he fixed me with a baleful stare. Gaetz was almost twenty years younger than me. I had not met him before, as was the case even with my congressman, Jamie Raskin. Gaetz clearly had no idea who I was, nor did he care. I was a witness who might have something to say that could damage the president, and in looking me quickly up and down, he decided that I was just some middle-aged female bureaucrat to intimidate. I stared right back and kept his gaze. This was ridiculous. Were we back in school or in the U.S. Congress? Did he even care what any of this was about?

After a while Gaetz dropped his eyes. I kept looking at him, watching and observing what he was up to. He was cocky, cavalier. This was all a big game. First he picked up some copies of newspapers at the end of the table, *The Hill* and *Politico*. He made a show of perusing them, although it was clear that he wasn't reading. He was ostentatiously signaling to me that I wasn't worth the effort. I was nobody. Then he engaged Jamie Raskin in an awkward discussion of the best restaurants to go to in Chevy Chase, an up-scale part of Congressman Raskin's district straddling the border between Maryland and Washington, D.C. Gaetz never looked up and back at me again. Eventually the word came that he should go, and off he went. Gaetz later held up the deposition of Pentagon official Laura Cooper in the same fashion for hours on end. Presumably he had by then perfected his shtick for staying around.

When the deposition finally got started after Gaetz's interruption, it lasted about ten hours. Coming out of those hearings, I was shocked at the zero-sum nature of U.S. partisan politics. I had been subjected not just to intense questioning but to political grandstanding and posturing. In addition to Congressman Gaetz's disruptive antics, some other members of Congress were in part falsely trying to claim that the government of Ukraine, not Russia, had intervened in the 2016 election. In their version of events, the Ukrainians had purportedly done so in support of Hillary Clinton. This spurious scenario was part of the congressional Republican defense of President Trump that would be presented a month later at the November public hearings and in the actual January impeachment trial.

The full transcript of my deposition, all 446 pages of it, including the Gaetz episode, was released in early November. On the assumption that most people would not have the fortitude to plow through hundreds of pages before the public hearings, I called out and repudiated the "alternative narrative" in my opening statement.

At the public hearings in Congress on November 21, I was there as a fact witness because of who I was professionally and what I did in government. Nonetheless, because I was a woman, my legal team's PR guru, Molly Levinson, stressed that how I looked would be an important element of how I presented myself and how people would approach my testimony. Indeed, the fact that I was a woman became a central feature in one memorable moment of my testimony, which touched on the double standards women face in the workplace. It summed up my experience at the NSC and in the closed-door deposition.

Trump's ambassador to the European Union, Gordon Sondland, testified publicly a few days before me. In his closed-door deposition ahead of the public testimony, Ambassador Sondland alleged that I had been "pretty emotional" in a meeting with him at the NSC. He also asserted that I had railed against the president and others and "was just upset about everything."

Based on the deposition transcript, which I carefully read through with Lee Wolosky and Sam Ungar ahead of my public appearance, it was clear that Sondland had conflated several meetings with me over our time working together. He never took notes in our meetings, so this was hardly a surprise. But I had in fact been particularly frustrated with him in our penultimate meeting a few months before, in July, before I left the NSC.

By the time of that meeting, it had become clear that U.S. national security policy toward Ukraine was going off the rails. Ukraine was not technically part of Ambassador Sondland's portfolio, yet he was seemingly involved in all kinds of meetings on Ukraine behind the scenes that he was not filling us in on. I pressed him for information. He demurred, telling me he was keeping the president, the chief of staff, the secretary of state, and the national security adviser in the loop. Why did he then have to tell me or anyone else what he was doing?

I was angry with Ambassador Sondland precisely because he was *not* telling us — at the NSC and at the State Department — what he was doing. In theory at least, Sondland was part of a team of people at his level (which included me and the assistant secretary of state for Europe), and he had a responsibility to fill us in. I pointed out that he could not reasonably expect the people at the very top of the government that he was keeping in the loop to turn around and immediately tell the rest of us what he was up to and why. I stressed the importance of coordination with all the officials working on Ukraine across the U.S. government, and I warned Ambassador Sondland that things could get out of hand and blow up in his face if he was in fact freelancing.

I had related this testy encounter in my own closed-door deposition on October 14, but it was not until the public testimony, once all the depositions were released and everyone had given their statements, that I fully understood what had been going on. While ostensibly I had been overseeing Ukraine policy at the NSC, Ambassador Sondland and others were, as I put it at the time, performing "a domestic errand" for President Trump. They were not freelancing; they were operating a parallel policy channel to persuade the Ukrainian government to announce investigations into Joe and Hunter Biden's purported activities in Ukraine. This had nothing whatsoever to do with American foreign policy. It was directly tied to President Trump's 2020 reelection bid and the fact that Joe Biden was likely to be his main competitor.

In the public testimony, I was asked by congressional Republican counsel Steve Castor about Ambassador Sondland's characterization of me as "emotional" and "upset." The question was framed with the clear intent of undermining me professionally and casting doubt on my credibility and thus my assessment of events. And having read through Ambassador Sondland's closed-door interview, I was obviously already on my guard. In his deposition, Sondland was very clearly trying to brush off my legitimate frustration with his conduct. He suggested that I was generally angry with everyone rather than specifically annoyed at him. In other words, Sondland was rejecting the idea that he could possibly have done something wrong.

The lawyer's question tapped into an ugly stereotype about my gender. Women are frequently deemed emotional or upset when they try to be as direct as men are in a given situation. I had learned long ago that women can't get away with showing "situational anger." It's immediately dismissed and labeled: "Oh, you're in a bad mood! What's wrong with you?" When I was younger, I was even asked if I was having my period if I directly criticized or challenged a man's actions: "What's the matter? Is this your time of the month, sweetie?" (Trump famously made the same comment about Fox News host Megyn Kelly. In an August 2015 interview, she pressed him on his history of misogynistic and sexist remarks. She had "blood coming out of her wherever," he said later, dismissing Kelly's comments and creating a media scandal.)

Women, moreover, are rarely given their due for holding their own in a debate or expressing themselves firmly. Being called "the Russia bitch" was just another example. Men use anger strategically. It's a show of strength in the workplace as well as in normal life. Men's anger is accepted and praised. Women's anger is not.

So I explained this whole situation to Castor and the committee as succinctly as I could: "To be honest I *was* angry with him . . . I hate to say it, but often when women show anger, it's not fully appreciated. It's often . . . pushed onto emotional issues, or perhaps deflected onto other people." With this comment, I suddenly found myself elevated to female icon status, both for speaking up and for offering a firsthand observation on the dynamic that plays out between men and women in the workplace. But I didn't feel like a female icon on November 21, 2019, or on most other days working at the NSC.

As one of a limited number of women in the national security field, I had always found it wearing to be the only woman in the room in the years before I went to the White House. Like most women, I was talked over and disregarded in professional settings. Gordon Sondland was one of many in a long line to dismiss or downplay what I had to say, purely based on my gender.

By this juncture, after my time in the White House and everything that had transpired in the months since I left, I wasn't just angry; I also was deeply concerned. America's postindustrial decline and dearth of opportunity — and its consequence: populist, partisan domestic politics — had become an obvious national security threat. If nothing was done to stop our political infighting and bridge the partisan divides, the United States would be perpetually vulnerable to the kind of operations that the Russian security services had launched in 2016 to disrupt our democratic processes. All any hostile state or nonstate actor would have to do was exploit what Americans were doing to fellow Americans in the name of domestic politics.

As it turned out, America would soon be overrun by a deadly enemy — one that would target our weakened country and prey on its divided people, regardless of which side of the chasm they were on. But it would not be the kind of opponent that I had in mind during my impeachment testimony.

13

The Horrible Year

In the immediate aftermath of President Trump's first impeachment trial came more vulnerabilities. Without any doubt, 2020 was a horrible year — and not just because of dramatic political upheavals that were bookended by two presidential impeachments.

January 2020 saw a novel coronavirus, COVID-19, turn into a global pandemic. It was the worst health crisis in a century, since the influenza pandemic of 1918. Other emergencies exacerbated and magnified its effects. The year was marked by the largest number of hurricanes on record battering the Gulf Coast and the Caribbean. There were widespread wildfires in California, droughts and floods across other parts of the country. On occasions it had an apocalyptic feel. Some unfortunate cities and regions, including some of the United States' poorest communities, got hit by different natural disasters multiple times.

This was a harbinger of difficult times ahead. Indeed, public health officials, scientists, and other analysts had warned for decades that we were in danger of a repeat of 1918. In a few years or decades, this *annus horribilis* of 2020 might not look so unusual, they said.

The coronavirus's apparent jump from an animal host to humans somewhere around Wuhan in China was perhaps just one consequence of environmental degradation as mankind continued to encroach on global ecosystems. Climate change further raised the specter of a permanently shifting Rust Belt across America — a swath of economic blight and urban decay that would no longer be confined to the country's former industrial regions. As some places in the United States became more risky or difficult to live in because of rising sea levels and more frequent catastrophic "weather events," people would have to move. This would compound the dislocation from deindustrialization and economic downturns since the 1980s and put new demographic pressure on regions and resources outside the climate danger zones. The surge in illegal immigration across the southern border from places like Guatemala and Honduras was already a warning sign, as people fled regions devastated by myriad hurricanes and laid waste by years of drought, where they could no longer subsist on small-scale farming.

In 2020, I went from sheltering in place for months at home in preparation for the impeachment process to sheltering in place at home in the collective effort to stem the transmission of the disease. In early March my day job as a senior fellow at the Brookings Institution became virtual, and it remained so extending through 2021. This, paradoxically, gave me time to contemplate the situation we were all in together and gave me space to write this book.

I was immediately struck by how much the U.S., the UK, and Russia, the three countries that had defined my personal and professional life, now resembled each other in their failure to mount a serious, well-coordinated response to dealing with the pandemic. All three countries had some of the world's highest levels of COVID-19 infection and devastating death rates among citizens and frontline health-care workers — as did other countries with populist politics and leaders, such as Brazil and India. In all of these places, scientific experts were drowned out by posturing populist politicians. Public health took a back seat to the exigencies of personalized politics. Political divisions became chasms over even the most basic medical advice, such as wearing masks and maintaining physical distance to slow the spread of the disease. Even the development of vaccines, such as Russia's Sputnik V, became an opportunity to play great power geopolitics rather than just focusing on getting people vaccinated.

Fast on the heels of the pandemic in the United States came the May 25, 2020, murder of George Floyd in Minneapolis. Floyd's death, his neck pressed beneath the knee of a police officer during a heavy-handed arrest, sparked nationwide protests against police brutality and highlighted the continued persecution of Black Americans decades after the civil rights movement. The United Kingdom was also swept up in the Black Lives Matter protests, as a younger generation of Brits contemplated the integral role the UK had played in the Atlantic slave trade and its own history of racism and heavy-handed policing.

Again I was struck by how inadequate the government-level responses were to address this painful and complex issue, especially against the backdrop of the coronavirus, which hit Black and other minority communities hard in both countries. In Russia, Vladimir Putin — faced with his own domestic problems, including the rampaging coronavirus and a growing opposition movement — did not waste an opportunity to comment on the situation and to criticize the United States for mishandling race relations. He was clearly only too happy to be able to divert the Russian public's attention away from deficiencies at home to debacles abroad.

Although I knew that things could always get worse, it was easy to think that we had reached the apogee of populism at home and abroad. In the Trump years, and especially in Trump's final year in office, the three countries that had shaped my personal and professional lives had reached a specific juncture where their fates completely intersected and entwined. All three had faced the challenges of managing major economic and technological shifts and had had to deal with the political consequences of postindustrial decline. Prime among those political consequences: governments seemingly without the interest or ability to solve the deadly serious challenges of the twenty-first century.

Since the 1980s and 1990s, large portions of the British, Russian, and American populations had found themselves stuck in hollowed-out towns and regions in their equivalent Rust Belts. In the case of Russia, millions were literally left out in the cold in frigid Siberian towns and cities thousands of miles from anywhere else. The despair that ravaged the three countries' forgotten places after decades of wrenching transition had fed populism and authoritarianism and undermined democracy. Lost generations in all three countries foresaw nothing but persistent disadvantage and lack of opportunity and wanted someone, preferably some strongman, to fix things for them with a series of bold moves.

The strongmen had arrived, but the rest of the populist dream had gone unfulfilled. And now life was upended. Everyone was imperiled by a deadly disease. The global pandemic was another shock to fragile systems, a negative force multiplier that compounded preexisting problems. If ever there was proof that the decline of opportunity posed an existential threat, this was it.

The Populists' Pandemic

Populist governments are, almost by definition, ill-suited to handle complex problems of governance. Style, swagger, and atmospherics, superficial and simplistic solutions, and enthusiastic sloganeering form the core of the populist's playbook — and are the antithesis of the toolkit needed to deal with a deadly pandemic.

To reach the levels of logistical organization required for implementing mass testing and other public health policies, as well as rolling out a nationwide vaccination program, a government must be methodical. It has to plan ahead, let seasoned experts take the lead, and pull people together around a clear set of goals and messages. Combating the coronavirus could not be done in an ad hoc manner, relying on a loose coalition of friends, family, and loyalists and pitting people against each other. It would take real leadership, and that was one thing that populists seemed wholly uninterested in providing.

Against the backdrop of high political drama, the United States hit a grim set of milestones over the course of the year. By Inauguration Day in January 2021, four hundred thousand Americans had died of COVID-19. Almost twenty-five million people had contracted the coronavirus, and close to two hundred thousand more were infected daily. This tragic trajectory would worsen over many more months until the advent of mass vaccination efforts in 2021.

This tsunami of infection and death was the consequence of the Trump administration's systematic dismissal of the gravity and extent of the pandemic, which the government's own watchdog agency, the General Accounting Office (GAO), pointed out in a damning 346-page report. The GAO report revealed that only 10 percent of its recommendations to address critical gaps in the medical supply chain had been implemented by the time Trump left office. Urgent action was still needed on this and multiple other fronts to deal with the "greatest public health pandemic in a hundred years."

In a negative report from the Lancet Commission in early 2021, the commission cochairs asserted that as many as 40 percent of U.S. deaths from COVID-19 in 2020 could have been prevented through better public health measures. They also laid part of the blame for the high mortality rate on the deterioration of the U.S. health system in the previous two decades and on the increase in America's socioeconomic and spatial inequalities. The commissioners noted that the United States' long-standing failure to provide full health insurance coverage for the American population, and Trump's efforts to weaken the Affordable Care Act since 2016, had all contributed to the impact of the pandemic.

Trump followed the same pattern on the pandemic that he had on foreign policy. In January 2021, Dr. Anthony Fauci, the director of the National Institute of Allergy and Infectious Diseases at the National Institutes of Health, and an adviser to several American presidents since the 1980s, gave an extensive interview to the *New York Times*. Dr. Fauci described in detail what it had been like to work with President Trump on the White House Coronavirus Task Force. He related experiences that were very similar to mine at the NSC in trying to work on national security issues.

Trump had been as dismissive of the U.S. government's medical experts as he was of other career professionals. He sought to remain the center of attention, push the government bureaucracy aside, downplay the virus, and play up his own "take charge" actions. Not wanting to appear weak, he refused to wear a mask in public and relentlessly made fun of anyone around him who did — even after he, his wife, his youngest son, and dozens of White House staffers contracted the virus in October. Similarly, the president solicited advice from friends and took their opinions, or whatever he heard on Fox News, more seriously than his advisers' recommendations on stemming transmission, treating the virus, and dealing with the overall crisis.

Dr. Fauci recounted how he had first been invited to the White House and told to "bring my white coat and stand there as he [President Trump] signed an executive order regarding something about influenza." Just like everyone else — be they a steelworker, a military general, or one of the West Wing Fox News–clone women staffers — Dr. Fauci was supposed to appear in costume. He had to look the part of a Central Casting medical doctor and take part in one of Trump's populist big shows.

At times Trump's press conferences on the pandemic took on the same qualities as the agony at the 2018 Helsinki summit with Putin. During one particularly mortifying event in April, Trump (having as usual paid little attention to his briefing materials) stoked public outrage by appearing to suggest that bleach could be injected to kill the virus. His comments on the virus and the means of combating it produced the same kind of word fog as his pronouncements on other topics, with the original meaning lost in transmission.

When the president offered this ludicrous suggestion on live television, the pained expression on the face of Dr. Deborah Birx, another professional member of the task force based at the White House, was captured vividly on camera. Her stricken look immediately brought back memories of my predicament at Helsinki. I wondered if she too was contemplating staging a fake medical emergency. But of course Dr. Birx was in the middle of a real one.

The consequences of this and other coronavirus press conferences that Trump botched were even more dire than Helsinki had been. At least a handful of people reported attempting to dose themselves prophylactically with sometimes toxic compounds seemingly endorsed by the president. As a result, Dr. Fauci found himself constantly having to correct the president to make sure that the American population received the appropriate public health message.

Before long, Dr. Fauci ended up not just on the "nasty list" but on the enemies list for crossing the president. Other people, loyalists with skimpy credentials for dealing with infectious diseases, were brought in to supersede him. Dr. Fauci was discouraged from giving public comments. He received death threats on the internet. An envelope filled with white powder was sent to his office. He had to be sprayed down by a hazmat team as a precaution. His wife and children were harassed with phone calls. Everything that I had experienced, Dr. Fauci suffered with more intensity. In the end he had to have a permanent security detail.

In many respects, the White House's approach to the pandemic had been prefigured at the very beginning of the Trump administration. In his 2018 book *The Fifth Risk,* the American author Michael Lewis recounted a series of interviews he had conducted with public servants as the outgoing Obama administration attempted to pass on information and responsibility to the incoming Trump team during the formal transition period in 2016–2017. Career officials and some of Obama's team told Lewis that most of the Trump appointees had little, if any, interest in learning what others had done or how the institutions they were taking over worked. They were determined to wing it. They thought they could simply start from scratch, steeped in the belief that every administration could approach ongoing issues as a blank slate — and in any case, "the other guys were idiots."

Lewis catalogued the five major things that career officials and appointees from the prior administration worried could go wrong. The fifth risk in the list was the one that proved the most prescient and consequential during the pandemic in 2020: incompetence and the failure of project management.

Trump's Slow-Motion Coup

Eventually Trump left office too. But before he did, for four years his supporters were duped. They were fed conspiracies and lies — on the internet, on social media platforms, and in speeches, interviews, and other public pronouncements — about the supposed actions of his enemies. Even the basic facts of events that could easily be documented and refuted by others were the subject of falsehoods, beginning with the size of the crowd at Trump's January 2017 inauguration.

The president told so many lies so often that it was more surprising when he told the truth. One of his top political consultants, Kellyanne Conway, referred to the president's lies as "alternative facts." The small lies gained the credence of truth when they were voiced by the president of the United States — especially for his voters. They paved the way for the Big Lie, Trump's whopper: the contention that "his enemies" had perpetrated a colossal voter fraud. Joe Biden had stolen the November 2020 election; he, Trump, actually had won. The people — his millions of followers — needed to rise in protest and take their country back. For him.

President Trump's time in the White House, the American people's house, came to an ignominious end in January 2021. In the course of a little over a year, Trump careened from one impeachment trial to another, becoming the first president in the history of the United States to be impeached twice by the U.S. Congress. Both impeachments were related to his attempts to stay in power for a second term. In the first, the president was caught behind the scenes trying to use foreign actors to harm a primary political opponent. In the second, the whole country watched him openly incite domestic actors to overturn the results of the 2020 election.

Trump had long made it clear that he was prepared to use every lever at his disposal as president. The storming of the U.S. Capitol Building on January 6, 2021, by a mob fired up by the president was just one episode in a long series of provocative moves to bend the system to his will. It was, in its essence, the culmination of a slow-motion coup attempt, perpetrated by Trump to keep himself in power even if he actually lost the election. Although coups historically tend to be the product of clandestine plots and sudden, violent military takeovers, Trump's attempt played out over a period of months. This did not make it any less threatening.

Trump's acquittal in his first Senate impeachment trial clearly had emboldened him. For four years he had stress-tested the U.S. democratic system to see if anyone would counter or rein him in. Whenever they did not, he pressed ahead. The failure of the first impeachment effort was proof positive for Trump that he could do whatever he wanted to hang on to power and get away with it. So it was little wonder that his unchecked behavior only grew worse.

Trump repeatedly stated that he "deserved" two or even three terms in office because he had been treated "unfairly" and "cheated" out of the first two years of his presidency by the "Russia hoax," the Mueller investigation, and then by the first impeachment trial. I myself heard him say that multiple times. Sometimes Trump would muse and tweet about the possibility of abolishing presidential term limits entirely and staying in power indefinitely. In the immediate aftermath of his acquittal in the January 2020 Senate impeachment trial, he retweeted a video suggesting that he would be president "4eva." He would float these ideas to see if anyone contradicted him. People rarely did. If there was some pushback in the media, he would say it was a joke, he was only kidding, and move on.

Perhaps because he had endured the ignominy of hosting the now-infamous Helsinki press conference, President Sauli Niinistö of Finland turned out to be one of the few who attempted to spotlight what President Trump was up to. During an October 2019 meeting in the Oval Office, the Finnish president listened quietly as Trump railed against Democrats, the news media, and the impending impeachment in response to reporters' questions. When attention finally turned to him, President Niinistö praised America's history of democratic development. He told Trump, "Mr. President, you have a great democracy. Keep it going on." Members of his staff, whom I worked with closely during my time at the NSC, later confided to me that President Niinistö was greatly concerned by Trump's words and attitudes. He didn't take Trump's comments as a joke at all. He could see where this all might lead.

The worst-case scenario, indeed, was exactly what happened. It became clear that Trump's intent was not simply to stress-test American democracy but to exploit the weak points that he found. He wanted to effect a "self-coup," along the lines of Charles Louis Napoleon Bonaparte's, who dissolved the French parliament and declared himself Emperor Napoleon III in December 1851, and Nicolas Maduro, the leader of Venezuela, who refused to step down after losing national elections in 2017.

But unlike Napoleon III and Maduro, Trump operated in plain sight and in full view of the American public and the media. There was no hidden plot. He made no attempt to conceal his objective. He talked openly and often about his intent to win the November 2020 election by every means possible. In doing so he normalized his actions. It was the political equivalent of the flashing that women had to put up with when I was growing up in the UK. Trump revealed himself, and people just got used to it. They were no longer shocked. They laughed it away, not thinking that his antisocial behavior and his words might translate into anti-constitutional and violent actions.

Trump continued to lay the groundwork for his self-coup throughout 2020. Whenever his poll ratings faltered, he declared that the November vote was sure to be "rigged." He would reference his own more favorable polling data, which indicated that he would win by a landslide and asserted that he could lose only if "they" stole the election. Trump maintained that mail-in ballots, which were necessary in a pandemic to reduce the numbers of people gathering in polling places, would be "faked" in favor of his opponent. Dead people and immigrants would vote illegally, he claimed. "They" would take votes for him and destroy them. "They" was a vast group of domestic enemies, led by Joe Biden and the Democratic Party, which Trump manufactured for his grassroots base to revolt against.

When November 2020 finally came around, even as the votes were still being counted, Trump preemptively declared "election fraud" on an enormous scale. When the election was called in favor of Joe Biden, Trump refused to concede. Just as he had deployed his personal lawyer, former New York City Mayor Rudy Giuliani, to pull off the Ukrainian gambit to investigate Joe Biden that had triggered the first impeachment, he now sent Giuliani and his legal team to contest election results in the courts. Giuliani was now a central player in two successive election-fixing efforts. Trump himself doubled down even further. He harangued state election officials in phone calls and in person to try to intimidate them into repudiating or changing vote tallies in key states such as Michigan, Pennsylvania, and Georgia. He pressed the U.S. Attorney General's Office to overturn the results in the Georgia election. He enlisted Republican members of Congress to object to the Electoral College votes for Arizona and Pennsylvania.

Finally, just before January 6, President Trump instructed Vice President Mike Pence to block the formal election certification process in Congress. This was beyond the vice president's constitutional authority, and, thankfully, he refused. But Pence's refusal prompted Trump to rally thousands of his supporters to "stop the steal" on Capitol Hill, in what would become the most pronounced and distressing example of the dangers of American populism and the consequences of the country's deep-rooted malaise.

Unlikely Saviors

The failure of Trump's slow-motion, in-plain-sight attempt at a self-coup was not preordained. Ultimately it was thwarted only by individuals at the key institutions that typically would be involved in executing such a plot. First and foremost, high-ranking members of the military resisted Trump's efforts to personalize their power, as they had—however haltingly—throughout his presidency. If they had gone along with it, the outcome of Trump's self-coup attempt could have been completely different.

On June 1, 2020, during protests by Black Lives Matter supporters in Washington, D.C., Trump had blatantly tried to see if he could transform the U.S. armed forces into a Praetorian Guard—a force that he could deploy in support of his personal interests. At the height of the protests, Trump drew Joint Chiefs chairman General Mark Milley and defense secretary Mark Esper out of a West Wing meeting to follow him across Lafayette Square in front of the White House. The president then staged a photo op, with Milley and Esper in the background, in which he brandished a Bible in front of a historic church that had been damaged during the protests, calling for the restoration of law and order. Ivanka had carried the Bible out to the church in her voluminous handbag. Paramilitary forces, including the Secret Service, U.S. Park Police, Bureau of Prisons officers, and other law enforcement agencies, cleared a crowd of protesters from the area ahead of Trump's appearance by using chemical irritants, flash grenades, and rubber bullets. The president's intent was obvious—and the public blowback was swift. Both General Milley and Secretary Esper understood the president's goal. They apologized for their participation in the episode and emphasized the apolitical position of the U.S. military.

In the subsequent months leading up to the election and the final handover of executive power on January 6, 2021, there was considerable public debate about the president's efforts to involve the U.S. military in the election. Some commentators even raised the possibility that Trump might find a pretext to declare martial law and halt the ballot certification. On January 3, underscoring this public concern, the ten living former U.S. defense secretaries — including Esper, whom Trump had forced out of office right after the election for insufficient loyalty — submitted an unprecedented public letter to the *Washington Post* in which they reminded Defense Department officials and U.S. military personnel of their oath to uphold the Constitution.

Other government institutions, like the military, also held firm. For instance, throughout his tenure, with the help of Republican lawmakers, Trump filled more than two hundred federal court vacancies with what he kept calling "his judges." He also successfully pushed through the appointments of three new Supreme Court justices. In doing so, he made his expectation clear that if the lower courts or the Supreme Court had to settle an election dispute, then these justices would tilt the verdict in his favor.

"Trump judges," all the way up to the Supreme Court, however, respected their oath of office. They rejected the president's appeals to overturn legitimate election results. State and local government election administrators also refused to be swayed. In the case of Georgia, the officials that the president tried to coerce into changing the results repeatedly called out the lie that he had won the election. They held press conferences and recorded him in a phone call demanding that they change the results. It was a disastrous repeat of his July 2019 phone call with Ukrainian President Zelensky and clearly now part of a pattern.

All these events, the facts about the actual outcome of the election, and details of Trump's behavior were reported by major media outlets. Social media flagged the president's falsehoods. But none of this was enough to prevent Trump's version of events from taking hold among his voters.

The increasing fragmentation of U.S. and international media space with the proliferation of online news sources in addition to those in print or on the airwaves provided ample opportunity for President Trump to disseminate lies. Unlike in the days before cable news, when families would gather together to listen to the nightly news on the radio or watch it on the big networks — ABC, CBS, and NBC in the U.S. and the BBC in the UK — there was no longer a fixed center, no agreed clearinghouse for transmitting accurate information to the public. Most people now received their "news" from a variety of sources. And Americans' policy preferences; professional backgrounds; cultural, religious, racial, linguistic, and generational markers; place of residence (whether in a rural or urban region); peer groups; and social networks were among the many influences shaping individuals' ideas of what was a "trusted" or "reliable" source.

To make matters worse, sources that were objectively trustworthy were disappearing. More than two thousand local newspapers in the U.S. that used to carry national and international news along with regional content steadily disappeared in a fifteen-year period, unable to compete with the proliferation of internet news and lacking the resources to move their reporting online. Surviving print publications and other media outlets that were dependent on subscriptions, not just advertising revenues, had been forced to pander to the interests and opinions of their audiences to retain them.

In this highly fluid and generally disorienting environment, every news outlet now seemed to have its own slant or spin. The resulting confusion meant that a charismatic populist like Trump, with a mass following, could easily push his supporters in a specific direction. What's more, some media outlets were complicit in Trump's attempt to retain power. His endorsement of their programming boosted their ratings and advertising revenues. They focused on catering almost exclusively to the millions of viewers and customers who tuned in from his base and on conveying Trump's view of the world, including his lies.

Throughout history, coup plotters have seized control of the main communications channels: the central telegraph or post office, and later the radio and TV towers. Trump put a loyalist in charge of the U.S. Post Office, which he knew would be heavily used by Democratic voters during the pandemic. Restructuring and cost-cutting measures implemented by the new postmaster general slowed down mail delivery ahead of the election, further fueling voters' concerns about the reliability of mail-in ballots.

Trump did not physically take radio and TV by storm, but he continuously discredited the "mainstream media" who were critical of his behavior. They were at the top of his enemies list: the "enemy of the people." This helped to turn his voters away from their programming and negative commentary on his conduct. Trump instead recruited Fox News, *Newsmax,* and One America Network (OAN) and used social media platforms like Twitter and Facebook to sway public opinion in his favor. Twitter became Trump's modern-day equivalent of the TV and radio tower. He directly messaged the eighty-eight million people who followed his account to propagate false self-serving narratives and blatant lies. Throughout his presidency, Trump exploited cable news and social media to reinforce messages that provided justification for his actions. Social media helped to mobilize his supporters into action. After the events of January 6, Twitter and Facebook belatedly acknowledged what Trump had done and cut off his accounts.

Finally, Trump's self-coup was headed off by his own vice president, Mike Pence. The vice president performed his constitutional role, along with the Republican Senate majority leader and most of the Senate, on January 6: they certified the election results and made Trump's electoral loss official.

The good news for the United States was that Trump's self-coup failed. The bad news was that his supporters still believed the Big Lie that he had won the 2020 presidential election. Millions of people thought the election was stolen. They still supported Trump the person and were prepared to take further action on his behalf. And in a sign of just how enduring his damage to American democracy would be, these voters' blind support for Trump extended to their political representatives — and to the party of which they were members.

In the end, even after the Capitol was seized by the violent mob, 147 Republican representatives, including House minority leader Kevin McCarthy, endorsed some of Trump's efforts to challenge the 2020 election results. So did Josh Hawley, Ted Cruz, and six other politically ambitious senators who wanted to tap into Trump's popular support. In this way they not only assisted his effort to overturn the constitutional order; they also signaled that their party would not part ways from Trump under any circumstances.

By January 2021, even though he had lost the election, Trump had successfully usurped the Republican Party. He claimed the more than 74 million who voted for him in November 2020 as his personal base — *his* popular support, not the GOP's. He openly threatened to destroy the careers of Republican members of Congress who did not favor overturning the election result, cowing them into submission. At the January 6 rally preceding the storming of the Capitol, Trump used the language of conflict, as he often had in his rallies, when he told his supporters to go out and "fight like hell" for him. At the same event, Trump's oldest son, Donald Jr., ominously stated that the GOP was now "Donald Trump's Republican Party."

The Authoritarian's Playbook

Populists feed off people's grievances and seek to exploit them. In the case of the United States, the grievances were manifold and posed considerable danger to the future of American democracy as well as the American dream. The country had become dangerously divided after decades of postindustrial decline and the loss of mining and manufacturing jobs, economic crisis, shrinking opportunity, and the lack of socioeconomic mobility for many Americans, as well as more recent and rapid demographic change. The haves and have-nots in America essentially lived in and experienced two different countries when Trump came along.

President Trump was a have-a-lot rather than a regular have or a perpetually disadvantaged have-not. But he sought to rule over both sides of America's unequal equation by channeling the despair of the have-nots into a powerful and unassailable political force. He was the self-declared champion of those in postindustrial towns or racially diversifying neighborhoods who no longer saw their reflection in the faces around them. His path to power — and his key to remaining in power, even after losing the presidency — was through the assertion of leadership over the disaffected.

Like Donald Trump, most populists, as well as revolutionaries, are not representative of the "unwashed masses" they seek to lead. All too frequently they are middle-class intellectuals or scions of the rich and privileged, like Trump. Fidel Castro, Che Guevara, Vladimir Lenin, Juan Perón, to list a few, did not start out poor. Karl Marx, the father of socialism, who called on the world's proletariat to unite, throw off their chains, and revolt, wrote his *Communist Manifesto* and *Das Kapital* in the reading room of the British Library in London, not some hovel in the shadow of a "dark satanic mill." Marx's writing was facilitated by Friedrich Engels, his close friend, intellectual collaborator, and sponsor. Engel's wealthy industrialist father owned several large textile factories around Manchester in the North of England as well as in Germany. In most of my studies of populists and social revolutionaries, I found that few had much of a direct relationship with the people and workers they presumed to speak for and mobilize. The Castros, Lenins, and Peróns of the past also sought to personalize their leadership and make everything about them.

For me, watching Trump's disorganized but deadly serious attempt at a coup unfold over the course of 2020, the clearest and most unmistakable parallels were with Russia. Russia has a long history of coups and succession crises dating back to the czarist era. In the modern period, a coup against Mikhail Gorbachev in August 1991, perpetrated by hardliners opposed to his reforms, helped bring down the Soviet Union. And even in its brief democratic interregnum, Russia had endured political violence of the sort that we had seen on January 6.

In October 1993, a bitter dispute between the Russian Duma (parliament) and President Boris Yeltsin over the respective powers of the legislature and the presidency in competing drafts of a new constitution degenerated into violence after the Duma refused to confirm Yeltsin's prime minister. President Yeltsin tried to dissolve the Duma. His vice president, Alexander Rutskoi, and the speaker of the Duma, Ruslan Khasbulatov, sought to impeach him. Yeltsin invoked "extraordinary powers." He eventually called out the Russian army to shell the Russian parliamentarians — who had holed themselves up in the "White House," the Duma building — into submission. Both sides claimed they were acting in the name of the Russian people. October 1993 was essentially a populist showdown between the parliament and the president. It was resolved by tank fire. President Yeltsin won. After this episode, Yeltsin pushed through his version of the constitution, which gave him sweeping powers and the possibility to rule by decree.

In early 2020, President Putin similarly wanted to amend the Russian constitution to beef up his presidential powers. He was particularly interested in removing the existing term limits so he could potentially stay on as president until 2036, giving him two additional terms, at which point he would be eighty-four years old, instead of wrapping up his already long tenure in 2024. But mindful of the unfortunate precedent of October 1993, Putin decided to take a different tack.

In Putin's view, populists always had to worry about being put against the wall and shot (not just metaphorically) when they lost power. Rutskoi and Khasbulatov had been shelled in the "White House," Nicolai Ceausescu had been shot by a firing squad in Romania at the end of the Cold War, and Muammar Gaddafi of Libya (whom Putin knew personally) had been shot in 2011 after he was deposed. Putin wanted to dispense with the risks of tank or gunfire. Instead he had Valentina Tereshkova, a Duma deputy and iconic figure as the first woman in space, who had joined the ruling party, United Russia, in the early 2000s, propose the amendments to the Duma. This was the first, crucial step in Putin's own self-coup.

Authoritarian leaders like Putin always prefer to use someone else to do their bidding to promote their interests in a softer, subtler way, if they can. It was telling, for instance, that Trump used Republican senators Josh Hawley and Ted Cruz, along with other GOP members of Congress, to contest the Electoral College count on January 6. In this instance, Vice President

Pence behaved more like Russian Vice President Rutskoi back in October 1993 in trying to block the president's constitutional challenge. (Like Rutskoi, Pence got targeted for his efforts. The mob that stormed the Capitol bayed for his blood.)

There were additional U.S. parallels to events in Russia in this timeframe. Following Tereshkova's proposal in the Duma, Valery Zorkin, the head of Russia's Constitutional Court, presided over a legal analysis that produced hundreds of pages laying out the legitimacy of amending the constitution in Putin's favor. Zorkin was a long-standing Putin loyalist and fervent advocate of strong executive power. Similarly, during Trump's first impeachment trial, Harvard professor Alan Dershowitz, who was part of Trump's defense team, argued in favor of a sweeping definition of executive power and privilege. Trump-appointed attorney general William Barr made similar speeches on maximizing presidential power, although in the end he refused to help overturn the results of the November election. Even enablers have their limits.

"The Old Pretender"

The events around the January 6 storming of the Capitol by the mob Trump had incited and his subsequent impeachment on January 13 were a populist flameout. Twitter and other social media finally cut him off, making him seem strangely absent for Americans used to waking up and going to bed against the backdrop of a constant stream of presidential consciousness in 140 characters. And, mercifully, Trump effectively cut himself off too — at least for what remained of his presidency.

After January 6, Trump refused to take on any public engagements for his last two weeks in office. He was either playing golf or stewing in the White House and conferring with close allies on how he might stay in office. He abandoned governing entirely, leaving the final mopping up and transfer of executive operations exclusively to Vice President Pence.

Trump departed from the presidency in a blaze of vainglory. He refused to attend Joe Biden's inauguration on January 21 — the first time an outgoing president had refused since 1869. He took his last flight on Air Force One out of Washington early in the morning, before the inaugural events took place, and headed to Florida, to political exile on his Mar-a-Lago estate.

Over the course of his presidency, Trump often seemed interested in creating a kind of elected monarchy out of the U.S. presidency and intent on crowning himself and his family as the new American dynasty. It had certainly appeared that way during the state visit to London in 2019. In early January 2021, Mam called to let me know that she had read that President Trump might be heading over to Turnberry ahead of the inauguration to play golf and avoid Washington. Prestwick Airport outside Glasgow had reportedly been contacted by the U.S. military. The White House denied the reports, and Scotland's first minister, Nicola Sturgeon, in any case quashed the possibility, saying that the president would not be welcome, as Scotland and the rest of the UK were in full pandemic lockdown.

Trump never made it to Turnberry in January 2021. But if he had, he would have brought himself back to where he started out, talking about America's "Brexit moment" in the summer of 2016. It would also have been strangely appropriate for him to claim the "American throne" from his Scottish golf course. In so doing, he would have been taking a page from an earlier history.

In 1715, not far from Trump's other Scottish golf course, in Aberdeen, the Earl of Mar had raised the Jacobite standard, the flag of James Edward Stuart, "the Old Pretender," to spark a rebellion. The Stuart family were Catholics. They were deposed in 1688, exiled to France, and replaced on the British throne by Protestant relatives from the Netherlands. They wanted the crown back and made several unsuccessful attempts to regain power.

During the 1715 Jacobite Rebellion, the Old Pretender sailed into Aberdeen to rally his army to victory. It was not enough. Eventually, in 1745, his son, "the Young Pretender," James Francis Edward Stuart, came to Scotland to lead the Highland Rebellion. He was thoroughly defeated at the Battle of Culloden, where some of my own ancestors joined the fray as Jacobite soldiers on the losing side. The lost Jacobite cause roiled Scottish and English politics for decades before the Stuarts eventually faded away. President Trump's mother's family, the MacLeods, like every other clan in Scotland, were likely caught up one way or another on various sides of the rebellion.

Succession crises and rebellions by deposed kings and queens calling up their own private armies were the dilemma of monarchies in earlier times. But in January 2021, America seemed to be embarking on one of its own, with the Trump family settling down at Mar-a-Lago, Trump's presidential "winter palace," to plot a comeback.

Even as the second impeachment process unfolded in the U.S. Congress and Senate, Donald Trump was holding court like the Old Pretender with leading members of the Republican Party flying down to pay homage to him ahead of the next set of congressional election cycles. Newspaper articles were also speculating which of the "young pretenders" — Donald Jr. or Ivanka or Eric Trump's wife, Lara — would be the first to run for office. They might begin with Senate seats in Florida, or by launching their own bids for the presidency.

In the aftermath of Trump's disastrous reign, it was tempting to breathe a sigh of relief. But that would have been premature, because there was no indication that his dynasty would fade away. And American populism looked like it was here to stay — unless we could find a way to mend our socioeconomic and political divisions.

PART IV
OUR HOUSE

14

The Great Reckoning

Trump's populist presidency had prioritized political opportunism over providing the economic opportunity that most of his voters had hoped for in 2016. His promises to his base and the American working class were left unfulfilled. Ultimately, Trump had played personal and polarizing politics rather than made policy. Not only the livelihoods but the *lives* of Americans were at stake. We needed to get our house, America, in order, not just fixate on which man was in the "people's house."

As the Trump family headed off for Florida in January 2021—all the while claiming the right to a comeback in the name of "the people," *real* Americans—individuals and families, low-income, working-class, and middle-class Americans from all racial and ethnic backgrounds—still needed their government to deliver something other than superficial solutions. By the end of the horrible year that was 2020, it was left to the new president, Joe Biden, to pick up the pieces from America's long-standing socioeconomic and political crisis as well as the pandemic. In his inaugural speech on January 20, 2021, President Biden considered how to start afresh and turn things around. He asked what America stands for: "What are the common objects we love that define us as Americans?" The first "common object" that he listed—before security, liberty, dignity, respect, honor, and the truth—was opportunity.

President Biden's message, which came in the wake of the January 6 storming of the Capitol, was that American democracy had prevailed, at least in terms of heading off a self-coup by his predecessor and successfully transferring executive power. But now Biden and his administration would need to show that American democracy could also deliver and restore people's faith in the capacity of the U.S. government to have a positive impact on their lives. The new administration would have a long road ahead to get a grip on the pandemic and stave off socioeconomic disaster. It had four years of gross mismanagement to overcome. Biden's campaign slogan was "build back better," but after Trump and COVID-19, there was no going back to what the United States had been before 2016.

Rather than building back better, America would have to *build forward together*. Americans would have to find ways to work together to overcome their internal partisan, socioeconomic, racial, and cultural divisions as well as deal with new challenges ahead. But how were they to do this? In an age of pandemic and decline, how could the United States deliver the common object of opportunity for the twenty-first century?

Picking at the Fissures

By the end of 2020, the fissures in America's social and political fabric that Trump had repeatedly picked at looked hard to repair and perhaps insuperable. The pandemic revealed that the United States could no longer be relied on for policy continuity. America's past successes no longer predicted its present performance.

Trump had been a one-man big show and his administration more of a personality cult than a representation of partisan politics. He was neither Republican nor conservative. He had thrown the existing Republican Party's ideological and government policy frames for addressing issues out the window but failed to replace them with anything more durable. He had no real fixed ideas, although there were plenty of things he didn't like or refused to contemplate and deal with.

In his time in the White House, Trump had made it his business to short-circuit representative democracy, embedded in Congress, political parties, and the full range of American institutions. He had weakened the checks and balances of the system, pushing out government watchdogs and pulling back oversight mechanisms. He had also tried to eliminate or push aside established political and social intermediaries. Populist systems always give a boost to those who are best funded and can shout the loudest, which is exactly what Trump was good at doing — drawing in money, setting up a myriad of political action committees, and drowning out everyone else. During his tenure, America veered toward plebiscitary democracy — a system driven by polling, popular opinion, and periodic personality-focused elections, precisely the kind of political territory carved out by Vladimir Putin over the twenty years of his rule in Russia.

Indeed, Russia offered a grim comparison and a portent of something much worse ahead. In the 1990s, President Yeltsin had fired on his parliament in the Russian "White House" to push through a constitution that gave him stronger executive powers. In the end, Yeltsin did not use those powers to their full effect. He too was a populist, but of a "softer" sort, and the Russian state was weaker under his tenure. Yeltsin's appointed successor, Vladimir Putin, however, had proven to be of a harder disposition. In the following years, Putin took the constitution's presidential powers and ran with them. He also enhanced them to the point of extending his own term in office essentially indefinitely. Likewise, President Trump's interpretation of executive power and his attempt to usurp the presidency may have paved the way for another, less personally insecure and more capable populist president — someone who actually did his or her homework and was skilled in project management — to pull a Putin in America.

All the false narratives about Russia and Ukraine that members of Congress had invoked during my October 2019 deposition and the events that led up to Trump's first impeachment trial had continued to spin out through the horrible year. They had threaded their way right through the 2020 presidential election campaign. Almost a year after my deposition, on October 7, 2020, one month before the vote, I had written an opinion editorial for the *New York Times*. In the article, titled "The Biggest Risk to This Election Is Not Russia. It's Us," I reiterated my concerns from the congressional hearings and my opening statement.

American political divisions had worsened. Partisan strife had contributed to the botched handling of the COVID-19 pandemic and eroded the United States' international reputation. A poll among American allies and partners, conducted by the well-respected Pew Research Center in summer 2020, showed a precipitous decline in U.S. favorability. Even closely aligned countries like the United Kingdom, which were suffering from their own problems in dealing with the pandemic, had turned sour on the United States. Only 41 percent of UK respondents held a favorable view of the U.S. The median positive view across all the countries surveyed was a meager 15 percent. In some countries President Trump's personal rating had sunk lower than President Putin's.

I had grown used to European colleagues and friends writing me alarmed notes about the "pitiful" state of affairs in the United States and the threats to America's democracy from its own president. Brookings colleagues looking at the link between U.S. domestic and foreign policy worried that America's lack of internal cohesion and cooperation had become a "top-tier national security concern" that could upend the U.S. role in maintaining "the rules-based global order." Their concern was justified: throughout 2020, President Trump had denounced the integrity of the U.S. electoral system and mobilized his supporters to "stop the steal." As the tension had mounted, the United States appeared to be on the brink of civil conflict, especially after the mid-October revelation by the FBI that its agents had thwarted a plot by armed militia groups to kidnap the Democratic governor of Michigan. They had been tracking a similar, early-stage plot targeting the Democratic governor of Virginia. In the opinion piece, I wrote that "we are our own worst enemies." We were tearing ourselves apart.

Persistent Patterns

Although the outcome of the 2020 presidential election was different from that of 2016 — Joe Biden, the Democratic Party candidate, was now president-elect — the results showed the remarkable persistence of the political patterns that had characterized Trump's election. The effects of the fissures in America's social and political fabric were evident. The final voter turnout was also historic — 67 percent — notwithstanding Trump's efforts to dissuade people from voting. It was in fact the largest turnout since the early 1900s, a time when the U.S. population was magnitudes smaller and neither women nor Black Americans were able to vote in national elections. Biden had selected Senator Kamala Harris of California as his vice president, and her Jamaican and Indian (South Asian) heritage as well as her gender made her a historic choice.

Given the high turnout, both Biden and Trump received unprecedented numbers of votes — respectively the highest and second highest vote tallies for any president. Biden won more than 80 million, over Trump's 74 million. In fact President Trump had attracted about 11 million more votes than he got in 2016.

There was no evidence to support any of Trump's claims of electoral fraud on a large scale. Domestic and international observers declared the 2020 election the most secure on record and commended its smooth conduct considering the difficulties created by the pandemic. And this time around, although reports from my old institution, the DNI, documented Russian security services' involvement in the 2020 election, there was no suspicion that Trump had received a significant assist from the outside.

For his part, President Putin mostly stayed out of the U.S. electoral fray. There was little left for him to do: the now former American president was a divisive element in U.S. politics in his own right, not just supported by the traditional Republican Party voter base but also standing at the forefront of a reactionary, increasingly violent populist movement. Still, Putin could not resist doing something to stir the pot and draw attention. In the weeks before the election, criminal groups attributed to Russia had launched ransomware attacks on a handful of hospital systems across the United States. In December 2020, private cybersecurity firms and the U.S. government also revealed that the Russian security services had launched an extensive, sophisticated, and successful attack to penetrate U.S. governmental systems and databases. Nonetheless, beyond reports of Russian military intelligence efforts to probe local electoral systems, the Russians had not attempted another large-scale 2016-style operation to target the presidential election.

Putin was conspicuously absent from the initial roster of world leader phone calls to the new American president. He delayed in congratulating Biden, clearly hedging on the outcome for as long as he could to gauge the mood in the U.S. and possibly get a sense of the direction that the new administration might take in international affairs through cabinet and other appointments. This was not atypical for Putin, as I had learned in my twenty years of tracking his activities. He eventually deigned to issue a recognition of President-elect Biden by old-fashioned telegram, once the Electoral College had confirmed Biden's victory on December 14, 2020.

In sum, the outcome of the November 2020 presidential election, with its more limited signs of Russian intervention, record voter turnout, and similar (but reversed) margins in the Electoral College, showed that the 2016 result and Trump's election in the United States had not been manufactured by Vladimir Putin. It was the homegrown outcome of a deeply and dangerously divided society.

The 2020 presidential election highlighted the United States' profound economic and regional disparities and racial discord. Exit polls also demonstrated that the voting population's overwhelming concerns were related to the performance of the economy and jobs — in other words, opportunity — and then, a little further down the list, racial inequality, followed by the national response to the COVID-19 pandemic. Foreign policy was not a significant factor. American voters had enough problems to contend with at home.

Fault Lines and Tipping Points

The electoral results had shown that as the United States entered its third decade of the twenty-first century, it was many Americas, not one. Joe Biden had won overwhelmingly in large urban areas, which accounted for more than 70 percent of the country's economic output, but Donald Trump had prevailed in rural areas and regions with the greatest economic insecurity. Biden was inheriting — and hoping to rehabilitate — a country that remained in fundamental ways at war with itself.

The nominally united states themselves were deeply divided. President Trump had dominated in states like Florida, increasing his number of votes over 2016. At the same time, voters in Florida had passed — on the very same ballot — a $15-an-hour minimum wage resolution, showing the locally diverse population's embrace of a core working-class economic demand. Trump also increased his votes among populations with no college education and among white evangelical Christians, who overwhelmingly voted for him. In contrast, Biden — at least in all the states that brought him the critical votes in the Electoral College — had secured majority votes from heavily white college-educated urban and suburban populations as well as younger or first-time voters. In addition, Biden drew a large turnout among Black Americans, especially women, in pivotal states like Georgia and Michigan.

America seemed genuinely polarized in the aftermath of the election, its population separated into all kinds of sectarian camps. Joe Biden appeared to be the president of the educated and economically advantaged, and Donald Trump the champion of the predominantly white working poor, the socially disaffected, and white evangelical Christians of all incomes. The fault lines ran along the edges of cities, suburbs, and towns, dividing educated white-collar professionals from blue-collar workers who had been denied similar educational opportunities.

In multiple analyses of the voting patterns, inequality as well as social grievance and cultural despair had undermined trust in democracy and fed populism. In a 2021 Quinnipiac University poll conducted immediately after the January 6 events, 56 percent of those surveyed stated that they fully anticipated that the country's partisan divisions would remain the same under the new president. The fissures and fault lines had been developing for a long time, and they were not going away anytime soon.

Historically, polarization and populism — and their close traveling companions, extremism and authoritarianism — emerge from the politics of cultural despair. They arise from and circle around the idea that a specific "someone" is guilty and to blame for the negative changes and existential angst that people experience when things are in flux. Back at home in the North East of England in the 1980s, we certainly blamed Margaret Thatcher for our downward trajectory. She was the architect of our misery. It was only later, when I moved away and proceeded with my studies and professional career, that I understood she was mostly responding to larger, impersonal economic forces, most of which were well beyond her control.

Economic and demographic change, as well as phenomena like sudden upsurges in the pace of immigration, shift people's sense of "you/me." "Others" can be blamed for this shift — for simply coming along, entering the economic, societal, or political arena, and contributing to the loss of the previously dominant group's status. Mass unemployment in the same timeframe, as the result of separate trade adjustments and technological developments, compounds the you/me shift with the loss of work identity as well as livelihood.

This had been the case with my father in the UK. Having lost his job as a coal miner, he lost his sense of self-esteem, belonging, and well-being. He was uprooted from a multigenerational community and a long-established set of work and social norms. Life became precarious and impecunious. For Dad, the fast pace of change was a trigger not just for anxiety but for nostalgia, a yearning for some supposed "halcyon days." He was always talking and reminiscing with friends and relatives about the golden age for Durham miners in the 1950s.

Trump had played on the U.S. "culture wars" and societal divisions to divide and conquer. Beginning with his inaugural address, which invoked the idea of "American carnage," a country being ripped to shreds by and at risk from new social forces, he had extolled the socially conservative values of the American working class rather than emphasizing what he would do to support their socioeconomic interests. He told them that their traditional place at the center of U.S. society was being taken away — stolen — by left-wing interlopers, alien immigrants, and all kinds of other deviants from their norms. It was *their* country, *their* America (his, "our" America), that *others* were taking away.

In his campaign speeches and public pronouncements, Trump particularly fueled white Christians' fears of losing their distinct religious identity and way of life because of demographic and societal change. He deliberately whipped up his voters' sentiment against the Black Lives Matter movement, denouncing it as a radical left-wing force bent on violence and destruction. Trump's words and actions — telling his base that they needed "to take [their] country back" from everyone else — further undermined societal cohesion. It added to an already prevailing sense of distrust among his supporters in the federal government and increasingly diminished the very idea of American democracy and unity. His two impeachment trials were a stark warning of how much trouble the United States was in socially and politically, and of the serious repercussions for its national security.

In April 2021, a study by Robert Pape, a professor at the University of Chicago, was widely featured and reported in the American press. Professor Pape examined the backgrounds of 377 Americans who were arrested after storming the U.S. Capitol Building on January 6. One critical factor stood out. They were mostly from counties in states where the non-Hispanic white population had sharply declined relative to minorities. The people arrested were predominantly white and male (95 percent and 85 percent, respectively) and clearly uncomfortable with the steady diversification of American society and their own communities. Notably, those arrested at the Capitol were older than the "usual protesters," trending toward middle age — more Generation X than Millennials or Generation Z. And they were not from the lowest U.S. income strata. Still other studies showed that many of them had lost assets or seen a negative change in their material circumstances with the economic downturn after the Great Recession in the 2010s.

In short, the people who had launched the vain attempt to keep Trump in the presidency had come from regions at a demographic tipping point, who believed their social status and economic prospects were impinged on. Their anxiety about the loss of their perceived racial and socioeconomic position had propelled them into an emergent populist political movement — a collective, desperate attempt to counter their change in circumstances.

Body Blows

America's polarization in the 2020s created another tipping point — this for the United States internationally. Partisan spectacles during the pandemic (as the summer 2020 Pew polls underscored) undermined the country's international standing as a democratic model and international authority on public health. Our inability to get our act together on most major policy issues (the fifth risk of incompetence and the failure of project management) hindered the projection of American soft power, essentially the power of our example. As a result, we reduced our overall global competitiveness with rising powers such as China.

Political polarization is ultimately a national security threat as well as a domestic challenge. It is a barrier to the collective action necessary for combating catastrophes like global pandemics, mitigating the effects of climate change, and, as I saw in my time at the White House, thwarting external threats from adversaries such as Russia. In the Trump administration, every peril was politicized. It was turned into fodder for personal gain and partisan games. Successive national security advisers, cabinet members, and their professional staffs were unable to mount a coherent response or defense to a national security threat in the face of personalized, chaotic, and at times simply opportunistic policymaking at the top.

Another egregious manifestation of this was the demonization of public service during my time at the NSC — the erosion of the ideas of nonpartisan expertise and public service as a value to society. Public servants, long-standing career officials such as Ambassador Yovanovitch and Dr. Fauci, were seen as beholden to a party or policy rather than focused on a common mission. They were trolled on the internet, attacked on all fronts, and, in the case of Masha Yovanovitch, hounded out of public service entirely by opportunists, lobbyists, and others pursuing personal, private agendas.

This behavior by domestic actors became a vulnerability. It laid us open to exploitation by Russian operatives. As I also witnessed at the White House and analyzed in my work tracking Russia's efforts to interfere in our politics, American-designed technology magnified the impact of once fringe ideas and subversive actors and became a tool in the hands of hostile state actors. National and international networking among extremists was greatly enhanced by entry into a digital world that operates on economically or commercially defined algorithms, which are specifically designed to attract people's attention and divide them into "affinity groups."

Social media platforms such as Facebook and Twitter facilitated the movement of social trends in extreme directions. They contributed to the fragmenting of American and other democracies, enabling authoritarian regimes like Vladimir Putin's to consolidate themselves. In Russia, Putin was able to deploy technology to stabilize his regime. In the United States, Putin was able to weaponize the same technology against us. Facebook, Twitter, and other platforms empowered marginalized groups, undermined social cohesion and social capital, and eroded Americans' sense of common, shared purpose. The Russian intelligence services used these American-designed digital tools to pile on. The fragmentation effects of partisan politics coupled with U.S. social media opened space for them to manipulate.

Grievances, resentments, anxieties, conspiracies, and groupthink all travel faster through the internet than efforts to counter them can travel through parliaments and policies. Virtual communities on the internet have no physical communal or even national allegiances. This is a boon to a seasoned intelligence operative like Putin, who might seek to divert the U.S. from tackling its socioeconomic disparities and inequities and getting its house in order and instead encourage it to fixate on culture wars and clashes of values — the very things he tries to avoid in his own home. A crisis to address at home becomes an opportunity to mess around abroad.

The 2016 presidential election had marked both an obvious tipping point and a turning point in the United States. But Vladimir Putin's intervention concealed it, precisely by diverting attention to him and Trump and what Putin might have done (or not done) to put Trump in office. Just like 2020, the 2016 election was, and should have been, an acknowledgment of and reckoning with long-neglected issues.

The voters who had swung the ballot for Donald Trump in critical counties in Wisconsin, Pennsylvania, and Michigan were swayed by consideration of their own personal, family, and communal circumstances, not by the fake internet personas devised by Russian intelligence services. Local economies were stuck in a crisis of opportunity. Like my home base of North East England, they had been devastated when coal mines, steel plants, and car factories closed as U.S. manufacturing moved overseas in search of lower labor costs, or failed to compete with cheaper imports from abroad. These same voters were hit again by the December 2007–June 2009 collapse of the U.S. housing market and subsequent global financial crisis. The Great Recession stripped the value from their homes, put small businesses under water, and wiped out their investments, savings, and pension plans.

In the United States in the early 2000s, just like in the UK in the 1980s, no one from the federal government came forward with sustainable long-term solutions to people's plight. Big banks and corporations got bailed out after the financial crisis, but not the American lower and middle classes, who took the body blows. In 2016 voters had been looking for someone to address their economic grievances, or at the very least give voice to them. By the 2020 presidential election, they wanted something more than that. They wanted someone to take concrete action, immediately.

President Trump did, in fairness, help to produce new low-skilled jobs through deregulation from 2017 to 2019. Unemployment was headed down during his tenure, and poverty rates were also trending toward all-time lows in 2019. Until the COVID-19 pandemic, many could cobble together a decent portfolio of part-time or contract work, or combine a full-time position with something additional and flexible in the service sector, like a rideshare job. But the portfolios of workers balancing part-time and contract work were precarious. Few new jobs came with benefits or the kind of decent wage the steelworkers were looking for when they stood around the president's desk in the Roosevelt Room in March 2018.

The COVID Accelerant

In the United States and globally, COVID-19 was an accelerant to existing fuel. It provided the kind of universal and immediate shock to the economy that the United States had not seen since the Great Depression of the 1920s and 1930s and Europe had not seen since World War II. It made the challenge of building forward together all the more necessary but all the more daunting.

With rare exceptions, the pandemic put everyone, unexpectedly, in the same precarious predicament. For many Americans, the experience of losing everything — including their lives — was in sudden stark relief. But the disease and its economic fallout had the greatest impact in the poorest regions and zip codes. Young people, low-income and low-skilled workers, those without a college degree, and women (from all backgrounds) disproportionately bore the brunt of the economic effects in those communities and across America. Low-income workers and racial minorities also died in higher numbers.

By 2021 everywhere looked like the Rust Belt with mass layoffs. By Inauguration Day almost twenty-six million Americans were officially out of work because of the pandemic, or they had been furloughed and had their hours reduced. Many of the new jobs created under the Trump administration had simply been wiped out.

Jobs that had expanded in the travel, hospitality, and leisure sectors were decimated as business trips and family vacations were curtailed and health restrictions forced most establishments to close their doors. Demand for trains, flights, hotels, restaurants, office space, and all the positions associated with them disappeared overnight. Service jobs that depended directly on consumer spending by America's affluent were dramatically cut by wealthy households forgoing cleaning, child care, eating out, and sports and entertainment during locally imposed lockdowns — or simply because people were concerned about contracting the virus and decided to self-isolate. Ride-share services like Uber and Lyft, which had offered part-time and supplemental opportunities for many workers on the bottom rung of the employment ladder, who were juggling several jobs at once to earn a decent income, were also hard-hit. Although the pandemic expanded the idea of "essential workers" to frontline employees in online shopping warehouses and delivery services, grocery stores, and food production — many of whom retained their jobs and had their pay increased — COVID-19 had a huge negative impact on their already precarious health. In U.S. meatpacking plants alone, 54,000 workers were infected by the coronavirus and at least 270 died.

The monthly average of unemployment claims was four times the level before the pandemic hit. Millions of Americans experienced months-long delays in getting any kind of unemployment benefits. Although poverty had declined between 2010 and 2019, now, with many employee protections stripped away after 2016 under the guise of not feeding "socialism," millions of Americans needed bailouts and handouts again. People who had entered the workforce with a mix of part-time jobs and temporary contracts found themselves with no unemployment insurance. Indeed, around 44 percent of U.S. jobs in 2020 came without benefits. In one survey at the end of the year, conducted by the U.S. Census Bureau's Household Pulse, eighty-three million adults reported having difficulty paying some of their bills or rent as well as covering essentials like food and medical care because of their reduced hours at work and straitened circumstances. Out-of-work Americans described sleeping in their cars with their families and lining up for food banks and other assistance from charitable organizations. COVID-19 had brutally laid everything bare, including the cupboard.

The Signal from the Compost Heap

The coronavirus created an enormous crisis of mobility for everyone as well as the loss of livelihood for millions. People had to stay at home and "telework" if they could. But of course not everyone could.

I was able to telework in my well-resourced suburb of Washington, D.C., thanks to a job in a think tank that was embedded in the new virtual world of the "knowledge economy." But those who worked in physical sectors — in factories, farms, and grocery stores across America, and in most of the jobs on the lower rungs of the economy, not to mention on the frontlines of dealing with the pandemic in hospitals and health care — had to show up in person.

Prior to the pandemic, on a trip to my hometown in September 2019 to bring my mother over to the U.S. for several weeks, I learned the hard way that even if you wanted to, you couldn't easily telework from a place like Bishop Auckland. None of the infrastructure was there, unless you could afford to install it yourself. My mother certainly couldn't, and her Wi-Fi — if you could even call it that — was barely functional. At her house, if I wanted to make a cell-phone call, I had to walk to the back of the garden and stand on top of the compost heap. I could never download all my email messages. As a result, I missed the drama back in the United States (including the release of the transcript of President Trump's call with Ukrainian President Zelensky) that would lead me to testify before Congress.

Bishop Auckland epitomized the crisis of cyber connectivity in places that had been stripped of their terrestrial connections and physical networks because of economic decline. Inadequate infrastructure contributed to the opportunity crisis. And the United States was full of Bishop Aucklands — small towns in predominantly rural areas not connected to a major city and not connected reliably to the internet or cell service.

On top of all the other blows, the pandemic and the new virtual world set back educational opportunities across the board, especially for the critical K-12 education sector. In theory, changes in technology made it possible to take classes online from home during the pandemic — as my daughter did, once her school was able to figure them out. But in practice, schools and children across the country did not have equal access to technology, including broadband, Wi-Fi, and personal computers. They became victims of the digital divide between the technological haves and have-nots. The new digital world and the role of big data and technology suddenly coalesced to form yet another obstacle to opportunity for disadvantaged kids.

This played out in a remarkable fashion in the UK in the summer of 2020, when the COVID-19 pandemic wreaked havoc on the higher education prospects of the entire national cohort of working-class kids applying to college. The digital divide in this case was manifested not by inadequate technological hardware and bandwidth but rather by the ones and zeroes that flowed through it and the human biases that they channeled.

With schools closed and students in lockdown to stem disease transmission, the spring A-level exams were canceled. The UK government's national exams and assessments regulatory board, known by its awkward acronym, Ofqual, decided to use a standardized statistical model instead of the exam to determine students' grades. Teachers were instructed to submit grade predictions, but the national exam board then adjusted these using the algorithm they had devised. This drew on the historic data of the school and the results of previous students taking the same subject-based exams.

When the A-level results were released in August 2020, 40 percent of teachers' recommended grades had been lowered. Students from disadvantaged backgrounds with stellar academic track records were hit hardest. At one comprehensive school in Rotherham, a former coal-mining and steel town in South Yorkshire, a staggering 84 percent of students received lower grades than anticipated. The computer algorithm was skewed toward kids from private schools and those in prosperous areas with long records of success. Almost 49 percent of students at private schools in England had received an A grade, in comparison with just under 22 percent of students in the state system. In some cases, pupils who might have passed the exam if they had actually been able to take it were assigned a failing grade simply on the basis of the data sets. Ofqual's own after-the-fact data analysis showed that pupils on free school meals in impoverished areas were more likely to have had their grades lowered or to have failed than any other category of students.

If this had been the approach to A-levels in 1984, my friends and I would surely have fallen into that unfortunate category. Bishop Barrington Comprehensive School had only a few years of A-level results in a smattering of subjects. There would have been no "historic" data for Ofqual to plug into its statistical model. In French, I didn't even have a teacher to offer a prediction. I had been studying on my own in the months leading up to the exam. I could hardly have written my own assessment and would probably have been assigned an "unclassified" grade.

Reading about the debacle from afar, I felt white-hot with sympathetic rage reading the students' stunned comments. One young woman told the *New York Times* that the results were "unfathomable. It felt like a reminder of my place, and it felt as though it was a way of the exam board saying your post code is more important than your potential. Your personal circumstances, your efforts overcoming adversity, it doesn't matter. Because a person like you, a person from your background, from your socioeconomic class, you aren't expected to do well."

Overwhelmed by the negative reactions and protests, Ofqual eventually allowed the teachers' assessments to stand. By then some students had already lost their highly competitive first-place choices at university.

In many respects, the bias in the data sets was inevitable — and it underscored the potential perils of the new digital age. If there had been more diversity in the educational backgrounds of UK government officials, someone might have spotted the deficiencies of the algorithm. UK ministers had little experience or even knowledge of the struggles of students at a disadvantaged school. Although the education secretary at the time, Gavin Williamson, had gone to a comprehensive school, 64 percent of Boris Johnson's cabinet in 2020 had studied at private schools, in contrast with only 7 percent of the overall population. Prime Minister Johnson himself had studied at one of England's most famous schools, Eton College, as had eighteen other British prime ministers over the centuries.

Biases shaped by place, class, and an elite education had all been fed by the official programmers into an algorithm that would determine who was going to be who in the UK during the pandemic.

And Up a Birch Tree

These dilemmas played out in myriad lesser forms elsewhere and everywhere simultaneously. COVID-19 cut tax revenues and with them local and national educational resources, so many schools did not have enough funding to give everyone a computer or Wi-Fi access. Public libraries were closed along with school buildings, putting both physical books and access to computers and free internet services out of reach. Many children with no reliable home internet service or personal computer strained to access classes on family smartphones. Even in my own case, we at first struggled with Wi-Fi bandwidth and had to equip our house with multiple routers, purchasing all kinds of expensive equipment. I could afford to do so, but millions across America could not. They had to relive my experience of trying to download my email on top of the compost heap in Mam's garden.

In one extreme example, a Russian student in a remote town in Siberia was forced, even in frigid temperatures, to climb up to the top of a birch tree in a field to get a strong enough signal to take his college courses. He posted a short video appeal on the social media platforms TikTok and Instagram to attract the attention of local authorities and appeal for better internet coverage. In the U.S., plenty of children and students, along with their parents, were sitting in cars in the parking lot of their school or local library, trying to work on their phones in icy cold weather or baking heat. As a result, by the end of 2020, educational standards and attainment scores were falling across the United States. In my home region of Montgomery County in Maryland, usually one of the more successful school districts in the country, failure rates in math and English increased by six times in some under-resourced schools in the first period of the 2020–2021 academic year.

Exams and other assessments had to be postponed in the U.S. (which fortunately didn't attempt any algorithmic alternatives), and educators fretted about the long-term effects on a generation of students. Students who were in their final year of high school or college worried about how to find a job during and after the pandemic, as many positions were cut or went virtual and competition increased. Would entry-level jobs simply be eliminated? How would they secure an interview over the internet? Where would they work if they did get a job? Could they move somewhere new during a pandemic? What would happen to the fall-back opportunities that temporary jobs typically provided as a bridge to something full-time and a way for students to support themselves through college? The kinds of bar, restaurant, and cleaning jobs I had relied on at school and in college disappeared. The year 2020 looked a lot like 1984, the year I left high school, when 90 percent of graduates had nothing permanent lined up on graduation day.

It also started to look like the 1980s and worse for working women. During the pandemic, women's gains in the labor force were effectively wiped out over the course of twelve months. Even single mothers who were their family's primary breadwinners and still had jobs were pushed from the workplace. They had to take themselves out because the services and facilities that working mothers relied on, including child-care centers, kindergartens, schools, and after-school activities, were physically closed for long stretches, if not most of the pandemic. Women with several kids found it impossible to work, look after small children, and run a home school (especially if it involved sitting in a parking lot in their cars). In families with two working parents, it was usually the mother who took a formal leave, reduced hours, or quit entirely while the father continued to work.

After the 1970s, the expansion of external child-care facilities as well as schools had played a critical role in enabling women to support their families; without access to either of these, working mothers were in a vicious chicken- (really mother-hen-) and-egg cycle. In summer 2020, one academic study concluded that one third of the women under forty interviewed for the survey had quit the labor force to take care of children. By January 2021, the official U.S. jobs report showed that more than one quarter of a million additional women had stopped working or looking for work for similar reasons.

U.S. economists and analysts concluded that women faced an "unsolvable dilemma" that was as much a personal crisis as a jobs crisis. The rates of women in the workplace had declined to levels last seen in the late 1980s, just as I arrived in the United States. This had an extremely negative impact on the economic circumstances of their children and families.

The only people who seemed to be thriving during the pandemic were billionaires — the group that Trump had favored in his deregulation and tax policies. They got richer while low-income and middle-class Americans got poorer. As of April 2021, the U.S. super-rich, a total of 719 people, had seen their collective wealth increase by over 50 percent since mid-March 2020, to $4.56 trillion.

The pandemic had accelerated the transformation of the U.S. economy already under way through long-term technological change. It increased the transition to teleworking and automation and boosted the fortunes of those who worked for or owned companies in digital commerce and the knowledge-based sectors of the economy. The pandemic was thus a preview of further shifts and dislocations to come, with the spread of automation into the transportation sector (self-driving vehicles) and the rise of artificial intelligence. As in the 1980s, with the decline in the industrial and manufacturing sectors, even after the pandemic was over and people could get back to work, the United States and other advanced economies would face a world with fewer jobs for their populations in the 2020s.

Something Ambitious

All this meant that we would need something significant to pull ourselves together individually and collectively and put the country on a different trajectory. Restoring the infrastructure of opportunity that was eroded by deindustrialization and almost destroyed by the pandemic was the first order of business, as President Biden acknowledged in his inaugural speech.

As a result of the sudden shock of the COVID-19 pandemic, the United States was now at the kind of inflection point that Europe had found itself at after the devastation of the Second World War. To make significant, measurable progress in reducing inequality, alleviating poverty, eliminating structural racism, and removing gender discrimination, the United States needed to take bold steps.

Creating a domestically focused agency to spearhead socioeconomic policy and coordinate programs could be one such step. After the terrorist attacks of September 11, 2001, provided a similar jolt in the national security sphere, for example, the U.S. created two new entities: the Office of the Director of National Intelligence (ODNI) to coordinate and oversee the country's sixteen intelligence agencies, and the Department of Homeland Security (DHS) to do the same for the twenty-two agencies covering public or domestic security. A new homeland or domestic development agency could play a similar role for overseeing or coordinating efforts to restore and create a new infrastructure of opportunity for the decades ahead.

Doing something on a mass scale would first require clear policy formulation at the national level. National leaders needed to acknowledge the fact that they were engaged in a deliberate and explicit *development* exercise. They needed to address a set of questions: What are you trying to do? What are your goals? What you will do to achieve them? What is the appropriate scale of funding and the right mechanism? Are you focused on short-term relief to promote recovery and stimulate the economy so other public and private actors will step in? Or do you want to do something more ambitious, like eliminate existing inequalities and the spatial, racial, gender, and other structural barriers to opportunity for current and future generations? If the latter, do you need to create a new institution or agency, or can you

adapt and augment current institutions to provide coordination and oversight?

In the United Kingdom after the war, for instance, the late 1940s became
a period of policy and institutional innovation. Despite a prolonged German aerial bombing campaign, most of the country's infrastructure was in-
tact, but the economy and population were beaten down. For five years the
UK had been cut off from commercial and other links with the rest of the
world. Its material and financial reserves were depleted.

It was a hard slog to rebuild. Food rationing for some staples continued
until 1954. The shadow of the war and its scarcities still hung over me as a
child growing up in the 1960s and 1970s. The lingering deprivation and the
knowledge that unemployment would also remain high for years — as was
the case after the First World War — led to the refinement of Britain's "welfare state" to help the population recover. The idea of pulling together *existing* public assistance programs to create a more comprehensive system
came under the rubric of "winning the peace." The system included not just
the establishment of the National Health Service but the introduction of a
"family allowance," a mix of direct payments and tax benefits to cover every child until he or she completed school; the provision of national insurance and pension reforms; and other benefits and subsidies (like free school
milk) to provide a safety net for children, the working poor, and the elderly.

As was the case in the UK before the formalization of the welfare state
and the NHS in the 1940s, the United States Congress in 2021 had already
allocated billions of dollars for domestic programs that fell under the rubric of "development." The federal government could fold into a new institution existing activities and funding, such as grants and other measures
to alleviate poverty, provide child benefits and unemployment assistance,
improve resources for K-12 public school education, and increase access
for the majority of the population to lifelong education, new skills development, and retraining, for example. With appropriate legislation, a more
focused American development organization could help expand affordable
health care, allocate specific resources to bridge the digital and other infrastructure divides, subsidize national child-care networks to help women get
back into the workforce, and oversee equity programs to remove racial barriers and close women's wage gaps.

Since 2016, think tanks like the Brookings Institution, congressional task
forces, and many development economists have generated ideas like these.

They have suggested drawing on the funding of the existing system of federal reserve banks across the country to administer grants and loans for regional reconstruction and setting up a new "American National Investment Bank" with an independent development-focused staff. Others have proposed creating a national wealth fund, similar to the state of Alaska's, for the whole country, which would provide annual dividends for low-income and middle-class Americans as well as local equity investment funds underneath an umbrella organization.

These were all good potential solutions to the challenges before us. But to implement any or all of these fixes, the United States needed a federal-level vision *and* an organizing principle for action at the state and local government and community levels. First and foremost, though, legislators needed to begin by focusing on *people*.

15

No More Forgotten People

People like me, who move literally from the coal house to the White House, tend to be the exception that proves the rule of how difficult it is to get ahead even in the best of times. Yet everyone should have the same and equal opportunity for social mobility, whether they are born in coal country or in the capital city. The infrastructure of opportunity and other amenities should be there in some form at every doorstep. This is not simply an ethical imperative; it is also an existential one, at least so far as our democracy is concerned.

Everyone can play a role in creating this infrastructure, even at the individual level. We all have agency and the power to do something to make a difference in the lives of other people. Sometimes simple acts like offering a ride to an interview or giving someone a suit to make a workplace transition are all that is needed to provide opportunity. In other cases, the acts required are braver and riskier: for instance, when individuals — such as people serving on scholarship committees or hiring managers for internships and job placements — have to confront discrimination and give people a chance to prove themselves no matter what they look or sound like or where they are from.

In all these cases, but especially those where discrimination is involved, people in positions of power must take it upon themselves to break down the barriers to opportunity that hold back the less powerful. Yet we all have some power. As citizens of a democracy, we are all responsible for effecting change, especially when doing so will shore up the political system that we have inherited and prevent disasters like the Trump presidency from happening again.

Many discriminatory barriers, as I discovered firsthand, are deliberately used by specific groups to reduce competition for scarce resources, including access to elite universities and jobs. I saw this in the UK, where the class system was explicitly used as a device to keep all but a tiny handful of working-class students out of places like Oxford and Cambridge for decades. Entrance exams and interviews were skewed in favor of children from middle- and upper-class backgrounds and private schools. Exam questions and the entire methodology for evaluating student potential and performance were similarly biased, as the A-level debacle of 2020 proved.

In the United States, race is the primary obstacle to opportunity. Racial prejudice has been woven into the country's social, economic, and political fabric over the centuries since the Atlantic slave trade began. Black and other minority Americans face the same constraints on opportunity as everyone else — poverty, socioeconomic class, place, and gender — but race plays into all of these. It amplifies the other disadvantages.

Biases and discriminatory barriers are systemic. They foster inequality. It takes concerted effort to break them down through targeted legislation and government policies at the federal and state level. Institutional reform is required alongside individual action. And this principle is not limited to discriminatory barriers alone.

Working- and middle-class Americans need cross-racial and cross-generational coalitions to overcome the existing barriers to opportunity, as well as the long-term effects of disadvantage on their health and well-being, educational attainment, and job prospects. As individual cohorts, the more diverse younger generations of Millennials and Generation Z (those like my daughter who were born between 1997 and 2015) have objectively less opportunity than their parents and grandparents. Having been hard hit by the 2008–2009 Great Recession, they must contend with the aftermath of the devastating 2020–2021 global pandemic.

On all these fronts, the people who are at the greatest disadvantage cannot overcome the barriers to opportunity on their own. Everyone needs to pitch in. Only by working together, individual to individual and as the individual constituents of a larger system, can we begin to break down barriers of the kind that I overcame, whether they are related to a person's place, class, gender, race, or other attribute or circumstance. Only then can we truly make strides toward addressing the socioeconomic costs of Thatcher's and Reagan's policies in the 1980s — and undoing the political damage inflicted by their populist heirs like Farage and Trump. Whether or not the damage is permanent, only time will tell. But if we don't rally together, we may never know if it can be fixed.

A Common Purpose

Spurring collective action across racial as well as generational lines is clearly a difficult political and societal task. As Isabel Wilkerson points out in her book *Caste,* in the United States, the manufactured idea of "white supremacy" was deliberately promoted after the American Civil War to pit working-class whites against Blacks. It was frequently deployed to undermine workers' solidarity in labor disputes. The concept and the racial categories underlying it were false, but that did not prevent it from taking hold and poisoning American race relations for generations.

This sad history of racial identity being weaponized by the powerful against working people is not limited to the United States. It was also evident in the United Kingdom after both world wars, when race was used as a deliberate tool for divisive policies to benefit the narrow interests of shipyard owners and other big businesses who wanted to hire cheaper and non-unionized immigrant labor to stave off organized British labor demands for access to jobs with higher pay. White mobs were deliberately incited against Black workers in shipyards and port cities, leading to riots, intercommunal violence, and the deaths of Black seamen and dockworkers who were accused of stealing jobs.

In the UK, despite this history, it is more obvious than in the U.S. that working-class Brits have common experiences and challenges irrespective of race and where they live. The United Kingdom does not have the same history of racial segregation in housing, taxation, education, employment, and social life, nor all the institutionalized restrictions and legal exclusions that marked the U.S. for centuries. Discrimination exists in many pernicious forms of bias and prejudice in the United Kingdom, but Britons from all racial and ethnic backgrounds were likely to find themselves living and working directly alongside each other in towns and cities across the country once immigration from the former British empire increased after World War II.

Black working-class students from across the UK at my alma mater, St. Andrews University, for example, in interviews with me in 2020, had the same concerns about accessibility and affordability in higher education and limited future job opportunities as white working-class students. These were exactly the same concerns that I had had in the 1980s. The limited representation of what the British term "Black, Asian and Minority Ethnic" (BAME) students at St. Andrews weighed heavily on them in our discussions, but they recognized that increasing their representation would not immediately overcome the other problems they faced. Race amplified the effects of deprivation. As a result, diverse groups of students had banded together in 2020 to push the university to implement a program of concrete changes to address accessibility and affordability.

The St. Andrews students were not outliers. Prominent UK cultural figures from mixed-race backgrounds — including some of my contemporaries from working-class towns and low-income households outside London — made similar points in articles and interviews. David Olusoga, the British-Nigerian historian, TV presenter, and author of the best-selling book *Black and British: A Forgotten History,* grew up on a council estate in Gateshead near Newcastle in the 1980s. He describes himself as "half white working class" on his mother's side. In an article in the *Guardian* in April 2019, Olusoga stressed that the two identities of being Black and working-class need not be in opposition. He noted the fact that people of all races in Britain lived in the same neighborhoods, worked in the same insecure jobs, and shared the same economic struggles. "As a result, working-class people are a diverse group," he asserted. After he read a June 2020 interview with me in the *Guardian,* in which I related some of my observations from my time in the Trump administration as well as reflected on growing up in North East England, Olusoga tweeted about the striking resonance in our class backgrounds.

Similarly, in an interview with the *Guardian* in December 2020, Roland Gift, the lead singer of one of the UK's most famous 1980s bands, the Fine Young Cannibals, and a talented actor, talked about growing up mixed-race in a council house in a working-class neighborhood of Hull, Yorkshire, in the 1970s. He made the same point as Olusoga. Where he grew up, class could at times transcend race: "I am half white, half black. So what? We all do the same things." Gift recounted a story in which he and some Irish friends strayed into a "posher area" of Hull. They encountered two other mixed-race children "in shiny shoes." "Their father," Gift recalled, "ushered them away from us. So it's not race. It's class. It's always class."

The fact that race is used as a political tool in the United States to divert attention from the vast opportunity gaps between low-income and wealthy Americans and to erase any shared feeling of class or socioeconomic commonality becomes glaringly obvious when you compare identity politics in the U.S. and the UK. Given the United Kingdom's demography and spatial divergence, its politicians have found it much more difficult to use race to play with the country's divisions and promote their agendas than politicians in the United States. Of course, this doesn't mean they haven't tried. Since the 1980s, white supremacist groups have managed to secure a foothold in towns like Bishop Auckland, even when those towns have no appreciable BAME representation or immigration. But the appeal of these groups has been limited.

Regional differences and perceived divides, as well as class and accent discrimination, mitigate against the development of a larger fixed sense of racial and at times even English solidarity. And as the divisive politics around Brexit underscored, white Europeans were subject to as much popular resentment as other immigrants to the UK. EU citizens were not necessarily welcomed because they shared some overarching racial identity. Similarly, UK citizens whose parents or grandparents came from the West Indies and described themselves as Afro-Caribbean see this as a distinct identity from those whose families emigrated from Africa. The UK additionally has a large population of South Asian origin that brings other concepts of individuality or group affiliation.

Identities are not rigid constructs in the UK, nor are they in America. This implies that there is still a chance to break down racial barriers and develop an infrastructure of equal opportunity for *all* low-income, working-class, and middle-class Americans, regardless of the color of their skin. But this will require the recognition of a common purpose.

The Importance of Education

Breaking down racial barriers, as well as other universal or generalized spatial and structural impediments to opportunity, requires large-scale intervention. This is especially true when it comes to the education system, where the current infrastructure of opportunity has become cluttered with hurdles in both the U.S. and the UK. Removing these hurdles is imperative for three key reasons. First, the decimation of low-skilled jobs during the COVID-19 pandemic underscored that finding a "good," well-paying job in the twenty-first century will be almost impossible without some form of post–high school education — a two- or four-year college degree or an apprenticeship or other specialized skill training. Because Blacks, other minorities, and women have faced the highest hurdles to education and training, as well as to retaining full-time employment in the face of family and child-care challenges, they will be the hardest hit by changes in the job market in the years ahead.

Second, focusing collective action on education is an important aspect in countering the national security crisis of polarization and fragmentation. Lack of education — in the sense of acquiring the critical thinking skills that a good K-12 and some form of college education can provide — breeds suspicion of government, skepticism toward science and expert knowledge, and resistance to the very idea that there are things like basic facts and objective information. Poor educational attainment leaves people vulnerable to populists and political operatives — a fact underscored by President Trump's persistently higher ratings among Americans without a college degree.

Third, ensuring that all people have access to a high-quality education is essential for increasing America's competitiveness on the world stage and positioning the United States for new tests ahead. For one thing, reforming the education system would enable the U.S. to build a more flexible economic system tied to the ongoing shifts in technology and the nature of work. But this in turn would position the U.S. to meet the greatest geopolitical challenges of the moment.

In this century (unlike the twentieth), the United States faces systemic competition not from Russia but from China. If it can't figure out a way to quickly raise its game, it risks the diminution of its previous position of unrivaled economic, political, and military power since the end of the Cold War and the 1990s. At 1.4 billion in 2020, China's population is four times that of the United States — a mismatch that gives the Chinese economy a huge domestic consumer base. In the early 2000s, China's economic growth was propelled by the government tapping into and investing in the development of its human capital, the Chinese population, as if it were any other natural or financial resource. Since the 1990s the Chinese government has moved millions of people from rural to urban areas. Between 2000 and 2010 the pace of urbanization was so high that China was constructing a new million-strong city practically every month. In the 1990s the Chinese government also created targeted programs to alleviate poverty. It made considerable strides in urban areas, less so in rural China.

Where the Chinese government was perhaps most successful in the early 2000s was in expanding education to produce a new labor force. Millions of children and young adults were enrolled in intense education programs at the government's expense, including at schools and top colleges in the United States. China set out to purposely and purposefully build a substantial technocratic urban elite as well as train a new generation of skilled workers. To say that it accomplished this goal is an understatement.

Education was a key motor of China's growth in the 2010s, whereas in the United States the K-12 educational system and underresourced universities outside elite institutions stagnated and lagged behind. Chinese students ultimately took advantage of opportunities, covered by their own government's grant programs, to study in top universities in the U.S. that were inaccessible to or unaffordable for most Americans. To compete with China in the twenty-first century, the United States will have to give similar precedence to education reform and expand access to educational and training opportunities for all Americans, not just a select or privileged few.

Most kids these days never have the opportunity to apply to college, either in the United States or in the United Kingdom. It's hard to get into college or any form of specialized technical training without first making it through a K-12 school and achieving the requisite basic qualifications. And as I learned when I got to St. Andrews University in 1984, it's very difficult to compensate for all the things you haven't learned or been exposed to once you get to college, no matter what resources are available or how hard you work.

A poor elementary and secondary education is the primary impediment to accessing all forms of higher education. You will always be left behind and running to catch up. Without mentorship and initiatives to pave the way and then foster a sense of inclusion for first-generation and minority college students, many never get over the first hurdle of applying, and they founder and drop out once they are in college. Sometimes, moreover, they find that the deck is stacked against them even when they perform exceptionally well, as low-income A-level students discovered during the UK algorithm debacle in summer 2020.

Interventions in elementary and secondary education are critical in expanding the infrastructure of opportunity, but national government programs frequently miss the mark, and not only when it comes to processes such as testing and issues such as algorithmic bias. Schools in both the UK and the United States get only a fraction of their funding from the central government. K-12 institutions are dependent on local government budgets and local income tax revenues. Unlike universities, which can tap into a mix of government funding, tuition fees, private endowments, and corporate sponsorship, schools outside the private educational sphere are dependent on their immediate ecosystem. In disadvantaged regions like the North East of England, where the industrial base has disappeared, taking tax revenues and jobs, elementary and secondary school budgets take a hit along with everything else.

Part of the problem in ensuring equal access to a quality education for young people in both the United Kingdom and the United States, irrespective of their place of origin or race or ethnic identity, is the current composition of elites. Those at the top of the educational and political system find it hard to grasp the problems of low-income and minority students unless they have experienced poverty, discrimination, and failing schools for themselves. Poor students are dismissed as insufficiently academically gifted or hardworking rather than acknowledged as deprived. No one takes account of the fact that they are engaged in a constant struggle with economic disadvantage on top of social discrimination.

Opportunity Hoarders

In 2017 my Brookings colleague Richard Reeves (also originally from the UK) wrote a book, *Dream Hoarders,* explaining how the educational system in the U.S. has become increasingly skewed in favor of the existing elites. He describes how upper-middle-class children become advantaged at birth thanks to a stable home in an affluent neighborhood, educated married parents, and access to the best schools. Over time the American upper middle class has become a self-perpetuating meritocracy. It reproduces and replicates itself through education and the acquisition of qualifications — the merits that it acquires but others cannot.

Richard relates how the upper middle class "engages in unfair opportunity hoarding," helping their children and those of their family, friends, and neighbors navigate admission to prestigious colleges (including through legacy admissions) as well as access to internships and other mechanisms for developing skills and credentials. Qualification barriers serve to keep others out of upper-middle-class networks, exacerbating inequality and widening the gap between the political elite and the working or middle class.

Here race also comes into the picture as a negative factor. Blacks and Hispanics face racial as well as geographically discriminatory wage and income gaps that keep them out of the upper middle class and its networks, even when they have a college degree. This in turn impedes their children's access to a college education. All of which suggests that any sustained initiatives to increase Black and Hispanic educational attainment will have to be accompanied by simultaneous efforts to eliminate wage and other disparities if they are going to be effective in promoting social mobility.

One of my closest friends from graduate school at Harvard, Bonnie Bertolaet, saw all of these embedded problems in the education system at first hand. Bonnie grew up in Michigan, where her father was a professor at the University of Michigan in Ann Arbor. I initially met her in Scotland. She was then an undergraduate at Amherst in Massachusetts but came as an exchange student to the University of Stirling, where my sister enrolled in the 1980s. They ended up being roommates. We would visit each other at weekends in either Stirling or St. Andrews. Bonnie and I were both surprised to later find ourselves in the same year of grad school at Harvard in 1989. Bonnie was in the chemistry PhD program and one of few women. There were also very few Black students in the Graduate School of Arts and Sciences, which we were both part of in the 1990s. This made a big impression on Bonnie as well as me. After living and working in San Diego, Bonnie returned to the Boston area in the 2010s as the head of Science Club for Girls of Greater Boston, a privately funded nonprofit organization that provides free programs for low-income girls from underrepresented communities to help them prepare for higher education and careers in STEM. Science Club for Girls established a stellar track record of assisting its members to go to college, including universities like Harvard and Howard.

When Bonnie first became involved with Science Club for Girls, she encountered surprising resistance to the program within some affluent communities in the Boston suburbs when she told people what she was doing. Many of her interlocutors saw Science Club for Girls in zero-sum terms — reducing opportunities for other children, *their* children, while increasing them for the underrepresented students. Some of the people she talked with criticized the fact that the girls did not have to pay for the program: they should have "skin in the game," not get something for free. Others complained that programs like this were increasing competition for places at Ivy League universities. One person asserted that a student from Science Club for Girls might take a highly competitive university place away from her son, implying that the girls were given an unfair advantage or special connections through the program.

Bonnie was dumbfounded. She frequently found herself explaining that Science Club for Girls had been created specifically to address the previous absence of girls from underrepresented communities in university science courses and careers. The intent of the programs was to increase accessibility and make what once seemed extraordinary the "new ordinary." It ought to be normal for every group in the United States to see people like themselves at college or in any profession.

Bonnie also stressed that it was hard work being poor and that low-income families had limited bandwidth. The program was free, and application was made simple, because she and her colleagues at Science Club for Girls had learned that filling out paperwork and going to interviews was a barrier to entry. Kids often had part-time jobs or long commutes to school and limited access to Wi-Fi and a computer at home. The group also needed to advertise the program widely throughout the school districts and hold its sessions at convenient locations, as otherwise girls would not know that opportunities like this were there in the first place. How could they know if no one told them?

Finally, Bonnie pointed out to critics that they were using a double standard. "You can't perpetuate the myth in America of rugged individualism forever," as she told me later. "Everyone benefits from networks and mentorships, but when men or people from affluent backgrounds network and mentor, nobody labels it like this. They are just 'helping each other out.'"

"Doubly Disadvantaged"

In the United States, private resources like Science Club for Girls substitute and fill in for the lack of publicly funded programs, but they are not available in every town and city, exacerbating geographic inequities. Seeing this, my friend who directed the Science Club for Girls had reconnected with her alma mater, Amherst College, which established a STEM incubator in 2020 tailored toward low-income high school and underrepresented students in Massachusetts, many of whom were the first in their family to go to university. The way in which Amherst designed its programs also highlights the unique needs of students from disadvantaged backgrounds who manage to get within reach of the particularly potent educational opportunities offered by elite institutions.

Prior to 2020, Amherst had already championed initiatives to bring disadvantaged students to its campus in the summer months before their formal enrollment for a series of special supplementary courses in the basic science and math subjects they needed to complete in their first year. The courses helped fill in the gaps between their high schools' curriculum and those of other students. Amherst scaled up the programs to accommodate the largest possible group, so individual students would not feel embarrassed or stigmatized by having to take remedial or bridging courses alone or during regular term time.

In 2019, Tony Jack, a professor of education at Harvard, who like Bonnie did his undergraduate degree at Amherst, published a deeply insightful book on the particular challenges for low-income kids going to college from underfunded, overcrowded U.S. public schools in impoverished neighborhoods. Professor Jack, who had grown up in a poor neighborhood in West Grove, Miami, Florida, recounted his experience of being the first person in his family to go to university. He was one of the few low-income Black students at Amherst in the early 2000s. He discussed the difficulties of transitioning to college from high school and the structural exclusion of low-income and minority students, who did not have the cultural capital or preparation for dealing with the informal social rules and expectations of college life.

Professor Jack had had a one-year scholarship to a private school in his senior year, just before his admission to Amherst. This helped him figure things out. As he noted in his book, around 50 percent of lower-income Black students at elite universities in the 2010s graduated from a private high school thanks to specially targeted scholarships such as these. This was the same for one third of lower-income Hispanics. Professor Jack describes these students as "the privileged poor." They were still economically disadvantaged, but the private school experience gave them a critical boost — similar to that of the working-class kids in the UK who passed the eleven-plus and headed to a grammar school in the old days.

Nevertheless, for these disadvantaged students, everything could still be lost in translation once they got to college. As one example, low-income students tended to do their academic work on their own rather than seek help from professors during office hours. They were either too intimidated or did not know this was an option. As I had done at St. Andrews, the low-income American students that Professor Jack surveyed also worked multiple campus jobs to stay afloat. This naturally meant that they often did not have time (let alone the money) to engage in regular college activities.

The real challenge, however, was that many of these low-income students were what Professor Jack called "doubly disadvantaged": they were academically gifted but had no prior exposure to elite networks and limited information on college opportunities. If they were to fully capitalize on the opportunity that college presented, they would need help in this crucial regard through the kind of bridging programs that colleges like Amherst had established.

Contact-Poor

My personal educational experience in the 1980s mirrored these observations and conclusions. The UK education system, just like that in the United States, was — and remains — heavily geared toward middle- and upper-class groups, who are already embedded in old-boy and old-girl networks that exclude state school and low-income students who don't manage to find a free place at private school. Not only are algorithms working against them, but poor kids tend to be network- and contact-poor — they lack social as well as cultural capital. In fact, this is one of the reasons that they are poor in the first place.

Poor people don't have resources or other people to help them identify opportunities and navigate their way to college and advance through life. This was certainly the case for my dad and his family. Part of fixing the infrastructure of opportunity thus involves creating networks and contacts for underprivileged kids and their families.

The fact that being contact-poor is a major disadvantage is underscored in a fascinating psychology book, *Connected: How Your Friends' Friends' Friends Affect Everything You Feel, Think, and Do*. The book describes how people's personal contacts and social networks influence every aspect of life, including personal relationships, health, and happiness. It points out that for many people, those networks are constrained by geography, socioeconomic status, technology, and even their genetic makeup. People "can't be friends with absolutely anybody," and they don't get to choose their birth family or initial family economic circumstances.

Similarly, in 2020 another Brookings colleague, Camille Busette, undertook a large-scale data analysis of social networks and their role in driving socioeconomic mobility in several U.S. cities, including Charlotte,

North Carolina, which ranked last in a set of fifty major American cities for promoting upward mobility. In Charlotte, Camille and her colleagues interviewed residents and then looked at more than thirty thousand interpersonal network configurations according to the number of people and family and professional connections, and the value of these connections as a source of assistance in obtaining housing, education, and jobs. They evaluated and compared social networks according to demographic group, race, income, and gender. And in the process they discovered some surprising things about how social networks provide access to support, information, power, and resources and how they play a critical role in shaping opportunity.

Camille's team observed that in the case of Charlotte, whites had the greatest network advantages — especially white men, who had broad networks of professional, family, and personal contacts that were important sources of information and advice, and for providing references. Fathers played a particularly critical role in promoting mobility, as they were usually the primary wage-earner, with more professional connections than mothers.

White wealth and support networks consistently cascaded down through successive generations, while such networks did not for Blacks and Hispanics, who constituted most of the city's low-income population. Middle-income residents had the broadest networks compared to poorer residents, and even to the most affluent. Those at the top of the economic ladder had small but superior social and support networks. They were elite in every respect.

Camille further concluded from the data sets that most social connections were formed through education in schools and colleges, then in the workplace. Exclusion from a good school or limited access to university, along with the loss of a job, was the primary means of losing valuable connections and social capital. Sadly, this happened to far too many already deprived people in Charlotte — and in all the other places the team surveyed.

Creating Networks

Obviously I did not grow up in such a racially or economically diverse setting as Charlotte, North Carolina. In addition to being predominantly White British, Bishop Auckland's majority population was low- to middle-income. In 2020, County Durham's average annual salary was £23,000, or just under $31,000. It was far lower than that back in the 1970s and 1980s, thanks to high and persistent unemployment.

My family had not accumulated wealth; no assets were passed down through the generations. But my parents *were* in the process of buying a house, and this helped to break the negative poverty-education cycle for me. Critically, my parents also helped me make all kinds of new social connections, including in our street and neighborhood. I started out contact-poor but ended up with a rich personal and professional network.

Two issues were key in creating networks in Bishop Auckland. First, Mam and Dad married and had children in their early thirties, making them older than the average parents locally. When Mam had my sister at age thirty-four, one of her close friends from school was already a grand-mother. But there were benefits to being outliers in this respect: with age and experience, they had fully processed the importance of education. My dad understood that his lack of formal education was one of the reasons for the economic disparity between himself and friends, relatives, and colleagues at the hospital, who had gone to college and then on to white-collar jobs. Mam had trained as a nurse. She had a résumé and commendations from her previous positions. Dad had no qualifications of any kind apart from the on-the-job training he acquired in the coal mines. With the pits closed, there was no one to vouch for him for another job.

Second, Mam and Dad set out examples for me to follow and signed me up for free music lessons, orchestras, choirs, sports programs, and school exchanges, all funded through Durham County Council. Mam pressed me and Angela into the Brownies and Girl Guides, which Mam herself had joined as a child in Billingham during World War II. As an adult, she ran a troop in a local church hall. Many other relatives were in the Guides or Scouts. One of Dad's older cousins was the local Guides commissioner. The Guides was a local, national, and international organization that provided strong regional networks as well as a way of meeting people from other parts of the country and social classes, if you stuck around long enough, as Mam did. The patrons of the Girl Guides and some of the commissioners were all middle- or even upper-class, the wives of the local landed gentry and philanthropic businessmen and a few professional women.

Angela and I resisted the Guides and were never enthusiasts, but Mam asserted that obtaining all the merit badges and becoming a Queen's Guide (the equivalent of an Eagle Scout) would help with university applications. I got my Queen's Guide badge and promptly left the troop. Angela fell one badge short a couple of years later, by not being able to complete her camping badge because of maintenance cuts for the public campsites that the Girl Guides relied on in poor areas.

Under Margaret Thatcher's government, beginning in 1981, local county councils had been selling off public parkland as well as "surplus" school playing fields to property developers to raise money. Over the course of the 1980s, about five thousand fields were sold, drastically curtailing free sports and other outdoor programs. While they lasted, however, these opportunities did create new networks and provide leadership and other skill development that I was able to list on my university and job applications. I am especially good at tying knots and map reading (always useful when the GPS fails), but I no longer play the violin, which is probably just as well, since it tortured me and everyone else for far too long.

Mam talked a great deal about her nursing training, the people she had met, and the success she had had in her career until she had had to leave work to take care of me and Angela. She would take us to visit Miss Lilian Dyke, the retired chief obstetrician and gynecologist from the hospital, who had been one of the first female NHS consultants and had delivered us both in the maternity ward. Mam deeply admired her. Miss Dyke was from the North East, had attended a local girls' private school, and had then studied medicine at Durham University in the 1930s. During World War II she served in the Royal Army Medical Corps in India and afterward trained at hospitals in Newcastle and Durham before becoming the consultant at Bishop Auckland in the 1950s. Miss Dyke mentored all the junior doctors and nurses and set up the local branches of the Red Cross. She had been forced to retire from the hospital because of ill health in the mid-1970s, but she kept up with the Red Cross. Thanks to her efforts, Bishop Auckland had the largest concentration of Red Cross activities in the UK and offered free practical training classes for schools and organizations like the Girl Guides.

Mam's and Dad's stories about the clever lasses — the older cousins from our working-class extended families who had gone to university after school — were also important. We would sometimes see them at holidays. Mam and Dad encouraged us to ask about their experiences when we did. My parents also introduced me to a couple of neighbors who had gone to university as well as grammar school. This was one of the benefits of living in our own house in the new neighborhood in town rather than in public housing on the council estate. The street was not the most affluent, but some residents had gone on to all forms of higher education and training and worked in white-collar jobs.

The message was clear: if these cousins and neighbors could go to college, then I could too. Mam and Dad drove the point home by observing that I did not have the same obstacles they themselves had faced either. Dad had left school at fourteen to go down the mines, and Grandad had left earlier, at thirteen — because they had no other choice. They had both been held back by timing and larger circumstances, not just poverty. I had more opportunities than they did. The timing was right. I should try to go forward with my education as far as it would take me.

My education had, of course, not taken me to Oxford. Even if I had applied decades later, I would have been no more likely to have been admitted, since I came from Bishop Barrington Comprehensive School. Contacts, and what Tony Jack, like many others, called cultural capital, remained key to opening the door.

Even in these rarefied spheres, to be sure, there were signs of progress. The dreaded Oxford entrance exam was abolished in 1997, more than a decade after I applied, a change that helped increase the number of state school students admitted to the university. The proportion rose to over 50 percent in the early 2000s. Louise Richardson, after becoming the Oxford chancellor in 2016, pushed to improve state school access over the next several years. In 2020–2021, Oxford had its highest recorded state school intake of over 68 percent. Cambridge had achieved 68 percent in 2019. Nonetheless, in this same timeframe, only a small percentage of poor kids like me from deprived areas were admitted to Oxford. It was still out of their league, as the botched algorithm and the 2020 A-level exams had underscored.

Rather than waiting for the universities or the government to do something, students were starting to take matters into their own hands to address the question of recruitment and Oxbridge access. They were creating their own infrastructure of opportunity — their own networks and mechanisms for success. A November 2020 article in the *Guardian* featured a group of underrepresented students who had set up a free network called Team Upside to help their counterparts get into elite universities. They ran mock Oxbridge interviews for students from underprivileged schools and regions. A group of similar students already at Oxbridge created a digital outreach site, Inside Uni, to advise state school applicants on how to apply and prepare for interviews. The website provided real-life accounts from students and was coordinated with Oxbridge admissions officers.

One of the students who created Team Upside explained his motivations in the interview with the *Guardian*: "We think it's unfair that some students who go to really top schools are provided with so much more support and guidance than other students, when every student deserves an equal opportunity to succeed. It's really just about levelling the playing field."

Lifelong Learning

Getting a university degree is not the only way to level the playing field of opportunity. From Dad's experiences and all the mass layoffs in the North East in the 1980s, I knew even before I left school that no one could keep a job forever. Even a university degree would likely not be enough to deal with the changes ahead in the nature of work. You would always need to upgrade your skills to keep up with social and technological change.

Further education and lifelong learning are essential in the twenty-first century, yet they remain all too rare. In the UK, according to government figures, 34 percent of college graduates are not in "high-skilled employment" commensurate with their degree, because many postgraduate positions are in new digital and technology fields that require additional skills and training (as do jobs in engineering, manufacturing, teaching, nursing, and other fields). Careers are no longer achievable after one step on the educational ladder; they require multiple progressions.

There are many options to pursue postsecondary or tertiary education in both the United Kingdom and the United States. In the UK in 2020, a little over 50 percent of students who completed secondary school went on to university, professional and technical training, or further (continuing) education tied to apprenticeships in the workplace. The initial enrollment rates in postsecondary education in the U.S. are much higher than in the UK — between 60 and 70 percent of high school graduates — but not everyone completes college or their training courses. Back in the 1980s, most of the friends I had started out with at Etherley Lane primary school did not go to university after completing comprehensive school. They tried to enter the workforce immediately, seeking an apprenticeship, or like my mam in the 1950s, they went off to nursing school or some similar professional training course.

After driving me around in his Mini to help me choose a university in the 1980s, Jeff — Mam's godson and my de facto brother — went on his own educational odyssey. Like many I grew up with, Jeff wanted to begin work as soon as possible in a craft apprenticeship. He had mild undiagnosed dys-lexia. He always reversed the "e" in his name on our birthday cards as a small child and complained that he couldn't read his own handwriting and notes from class. Teachers at his elementary and comprehensive schools wrote him off as "lazy and could do better" in their reports.

Jeff's educational chances came after school, when the North East's ship-yards closed. At sixteen, in the late 1970s, Jeff enrolled in a British Ship-builders apprenticeship program to become a mechanical fitter in Smith's Dock in Middlesbrough. This opened a variety of opportunities. First, the apprenticeship put him through courses at Stockton-Billingham Technical College (the equivalent of a U.S. community college). Then, taking advan-tage of other on-the-job educational programs, Jeff went to night school in electronics at the same Tech.

Smith's Dock closed in February 1987. But even in this moment Jeff found new opportunities. He was among the last to go when orders wrapped up at the shipyard in 1985–1986. He then took a package for laid-off workers that included an "enterprise allowance scheme" for retraining. The allowance was partly funded by the UK government and the EU. It covered 75 percent of his base pay for the retraining period.

Like the early 2000s, that was a tough time to find permanent work — UK unemployment peaked for women at just under 12 percent in March–June 1984 and for men at 12.7 percent in December 1992–March 1993. With so many people across the country looking for a job all at once after the widespread industrial closures, the challenge was how to find a training program for a sector that would guarantee something longer-term. Elec-tronics and technology proved to be one area.

Jeff heard from a colleague about a computer course in Leeds which was tied to entry-level positions with the American mainframe company Con-trol Data Corporation (CDC). He enrolled in the course, got a job, and worked his way through various computer technology companies, includ-ing Siemens and Fujitsu in the North East. Once in a new permanent job, Jeff enrolled in a degree program at the Open University, the UK's larg-est public university, which offers off-campus, commuter, online, and fur-ther education courses. The degree was sponsored by his company. They paid half the fees and gave Jeff a week off to attend summer school. He also attended courses at nights and weekends at Teesside Polytechnic (now Teesside University) in Middlesbrough, which hosted the Open University classes.

Jeff graduated with a BSc in technology and systems. He parlayed the degree into a senior position as systems engineer for mainframes and networks. His additional training and education provided an immediate boost to his employment prospects and ability to generate wealth. Most importantly, like me, Jeff did all this without accruing any educational debt. As his experience demonstrated, there were different routes to a good job and educational attainment. You didn't have to take the route to an undergraduate degree that I did and head off to an elite university. But further education and training were critical elements of Jeff's success — and of mine.

Seizing Opportunity

In the UK, changes in the educational system in the 1960s and 1970s shaped my infrastructure of opportunity. Government reforms expanded the equivalent of K-12 education for working-class children and offered access to opportunities that my grandparents and parents did not have. Although my middle and high school, Bishop Barrington Comprehensive School, was chronically underresourced (and in this sense had the same problems that similar schools in the United States have had recently), Durham County Council's education authority nevertheless offered subsidized programs for music lessons, sports, and school trips and exchanges, and additional assistance in cases of real hardship. Most of these opportunities were extracurricular, which meant that they involved some legwork and personal initiative. They were not handed to you, nor were they always particularly well advertised; you needed to seek them out, reach out, and grab them on your own.

School exchanges played an especially important role in my social mobility by giving me early opportunities to study in Europe (in Germany and France), improve my language skills, make new contacts, and see how other people lived. County Durham's exchanges were part of a broader post–World War II European initiative to promote reconciliation among former adversaries. They increased in popularity after the UK joined the EU in the 1970s. Many of the school exchanges were facilitated through "town twinning" or "sister city" networks that were formalized by local governments. U.S. towns and cities were also included in the programs. Exchanges were paid for by local education authorities and relied on host family volunteers.

Beyond the school exchanges, in the 1980s, County Durham paid the fees for my entire university education. The county awarded me an additional "maintenance grant" that covered housing, living expenses, and student materials. I received the maximum grant available, based on a means test and the low income of my parents. I was able to study anywhere in the United Kingdom with that funding. I could pursue any degree or training course. There was no restriction stipulating that I had to enroll in a local university or technical college. If I had opted for an institution close to home, I would simply not have received the full maintenance grant. I might have been encouraged to live with my parents.

In the United States, my husband and all his siblings had their college education covered on the same basis by federal grants, which were supplemented by other scholarships. Those grants were game-changers for me and my husband. We both graduated without debt, which is another obstacle to opportunity. My university education at St. Andrews, and the funding for my year abroad in Moscow through the Russian Language Undergraduate Study Committee, which was administered by the British Council, was especially consequential. It opened the door to a different life.

For educational programs and studies out of area or abroad that were not covered by Durham County Council, I found supplemental sources of funding thanks to tips from relatives and neighbors. The Durham Miners' Association, part of the National Union of Mineworkers, was especially helpful, as was the local business community via the Rotary Club. I was directed to small grants and subsidized programs through my local library and its in-house Citizens Advice Bureau, which was staffed by volunteers. These were usually retired white-collar professionals with very different backgrounds and experiences from those of my family and relatives. They offered me access to their networks of contacts just by sitting in the library. By volunteering in this way, all these individuals helped bridge generational, class, and informational divides. They had already achieved professional status, had stable incomes, and had insight into how things worked at the local and national levels.

In the same way, my member of Parliament, Derek Foster, and his constituent offices played an important role in social mobility. He and his staff visited local schools and regularly checked in with children and their parents to tell them about government programs they might be eligible for. Local council members were equally engaged with schools, as were the representatives of the community's churches (the town was predominantly Christian). Even if you weren't part of their denomination or congregation, the town's churches would welcome you to their youth clubs. Poor local kids could sign up for vacation activities, including summer day trips to the seaside. Trade unions, community churches, workplace associations, Girl Guides, and other local groups like the Red Cross helped provide me and others with new experiences and skills.

Most of these educational opportunities that brought me from the UK to America came through ad hoc initiatives and stand-alone funding sources. They were not part of some comprehensive national or regional program intended to promote social mobility. There was no room for passivity. You had to be persistent and active in looking for opportunity. Once you knew a prospect for advancement was there — like hearing about the scholarships to Harvard and other American universities from a chance encounter in Moscow — then you had to seize the initiative.

Systematizing Opportunity

Individual agency will always be essential, but a systematic, coordinated approach to developing the infrastructure of opportunity would ease the way for more people to succeed. Back in my early graduate student days at Harvard, my economics professor, János Kornai, introduced the concept of "social protection funds" to assist former state industrial workers in the old Eastern bloc to retrain for the new market economy. That idea was passed over by would-be reformers in Eastern Europe and Russia in the 1990s, but this proposal could still be useful today.

Just as Mam's godson, Jeff, was able to use UK and EU government funds to retool for a new technology job, similar funds could be used for any disadvantaged group to acquire the skills they need for the future market and workplace. For example, educational programs like the Science Club for Girls of Greater Boston that my Harvard Graduate School friend Bonnie Bertolaet chairs shouldn't be confined to large metropolitan areas. These kinds of programs need stakeholders to band together to fund and scale them up into national networks. All girls and low-income kids interested in STEM should have access to something close by.

Philanthropists and nonprofit organizations can play a critical role in creating and replicating programs for K-12 students, but so can universities, large library systems, and private-sector companies. They can work together to get buy-in for programs from schools, parents, and kids. Educational programs inside and outside schools need to be tied to the idea of preparing students for college and the workplace simultaneously. Education should be linked to jobs.

Pro bono volunteering by senior people in universities and companies can help incubate and expand programs such as these. Bonnie Bertolaet, for example, tapped into her contacts at the Harvard Graduate School and local tech companies for advisers. Individuals in both universities and the private sector can act as skills builders for young people enrolled in programs to create "career escalators." Anyone at any stage further up the career ladder can explain the next steps that a student might have to take in her or his formal education and training. Would-be mentors don't have to wait until they have "made it" or retired, like the volunteers in Bishop Auckland's Citizens Advice Bureau.

Temporary internships for schoolkids also play a role in skills and career development. When I was in secondary school, I enrolled in a couple of short-term job placement schemes managed, again, by Durham County Council. The county relied on local businesses stepping up to assist the program. Unfortunately, the options were few and far between, given the dearth of large businesses and transportation constraints. Many of the local small businesses didn't have the resources or time to set aside to bring schoolkids on board, and those that signed up could have benefited from some additional program funding. Still, they provided me with experience, which is more than I had had before.

I spent a couple of memorable weeks tramping around agricultural shows and interviewing farmers for one of the local newspapers, the *Teesdale Mercury,* in the nearby town of Barnard Castle. I rode the fourteen miles there and back every day on my bicycle, as well as to the interviews. I got my own byline for an article on an extraordinarily large leek grown in someone's garden, "Bob Grows a Whopper!" I also spent a short period of time trying to sell patio doors, not very successfully, for Castlewood Enterprises, a call center in Bishop Auckland's Railway Street. Some of the old buildings that used to serve the Stockton-Darlington railway had been converted into cheap office space, and although most of the enterprises on Railway Street went under quickly, call centers flourished for a while in Bishop Auckland — then went to India.

Neither of these experiences made a big difference, but they helped me figure out that I wanted to stick with the plan of going to university. It was also clear to me, even as a teenager in the 1980s, that programs like this needed to be at scale to be effective. County Durham and the surrounding communities did their best with limited resources, but there was no larger set of national funding to tap into for more robust programs. Many of my school friends didn't bother with the job placement scheme because of the lack of options.

In the United States, private-sector interventions could easily assist public-sector efforts at the local and state level in establishing larger internships and job placement schemes for schools. Big tech companies could help bridge the digital divide for schools in rural communities to access information about programs as well as online programming.

Based on my family's experience with the Durham Miners' Association, labor unions and workers' collectives have a role to play alongside private companies. Even though in the 1970s and 1980s it seemed like trade unions were fixated on nothing more than pay disputes and strikes, the older workers' collectives like the DMA focused on creating dignity and respect in work. Continuous on-the-job learning and lifetime skills acquisition for workers and their families was a core feature. DMA dues created all kinds of opportunities for my family, such as the miners' welfare clubs that Grandad and Dad took part in and the small grants and scholarships I tapped into. The DMA was also fully engaged in the broader communities where their members lived.

Perhaps more than anything else, opportunities such as these show aspiring but disadvantaged people that there is a world beyond their immediate horizons. They give people hope, and permission to dream. Occasionally they even give people access to new places.

Given the geographic disparities across the UK, I often thought that a system of exchanges or "twinning" arrangements like the ones I'd seen abroad would have been useful at home. When I left the UK in 1989, despite the country's small size, I knew little about what life was like for people living outside of the North East and Scotland, nor what it was like to be a middle-class student at a well-equipped private school. I could only imagine.

Such a system could have political benefits as well as personal ones. In the United States, a formal domestic program of school exchanges embedded in twin towns and sister cities across every state could assist in bridging some of America's divides at the individual level. Short-term physical exchanges supported by host families could be supplemented by larger virtual exchanges with groups of schools, both public and private. Virtual exchanges could foster cross-county friendships through regular small group online chats or meetings. "Sister schools" could offer joint curricula and classes through digital platforms, which would also enable teachers to share best practices on new teaching methods.

There are so many ways in which we can learn from each other, and so many reasons that we should. But there also are many ways in which places, as much as people, hold the key to unlocking opportunity. Education is the beating heart of the infrastructure of opportunity, but place — where you live — is the body that holds it. Place frames everything else. It has the greatest impact on an individual's educational and economic opportunity and ability to build wealth. It can hold someone back from finding opportunity or provide a direct pathway to it. For all these reasons, unlocking the potential of place is one of the greatest imperatives of the twenty-first century.

16

No More Forgotten Places

In the 1980s my dad told me to get out of Bishop Auckland and the North East of England with five fateful words: "There's nothing for you here." But of course there *should* have been something for me and others there, at home in County Durham, and elsewhere in the United Kingdom. I should not have had to leave my family, friends, and hometown behind in order to make a meaningful life for myself.

In the final reckoning, in both the United Kingdom and the United States, there should be no such thing as the wrong place to live. And in America, our currently polarized partisan politics and fragmented sectarian society would look very different if we were able to realize the vision of a more inclusive nation where opportunity is spread more evenly across the country's vast landscape and its population.

Young people in both the UK and the U.S. should have equal opportunity to stay in their hometowns or go back home after college and contribute to the future of their community if they want to. No one should have to think that social mobility can come only from geographic mobility — that they have to move, like I did and like my sister did, in order to find a future for themselves.

After leaving Bishop Auckland, Angela found a job in London, ostensibly the hub of opportunity in the UK. But she was ultimately defeated by the impossible task of trying to make ends meet in one of the world's most expensive cities. She now lives and works as a teacher in Spain. Neither of us regrets moving and becoming citizens of other countries, but neither do we have any illusions that this is a solution for the majority of people from our hometown or places like it.

Many of our friends in Bishop Auckland did not want to leave the North East of England. Some left and then went back because pockets of regional development — in cities like Newcastle — and shifts in technology made it possible to do so. Others stayed put all along, doing whatever it took to get by.

The people who stayed in Bishop Auckland did so for the same reasons that anyone gives for wanting to remain at home. They wanted to be where their grandparents and parents had put down roots. They didn't want to be transplants in some other place. They wanted a job and the feeling that they were living somewhere that mattered to them — in a tight-knit community where they belonged, where people knew their names, and where no one was going to make fun of their accents.

None of this should be too much to ask for anyone. But making even these modest goals achievable will require building forward together in a very literal sense. Unless and until we do, the fundamental challenges for America, the United Kingdom, and other struggling countries will remain unsolved.

Starting from Scratch

Of course, just as everyone is disadvantaged differently, opportunity also will never be completely evenly distributed. In some places jobs will remain scarce, while in others demand for workers will exceed supply in the local population. Some people will also *want* to move in search of new opportunity. In such cases we need national programs to facilitate domestic relocation for those on the lower rungs of the economic ladder. Leaving family and friends and social networks is always a risky proposition. It requires the physical ability to move as well as the financial means to cover travel and accommodation. You need access to information on jobs and places to live and on local schools for children.

In the United States, until recently, economic growth, affordable cars, cheap gas, extensive rental and federally backed mortgage markets, and the low price of consumer goods made pulling up stakes far easier than in most other countries. My in-laws, the Keens, took geographic and social mobility for granted when they packed their kids into a station wagon and headed off from Mitchell, South Dakota, to Minneapolis and then to the

Chicago suburbs in the 1950s and 1960s. They figured something would always work out.

But the 2008–2009 housing bubble and financial crisis helped put an end to Americans' ease of mobility. According to my colleague William Frey at the Brookings Institution, in 2019 — before the pandemic forced everyone to shelter in place and work at home — migration and mobility in the U.S. had declined to their lowest rates since 1947. Migration is different from emigration — the latter sometimes the result of being unable to overcome the barriers to opportunity at home. Emigration strips a country of its human capital and talent. Migration retains it.

In the United Kingdom it was never easy to move or migrate, even with a guaranteed job. For someone like me in the North East of England, it was simpler to move to Australia, Canada, or the United States than it was to relocate to the South of England, where you knew no one, you might face class or accent discrimination, and you were priced out of the housing market. Too often such barriers cause people to pass up opportunities, much as I had been forced to pass up the chance to go to a better school because of the cost of the uniforms, books, and sports equipment.

In the early 1990s, Mam's godson, Jeff, had the opportunity for a promotion and job relocation to Bracknell, near London. The discrepancy in house prices proved an insurmountable barrier. Based on what he saw was available in the classified advertisements, if Jeff had sold his house in Billingham, he would have been lucky to buy a shed or a parking space in London. He didn't know anybody in London to stay with or to help him look for something in advance. So many things were in flux in the UK economy at the time that he also feared the promised job might eventually be cut or restructured. Then he would be stranded in the South. So Jeff turned down the promotion and stayed put in the North East.

Conversely, when my sister got her first job in London, she initially heard about the vacancy from an advertisement in the *Guardian* after enrolling in a government employment training scheme in computing and data entry. The training scheme paid the train fare for her to go to her interview. The older brothers of two classmates from Bishop Barrington had already moved south and rented a small house. They offered Angela their spare room once she got the job. Without the government assistance and then those personal connections, Angela might have stayed put too.

In the 1990s, many of the "rough sleepers" on London's streets were from the North East. They moved to look for work and couldn't find anywhere to stay. They didn't have support networks or relatives to reach out to. There was no "North East consulate" or domestic migrant network if they got into trouble. Before Brexit made it harder for foreign workers to move to the British capital in search of opportunity, it was easier for someone from Warsaw than from Wallsend, near Newcastle, to move to London. The Poles set up all kinds of mutual support networks for their compatriots; there was no such mechanism for Brits.

When there are no formal mechanisms to assist relocation, it's hard to start from scratch in your own country. Angela's and Jeff's anecdotal experiences underscore what Camille Busette at Brookings and her research team discovered in examining social mobility in Charlotte, North Carolina, and other U.S. cities. Personal and family contacts and social networks play a determinative role in social mobility. When people are forced to move because of social and economic upheaval, they rupture and lose their personal infrastructure of opportunity. They leave behind their geographic, place-based social group and family support networks. They are displaced. They become contact-poor. Without family, friends, neighbors, workers' collectives, church groups, and other sources of mutual aid, they have no one to help them get by.

There are, however, some very simple but effective ways in which governments and institutions can provide support for necessary relocations. For instance, my relatives who moved from the North East of England to Australia in the 1960s had everything set up for them. They just needed the courage and determination to emigrate. The Australian government paid for their flights. Once they got there, a government relocation program directed them to regions that needed workers. The program offered additional subsidies for transportation and housing. They had all the information and resources to find a new job and build a new life.

In effect, I had the same experience when I moved to the United States. With a Harvard scholarship, a special administrative unit within the Harvard Graduate School of Arts and Sciences, a defined course of study, and somewhere to live set up for me (in a dormitory), I ended up with all the infrastructure for new opportunity. This included a ready-made set of contacts.

The challenge for us today is to create these kinds of mechanisms and networks for domestic relocation. Of course, these support systems cannot substitute for improving the overall quality of life in places like Bishop Auckland and small-town America, so people can stay where they already are, at home. But if people must leave to seek opportunity elsewhere, they should have a shot at doing so.

Out of Pocket

For many people, "quality of life" is one of those sometimes nebulous terms that has subjective as well as objective elements. What provides a boost for some, like easy access to particular sets of amenities such as parks and sports fields, might be less important to others. Towns can take care of some of these kinds of boosters themselves, whereas other structural and essential institutional elements that contribute directly to quality of life, in terms of affecting people's physical health and overall well-being, may be far beyond the extent of a municipality's resources or organizational capacities and authorities. In the United States, for example, many people fear moving — changing jobs and place — because of the risk of losing their health-care benefits or of ending up somewhere with limited access to a hospital and other medical services. Towns cannot fix these kinds of problems on their own.

In the U.S. social system, unequal and inadequate access to health care is one of the greatest vulnerabilities for individuals and families, as COVID-19 underscored in 2020. In this respect, the United States is more like Russia in the 1990s than the United Kingdom. In both the U.S. and Russia, people lost their health care when their factories closed or they lost their jobs. Medical care and employment have been bound together for most Americans since World War II. After the U.S. government imposed wage controls in 1942, companies began offering work benefits like health insurance in lieu of higher wages. The following year, health insurance was made non-taxable by the IRS, rendering it cheaper for workers to get insurance through their employer than on the open market. Only those with a very low income, the elderly, the disabled, and serving members of the military and veterans have had their health care funded under government programs. In 2019, thirty million Americans (9 percent of the total population) were uninsured, with premiums for health insurance well beyond their or their employer's financial reach. As with education, reforming health care in the United States will play a pivotal role in improving the country's competitiveness in the twenty-first century.

This is one area in which the United Kingdom is well ahead of the United States — and other English-speaking nations are further ahead still. In the

UK, equal access to some form of health care played an important factor in both alleviating the effects of poverty after World War II and enabling people to manage a portfolio of part-time jobs or move to another town for work. They had health care no matter what. This was not a constraint or an obstacle. In some advanced-economic countries, such as Canada, access to health care as well as good K-12 education are essentially the same no matter where you live. There is not the kind of spatial inequality in the infrastructure of opportunity for Canadians that Americans and Brits have to contend with.

In my case, the National Health Service was pivotal on two fronts for my family. First, the NHS provided basic medical services, regular childhood well-being checks, and emergency treatment. It gave me the opportunity to be healthy and thrive. The NHS was anything but perfect, but it was particularly good at the care side of health care rather than at meeting demands for the expensive medical tests and novel treatments that have pushed up costs in both the UK and the U.S. in recent years. For the latter there could be lengthy waiting lists or simply no availability. The NHS was also strong on cradle-to-grave interventions like pre- and postnatal care, childhood vaccinations, and end-of-life hospice care.

My parents were already leaving school when the NHS came along in the late 1940s, but I was born in the mid-1960s, when it was in full swing. The NHS made all the difference between life and death. I was very ill at one point as a child and needed treatment for the best part of a year. Much of that treatment ended up being at home, with visiting doctors and nurses. At various points each of my parents was in hospital for short periods, for either illness or acute injury. My father needed in-home care in the last year of his life, when he suffered from congestive heart failure. The NHS helped with the provision of home hospice care and any equipment he needed, which came on loan. Our family doctor's office coordinated the care, along with the local social services. We didn't have to seek it out. Specialist appointments and medical tests may not always have been easy to schedule and sometimes required traveling out of town. But no one was out of pocket or bankrupted by any of these services.

In addition to benefiting health-care consumers (as they are sometimes called today in the United States), the NHS provided many people in the United Kingdom with a job, especially as postindustrial decline accelerated in the 1970s and 1980s. As I've mentioned, both of my parents found long-term work at Bishop Auckland General Hospital, for instance. Before the pandemic, the "care economy" was a major source of employment in Bishop Auckland, in the local hospital, in nursing homes, through home care, and in child-care facilities as well as in dentists' offices, pharmacies, chiropodists' offices, optometrists' offices, and the whole range of entities that make up the health-care sector. Women especially benefited from these opportunities, but not exclusively: when Dad's coal mine closed in the 1960s, funding for retraining was not available, but auxiliary jobs at the hospital provided the lifeline. And it was my mother's job as a nurse and midwife with the NHS that paved the way for us to buy a house. Nursing was a good, solid, respected working-class profession. Living in our own house in a new neighborhood, a mini-community within the larger town, gave us a chance to meet new people and build new social networks. Our neighbors in turn helped us through difficult times in my childhood, forming a sort of secondary safety net. Similarly, the next generation of neighbors in our street helped Mam stay in her own home in her old age. And the NHS dispatched a range of health visitors and carers to her house to deal with health issues.

The health-care economy in the U.S., as in the UK, became the bastion of reliable jobs when the manufacturing sector declined, including for a manual worker like my father, whose coal-mining skills were not easily transferable. As a March 2020 Brookings Institution report underscored, America's health-care sector has been one of the most significant growth areas in the U.S. economy since the turn of the century. It employs 11 percent of U.S. workers and accounts for 24 percent of government spending as well as just over 8 percent of consumer spending. In other research in the United States, the health-care sector generated 56 percent of the growth of low-wage jobs in the 1980s and almost 75 percent by the 2000s. And it became the mainstay of jobs in former industrial regions, such as the old coal and steel towns of Ohio, Pennsylvania, and West Virginia, accounting for more than one fifth of employment for otherwise "left-behind workers."

There is a dark underside to this safety net, however. As the February 2021 Lancet Commission on the U.S. government's approach to handling COVID-19 underscored, the impacts of the pandemic were exacerbated by the deficiencies in America's public health system, including the strain put on undertrained, underpaid, overworked staff on the lower rungs of the care economy, in places like nursing homes. People like my father, working as hospital porters, orderlies, and cleaners, suddenly found themselves at the tip of the spear as frontline workers alongside doctors and nurses, all of them confronting a mysterious and deadly new threat without anywhere close to the level of support that they and their patients needed.

The pandemic highlighted the vital importance of finding ways to fix the overall system. Some of the commissioners recommended the creation of a socialized or universal single-payer health-care system as in the UK and Europe. For most Brits and Europeans who settle in the United States, the creation of a single-payer health-care system seems long overdue. The politics that swirl around this issue are nothing short of baffling. Why is universal access to health care an example of the "evils of socialism"? Socialized medicine exists already in the United States in the form of Medicare and Medicaid funding. It is also a feature of the hospital networks of the Veterans Affairs system and of large privately funded health maintenance organizations, as well as in specific state-based initiatives such as Massachusetts' Blue Cross Blue Shield system, which I used when I lived in the state in the 1990s.

There are many similarly practical ways to approach this issue. In December 2020, for example, Brookings scholar Stuart Butler — who was also born in the UK — provided a detailed blueprint for building on existing elements to create a new comprehensive American health system. Stuart recommended a mixture of universal subsidies, grassroots community health centers, and programs tailored to the needs of individual states. His emphasis was on creating a flexible, networked system with regional and local differentiation. In many respects this is what the UK's National Health Service did when it was formed in the 1940s. The NHS was created through the amalgamation of a series of existing private, voluntary, charitable, and public networks. It wasn't created entirely from scratch, and even after it came on the scene, private medical practices never completely disappeared.

Over the decades since the creation of the NHS, the UK's primary problem has been the systematic government defunding of the NHS, not the basic provision of care, alongside the difficulties of implementing a wholescale reform of the system to keep up with the population's growing demand for medical services. These are all problems that could be factored in and addressed at the outset in the United States with the kind of mixed approach recommended by Stuart Butler.

The U.S. could learn from the UK in other regards as well. In the UK, in addition to the NHS, other national networks and mechanisms helped alleviate poverty, contribute to well-being, and provide children and their families across the country with a modest hand up, no matter where they lived.

My parents benefited from long-standing mutual assistance programs, conceived nationally but accessed through locally organized networks, including the Co-operative (Co-op) shops for accessing food and basic household items, and building societies for buying a house. Building societies were a form of credit union or cooperative savings association specifically targeted at funding mortgages for low-income workers. They were first developed as part of a network of citizens' mutual aid societies during the rapid urban growth of the industrial revolution in the late nineteenth century. As low-income borrowers, Mam and Dad had an interest rate reduction guaranteed by the government as well as a twenty-five-year term. Similarly, at the national level, the family allowance (which later became the child benefit) helped lift mothers and children out of crushing poverty when I was a child. This was initially a combination of direct payments and a tax benefit, which was paid directly to mothers for each individual child from infancy until the child left school.

Similar payments for children and families have long been considered in the United States, and local financial institutions like community banks and credit unions that were shuttered in the wake of the Great Recession could be revived as part of a newly targeted national development program. In these and so many other ways, the solutions to our broken health-care and other parts of the social support system are staring us in the face. All it would take to implement them is political will.

A Marshall Plan for America

All these ideas — including for providing health-care networks at the grassroots level, in the communities where people actually live — fit within a broader framework of ideas and projects organized around the concept of place-based regeneration or "transformative placemaking."

In the United States, the political agenda for developing the economy is usually initiated at the federal level. As a result, it changes with every new administration. But state and local problems remain the same — their development issues persist irrespective of who is in the White House. To create and restore the infrastructure of opportunity after the coronavirus pandemic, the United States will have to balance a place-based and local- and state-driven development agenda with national-level programs. America's towns and cities and rural areas need continuity of policy. And this modest goal is within their reach. After four years of the Trump administration, the government agencies dealing with economic development issues were hollowed out and their career staffs demonized like other public servants. In contrast, local and regional institutions and leaders retained reasonably high levels of trust. So it is perhaps no surprise that some of them have taken up the standard of place-based regeneration that so often has been set aside by the federal government.

In November 2020, a group of eight mayors from Pennsylvania, Ohio, West Virginia, and Kentucky — in the Appalachian region of the greater Ohio River Valley — called for a "Marshall Plan for Middle America," a variant of the Marshall Plan, or European recovery program, that the U.S. initiated in Europe after World War II. They noted that the plan's architect, U.S. secretary of state George C. Marshall, had been born in Uniontown, Pennsylvania, and they advocated for a similarly large-scale, multiyear, regionally focused federal program for that region and others like it in the United States.

The original Marshall Plan was conceived as an investment in postwar Europe's financial stability and its political future, and it helped forge a transatlantic alliance system that lasted for the next eight decades. The plan was a response to the physical and economic devastation of Europe after years of heavy combat during World War II. Much of Europe's infrastructure had to be rebuilt — entire cities, roads and rail connections, power plants, and industries. The U.S. feared that the destruction and dislocation of the war, with millions of refugees, mass unemployment, and poverty, would undermine European democracies and increase the appeal of Communist and other extremist parties across the continent. Faced with that prospect, over a relatively short time, from 1948 to 1951, the United States dispensed more than $13 billion in grants and loans.

The original Marshall Plan does offer a useful overarching frame for the United States at a critical time in the country's history. But it was a one-time injection of money, not a sustained long-term development effort. The focus was primarily on relief and recovery. Under the Marshall Plan, individual European countries drew on central resources to kick-start their own investment strategies. Local leadership and public-private efforts continued projects beyond the scope of the plan.

The longer-term development goals were later picked up on a permanent basis by the International Bank for Reconstruction and Development — the World Bank — which established specific in-country programs that eventually expanded from Europe to the rest of the world. Similarly, after the Cold War, the U.S. helped with the creation of the European Bank for Reconstruction and Development (EBRD) for the redevelopment of the former Soviet Union and Eastern Europe. The Washington, D.C.–based Eurasia Foundation, where I worked in the late 1990s, was set up by funding allocated by the U.S. Congress to complement EBRD and other programs by taking grant-making down to the grassroots level in the former Soviet republics. Funding had to be aligned with local needs. Community groups came up with their own development strategies and proposals.

The whole point of U.S.-led international development programs was to invest directly in people, their communities, institutions, and private businesses so they could strengthen their own capacity for action. We need to do the same for the United States, so that Americans can access and create the infrastructure of opportunity for themselves.

In early 2021, building on these kinds of global development initiatives and the idea of the mayors from Appalachian cities, Tony Pipa at the Brookings Institution issued a report recommending the creation of a "domestic development corporation" specifically designed for rural America. Rural America accounts for 14 percent of the U.S. population, or forty-six million people who live outside large metropolitan areas and their suburbs. Since 2005 rural America has fallen through the gaps in every U.S. government program, hemorrhaging vital services, including access to health care, which put its population in a precarious situation ahead of the pandemic. In a ten-year period, for example, 176 rural hospitals and associated medical centers closed, forcing residents to drive long distances, sometimes for hours, even for emergency treatment.

As in the case of similar proposals, Tony recommended pulling together and streamlining existing funds and setting clear development goals. His report pointed out that millions of dollars of funding were already being dispensed but were buried across four hundred federal programs, thirteen departments, and ten independent agencies as well as over fifty offices and subagencies. No fewer than fourteen congressional committees had some form of responsibility for legislation concerning rural-eligible programs. The obvious solution was a single national program for rural America that could be part of a larger federal development agency or effort.

The original Marshall Plan was a huge transfer of funds to modernize industry, restore infrastructure, break trade barriers, and head off communism. Today America needs something broader — an intervention at all levels that is more than just an injection of money or a one-off series of capital investments in roads and railways. The Marshall Plan was also a government-to-government program. In the United States, the government is no longer the primary mover, and private actors play critical roles in providing place-based programs and services. The key is to empower them to take development into their own hands, making it a virtuous cycle to counteract the vicious cycles that have dominated in America's forgotten places for so long.

Aiding Outside the Box

Once national and regional frameworks are in place and targeted development programs are under way, individuals and private groups can step in to bolster the infrastructure of opportunity. This is what happened in the former Soviet Union, for example, in the 1990s and early 2000s. And the same approach could easily be adapted and applied in the United States in the 2020s.

In the former USSR, international organizations like the World Bank and American and European government development agencies provided large-scale funding for major programs. Independent organizations such as the Eurasia Foundation focused on supporting grassroots organizations at the local level by disbursing small grants and promoting collaboration among them. With its own government funding and contacts with the U.S. State Department, Congress, the U.S. Agency for International Development and similar European entities, the Eurasia Foundation played a critical networking and coordinating role. It helped to connect governmental agencies to nonprofits on the ground in specific countries. And it created linkages among the local and community-level organizations to encourage relationship-building for initiatives, such as developing regional educational and employment programs for people with disabilities or creating trading networks for small-scale agricultural and food producers.

The Eurasia Foundation and similar independent entities became clearinghouses and conveners, as well as training providers and advisers for grantees on how to use technology, measure the performance of their programs, and make sure funds were spent properly. They helped to create information systems for their grassroots grantees to encourage and support research and development initiatives, and they provided platforms to share best practices.

None of these services were time- or country-specific. Because of that, the post-Soviet programs of organizations such as the World Bank and the Eurasia Foundation can serve as a model, a template, for organizations in other struggling countries to follow. Indeed, the Eurasia Foundation is still in operation and has expanded its work to the Middle East and Afghanistan.

Foundations and individual philanthropists can also play a critical role in scaling up in the United States once there is a shared vision and broader context for action. America has long been a world leader in individual philanthropy. In December 2020, for example, MacKenzie Scott, the former wife of Amazon founder Jeff Bezos, donated more than $4 billion to a wide range of long-established but underresourced entities in direct response to the ravages of the coronavirus pandemic. These included historically Black universities and colleges and nonprofits with programs targeted at working-class Americans, alleviating economic hardship and promoting upward mobility. Ms. Scott's focus was on "no strings attached" philanthropy. Although she and others acknowledged that her donations could not substitute for government funding, they would make a significant difference. In most cases her gifts were the largest donations a group had ever received.

Ms. Scott's actions were a far more sophisticated and well-resourced version of the kind of individual, scattershot philanthropy usually seen in County Durham and U.S. rural areas. In Blackhall Colliery, for example, a particularly impoverished former pit village on the County Durham coast, not far from Bishop Auckland, two anonymous benefactors literally dropped packets of money in the street over a six-year period. They wanted to help local people in the wake of the Great Recession, but no institution was available to pass money through to the community. They took the risk that whoever found the money would figure out something beneficial to do with it.

In Bishop Auckland, a school friend, Aidan Davison, who went off to play soccer in the Premier League, tried to play the same kind of Good Samaritan role in Close House, one of the poorest parts of the area, where his grandparents had raised him in a council house. Affordable decent rental housing was still practically nonexistent, so Aidan bought several abandoned rowhouses and renovated them, hoping to achieve sufficient scale that everything would eventually pay for itself. Without a larger housing program or developmental framework to slot into, Aidan's venture proved too difficult to manage solo from a distance. Many of the properties ended up vandalized. He couldn't keep up with repairs. As he told me later, he "lost his shirt." Aidan would have benefited from a larger initiative through which he and others with similar goals could pool philanthropic monies to create a local asset-based housing fund and pay for a small staff or attract volunteers to manage the project.

In 2020, several initiatives tried to address this same problem for place-based projects in the United States. One think-tank report promoted the idea of the federal government creating a national service-year program and "scholarships for service" as part of a domestic version of the Peace Corps. Recent college graduates would enroll for one to two years of paid voluntary service and be placed within distressed communities across the United States. They would be matched up with local development projects, nonprofits, charities, and schools. The federal government would also forgive student loans for the period of service. The National Commission on Military, National, and Public Service, which was set up in 2017, proposed a similar idea in its final report in 2020. The commission advocated legislation to secure funding for national service and volunteering on a large scale that would enable young people and skilled adults to build new networks and help achieve sustainability for local institutions in every U.S. state.

Building on Local Assets

In this spirit, many towns and cities in America have established local development corporations to promote public-private collaborations and build on existing assets. Some of these have been quite successful in creating new jobs and economic opportunity.

My former Brookings colleague Tesia Mamassian works as the vice president of operations of the Detroit Regional Partnership (DRP) in Michigan, a regional economic development nonprofit serving the eleven counties around the city of Detroit and their 5.4 million residents. The DRP covers a diverse collection of communities and industrial and technology centers spread over a large area. It coordinates with Michigan's state and local governments to attract new business and investment to the region and produces reports on improving the business climate, as well as informing programs on workforce development. The DRP helps big companies in the Detroit region, such as the Ford Motor Company and General Motors, connect with smaller firms in the new automotive and "mobility technology" sector (self-driving cars and electric vehicles) to create a business network focused on developing technology clusters. In 2020 alone the DRP's model of bringing together private companies and local government officials brought over $450 million in new investment into the Detroit region and created 1,745 new jobs.

In the Lehigh Valley, where Dad might have ended up back in the 1960s had he actually emigrated, the city of Bethlehem set up a similar public-private partnership, the Lehigh Valley Economic Development Corporation. In the period from 2015 to 2020, the corporation created twenty-six thousand jobs by working with local universities and community colleges, building office parks, and offering tax credits to bring in new companies.

Across the United Kingdom and the United States since the 1990s, state and local governments have often tried to attract new businesses through similar methods, and by deploying tax breaks and other subsidies. If these inducements worked, old industrial towns in the UK might get a megastore such as an Asda. Those in the U.S. might get a Walmart (Asda's parent company). They might get a meatpacking plant, or a big warehouse and shipping center for Amazon or another multinational company. In some places the tax breaks would bring a series of small factories — Black & Decker, Hitachi, and others came to the Bishop Auckland area. Generous subsidies might attract a car assembly line (Nissan came to Sunderland).

But the new jobs and revenues that these subsidies generated for the local economy were never on the same scale as the old mass manufacturing industries, and sometimes they were temporary. Salaries and workers' benefits were far less than they had been before as well. This predicament gave rise to some unfortunate developments. In some towns the government, or a private company, might decide to take advantage of the cheaper local labor market and the eagerness of the regional authorities to provide incentives to build a maximum-security prison. This was more secure as a source of jobs (in every sense) than the megastores, warehouses, and new factories. Once a prison was built, it stayed put.

But in other cases, as soon as the government tax breaks and subsidies ended, commercial businesses would take off for somewhere with even cheaper wages and more inducements. I have friends and family in Bishop Auckland and the North East who repeatedly lost good jobs after a few years and had to start again under these circumstances.

The problem is that tax breaks and subsidies as well as stand-alone economic development corporations don't work particularly well in small towns without existing industrial clusters. Nor do they work in places with few large private businesses to provide matching dollars for external funds and for outmoded infrastructure.

In the 1990s and early 2000s, Bishop Auckland's immediate district in County Durham attempted to create a local development agency along the same lines as those in Detroit and Bethlehem, pulling together a group of small towns and villages under the rubric "Wear Valley." It had little success, and Wear Valley was disbanded, although of course none of the towns and villages went anywhere. They didn't disappear; they simply didn't develop, and thus continued to decay. Across the North East of England after 1981, there were more than fifty similar failed structures and attempts to spur local growth.

Point A to Point B

Old industrial towns like Bishop Auckland and its counterparts in rural America are poorly connected in terms of their physical infrastructure and also their business and national relationships. The paucity of physical connectivity holds them back, much like people when they are contact- and network-poor. In places like County Durham or its correlate of Carbon County in Pennsylvania, everything used to serve the old central coal mine or factory or link to a larger regional hub. Smaller places were often cut off from each other. Not having a car was a big problem when the rail and bus routes were cut back and jobs moved somewhere that was no longer close to home.

Fifteen miles away from where I live in Maryland is the historic Black community of Tobytown, which is adjacent to one of the region's most affluent suburbs, Potomac. Few of Tobytown's residents have cars. Tobytown has no nearby bus stop or bus route into town. To get to the nearest stop on the regional Metro line (close to my house) requires first a trek to find a bus stop and route and then multiple changes. Factoring in all the stops, getting to the Metro on the bus would take about an hour and half, if you were lucky. Your alternative would be a cycle ride along busy roads or a four-and-a-half-hour walk. Unemployment in the community is persistently high. People have homes but no way of getting to a job in a reasonable period, even if they work in one of the limited number of positions in a grocery store in Potomac, about five and a half miles away. Again, there is no direct bus.

Various attempts to set up something for the community have faltered, in large part because there is no broader sustained local demand for buses. The far more affluent residents of Potomac all have their own cars. Anything to serve Tobytown would have to be on a small scale, specifically targeted for a few individuals. So who would pay to maintain a micro transportation route indefinitely?

When I was growing up, I was in the same predicament as the residents of Tobytown. One of the biggest obstacles to my family's opportunity was distance. Navigating the eight miles from Granny and Grandad's house in Roddymoor to home in Bishop Auckland was daunting without a car when all the bus routes were cut back. Similarly, throughout the UK, most of the country's transportation development was focused on increasing linkages to London or other big cities with large populations, like Birmingham, Manchester, and Newcastle. The rest of the country was poorly served by road and rail services. Everything in terms of dense infrastructure networks in the UK seemed to be concentrated in a triangle in the South connecting Oxford-Cambridge-London.

The dynamic is the same today in individual U.S. states, including in regions where the distances are far greater than from Tobytown to Potomac and to Washington, D.C. Poor areas in the United States become even poorer when people have no bus or commuter train service to get to a job and can't afford a car, even though there may be ample jobs nearby in more affluent communities. Infrastructure improvements, for basic transportation to get to work and Wi-Fi to enable people to work from home without climbing to the top of a compost heap or a birch tree, have to be developed with federal grants and low-interest community loans.

Places like Tobytown often need a philanthropic benefactor or private-sector group to step into the void to obtain a vital service. More often than not, however, no one materializes, because of an overall shortage of major local donors. In County Durham and Wear Valley for most of the past twenty years, for example, in stark contrast to Detroit, no big firms on the scale of a Ford or General Motors were left in the region after deindustrialization in the 1980s, nor were there any large philanthropic foundations. The big North East industrialist philanthropists of the nineteenth century, who built the region's parks, museums, and libraries, disappeared along with the heavy industry in the twentieth century. Unlike the Rockefellers and Carnegies in the United States, they didn't leave foundations behind. In the North East of England, local councils like County Durham's became the essential actors, but they were starved of funds.

One of Margaret Thatcher's reforms in the 1980s involved the consolidation and centralization of the UK government, in sharp contrast to the situation in the United States. The 1980s saw the abolition of larger regional and municipal authorities in the UK, the erosion of their autonomy, and the creation of smaller entities. City mayors, including in London, lost political influence and their revenue-raising authority. Before 2013, roughly 90 percent of UK local taxes went to the central government in Westminster. Because regional governments in the UK, unlike American states, have no financial independence from the central government, they have no scope for engaging in fiscal innovation to raise money for place-based development projects. Before Brexit cut off funding streams from Brussels, some special grant funds were available from the European Union as well as from various departments of the UK government, but regional authorities had to find matching private-sector or charitable resources before they could come up with a project proposal. The North East also had to compete with other regions across Europe for any EU structural and investment funds. For years, ideas for reconstruction and renewal tended to stall at the first set of hurdles.

The Living Museum of the North

In the absence of corporate development prospects, County Durham, like its "twin," Carbon County in Pennsylvania, turned to its past as a base of development. The local government attempted to use history, nostalgia, and scenery to create jobs. In Pennsylvania, Jim Thorpe has used its coal-mining heritage and the outstanding scenic beauty of the Pocono Mountains to build up a tourist industry. Local industrialist Asa Packer's mansion, the Lehigh Gorge Scenic Railway, the number 9 mine, and several other museums and cultural centers, along with cycling trails, hiking, and white-water rafting, have all become part of a network of tourist attractions. These are managed by the town council, local business associations like the Lions Club, and small businesses. In County Durham, despite all the cuts to its other budgets, the council retained its cultural funds and has taken the same approach.

In the 1970s, County Durham created a unique open-air museum, the Living Museum of the North, built around a drift mine and pit village in a tiny place called Beamish. This was the first museum in the UK that was financed by a consortium of county councils. Durham pooled its limited resources with those of its immediate neighbors, Cleveland (Teesside), Northumberland, and Tyne and Wear. Historic buildings and significant industrial artifacts from across the region — including a vintage pub, the Sun Inn, from Bishop Auckland — were dismantled and taken to Beamish to create an entire main street. Local people, including my parents and extended family, donated household items and period clothing. There are miners' cottages in Beamish that look just like Granny and Grandad Hill's house in Roddymoor before modernization. There are allotments with sheds and "pigeon crees" — hand-crafted wooden houses for miners' prized racing or breeding birds — alongside a Methodist chapel, a small school, and other features of the once-vibrant Durham miners' communities. Locals became paid employees, including former coal miners who take people down the Beamish drift mine and maintain it in good working order.

Beamish took decades to build up. It was an enormous collective effort. Before the pandemic, it was one of the North East's biggest tourist attractions, a staple for school trips and educational programs, with around 450,000 annual visitors. Beamish received some national government funding, but it was almost entirely supported by admission fees by 2020. Elsewhere, in Shildon near Bishop Auckland, where the last major manufacturer, the Wagon Works, closed in the early 1980s, the county turned part of the huge plant into the Locomotion Museum. The museum, and a similar Head of Steam railway museum in nearby Darlington, celebrates County Durham's role as the world's cradle of industrial and passenger railways.

All these museums were the product of local grassroots efforts. Previously in the North East, people worked for big impersonal companies or industrialists, which tended to stifle the region's entrepreneurial spirit. The public museums and volunteering offered a new infrastructure of opportunity for individuals to do something for themselves. Although these cultural projects were insufficient to turn the economy around, in aggregate they had transformational potential, especially if they became part of a larger regional or national development initiative.

Buying Bishop Auckland

In the 2010s, Durham County's emphasis on public history did in fact become the basis for a specific large-scale philanthropic venture. It was a surprise opportunity, a one-off. It was also not something that every forgotten place in either the UK or the U.S. can replicate, unless someone with the resources of a MacKenzie Scott decides to intervene and focus all her donations on a single initiative. But sometimes places, like people, just get lucky.

Right around the time that the "Viva Bish Vegas" video captured the town's state of seemingly terminal decay, a wealthy London-based investor turned philanthropist, Jonathan Ruffer, came in and essentially bought Bishop Auckland.

Ruffer had not initially wanted to buy a town. He had his sights set on some internationally famous paintings by the Spanish painter Francisco de Zurbarán that had been housed in the Bishop's Palace since 1756. His purchase was complicated by the fact that the paintings and the building were joined in a bequest from a former bishop of Durham. The palace conveyed.

Struck by Bishop Auckland's overall sorry state, as well as by the local history and raw potential, Ruffer decided to go all in. He set up an ambitious Auckland Project to redevelop the historic core of the town as a tourist attraction. Ruffer purchased almost every notable building in the town's marketplace and the nearby Roman fort. He forged alliances with Durham University and regional museums, the British Museum in London, and even the Prado in Madrid, to create a Spanish art museum. He used the paintings he had originally set out to purchase as an enticement, promising to send them on tour. Ruffer had a strong sense of the importance of organized religion in community-building and a deep interest in the history of Christianity in the North East. One of his ventures was to create a museum of faith, charting the development of all religions in England, within a restored wing of the Bishop's Palace. He engaged the bishop of Durham and other local church leaders in the initiative, which was launched in 2012.

The Auckland Project was one man's contribution to the infrastructure of opportunity. Ruffer anticipated that other funding would follow to fix the overall physical infrastructure: "Build it and they will come." He understood that people in Bishop Auckland wanted a sense of common purpose and a boost to local pride. Inspired by a theme park with a live-action show that had helped turn around the fortunes of a relatively remote rural area in France, Puy du Fou, Ruffer decided to do the same thing. He brought in the French team from Puy du Fou to get things going, bought an old golf course down by the River Wear as a permanent site, and developed a show, *Kynren: The Story of Us*. It would be linked to the Auckland Project to generate additional money and national attention but managed separately. "Kynren" means kin, family, or generation in Anglo-Saxon. The show fused Bishop

Auckland and its history with the North East's industrial legacy and the broad sweep of British history.

Both the *Kynren* show and the Auckland Project relied heavily on local people volunteering — in their hundreds in the case of *Kynren*. They traded their time in return for training, learning new skills, and eventually (for some) securing permanent or seasonal jobs on-site and through spinoffs for local crafts and food production. Some skills in construction, stage production and lighting, costume design and manufacturing, and large-scale project management were clearly transferable. It wasn't immediately clear how learning to fire flaming arrows as an archer in an ancient battle would translate into a new job, but many of the local volunteers in *Kynren* — like a family friend who was a taxi driver by day and a flaming archer by night — were genuinely grateful for the morale boost.

The Auckland Project did open opportunities for the town that had been elusive in the past. Jonathan Ruffer's upfront commitment of tens of millions of pounds, and his efforts to bring in matching contributions from other private and public sources as well as development know-how, helped create a critical density of philanthropic activity. Bishop Auckland suddenly had some assets.

Alongside County Durham's other public history projects, this windfall in Bishop Auckland became the stimulus for additional funding applications to large national charitable organizations and development programs. In 2021 the UK government offered Bishop Auckland the possibility to apply for a grant to revitalize "the golden mile," the much-neglected Newgate Street, through a new Future High Streets Fund, and to transform itself into a "world-class visitor destination" through an ultimately successful multi-million-pound bid to a larger UK Stronger Towns Fund.

In terms of its size and long-term commitment, Jonathan Ruffer's intervention underscores the level of funding and collective effort necessary to make an impact in a forgotten place like Bishop Auckland. Other philanthropic commitments by local corporations illustrate the same point.

In 2012, when Ruffer launched the Auckland Project, a local entrepreneur, John Elliott, turned his company into a trust, the Ebac Foundation. Elliott wanted to bind Ebac to the area and guarantee jobs for its two hundred–plus employees, reinvest profits, and provide ongoing support to the community. Ebac, which Elliott founded to make dehumidifiers and water coolers in Bishop Auckland in 1973, relocated to nearby Newton Aycliffe af-

ter expanding its production to air conditioners and washing machines. Elliott, who left school at fifteen to become an electrical engineering apprentice, wanted to ensure that local low-skilled workers would have the same
opportunity that he had had to access a good manufacturing job. In an interview with the local newspaper, the *Northern Echo*, Elliott summed up
his ethos: "As an employer you have a responsibility to support worthwhile
causes in your community. We don't try to make things easy for people, but
to make things possible for them."

In the United States, on a much bigger scale, Hamdi Ulukaya, founder
of the yogurt company Chobani, launched a similar program in 2016 to
turn workers into stakeholders and support community projects. Ulukaya,
a Kurdish immigrant to the United States, offered 10 percent of the company's stock to its more than two thousand workers. He also set up the Chobani Food Incubator to support food-processing startups in New York State
and Twin Falls, Idaho, around Chobani's plants and headquarters.

The Antidote to Populism

Individual philanthropy like MacKenzie Scott's and Jonathan Ruffer's, as
well as company-driven worker and community projects like Ebac's and
Chobani's, can all strengthen the infrastructure of opportunity if a comprehensive national framework and vision are in place. Individuals and institutions can pool resources of money and time to create local assets and re-
claim forgotten towns. What was lost in the past should not be an obstacle
for creating opportunity in the present or future.

In forgotten towns, the people who live there clearly have a stake in how
things develop. People in these places need to help set their own conditions
for building personal, professional, and community relationships. Everyone
needs to feel they are part of any process of change to also then feel connected to and part of something larger than themselves, something that extends beyond their community to the national level. And when they don't,
personal and political catastrophes are sure to follow.

The 2008–2009 financial crisis and the widening opportunity gap in the
United States paved the way for the advent of ruinous populist and sectarian politics in 2016. COVID-19 and the recession in its wake could pave the
way for more political upheaval unless American democracy delivers tan-
gible results. Populists are particularly adept at PR and sloganeering. When
they take control of the national media, or dominate and manipulate it as

President Trump did, then they get away with making promises without achieving anything significant.

Real communities and physical connections offer the antidote to populism. Real relationships offer support and mentoring and improve well-being. They provide "best interest," not just "self-interest." They give individuals contact with people they care about. They make them feel as if they have a future. There can be no collective progress without this individual progress, just as there can be no national progress without local progress. In this as in so many other ways, the macro is dependent on the micro.

The well-being of the national economy and polity hinges on people's quality of life and on their ability to fulfil their potential at the local level. When the physical as well as the information space is fragmented, voters don't know whom to trust. But when people see concrete, personally measurable examples of positive change within their own immediate physical communities — programs and initiatives that bring real benefits to them and their families — they reach their own conclusions. They become more discerning and hopeful. And they become less susceptible to manipulation by people who profess to have their best interests at heart but in truth are only out for themselves.

CONCLUSION

To get our house in order for the rest of this century, America needs political and economic reforms to be tied together — and honest assessments of why some issues are so difficult to tackle and what works and what does not. National programs need to bring government action and accountability down from the top, federal level to the ground into small towns and neighborhoods. Places and the real people living in them need to be seen, recognized, and rediscovered. And real people need to see reflections of themselves in the people at the top.

The best way for this to happen is through investment in people where they live — particularly through education. Education can lower the barriers to opportunity in a way that nothing else can. It offers everyone the chance not only to develop knowledge and learn skills but also to continue to transform themselves and their communities and both adapt and rise to new demands and challenges.

Education can be a great social and economic equalizer if, in theory, everyone has access to the same quality of public or state schools. But in the United Kingdom and the United States today, the quality and content of an education still vary widely across geographic regions. In the U.S., race has a similar negative impact on educational opportunity as place and social class do in the UK. In the U.S., Black, Hispanic, Native American, and other minority students dominate the lower income brackets and frequently find themselves in marginalized neighborhoods and inadequate schools.

Poverty, not innate ability or the lack thereof, is the key predictor of poor educational attainment. This was the same when my grandparents and parents went to school, the same for me in the 1970s and 1980s, and the same for children and students in the United Kingdom and the United States in the 2000s. Poor student achievement in schools in impoverished areas, in both the UK and the U.S., reflects the demographics and the economy of the surrounding region. It does not indicate deficiencies in the talent, potential, and aspirations of individual students. In another environment, with more focused investment in the quality of their education, these students would flourish. Place, class, race, and gender all come into play in limiting educational outcomes for children — and for adults as they move on with their careers and have to adjust to changing circumstances and find ways to retrain and retool.

I defied this grim prediction through a combination of factors. Higher education was my primary pathway to opportunity after I left Bishop Auckland, and if there were many impediments to success along that path, I also received many lucky boosts along the way. Some of the challenges, such as the stigmas attached to being working-class and to being a woman, were systemic and at times pernicious, but there were also ways for me to overcome them. Family and community support groups were critical in ensuring my first steps toward university. Personal and professional networks then became the accelerators of progress.

Most people are not as lucky as I have been. A low income remains the key barrier to private educational opportunities in the absence of a grant or subsidy, but state-sponsored educational outcomes are further shaped by the physical state of school facilities as well as by the qualifications and training of teachers and the nature of the curriculum. Place, class, and race also matter in equal measure to poverty — where you go to school and who people think you are.

To find a job, avoid poverty, and get ahead in this century, you need knowledge and skills tailored to the current economic environment. You also need the ability to adapt over a working lifetime to deal with sudden universal shocks (like a recession, war, or global pandemic) but also to other changing circumstances, including the nature and forms of work, the advent of new technologies, and the increasing social and political complexity of modern democracies.

Changes in technology come roughly every five to seven years, so no one can ever have any expectation of permanence in the workplace. People's skills will always need upgrading. But the right kind of education for the twenty-first century is the one that prepares us to weather these changes — and which does so equally, without regard to where we are from or what our parents do.

Educational success and participation in all forms of higher education (academic, professional, technical training, skills development) are influenced by seeing others blaze a trail and setting examples that people can follow. If everyone you know has headed in the same direction by leaving school early to work in a coal mine or a factory or in the local retail or agricultural sectors, then that tends to shape the realm of possibilities. Especially if you want to break out of a local employment pattern or go to college, mentorship is critical. If you don't have parental or family examples of higher education to fall back on, then you need teachers, school counselors, and representatives of the broader community to point out the possibilities and help you access opportunities.

When "there is nothing for you here" in terms of college or job prospects, the best and the brightest — those with talent and educational attainment — leave after they finish school to look for something elsewhere. Most of them, like me, move away and don't come back. They become part of a brain drain, taking their educational perspectives and personal networks with them to benefit other towns, cities, and countries.

Higher education in this case splits families and diminishes communities rather than building them up. It becomes a way out of a beleaguered town, not a way of bringing in new skills and ideas to fix things. Aspiring students have no one to look up to on the educational path or to refer to when looking for advice on how to do things, including dealing with the next steps on the academic ladder and tailoring course choices to future job prospects. When all the people ahead of you with that kind of knowledge have left, you are on your own.

In recent years, two best-selling books in the United States described the challenge of getting out of poverty and getting an education in low-income and divided America. J. D. Vance in *Hillbilly Elegy* and Tara Westover in *Educated* focused on how they as individuals succeeded against the odds and moved from blighted economic regions and harsh family circumstances to prestigious universities such as Yale and Harvard. Getting into college was the pinnacle of achievement. Neither offered much in the way of observation about how others might follow their path. Vance's and Westover's accomplishments were something completely remarkable, not replicable.

Indeed, in 2020, *Hillbilly Elegy* was turned into a Hollywood movie, underscoring the unique nature of Vance's childhood and adult success.

The reason others could not and cannot emulate the individual academic and life successes of J. D. Vance and Tara Westover is rooted in the particulars of the crisis of opportunity. Their stories underscore the persistence of deep structural barriers, including discrimination against low-income students, the inadequacies of K-12 education in impoverished areas, and racial and gender disparities in access to education. Poor children are more likely to become poor adults. Poverty then extends across generations, as I experienced with my own family. My dad could not break out of his parents' pattern. They did not break out of their parents'. I succeeded at school and won a place at university not because I was exceptional but because I had help. No one does anything completely alone. Life is a team sport.

Of all the breaks that I got in life, my luckiest was timing. The UK educational system was changing just as I was born in the 1960s, opening new opportunities for working-class kids. By the time I started elementary school in the 1970s, the United Kingdom had devised a reasonably robust social program for education. Poor kids could get a hand up, not just a handout. This included funding for school exchange programs, job placement schemes, and extracurricular activities as well as for college tuition and living expenses from local education authorities for those who needed it — and who actually applied for the programs.

For every rung of the educational ladder I found a subsidy or a grant to pull me up. Of course, you had to know the programs and grants were there in the first place. I found out about them because my parents were rooted in strong extended family and community networks that we could draw upon. I had generous mentors and even benefactors in the UK — relatives, neighbors, teachers, my local member of Parliament, prominent alumni of St. Andrews University — who pointed out these opportunities to me. They gave me access to their personal and professional connections: people I could talk to for the advice to help me advance further. I ultimately had the same experience in the United States, thanks to access to new university-based networks and contacts from Harvard.

Far too many people who were born into similar circumstances in the generations after me did not have the same opportunities. Deprived and disadvantaged, they will continue to be preyed upon by unscrupulous politicians who offer them a promise of opportunity in return for their votes.

These left-behind people deserve better. But their problems are everyone's. They are our fellow Americans and fellow Brits, in some cases our family members and friends. Helping them will not be purely a selfless act. Because as long as they feel that there is no hope for them, there will be no hope for the rest of us. There will be nothing for us, anywhere.

AFTERWORD

Creating Opportunity in the Twenty-First Century

While federal, state, and local governments, large foundations, and wealthy individual philanthropists play critical roles in creating opportunities for underprivileged Americans, each of us as an individual actor can help create what I describe in this book as the infrastructure of opportunity. The greater your wealth is, the more positional authority you have; the more free time you enjoy and the larger your personal and professional networks are, the more you can do. But everyone can and should play a role in helping to break down barriers and even the playing field.

If you are a CEO or an executive of a corporation or other large organization:

1. Create mentoring programs, job placement schemes, and internships that provide disadvantaged youth with opportunities to learn and gain experience that will help them build the foundation for long-term career success.
2. Demonstrate the courage to acknowledge, confront, and overcome the systemic biases — racial, social, or gender-based — that are embedded in your current recruiting, promotion, and compensation practices.
3. Set aggressive hiring targets for women, minorities, and underrepresented groups, including those from low-income, working-class backgrounds who are the first in their families to go to college. Re-

ward the individuals and corporate functions that achieve their targets; make those that do not pay a penalty.

4. Recruit at educational institutions that serve historically deprived groups. Look beyond the formal résumé. Take chances on candidates who may lack the requisite experience but demonstrate determination and ambition.

If you are retired and have free time:

1. Volunteer as a mentor or teacher for one of the many social service and nonprofit organizations that serve the disadvantaged, including local schools.

2. Act as a local ambassador for public and national service programs, volunteering schemes, and other community-wide initiatives. Raise awareness about the benefits and importance of assisting these organizations within your own peer and social groups with a concrete call to action. Ensure that those with more limited access to information or resources also know about these ventures.

3. Participate in intragenerational exchanges and collaborations. Offer counsel to younger groups, especially those from underrepresented communities and youth with no parental or mentor figures in their lives. Encourage them to be purposeful and help break barriers. Tell your own stories. Communicate your regrets and failures, including what you have learned from your personal experiences.

4. If logistically possible, consider acting as a host by offering free or affordable housing to students, school exchange participants, interns, volunteers, or young professionals who have limited financial means, including in exchange for housekeeping or other services.

If you are an experienced working professional:

1. Make a conscious effort to nurture diverse talent within your workplace and help prepare younger colleagues — especially women, racial minorities, and other underrepresented groups — for leadership roles. Equip them with the necessary skills and confidence to succeed.

2. Act as a professional connector between people from different social, economic, racial, and geographic (rural/urban) backgrounds. Convene groups inside and outside the workplace with diverse sets of perspectives and experiences to encourage nontraditional synergies.

3. Build active mentor-mentee relationships with young professionals, especially those coming from less advantaged backgrounds. If you know others who might be better equipped to play the mentor role for a certain individual, facilitate an introduction.

4. Reach back to your college alumni networks as well as to local further education institutions to offer mentoring or opportunities for current students to seek career advice.

If you are a young professional:

1. Create peer networks within your organization to assist colleagues from nontraditional backgrounds who may be struggling in the workplace.

2. Maintain ties with alumni networks for college and high school to offer next-steps career guidance. Volunteer to host physical or virtual career fairs at your organization.

3. Act as a mentor or volunteer for a local social service or nonprofit with educational programs for disadvantaged youth.

4. Pool resources with other young professionals to sponsor a young person from the local community to cover the costs for that person to take advantage of opportunities that might otherwise be out of reach, such as attending an educational summer camp or taking part in sports or other enrichment programs.

If you are a college professor or administrator:

1. Open courses virtually to high school students from underprivileged backgrounds to give them a taste of college. Partner with organizations that fund educational programs in high-poverty areas. Pair school and college students who enroll in these courses together for further content discussions and to foster mentoring relationships that will help disadvantaged kids apply to college.

2. Establish bridge and advisory programs for incoming students from underresourced public schools and those who are the first in their families to attend college to assist them with the academic, social, and cultural transition to the first year.

3. Create initiatives that encourage students from different backgrounds to participate in study or peer groups to listen and learn from each other's perspectives, not just review course materials.

4. Offer students course credit for mentoring K-12 students and volunteering in local community projects, nonprofits, and other organizations that offer programs for disadvantaged youth.

If you are a college student:

1. Use volunteer time as an opportunity to explore potential career paths as well as gain new skills for professional development. Identify service opportunities and organizations that make a local impact and raise campus awareness about their activities. Consider taking college courses with a service component.

2. Initiate collaborations with peers from other academic institutions, including community colleges and universities with historically underrepresented student populations. Encourage faculty members to develop joint virtual programming on areas of common interest.

3. Take an alternative spring break. Ask your friends and classmates to volunteer with you and make a difference together. Seek out opportunities to volunteer in geographies (rural/urban) and communities different from your own.

4. Provide free tutoring to middle and high school students. Prioritize students from underprivileged communities as well as students with learning difficulties and disabilities. Offer insight and assistance on choosing future courses of study. Share your own experiences.

If you are a teacher:

1. Ensure that all students in class are able to access the full range of federal, state, and community programs and other social and academic assistance they are eligible for. In some cases their families may simply not know that resources are available.

2. Pay particular attention to children with no parental or mentor figures in their lives. Consider how they can tap into school or community networks, including counselors, other teachers, nonprofit organizations, and recent alumni who can assist them.

3. Explore opportunities to create ties with teachers in other schools for virtual class exchanges and to share best practices. If you are a private-school teacher, reach out to a public-school counterpart in a disadvantaged area. Conversely, connect with another teacher and his or her class in a more racially diverse or different type of (rural/urban) school system.

4. Encourage underprivileged students to think about college early in their K-12 education, and enroll in service learning, local community projects, and sports and other groups that offer summer camps, tutoring, and other preparatory programs for disadvantaged children. Consider partnering your class with specific local organizations.

ACKNOWLEDGMENTS

This book is the product not just of the months that were devoted to its immediate research and writing but also of several years of discussions and joint work with colleagues at the Brookings Institution, dating back to 2000 and especially surrounding the contentious American presidential election of 2016. It is also the result of personal and professional experiences, extensive reading, and detailed notes made in the years before.

I received ideas from many sources, particularly from family members and close friends on both sides of the Atlantic. I am especially grateful to my in-laws — all the immediate and extended members of the Keen family spread over Illinois, Iowa, Nebraska, South Dakota, Wisconsin, and other states — who have shared their thoughts and views with me at countless family events and meetings since the early 1990s and in recent phone calls. Younger generations of the Keens, Millennials and Generation Z, offered important insight and their own perspectives on the topics in the book as I began thinking it through: Caleb Keen, Ellie Keen, Eric Keen, Levi Keen, Malika Hill Keen, Marie Louise Keen, Michael Keen, Noel Keen, Andy Kirchoff, Joe Kirchoff, Martin Kirchoff, Matthew Kirchoff, and Tim Kirchoff. Members of my own extended family in the U.S., including Sue Anne Mather, Scott LeVine, and other relatives, also offered their thoughts.

Back home in North East England, my parents and grandparents and the older cousins of my parents' generation played an important role in shaping my perspectives on the theme of opportunity and what individuals can do to create the infrastructure of opportunity in forgotten places. "Uncle" Gordon Encinias, who was born in Bishop Auckland but moved to Coatbridge, outside Glasgow — the "Iron Burgh," once one of the largest coal- and steel-producing towns in the UK before it lost its industry — spent years trying to help his struggling community. After serving as the head of the local tenants' housing association, he became a town councilor in his old age, just as he had been diagnosed with what would prove to be terminal cancer. He turned his own hard life of poverty, raised by a single mother after World War II, into the basis for public service. His first order of business was to fix the broken playground in his blighted neighborhood to make sure local children had somewhere safe to play. "Uncle" Gordon, along with "Uncle" Charlie Crabtree and Dorothy Long, who encouraged me to study Russian during the 1980s "war scare," believed that anyone (no matter what their background) could be an agent of change if they put their mind to it.

The "clever lasses" from the extended Hill family — Jennifer Bogan, Elizabeth Fisher, Clare Hammond, Kathleen Kirby, Julia McGill, and Susan McKenzie — blazed a trail for working-class girls like me to go to university. They showed me it was possible. Other family members — Jeff Goodman, Malcolm and Rosemary Murray, Alastair and Ian Newton, and Florence and Ray Rix — kindly functioned as family focus groups and sounding boards as I started on the book proposal. They then provided information at key points along the way. Mam, June Hill, acted as an unpaid research assistant, sending me a large stash of family archive materials as well as articles from the *Northern Echo* and the *Bishop Press*.

Friends and neighbors over many decades and generations in Bishop Auckland, some of whom are sadly no longer alive, were instrumental in shaping my thinking. My godparents, John and Bessie Williams, regaled me with tales of the Welsh slate-mining villages of Snowdonia and the difficulties they faced as native Welsh-speakers, including being beaten at school for conversing in their own language. John and Bessie gave me material and practical support, including driving me to out-of-school activities and local job interviews when I couldn't get there on the bus or my bike. They, along with other neighbors from our cul-de-sac — Sidney and Hilda Lockey, Billy and Linda Dixon, Steve and Linda Owers, Paul and Viviane Wayne, the Roche family, Cynthia Bland, and Keith and Michelle Stapleton — all played pivotal roles at different stages in my life. School friends from Etherley Lane and Bishop Barrington — Stew Crombie, Craig Currie, Aidan Davison, Danny Gibson, Sue Elgey Hare, Lorraine Joyce, Carolyn Miller, Mandy Roche Padfield, Jane Burrell Redfern, Martin Russell, Peter Scott, Ariadne Shore-Pullen — all shared ideas that informed this book. They filled me in on their children's experiences with the same issues that we faced in the 1980s. Teachers at Etherley Lane and Bishop Barrington School — Mr. Armstrong, Mr. Davidson, Mr. Everett, Mr. Gibson, Dr. Marshall, Mr. Noble-Eddy, Miss Wilson; our late member of Parliament, Lord Derek Foster; and Tony Sutcliffe, who directed County Durham's international school exchanges, and his wife, Catherine, helped me navigate my early educational journey.

I am also extremely grateful to Jane and John Armstrong, Jean Clarke, John Letherbridge, Peter Moore, and other staff and volunteers at Woodhouse Close Community Church; Allison McInnes (a Bishop Barrington classmate), from Northumbria University's Department of Social Work, Education, and Community Well-being; Brian Stobie, from Durham County Council's International Office; and Alison Tweddle, from the Auckland Project, for providing insight into current circumstances in Bishop Auckland, County Durham, and the North East related to the themes of the book. And I am similarly grateful to the new generation of students from Bishop Auckland, including Niall Cronin and Thomas Hodgson, who got in touch to fill me in on their travails and successes of applying to university and finding jobs. Niall experienced the same challenges I had in overcoming the opportunity barrier of a North East accent in addition to the difficulties of job-hunting from the vantage point of County Durham after college. Almost four decades later, in 2021, as the first in his family to apply to college, Thomas had a similar experience to mine with Oxford University and opted to go to St. Andrews in its aftermath.

Outside Bishop Auckland, Peter Hughes, a transplant to the United States from the coal-mining town of Stanley, County Durham, provided additional insight into life in the pit villages around World War II and in the 1950s. Peter's uncle, Jack Hughes, was a British union activist and member of Parliament for the Labour Party. As "Red Jack," he became famous for his protests against Margaret Thatcher's social policies in the late 1980s. Peter made his own transition from the coal house to the White House, immigrating to America as a young man and later working in the Reagan administration. He was an early proponent of the book, along with Alan Capps and Richard Pomfret, other refugees from the British class system. I also found great personal inspiration in William Woodruff's 1993 autobiography, *The Road to Nab End: An Extraordinary Northern Childhood,* a story of growing up in poverty in Blackburn, a Lancashire textile town, just after the First World War, before making a remarkable educational journey in the UK and ending up as a renowned professor of world history, including at the University of Illinois, Melbourne in Australia, Princeton, and the University of Florida. Professor Woodruff's life story is fused with British social history from half a century before mine. He was part of the generation between my grandparents and parents. He made it to Oxford in the late 1930s, despite an entirely unconventional education, including working in an iron foundry while he put himself through night school. The university waived the exam for him.

A current generation of St. Andrews students filled me in on the difficulties of navigating the UK university system in the 2020s, including Chris Anderson, Stella Ezeh, Leo Kelly, Morgan Morris, Manhattan Murphy-Brown, Hampton Toole, and Julia Whalen. I also greatly appreciated my conversations with St. Andrews principal Sally Mapstone, chancellor Lord Menzies Campbell, rector Leyla Hussein, former rector Catherine Stihler, rectorial candidate Ken Cochran, professor Brad MacKay, and Moira Sharkey. I owe a great deal of debt to Lord George Robertson, the late John Sullivan, and Frank Quinault for their support while I was a student at the university; and to Mike Bird of the British Council for all his efforts to help me apply to scholarships to Harvard and the United States in the late 1980s. And of course I am indebted to professor Robert Legvold for telling me about the educational opportunities in the U.S. and showing me how to use a drip coffee machine in Moscow in 1988.

Professor Graham Allison, professors Abe and Toni Chayes, dean Margot Gill, professor Akira Iriye, professor János Kornai, Joe and Marina McCarthy, professor Richard Pipes, professor Jurij and Emanuela Striedter, Patty Walsh, Dr. Dorothy Zinberg, and other inspirational professors and close colleagues at Harvard were instrumental in helping me set off on my career path. They and Bill Maynes, who hired me out of Harvard to the Eurasia Foundation and then recommended me to Richard Haass, who was then at the Brookings Institution, for my research fellow position, all took a chance on me. They pushed me forward. Cliff Gaddy, my long-term scholarly collaborator at Brookings, provided me with a decades-long master class in economics, for which I am particularly grateful. All my male mentors had something in common: accomplished wives who were equal partners in their relationships. In some cases they also had daughters whose lives and future careers they were fully engaged in — much like my own father.

This book was written between October 2020 and May 2021. In writing the final manuscript, I benefited from the ongoing research of many colleagues at the Brookings Institution, who generously took the time to brainstorm on core concepts, shared sources, and offered critiques and cautions. Participation in numerous Brookings conferences, seminars, and private meetings gave me a unique opportunity to engage in one-on-one or small group discussions with a range of Brookings scholars and staff working on the topics covered in the book: Stephanie Aaronson, John Austin, Dany Bahar, Alan Berube, Sarah Binder, Gary Burtless, Camille Busette, Stuart Butler, E. J. Dionne, David Dollar, Leah Dreyfuss, Courtney Dunakin, Wendy Edelberg, Bob Einhorn, Marcela Escobari, Vanda Felbab-Brown, Jeff Feltman, Bill Finan, William Frey, Bill Galston, Josh Gotbaum, Ryan Hass, Susan Hennessey, Bruce Jones, Bob Kagan, Marvin Kalb, Elaine Kamarck, Molly Kinder, Aaron Klein, Amy Liu, Tanvi Madan, Chris Meserole, Mark Muro, Andre Perry, Ted Piccone, Tony Pipa, Jonathan Rauch, Rashawn Ray, Sarah Reber, Richard Reeves, Bruce Riedel, Molly Reynolds, Frank Rose, Martha Ross, Ashley Ruttenberg, Natan Sachs, Belle Sawhill, Mireya Solis, Shibley Telhami, Jennifer Vey, David Wessel, Darrell West, Vanessa Williamson, Rebecca Winthrop, Ben Wittes, and Tamara Wittes. I am extremely grateful to all of them for sharing their research conclusions and firsthand experiences, as well as for offering me their analyses of developments in the United States and opinions on the project. I have benefited greatly from their articles, blog posts, and public commentary, and from the work of the late and much-missed Alice Rivlin.

I owe a special note of thanks to the Robert Bosch Foundation for ongoing support to the Brookings Institution and my research there, as well as to Brookings donors and trustees Bob Abernethy, Alan Batkin, Jonathan Colby, Susan Crown, Nancy Hewett, Lou Anne Jensen, David Weinberg, and Daniel Yergin, and to Brookings colleagues who encouraged me in writing this book and helped me carve out space to get it done: Brookings Institution president John Allen, special adviser Corey Broschak, chief of staff Elliot Fleming; Patrick Cole, Lucy Kim, Jesse Kornbluth, and Miguel Vieira of the Brookings development team; and other key Brookings staff, including Irena Barisic, Jackie Basile, Cy Behroozi, Michael Cavadel, Ian Dubin, Wakeen Edwards, Julia McManus, April McWilliams, Sean Meehan, Laura Mooney, Robert Moss, John Parker, and Sandra Peters. Brookings Foreign Policy Program vice president Suzanne Maloney, Center on the U.S. and Europe (CUSE) director Tom Wright, Foreign Policy Program research director Mike O'Hanlon, Leo Pasvolsky, senior fellow Carol Graham, president emeritus Strobe Talbott, and close colleagues Pavel Baev, Carlo Bastasin, Célia Belin, Natalie Britton, Giovanna De Maio, Sam Denney, Jim Goldgeier, Emilie Kimball, Jamie Kirchick, Kemal Kirisci, Caroline Klaff, Andy Moffatt, Anna Newby, Steve Pifer, Doug Rediker, Kevin Scott, Javier Solana, Constanze Stelzenmüller, and Torrey Taussig all shared ideas and perspectives. They also helped with source materials and offered moral support. Brookings interns who took part in discussions with me over the course of writing the book—A'ndre Gonawela, Gibbs McKinley, Jerôme Nicolaï, Lucy Seavey, and Chloe Suzman—and Clara O'Donnell fellows Khrystyna Parandii, Katherine Pye, and Leonard Schuette also helped me with ideas and materials.

Outside the Brookings Institution, several groups invited me to participate in workshops related to the book topics in 2020–2021. Director James Arroyo, Emerson Csorba, Natasha Whitmill, and other staff at Ditchley Park in the UK included me in a series of virtual workshops and summits with the Lumina Foundation. These meetings brought together UK government ministers, mayors from the U.S. Midwest and UK North East, the heads of other prominent foundations, nonprofits, and universities, and youth representatives to discuss UK-U.S. relations, comparative deprivation, the challenge of renewing democracies, the role of education, recognizing talent and regaining aspiration and opportunity, and how to bridge geographic divides. As I wrapped up work on the manuscript, Jamie Merisotis of the Lumina Foundation shared perspectives from his book *Human Work in the Age of Smart Machines,* and Ben Delo, Jeremy Hildreth, and Jamie MacFarlane offered their perspectives on the role of philanthropy in shaping opportunity. In the U.S., Daniel Stid at the Hewlett Foundation brought me into various seminars for reviewing themes and provided insights into his and Hewlett grantees' work on renewing democracy; Maya MacGuineas and Mike Murphy at FixUS shared their insights with me, as did Lukas Haynes from the David Rockefeller Fund and Max Stier from the Partnership for Public Service. Mike Berkowitz and Rachel Pritzker included me in their "Patriots and Pragmatists" meetings. They offered invaluable insights and inspiration.

As I worked on the original proposal and then moved forward with the research and manuscript, many people shared their reactions, including Michael Abramowitz, Richard Ades, David Agranovich, Douglas Alexander, Danielle Allen, Joe Amprey, Anne Applebaum, Ellen Archer, Tim Ash, Cathy Ashton, Brian Bacon, Thomas Bagger, Peter Baker, Shachar Bar-On,

Preet Bharara, David Becker, Horton Beebe-Center, Miji Bell, John Bellinger, Gina Bennett, Charlie Bergen, Brad Berkley, Carl Bernstein, Bonnie Bertolaet, Emily Alinikoff Bilbao, Martha Blaxall, Mark Blyth, Charles and Ché Bolden, Julian Borger, Chris Bort, Berkeley and Heather Breathed, John Bridgeland, Reuben Brigety, Ian Brodie, Christian Brook, Archie Brown, Christopher Broxholme, Lauren Buitta, Richard Burger, Vince Cable, Michael Calingaert, Ash Carter, Eric Ciaramella, Emily Carrier, Christian Caryl, Seth Center, Julian Chang, Sam Charap, Chris Chivvis, Adrian Cleasby, Peter Clement, Elliot Cohen, Lisa Coll, Tim Colton, Alex Cooley, Tom Cosgrove, Vassilis Coutifaris, Gretchen Crosby-Sims, Stephen Crowley, Alan Cullison, Keith Darden, Kim Darroch, Janine Davidson, Sarah Davies, Emma Dench, Georgi Derlugian, Barry Didcock, Pawel Dobrowolski, Fiona Dogan, Karen Donfried, Chris Donnelly, Ona Dosunmu, Bill Drozdiak, Daphne Dufresne, Markus Ederer, Doug Elliott, Adam Entous, Steve Erlanger, Philippe Etienne, Alexander Evans, Lara Flint, Michèle Flournoy, Dan Fried, Julia Friedlander, Michael Fullilove, Regina Galer, Robin Gellman, Geoffrey Gertz, Sarah Gilbert, Susan Glasser, Dan Goldberg, Amy Gordon, Nigel Gould-Davies, J. J. Green, the late and much-missed Shane Green, Barbara Grewe, Brian Grzelkowski, Sergei Guriev, Richard Haass, Emily Haber, Nina Hachigian, Avril Haines, John Hamre, Simon Hare, Geoffrey Harris, Shane Harris, Mark Harvey, Hitesh Hathi, John Henriksen, Maura Henry, Francis Hills, Peter Hirst, Jess Hobart, Dan Hoffman, Martin Indyk, Connie Irons, Nick Irons, Andrew Jack, Aaron James, Pam Jewett, Lee Johnson, Timothy Jones, Ludmilla Jordanova, Steve Kaplan, Kirsti Kauppi, Kathy Kavalec, Michele Kelemen, Maura Reynolds Kelley, Bridget Kendall, Paul Kennedy, Thomas Kent, Barbara Keys, Nina Khrushcheva, Keertan Kini, Paul Kolbe, Chris Kojm, Jonathan Koppell, David Kramer, Chris Krebs, Ben Krueger, Charlie Kupchan, Matt Lantz, Susan Lazorchick, Natasha Lebedeva, Philippe Le Corre, Martha Leishman, Paul Lekas, Yuval Levin, Jim Levinsohn, Kadri Liik, Johannes Linn, Ava and Paul Linton, John Lloyd, Eric Liu, Jenny Lo, Viviana Lopez-Green, Edward Lucas, Jennifer Luff, Mark Malcomson, Tesia Mamassian, Sigal Mandelker, Stuart McCormick, Anne McElvoy, Ellen McHugh, Cathy McLaughlin, H. R. McMaster, Tom McTague, Anand Menon, Claire and David Merkel, Greg Miller, Molly Montgomery, Sarah Moor, Edwina Morton, Simon Marks, Yascha Mounk, Daniel Mulhall, Michael Mullen, Grant Murphy, Vivek Murthy, Nancy Nachbar, Elena Nachmanoff, Ellen Nakashima, James Nixey, Toria Nuland, Melanie Okuneye, Arkady Ostrovsky, Meghan O'Sullivan, Bob Otto, Gene

Park, Bruce Parrott, Norma Percy, Emily Perkins, Tom Pickering, Karen Pierce, Alexander Pivovarsky, Ruth Pojman, Jane Prokop, Manveen Rana, Jamie Raskin, Brian Reed, Dakota Roberson, Lori Robinson, Chuck Rosenberg, Jonathan Rozenberg, Trudy Rubin, Blair Ruble, Andrew Sanders, John Scarlett, Lucas Schoch, Daniela Schwarzer, Jim Sciutto, Anula Seelawathie, Klaus Segbers, Demetri Sevastopulo, Minouche Shafik, Jeremy Shapiro, David Shimer, Zach Shore, Katy Simmons, Amanda Sloat, Ben Smith, Jason Smith, Stephen Kennedy Smith, Yuri Somov, David Speedie, Lesley Stahl, Paul Starobin, Danica Starks, Angela Stent, "Sully" Sullenberger, Tammy Sun, Barrett Takesian, Michael Tatham, Bill Taylor, David Taylor, Kim Teri, Hannah Thoburn, Harold Trinkunas, Robert Tsai, Misha Tsypkin, Charlie Undeland, Alexandra Vacroux, Justin Vaisse, Ian Vasey, Alex Vindman, Tessa Walker, Joe Wang, Melissa Weintraub, Andrew Weiss, Gavin Wilde, Clete Willems, Ted Wittenstein, Martin Wolf, Beatrix von Watzdorf, Casimir Yost, Marie Yovanovitch, Daniel Ziblatt, Tim Ziemer, and Fabian Zuleeg.

Many of this large group of friends, colleagues, and distant acquaintances provided insights and raised important questions about core ideas. They also flagged articles in the press that I might not otherwise have seen, suggested individuals I should approach for interviews, and sent me their own and other publications for reference. Some even allowed themselves to be interviewed and then agreed to be featured or referenced in the book, for which I am extremely grateful. Although I did not hesitate to impose on them and others to ask for their input, I alone bear responsibility for any errors or misinterpretations of their perspectives. The generosity of those mentioned in assisting me should in no way be interpreted as their personal endorsement of my ideas and interpretations, nor of the accuracy of the information presented.

I am especially grateful to Agneska Bloch, Angela Hill, Ken Keen, Filippos Letsas, and Chuck Young for brainstorming all the way along, reading the first drafts, and offering advice on how to improve the book. Editor Alex Littlefield and the team at Houghton Mifflin Harcourt — Megan Wilson, Deb Brody, Lori Glazer, Liz Duvall — and agents Andrew Nurnberg and Jenny Savill, along with Charlotte Merritt and Saskia Willis and all their colleagues, are the people who made this book possible. They had faith in the idea in the first place, provided thematic suggestions, critical feedback, important editorial advice, and support at all points along the way. This manuscript would also not have happened without the team who got me through my congressional testimony and its aftermath in 2019–2020: my lawyers, Sam Ungar and Lee Wolosky; Mia Wolosky, who came to sit behind me and offer moral support during the public hearing; and the PR gurus of the Levinson Group — Molly Levinson, Caitlin Klevorick, Kylie McKenna, Colin Reed, and Kristin Rudman — who helped me navigate my unexpected moment in the international spotlight.

I would finally like to thank everyone I served with at the NIC, ODNI, the NSC, the White House, and the U.S. government, many of whom helped prompt me to write this through endless conversations and shared experiences. And to all the people who wrote to me in 2019–2020 and continue to do so, thank you! Your letters informed this book, and I am very grateful for the personal gifts and mementos.

Fiona Hill
Washington, D.C., June 2021

NOTES

PROLOGUE: THE "IMPROBABLE" FIONA HILL

page

2   *"Their testimony was pointed"*: Robin Givhan, "Their testimony was pointed. Their clothes were reassuringly dull," *Washington Post,* November 21, 2019, https://www.washingtonpost.com/lifestyle/2019/11/21/their-testimony-was-pointed-their-clothes-were-reassuringly-dull/.

5   *the "improbable" Fiona Hill*: Demetri Sevastopulo, "Fiona Hill: 'I knew more about what was going on in the Kremlin,'" *Financial Times,* June 12, 2020, https://www.ft.com/content/e51f701e-aa62-11ea-a766-7c300513fe47.

INTRODUCTION: FROM THE COAL HOUSE TO THE WHITE HOUSE

7   *only 10 percent . . . had something lined up*: Martin Cooper, "The youth unemployment 'crisis' of the 1980s: How two comprehensive schools have responded," *Evaluation & Research in Education* 3, no. 2 (1989): 81–88.

11   *"the authoritarians' playbook"*: See Anne Applebaum, *Twilight of Democracy: The Seductive Lure of Authoritarianism* (New York: Doubleday, 2020); Theodor W. Adorno, Else Frenkel-Brunswik, Daniel Levinson, and Nevitt Sanford, *The Authoritarian Personality* (New York: Harper & Brothers, 1950); David Runciman, *How Democracy Ends* (London: Profile, 2019); Timothy Snyder, *On Tyranny: Twenty Lessons from the Twentieth Century* (New Tork: Tim Duggan, 2017); Timothy Snyder, *The Road to Unfreedom: Russia, Europe, America* (New York: Vintage, 2018); Daniel Ziblatt and Steven Levitsky, *How Democracies Die* (New York: Crown, 2019).

1. "CALL THE UNITED NATIONS"

18   *acutely class-based society:* Mike Savage, *Social Class in the 21st Century* (London: Pelican, 2015).

23   *Margaret Thatcher was a trailblazer:* Peter Jenkins, *Mrs. Thatcher's Revolution: The Ending of the Socialist Era* (Cambridge: Harvard University Press, 1988).
      commanding heights: Daniel Yergin and Joseph Stanislaw, *The Commanding Heights: The Battle Between Government and the Marketplace* (New York: Simon & Schuster, 2002).
      last pit in County Durham: "Coal Mining and Durham Collieries," Durham County Record Office, accessed March 10, 2021, http://www.durhamrecordoffice.org.uk/article/10560/Coal-Mining-and-Durham-Collieries.
      the last shipment: Chris Robinson, "Last coal shipment leaves River Tyne," *BBC News,* February 18, 2021, https://www.bbc.com/news/uk-england-tyne-56071386.

24   *the rise of coal: Coal Mining in County Durham* (Durham: Durham County Environmental Education Curriculum Group, 1993).

31   *2,600 people on its books:* John Sansick, "The jewel in British rail's crown: an account of the closure at Shildon Wagon Works" (PhD diss., Durham University, 1990), 29, http://etheses.dur.ac.uk/6230/1/6230_3585.PDF?UkUDh:CyT.
      also closed: Chris Lloyd, "From the Archive: Shildon Wagon Works," *Northern Echo,* March 14, 2015, https://www.thenorthernecho.co.uk/history/11856977.archive-shildon-wagon-works/.

2. GRASPING AT THE FUTURE

39   *government poverty level:* "2021 Poverty Guidelines," Office of the Assistant Secretary for Planning and Evaluation, January 26, 2021, https://aspe.hhs.gov/2021-poverty-guidelines.
      Real wages dropped: Ciaren Taylor, Andrew Jowett, and Michael Hardie, *An Examination of Falling Real Wages, 2010–2013* (Newport: Office for National Statistics, 2014), 3, https://webarchive.nationalarchives.gov.uk/20160108042646/http://www.ons.gov.uk/ons/dcp171766_351467.pdf.

3. OUT OF YOUR LEAGUE

46   *students admitted to college:* "Research Starters: The GI Bill," National WWII Museum, accessed April 25, 2021, https://www.nationalww2museum.org/students-teachers/student-resources/research-starters/research-starters-gi-bill.

47   *uproot the select few:* Lynsey Hanley, *Respectable: The Experience of Class* (London: Allen Lane, 2016).
      Fewer than 10 percent: Paul Bolton, *Education; Historical statistics* (London: House of Commons Library, 2012), 14.

58   *country of individuals:* Margaret Thatcher, "Interview for *Woman's Own* ('no such thing as society')," interview by Douglas Keay, *Woman's Own,* September 23, 1987.

60   *1983 "war scare":* Fiona Hill and Clifford Gaddy, "The American Education of Mr. Putin," in *Mr. Putin: Operative in the Kremlin* (Washington: Brookings Institution, 2015), 285–311.

66   *9 percent of Oxford students:* Claire Hann Danny Dorling, "The Oxbridge access question has not been settled," *Times Higher Education,* October 17, 2019, https://www.timeshighereducation.com/opinion/oxbridge-access-question-has-not-been-settled.

      did not become co-ed: Catherine Bennett, "Oxford University went co-ed 40 years ago. And look how far we've come," *Guardian,* June 21, 2014, https://www.theguardian.com/commentisfree/2014/jun/21/oxbridge-co-ed-40-years-women-feminism-arts.

4. COMMON NORTHERNER

71   *767,000 Africans were shipped:* David Olusoga, *Black and British: A Forgotten History* (London: Pan, 2017), 222–223.

      infamous speech on immigration: Enoch Powell, "Rivers of Blood," speech, Conservative Association meeting, Birmingham, April 20, 1968, https://anth1001.files.wordpress.com/2014/04/enoch-powell_speech.pdf.

      Rampaging and pillaging: Bill Buford, *Among the Thugs* (New York: Vintage, 1993).

72   *killed in clashes:* Martin Adeney and John Lloyd, *The Miners' Strike 1984–1985: Loss Without Limit* (London: Routledge and Kegan Paul, 1986), 126, 224–225.

73   *built by coal mining:* Adeney and Lloyd, *The Miners' Strike.*

85   *new generational movement:* Joanna Stingray and Madison Stingray, *Red Wave: An American in the Soviet Music Underground* (Los Angeles: DoppelHouse, 2020).

89   *North-South divide:* Dan Jackson, *The Northumbrians: North-East England and Its People: A New History* (London: C. Hurst, 2019).

5. THE LAND OF OPPORTUNITY

94   *trajectory of industrial development:* For further reading, see Paul Kennedy, *The Rise and Fall of the Great Powers: Economic Change and Military Conflict from 1500 to 2000* (New York: Penguin Random House, 1989).

95   *the USSR came apart:* Svetlana Alexievich, *Secondhand Time: The Last of the Soviets: An Oral History* (New York: Random House Trade Paperbacks, 2017).

98   *self-perpetuating dynasty:* Andy Beckett, "PPE: the Oxford degree that runs Britain," *Guardian,* February 23, 2017, https://www.theguardian.com/education/2017/feb/23/ppe-oxford-university-degree-that-rules-britain.

101   *I had just written:* Hill and Gaddy, *Mr. Putin.*

104   *experienced at home:* Katherine D. Kinzler, *How You Say It: Why We Judge Others by the Way They Talk — And the Costs of This Hidden Bias* (Boston: Houghton Mifflin Harcourt, 2021).

       distinct British ethnic groups: Travellers were recognized as a separate ethnic group in the UK in 2002, although only the Gypsy Roma and those of Irish heritage have official status. There are about three hundred thousand across the country, and they are one of the most disadvantaged groups in the United Kingdom. In addition to the officially recognized groups, the UK also has Welsh and Scottish Travellers. Records of all the groups date back centuries. Traveller groups have also intermingled over time. My dad's paternal grandmother's family were "hawkers" and part of the Scottish Lowland Traveller community who moved around the borders of Scotland and North East England until they settled in one of the villages outside Bishop Auckland. My mother's paternal grandfather's family were Scottish cattle drovers who similarly moved between cattle markets in Scotland and the North East.

108   *an entirely different frame:* Nancy Isenberg, *White Trash: The 400-Year Untold History of Class in America* (New York: Penguin, 2017).

       fixed caste system: Isabel Wilkerson, *Caste: The Origins of Our Discontent* (New York: Random House, 2020).

114   *economics of shortage:* János Kornai, *Economics of Shortage* (Amsterdam: North-Holland, 1980).

115   The Road to a Free Economy: János Kornai, *The Road to a Free Economy: Shifting from a Socialist System: The Example of Hungary* (New York: W. W. Norton, 1990).

6. SHOCK THERAPY

119   *keep production going:* Clifford G. Gaddy and Barry W. Ickes, *Russia's Virtual Economy* (Washington: Brookings Institution, 2002).

       most women in Russia: Mary Buckley, "Women in the Soviet Union," *Feminist Review,* no. 8 (1981): 80.

120   *drove people to drink:* Oliver Bullough, *The Last Man in Russia: The Struggle to Save a Dying Nation* (New York: Basic, 2013).

       council house tenants: Andy Beckett, "The right to buy: the housing crisis that Thatcher built," *Guardian,* August 26, 2015, https://www.theguardian.com/society/2015/aug/26/right-to-buy-margaret-thatcher-david-cameron-housing-crisis.

       allocated by the Communist Party: Nadezhda Kosareva and Raymond Struyk, "Housing Privatization in the Russian Federation," *Housing Policy Debate* 4, no. 1 (1993): 82, https://www.innovations.harvard.edu/sites/default/files/hpd_0401_kosareva.pdf.

123   *most remote cities:* Fiona Hill and Clifford Gaddy, *The Siberian Curse: How Com-*

munist Planners Left Russia Out in the Cold (Washington: Brookings Institution, 2003), 119.

World Bank pilot program: Hill and Gaddy, *The Siberian Curse,* 126–129.

124   *Gender inequality still persists: Women in higher education: has the female advantage put an end to gender inequalities?* (Caracas: UNESCO International Institute for Higher Education in Latin America and the Caribbean, 2021), 45, https://www.iesalc.unesco.org/en/wp-content/uploads/2021/03/Women-Report-EN-080321.pdf.

128   *60 percent of schoolgirls:* Denise Hamilton, "Changing Lifestyles: Prostitution Rising as Tough Times Wear on Soviet People," *Los Angeles Times,* November 12, 1991, https://www.latimes.com/archives/la-xpm-1991-11-12-wr-1528-story.html.

130   Essence of Decision: Graham T. Allison, *Essence of Decision: Explaining the Cuban Missile Crisis* (Boston: Little, Brown, 1971).

132   *push the bank:* Elena Fabrichnaya, "How Russia's central bank chief held the line," Reuters, September 26, 2016, https://www.reuters.com/article/us-russia-cenbank-nabiullina-insight-idUSKCN11W166.

133   *"combat the strong stereotypes":* Hill and Gaddy, *Mr. Putin,* 462–463.

     so close to him: Clifford G. Gaddy and Fiona Hill, "Putin's Next Move in Russia: Observations from the 8th Annual Valdai International Discussion Club," Brookings Institution, December 12, 2011, https://www.brookings.edu/on-the-record/putins-next-move-in-russia-observations-from-the-8th-annual-valdai-international-discussion-club/.

7. WOMEN'S WORK

136   *40 percent of women voters:* "An examination of the 2016 electorate, based on validated voters," Pew Research Center, August 9, 2018, https://www.pewresearch.org/politics/2018/08/09/an-examination-of-the-2016-electorate-based-on-validated-voters/.

138   *frequently denied the salary:* Benjamin Artz, Amanda Goodall, and Andrew J. Oswald, "Research: Women Ask for Raises as Often as Men, But Are Less Likely to Get Them," *Harvard Business Review,* June 25, 2018, https://hbr.org/2018/06/research-women-ask-for-raises-as-often-as-men-but-are-less-likely-to-get-them.

145   *more than 40 percent of women:* Isabel Sawhill, *The Forgotten Americans: An Economic Agenda for a Divided Nation* (New Haven: Yale University Press, 2018), 168–169.

     Seventy-one percent of these single parents: "Family Homelessness Facts," Green Doors, accessed April 29, 2021, https://www.greendoors.org/facts/family-homelessness.php.

146   *headed by a single mother:* "Family Homelessness Facts."

     just over 13 percent: "U.S. Census Bureau QuickFacts: United States," U.S. Census

Bureau, accessed May 12, 2021, https://www.census.gov/quickfacts/fact/table/US/PST045219.

the role that families play: Pamela Braboy Jackson and Rashawn Ray, *How Families Matter: Simply Complicated Intersections of Race, Gender, and Work* (Lanham, MD: Lexington, 2018).

147   *the United States is an outlier:* Gretchen Livingston and Deja Thomas, "Among 41 countries, only U.S. lacks paid parental leave," Pew Research Center, December 16, 2019, https://www.pewresearch.org/fact-tank/2019/12/16/u-s-lacks-mandated-paid-parental-leave/.

8. UNLUCKY GENERATIONS

149   *Only 3 percent came from the poorest:* David Brooks, "Who Is Driving Inequality? You Are," *New York Times,* April 23, 2020, https://www.nytimes.com/2020/04/23/opinion/income-inequality.html.

150   *"unluckiest generation":* Andrew Van Dam, "The unluckiest generation in U.S. history," *Washington Post,* June 5, 2020, https://www.washingtonpost.com/business/2020/05/27/millennial-recession-covid/.

unable to cover $1,000: Megan Leonhardt, "60 percent of millennials don't have enough money to cover a $1,000 emergency," CNBC, December 20, 2018, https://www.cnbc.com/2018/12/19/60-percent-of-millennials-cant-cover-a-1000-dollar-emergency.html.

chance of making more money: Raj Chetty et al., "The fading American dream: Trends in absolute income mobility since 1940," *Science* 356, no. 6336 (April 2017): 398–406.

consequences of socioeconomic divisions: Robert D. Putnam, *Our Kids: The American Dream in Crisis* (New York: Simon & Schuster, 2015).

152   *$1.6 trillion in total:* Erica L. Green, Luke Broadwater, and Stacy Cowley, "Student Loan Cancellation Sets Up Clash Between Biden and the Left," *New York Times,* December 10, 2020, https://www.nytimes.com/2020/12/10/us/politics/biden-student-loans.html; Oksana Leukhina, "Rising Student Debt and the Great Recession," Federal Reserve Bank of St. Louis, January 14, 2020, https://www.stlouisfed.org/on-the-economy/2020/january/rising-student-debt-great-recession.

from higher-income households: Sandy Baum and Adam Looney, "Who owes most in student loans: New data from the Fed," *Up Front* (blog), Brookings Institution, October 9, 2020, https://www.brookings.edu/blog/up-front/2020/10/09/who-owes-the-most-in-student-loans-new-data-from-the-fed/.

in the years following graduation: Judith Scott-Clayton and Jing Li, *Black-white disparity in student loan debt more than triples after graduation* (Washington: Brookings Institution, 2016), https://www.brookings.edu/research/black-white-disparity-in-student-loan-debt-more-than-triples-after-graduation/.

did not finish: "Status and Trends in the Education of Racial and Ethnic Groups: Indicator 23: Postsecondary Graduation Rates," National Center for Education Statistics, last updated February 2019, https://nces.ed.gov/programs/raceindicators/indicator_red.asp.

The provision of student grants: "Michigan wants to increase residents' college enrollment, but student debt is holding them back," *The Avenue* (blog), Brookings Institution, March 15, 2021, https://www.brookings.edu/blog/the-avenue/2021/03/15/michigan-wants-to-increase-residents-college-enrollment-but-student-debt-is-holding-them-back/.

154 *dominated by men:* "Women in Academia: Quick Take," Catalyst, January 23, 2020, https://www.catalyst.org/research/women-in-academia/.

inside and outside Congress: Theda Skocpol and Vanessa Williamson: *The Tea Party and the Remaking of Republican Conservatism* (Oxford: Oxford University Press, 2016).

155 *dissolution of the British empire:* Fintan O'Toole, *The Politics of Pain: Postwar England and the Rise of Nationalism* (New York: W. W. Norton, 2019).

baby boomers: Kim Parker and Ruth Igielnik, "On the Cusp of Adulthood and Facing an Uncertain Future: What We Know About Gen Z So Far," Pew Research Center, https://www.pewresearch.org/social-trends/2020/05/14/on-the-cusp-of-adulthood-and-facing-an-uncertain-future-what-we-know-about-gen-z-so-far-2/.

"majority minority": William H. Frey, "The US will become 'minority white' in 2045, Census projects," *The Avenue* (blog), Brookings Institution, March 14, 2018, https://www.brookings.edu/blog/the-avenue/2018/03/14/the-us-will-become-minority-white-in-2045-census-projects/.

156 *predicament of distressed towns:* See Amy Goldstein, *Janesville: An American Story* (New York: Simon & Schuster, 2018); Arlie Russell Hochschild, *Strangers in Their Own Land: Anger and Mourning on the American Right* (New York: New Press, 2016); George Packer, *The Unwinding: An Inner History of the New America* (New York: Farrar, Straus and Giroux, 2013); and Jennifer Silva, *We're Still Here: Pain and Politics in the Heart of America* (Oxford: Oxford University Press, 2019).

"cultural despair": Fritz Stern, *The Politics of Cultural Despair: A Study in the Rise of German Ideology* (Oakland: University of California Press, 1974).

circumstances of the 1930s: For further reading on the economic dilemmas of the 2000s, see Paul Collier, *The Future of Capitalism: Facing the New Anxieties* (New York: HarperCollins, 2018); Michael Graetz and Ian Shapiro, *The Wolf at the Door: The Menace of Economic Insecurity and How to Fight It* (Cambridge: Harvard University Press, 2020); and Michael Sandbu, *The Economics of Belonging: A Radical Plan to Win Back the Left Behind and Achieve Prosperity for All* (Princeton: Princeton University Press, 2020).

make their way to the top: "Americans overestimate social mobility in their country," *Economist,* February 14, 2018, https://www.economist.com/graphic-detail/
2018/02/14/americans-overestimate-social-mobility-in-their-country.

157   *below the official poverty line:* Mark R. Rank, "Five myths about poverty,"
Washington Post, March 26, 2021, https://www.washingtonpost.com/outlook/
five-myths/5-myths-about-poverty/2021/03/25/bf75d5f4-8cfe-11eb-a6bd-0eb91c
03305a_story.html. See also Mark Robert Rank, Lawrence M. Eppard, and
Heather E. Bullock, *Poorly Understood: What America Gets Wrong About Poverty*
(New York: Oxford University Press, 2021).

statistical divergence: John R. Allen and Darrell M. West, *Ways to reconcile and
heal America* (Washington: Brookings Institution, 2021), 17, https://www.brook
ings.edu/research/ways-to-reconcile-and-heal-america/. See also Dominic Sand-
brook, *Who Dares Wins: Britain 1979–1982* (London: Allen Lane, 2019). Sand-
brook deems 1981 the UK's "worst year."

American fathers passed on: Rank, "Five myths about poverty."

ten times less: Kriston McIntosh, Emily Moss, Ryan Nunn, and Jay Shambaugh,
"Examining the Black-white wealth gap," *Up Front* (blog), Brookings Institution,
February 27, 2020, https://www.brookings.edu/blog/up-front/2020/02/27/exam
ining-the-black-white-wealth-gap/.

far less likely to own: Jung Hyun Choi, "Breaking Down the Black-White Home-
ownership Gap," Urban Institute, February 21, 2020, https://www.urban.org/
urban-wire/breaking-down-black-white-homeownership-gap.

due to the legacy: Andre Perry, *Know Your Price: Valuing Black Lives and Property
in America's Black Cities* (Washington: Brookings Institution, 2020); Dorothy A.
Brown, *The Whiteness of Wealth: How the Tax System Impoverishes Black Americans — and How We Can Fix It* (New York: Crown, 2021).

lived seven years longer: David Leonhardt and Yaruna Serkez, "America Will
Struggle After Coronavirus. These Charts Show Why," *New York Times,* April
10, 2020, https://www.nytimes.com/interactive/2020/04/10/opinion/coronavirus-
us-economy-inequality.html.

no health insurance: Kenneth Finegold et al., *Trends in the U.S. Uninsured Population, 2010–2020* (Washington: ASPE Office of Health Policy, 2021), https://aspe.
hhs.gov/system/files/pdf/265041/trends-in-the-us-uninsured.pdf.

158   *"deaths of despair":* Anne Case and Angus Deaton, *Deaths of Despair and the
Future of Capitalism* (Princeton: Princeton University Press, 2020); Carol Graham, *America's crisis of despair: A federal task force for economic recovery and
societal well-being* (Washington: Brookings Institution, 2021), https://www.
brookings.edu/research/americas-crisis-of-despair-a-federal-task-force-for-eco
nomic-recovery-and-societal-well-being/; Carol Graham, *Happiness for All? Unequal Hopes and Lives in Pursuit of the American Dream* (Princeton: Princeton
University Press, 2017); Carol Graham and Stefano Pettinato, *Happiness & Hard-*

ship: Opportunity and Insecurity in New Market Economies (Washington: Brookings Institution, 2001).

159   *report from his UK visit:* United Nations, Human Rights Council, *Visit to the United Kingdom of Great Britain and Northern Ireland: Report of the Special Rapporteur on extreme poverty and human rights,* A/HRC/41/39 (April 23, 2019), https://undocs.org/A/HRC/41/39/Add.1.

160   *October 2019 interview:* Michael Goldhaber, "Professor Philip Alston, UN Special Rapporteur on extreme poverty and human rights," International Bar Association, October 14, 2019, https://www.ibanet.org/Article/NewDetail.aspx?ArticleUid=33B6F2D1-D47F-419A-98B4-A2DC19BA6BC8.

163   *minorities tended:* Sean Coughlan, "The 'taboo' about who doesn't go to university," BBC, September 27, 2020, https://www.bbc.com/news/education-54278727.

164   *"White teenagers" on free school meals:* Sean Coughlan, "Poor white teens in 'left behind' towns not going to uni," BBC, January 26, 2021, https://www.bbc.com/news/education-55804123.

165   *45 percent of the population:* "Regional ethnic diversity," UK Government Ethnicity facts and figures, updated August 7, 2020 https://www.ethnicity-facts-figures.service.gov.uk/uk-population-by-ethnicity/national-and-regional-populations/regional-ethnic-diversity/latest; "2011 Census: Key Statistics for England and Wales, March 2011," Office for National Statistics, December 11, 2012, https://www.ons.gov.uk/peoplepopulationandcommunity/populationandmigration/populationestimates/bulletins/2011censuskeystatisticsforenglandandwales/2012-12-11#usual-residents-born-outside-the-uk.

      outer city boroughs: Neil Kaye, *BME populations in London: Statistical analysis of the latest UK census* (London: Middlesex University, 2013), http://sprc.info/wp-content/uploads/2013/07/BME-communities-statistical-profile1.pdf.

      proceeded to higher education: Coughlan, "The 'taboo' about who doesn't go to university."

      just over a quarter: "Widening participation in higher education," Gov.uk, July 30, 2020, https://www.gov.uk/government/statistics/widening-participation-in-higher-education-2020.

      the rest of the country: Edwina Moreton, email message to author, December 10, 2020.

9. ME THE PEOPLE

170   *electorate turned out:* "Results and turnout at the EU referendum: National totals," Electoral Commission, last updated September 25, 2019, https://www.electoralcommission.org.uk/who-we-are-and-what-we-do/elections-and-referendums/past-elections-and-referendums/eu-referendum/results-and-turnout-eu-referendum.

171   *opted for Brexit:* "Bishop Auckland parliamentary constituency," *Democratic Dashboard,* accessed April 25, 2021, https://democraticdashboard.com/constituency/bishop-auckland.

Trump predicted: Ali Vitali, "Trump Says U.S. Election Result Will Be Like 'Brexit Times Five,'" *NBC News,* October 21, 2016, https://www.nbcnews.com/politics/2016-election/trump-says-u-s-election-result-will-be-brexit-times-n67 1081.

nothing conclusive: Russia (London: Intelligence and Security Committee of Parliament of the United Kingdom, 2020), https://www.globalsecurity.org/intell/library/reports/2020/russia-report_uk-isc_20200721.pdf.

essence of populism: For further discussion of populism, see Cas Mudde and Cristóbal Rovira Kaltwasser, *Populism: A Very Short Introduction* (Oxford: Oxford University Press, 2017), and Jan-Werner Müller, *What Is Populism?* (Philadelphia: University of Pennsylvania Press, 2016).

175   *"to be seen with it":* Alexander Brown, "Nigel Farage drinks beer 'to be seen with it' and actually 'prefers wine,'" *Daily Star,* May 7, 2019, https://www.dailystar.co.uk/news/latest-news/nigel-farage-beer-brexit-party-16770301.

176   *people outside elite circles:* Joan C. Williams, *White Working Class: Overcoming Class Cluelessness in America* (Cambridge: Harvard Business Review, 2017).

"people's champion": Michael Edison Hayden, "Ivanka Trump Introduces Her Father Donald at the RNC: He Is 'the People's Champion,'" *ABC News,* July 21, 2016, https://abcnews.go.com/Politics/ivanka-trump-introduces-father-donald-rnc-peoples-champion/story?id=40783780.

177   *over fifty thousand American miners:* Chuck Jones, "The Coal Industry Has Lost Almost One Thousand Jobs Since Trump Became President," *Washington Post,* March 7, 2020, https://www.forbes.com/sites/chuckjones/2020/03/07/the-coal-industry-has-lost-almost-one-thousand-jobs-since-trump-became-president/?sh=1b414df52e29.

eighty-five thousand workers in blast furnaces: "Iron and steel industry in the United States — employment 2013–2019," Statista Research Department, February 21, 2020, https://www.statista.com/statistics/813419/employment-in-the-us-steel-industry/.

25 percent tariffs: Ana Swanson, "Trump to Impose Sweeping Steel and Aluminum Tariffs," *New York Times,* March 1, 2018, https://www.nytimes.com/2018/03/01/business/trump-tariffs.html.

filed for bankruptcy: Oliver Milman, "'My friends were lied to': Will coalminers stand by Trump as jobs disappear?," *Guardian,* September 24, 2020, https://www.theguardian.com/us-news/2020/sep/24/donald-trump-coal-miners-us-election.

the steel industry had been dead: Lori Robertson and Eugene Kiely, "Trump's Steel Industry Claims," Factcheck, August 29, 2019, https://www.factcheck.org/2019/08/trumps-steel-industry-claims/.

179 *closed down in 2015:* Sean Farrell and Dominic Smith, "Redcar steel plant to close with 1,700 job losses," *Guardian,* https://www.theguardian.com/business/2015/sep/28/redcar-steel-plant-to-close-with-1700-job-losses.

180 *efforts to defame:* Russ Buettner and Charles V. Bagli, "How Donald Trump Bankrupted His Atlantic City Casinos, but Still Earned Millions," *New York Times,* June 11, 2016, https://www.nytimes.com/2016/06/12/nyregion/donald-trump-atlantic-city.html; Michelle Lee, "Fact Check: Has Trump declared bankruptcy four or six times?," *Washington Post,* September 26, 2016, https://www.washington post.com/politics/2016/live-updates/general-election/real-time-fact-checking-and-analysis-of-the-first-presidential-debate/fact-check-has-trump-declared-bankruptcy-four-or-six-times/.

"No politician in history": Lauren Gambino and Tom McCarthy, "Trump: 'No politician in history has been treated more unfairly," *Guardian,* May 17, 2017, https://www.theguardian.com/us-news/2017/may/17/donald-trump-presidency-media-coverage-russia-scandal.

This was "socialism": David A. Graham, "Trump's New Red Scare," *Atlantic,* February 20, 2019, https://www.theatlantic.com/politics/archive/2019/02/trump-socialism-venezuela-bernie-sanders-ocasio-cortez/583135/.

181 *top-down approach:* Katie Lobosco, "Employers commit to train 3.8 million workers under Trump executive order," CNN, July 19, 2018, https://www.cnn.com/2018/07/19/politics/trump-executive-order-job-training/index.html.

ephemeral: Brooks Jackson, "Trump's Numbers January 2020 Update," Factcheck, January 20, 2020, https://www.factcheck.org/2020/01/trumps-numbers-january-2020-update/.

went after trade unions' efforts: Margaret Poydock, "President Trump has attacked workers' safety, rights, and wages since Day One," Economic Policy Institute, September 17, 2020, https://www.epi.org/blog/president-trump-has-attacked-workers-safety-wages-and-rights-since-day-one/.

184 *79,646 votes:* Philip Bump, "Donald Trump will be president thanks to 80,000 people in three states," *Washington Post,* December 1, 2016, https://www.washingtonpost.com/news/the-fix/wp/2016/12/01/donald-trump-will-be-president-thanks-to-80000-people-in-three-states/.

contacts with Wikileaks: David Shimer, *Rigged: America, Russia, and One Hundred Years of Covert Electoral Interference* (New York: Knopf, 2020); Catherine Belton, *Putin's People: How the KGB Took Back Russia and Then Took on the West* (New York: Farrar, Straus and Giroux, 2020); Annie Karni and Maggie Haberman, "Roger Stone's Dirty Tricks Put Him Where He's Always Wanted to Be: Center Stage," *New York Times,* January 25, 2019, https://www.nytimes.com/2019/01/25/us/politics/who-is-roger-stone.html; *Get Me Roger Stone,* directed by Dylan Bank, Daniel DiMauro, and Morgan Pehme, aired April 23, 2017, on Netflix, https://www.netflix.com/title/80114666.

185   *report from Mueller:* Robert S. Mueller, III, *Report on the Investigation Into Russian Interference in the 2016 Presidential Election* (Washington: U.S. Department of Justice, 2019), https://www.justice.gov/archives/sco/file/1373816/download.

     avoid reimbursing contractors: Steve Reilly, "USA TODAY exclusive: Hundreds allege Donald Trump doesn't pay his bills," *USA Today,* June 9, 2016, https://www.usatoday.com/story/news/politics/elections/2016/06/09/donald-trump-unpaid-bills-republican-president-laswuits/85297274/.

186   *approach to foreign policy:* Jim Sciutto, *The Madman Theory: Trump Takes on the World* (New York: HarperCollins, 2020).

188   *"Central Casting":* Adam Entous, "What Fiona Hill Learned in the White House," *New Yorker,* June 22, 2020, https://www.newyorker.com/magazine/2020/06/29/what-fiona-hill-learned-in-the-white-house.

     up in heaven: "Trump assumes steelworker's father is dead; steelworker corrects him," *Washington Post,* March 8, 2018, https://www.washingtonpost.com/video/politics/trump-assumes-steelworkers-father-is-dead-steelworker-corrects-him/2018/03/08/21bf1504-2317-11e8-946c-9420060cb7bd_video.html.

189   *"good American jobs":* Jeffrey Bonior, "For These Steelworkers, a Trip to the White House Is Another Step in a Decades-Long Fight," *United Steelworkers,* March 13, 2018, https://www.usw.org/blog/2018/for-these-steelworkers-a-trip-to-the-white-house-is-another-step-in-a-decades-long-fight.

190   *"his America":* Peter Baker, "For Trump It's Not the United States, It's Red and Blue States," *New York Times,* September 17, 2020, https://www.nytimes.com/2020/09/17/us/politics/trump-america.html.

10. "RUSSIA BITCH"

193   *designated as the deputy:* K. T. McFarland, *Revolution: Trump, Washington and "We the People"* (New York: Post Hill, 2020).

194   *H. R. McMaster:* H. R. McMaster, *Battlegrounds: The Fight to Defend the Free World* (New York: HarperCollins, 2020).

     malicious leaks: Entous, "What Fiona Hill Learned in the White House."

198   *"Tariff Man":* Jen Kirby, "Trump called himself 'Tariff Man.' The internet did the rest," *Vox,* December 4, 2018, https://www.vox.com/policy-and-politics/2018/12/4/18126061/tariff-man-trump-china-tweets-memes-stock-market.

     "ultimate catastrophe": Glenn Plaskin, "The Playboy Interview with Donald Trump," *Playboy Magazine,* March 1, 1990, https://www.playboy.com/read/playboy-interview-donald-trump-1990.

     fruitless effort: Paula Span, "From the archives: When Trump hoped to meet Gorbachev in Manhattan," *Washington Post,* December 3, 1988, https://www.washingtonpost.com/lifestyle/style/from-the-archives-when-trump-hoped-to-meet-gorbachev-in-manhattan/2017/07/10/3f570b42-658c-11e7-a1d7-9a32c91c6f40_story.html.

199   *his particular interests:* Alex Ward, "'The end of arms control as we know it,'" *Vox,* August 3, 2020, https://www.vox.com/world/21131449/trump-putin-nuclear-usa-russia-arms-control-new-start.

        strong executive power: See Archie Brown, *The Human Factor: Gorbachev, Reagan, and Thatcher, and the End of the Cold War* (Oxford: Oxford University Press, 2020).

200   *roster of officials:* Kathryn Dunn Tenpas, *Tracking turnover in the Trump administration* (Washington: Brookings Institution, 2021), https://www.brookings.edu/research/tracking-turnover-in-the-trump-administration/.

204   *"anonymous source":* Greg Miller, Greg Jaffe, and Philip Rucker, "Doubting the intelligence, Trump pursues Putin and leaves a Russian threat unchecked," *Washington Post,* December 14, 2017, https://www.washingtonpost.com/graphics/2017/world/national-security/donald-trump-pursues-vladimir-putin-russian-election-hacking/.

205   *legal requirement for record-keeping:* Deb Riechmann, "Will Trump's mishandling of records leave a hole in history?," Associated Press, January 16, 2021, https://apnews.com/article/donald-trump-technology-politics-vladimir-putin-russia-65748b70e3cf3f7eecffa265da9ccae7.

        lengthy article: Entous, "What Fiona Hill Learned in the White House."

209   kompromat: Zachary Basu, "Woodward book: Former intel chief Dan Coats believed 'Putin had something on Trump,'" *Axios,* September 9, 2020, https://www.axios.com/bob-woodward-book-trump-putin-russia-dan-coats-b3994f91-8791-4fdc-9adb-ad093141592b.html.

        soured on President Trump: John Bolton, *The Room Where It Happened: A White House Memoir* (New York: Simon & Schuster, 2020).

210   *Trump called Putin:* Zeeshan Aleem, "Trump appears delighted that Putin has 'very nice things' to say about him," *Vox,* December 15, 2017, https://www.vox.com/world/2017/12/15/16780414/trump-putin-economy-russia-scandal.

        "I wish I had known": Maxwell Tani, "A reporter confronts Greek prime minister at press conference with Trump over past comments calling him 'evil,'" *Business Insider,* October 17, 2017, https://www.businessinsider.com/greek-prime-minister-trump-evil-2017-10.

211   *Trump's "nasty list":* Aaron Blake, "'Nasty' is Trump's insult of choice for women, but he uses it plenty on men too," *Washington Post,* August 21, 2019, https://www.washingtonpost.com/politics/2019/08/21/nasty-is-trumps-insult-choice-women-he-uses-it-plenty-men-too/.

        perpetually aggrieved: For an in-depth firsthand explanation of this conundrum, see Mary L. Trump, *Too Much and Never Enough: How My Family Created the World's Most Dangerous Man* (New York: Simon & Schuster, 2020).

212   *welcome guest:* Matthew Weaver, "Timeline: Donald Trump's feud with Sadiq Khan," *Guardian,* June 15, 2019, https://www.theguardian.com/us-news/2019/jun/03/timeline-donald-trump-feud-with-sadiq-khan.

213   *the president's UK "nasty list":* Labour leader Jeremy Corbyn, Scottish first minister Nicola Sturgeon, the Queen's grandson Prince Harry's wife, Megan, and numerous others were also on Trump's "nasty list" in the UK. See Blake, "'Nasty' is Trump's insult of choice."

216   *prince's points:* "Trump says 'climate change goes both ways,'" BBC, June 5, 2019, https://www.bbc.com/news/world-us-canada-48531019.

217   *call him out: Trump Takes on the World,* "Episode 1," directed by Tim Stirzaker, aired February 10, 2021, on BBC Two, https://www.bbc.co.uk/programmes/m0o0s5zl.

11. THE PRICE OF POPULISM

218   *perverse machismo and personalization:* See Susan Hennessey and Benjamin Wittes, *Unmaking the Presidency: Donald Trump's War on the World's Most Powerful Office* (New York: Farrar, Straus and Giroux, 2020).

219   *increasingly appealed to:* Keeanga-Yamahtta Taylor, "The Bitter Fruits of Trump's White Power Presidency," *New Yorker,* January 12, 2021, https://www.newyorker.com/news/our-columnists/the-bitter-fruits-of-trumps-white-power-presidency.
       shoot someone: Colin Dwyer, "Donald Trump: 'I Could . . . Shoot Somebody, And I Wouldn't Lose Any Voters,'" NPR, January 23, 2016, https://www.npr.org/sections/thetwo-way/2016/01/23/464129029/donald-trump-i-could-shoot-somebody-and-i-wouldnt-lose-any-voters.
       "It's funny": Orion Rummler, "Trump says he gets along better with world leaders 'the tougher and meaner they are,'" *Axios,* September 14, 2020, https://www.axios.com/trump-woodward-foreign-leaders-934d6cfe-d93e-438c-9f1b-01bc258864ff.html.

220   *"I can tell you":* Franklin Foer, "Viktor Orbán's War on Intellect," *Atlantic,* June 2019, https://www.theatlantic.com/magazine/archive/2019/06/george-soros-viktor-orban-ceu/588070/.

221   *richest man in the world:* Hill and Gaddy, *Mr. Putin*; Karen Dawisha, *Putin's Kleptocracy: Who Owns Russia?* (New York: Simon & Schuster, 2015).
       seemed to look up to Putin: Ashley Parker and Rosalind S. Helderman, "In new book, former Trump lawyer Michael Cohen describes alleged episodes of racism and says president likes how Putin runs Russia," *Washington Post,* September 5, 2020, https://www.washingtonpost.com/politics/cohen-trump-book/2020/09/05/235aa10a-ef96-11ea-ab4e-581edb849379_story.html.

222   *frequently featured:* Hill and Gaddy, *Mr. Putin,* 177–178.
       Trump called Mary Barra: Kevin Liptak, "Trump says he was 'very tough' on GM's Barra over plant closures," CNN, November 27, 2018, https://www.cnn.com/2018/11/26/politics/trump-barra-gm-closures/index.html.
       "the people who": Dmitri Trenin, "Russia Redefines Itself and Its Relations with the West," *Washington Quarterly* 30, no. 2 (Spring 2007): 95–105.

223 *systematically attempted:* Josh Sawsey and Isaac Arnsdorf, "Trump doling out plum adviser jobs to rich friends," *Politico,* January 22, 2017, https://www.politico.com/story/2017/01/trump-jobs-rich-allies-233975.

made him "smart": Dan Mangan, "Trump brags about not paying taxes: 'That makes me smart,'" CNBC, September 16, 2016, https://www.cnbc.com/2016/09/26/trump-brags-about-not-paying-taxes-that-makes-me-smart.html.

224 *Putin's supporters:* Anne Garrels, *Putin Country: A Journey into the Real Russia* (New York: Farrar, Straus and Giroux, 2015); Nina Khrushcheva, *The Lost Khrushchev: A Journey into the Gulag of the Russian Mind* (Mustang, OK: Tate, 2014); Nina Khrushcheva and Jeffrey Tayler, *In Putin's Footsteps: Searching for the Soul of an Empire Across Russia's Eleven Time Zones* (New York: St. Martin's, 2019).

"stand back and stand by": Kathleen Ronayne and Michael Kunzelman, "Trump to far-right extremists: 'Stand back and stand by,'" Associated Press, September 30, 2020, https://apnews.com/article/election-2020-joe-biden-race-and-ethnicity-donald-trump-chris-wallace-0b32339da25fbc9e8b7c7c7066a1db0f.

exploitation of the media: Peter Pomerantsev, *Nothing Is True and Everything Is Possible: The Surreal Heart of the New Russia* (New York: PublicAffairs, 2015); Peter Pomerantsev, *This Is Not Propaganda: Adventures in the War Against Reality* (New York: PublicAffairs, 2015).

225 *one synthetic Russian culture:* Hill and Gaddy, *Mr. Putin,* 59–62.

226 *"Russian candidate":* Peter Strzok, *Compromised: Counterintelligence and the Threat of Donald J. Trump* (Boston: Houghton Mifflin Harcourt, 2020).

228 *"Turkey Day":* Western journalists and think tank colleagues relating official Turkish comments to author, November 2020.

229 *Russian intelligence agents: United States vs. Viktor Borisovich Netyksho, Boris Alekseyevich Antonov, Dmitriy Sergeyevich Badin, et al.,* 1:18-cr-00215-ABJ (D.D.C., 2018), https://www.justice.gov/opa/pr/grand-jury-indicts-thirteen-russian-individuals-and-three-russian-companies-scheme-interfere.

230 *best-selling book,* Red Notice: Bill Browder, *Red Notice: A True Story of High Finance, Murder, and One Man's Fight for Justice* (New York: Simon & Schuster, 2015).

a full list: Samantha Schmidt, "Outrage erupts over Trump-Putin 'conversation' about letting Russia interrogate ex-U.S. diplomat Michael McFaul," *Washington Post,* July 19, 2018, https://www.washingtonpost.com/news/morning-mix/wp/2018/07/19/trump-putin-conversation-about-russian-interrogation-of-u-s-diplomat-prompts-outrage-astonishment/; Entous, "What Fiona Hill Learned in the White House."

231 *taking the U.S. interpreter's notes:* Greg Miller, "Trump has concealed details of his face-to-face encounters with Putin from senior officials in administration," *Washington Post,* January 13, 2019, https://www.washingtonpost.com/world/

national-security/trump-has-concealed-details-of-his-face-to-face-encounters-with-putin-from-senior-officials-in-administration/2019/01/12/65f6686c-1434-11e9-b6ad-9cfd62dbb0a8_story.html.

232 *"never do it again?"*: Jennie Neufeld, "Read the full transcript of the Helsinki press conference," *Vox*, July 17, 2018, https://www.vox.com/2018/7/16/17576956/tran script-putin-trump-russia-helsinki-press-conference.

convoluted conspiracy theory: Allan Smith, "'Enough.'": Trump's ex-homeland security adviser 'disturbed,' 'frustrated' by Ukraine allegations, says president must let 2016 go," *NBC News*, September 29, 2019, https://www.nbcnews.com/politics/donald-trump/enough-trump-s-former-homeland-security-adviser-disturbed-ukraine-allegations-n1060051.

"Where is the server?": Neufeld, "Read the full transcript."

234 *"incontrovertible"*: David E. Sanger, "Trump's National Security Chief Calls Russian Interference 'Incontrovertible,'" *New York Times*, February 17, 2018, https://www.nytimes.com/2018/02/17/world/europe/russia-meddling-mcmaster.html.

"General McMaster forgot": "The Latest: Trump tweet undercuts McMaster Russia claims," Associated Press, February 18, 2018, https://apnews.com/article/north-america-donald-trump-ap-top-news-elections-indictments-966d5d2c b614e4c9da8e6200505c9f6.

the president's immediate circle: Entous, "What Fiona Hill Learned in the White House."

235 *building up nuclear arsenals*: Steven Pifer, "Nuclear Arms Control Choices for the Next Administration," Brookings report, October 2016, https://www.brookings.edu/research/nuclear-arms-control-choices-for-the-next-administration/.

236 *scrambling for a new approach*: Bolton, *The Room Where It Happened*.

12. OFF WITH THEIR HEADS

239 *compromising information*: Entous, "What Fiona Hill Learned in the White House."

240 *Fruman recorded*: Katherine Faulders et al., "'Take her out': Recording appears to capture Trump at private dinner saying he wants Ukraine ambassador fired," *ABC News*, January 24, 2020, https://abcnews.go.com/Politics/recording-appears-cap ture-trump-private-dinner-ukraine-ambassador/story?id=68506437.

241 *Trump railed against*: Eli Watkins, "Trump's top economic aide on Trudeau: 'It was a betrayal,'" CNN, June 10, 2018, https://www.cnn.com/2018/06/10/politics/larry-kudlow-donald-trump-justin-trudeau/index.html.

"go through some things": Sheryl Gay Stolberg, "Ex-Envoy to Ukraine 'Devastated' as Trump Vilified Her," *New York Times*, November 15, 2019, https://www.ny times.com/2019/11/15/us/politics/marie-yovanovitch-testimony.html.

family ties: Bryan Talbot, *Alice in Sunderland* (Milkwaukee: Dark Horse, 2007).

"ungovernable passion": Cited in A. S. Byatt, "Queen of hearts and minds," *Guardian,* December 14, 2002, https://www.theguardian.com/books/2002/dec/14/classics.asbyatt.

"one way of settling all difficulties": Lewis Carroll, *Alice in Wonderland* (London, 1865; Project Gutenberg, 2008), chap. 8, https://www.gutenberg.org/ebooks/11.

"the Russia hoax": Alex Marquardt, Zachary Cohen, and Jeremy Herb, "Grenell takes parting shot at Democrats as he exits top intelligence job," CNN, May 26, 2020, https://www.cnn.com/2020/05/26/politics/grenell-director-of-national-intelligence-final-days/index.html.

242   *highest cabinet turnover*: Tenpas, *Tracking Turnover in the Trump Administration.*

243   *internet conspiracy theories*: Dan Evon, "Is This a Photo of Vladimir Putin with Fiona Hill?," *Snopes,* https://www.snopes.com/fact-check/vladimir-putin-with-fiona-hill/.

245   *I featured on* Infowars: Timothy Johnson, "Alex Jones presses on with Roger Stone's smear campaign against Fiona Hill," *Media Matters,* November 25, 2019, https://www.mediamatters.org/alex-jones/alex-jones-presses-roger-stones-smear-campaign-against-fiona-hill.

246   *Mack had sold me out*: Entous, "What Fiona Hill Learned in the White House."

I later learned: Entous, "What Fiona Hill Learned in the White House."

247   *left-wing political activities*: Emily Tamkin, *The Influence of Soros: Politics, Power, and the Struggle for an Open Society* (New York: HarperCollins, 2020).

was apologetic: Entous, "What Fiona Hill Learned in the White House."

traded in disinformation: Thomas Rid, *Active Measures: The Secret History of Disinformation and Political Warfare* (New York: Farrar, Straus and Giroux, 2020).

248   *"Soros conspiracy"*: Hannes Grassegger, "The Unbelievable Story of the Plot Against George Soros," *BuzzFeed News,* January 20, 2019, https://www.buzzfeednews.com/article/hnsgrassegger/george-soros-conspiracy-finkelstein-birnbaum-orban-netanyahu.

anti-Semitic undertones: Steven J. Zipperstein, "The Conspiracy Theory to Rule Them All," *Atlantic,* August 25, 2020, https://www.theatlantic.com/politics/archive/2020/08/conspiracy-theory-rule-them-all/615550/.

249   *featured in* Mein Kampf: Richard Evans, *The Hitler Conspiracies: The Third Reich and the Paranoid Imagination* (London: Penguin, 2021); Timothy Snyder, "The American Abyss," *New York Times,* January 9, 2021, https://www.nytimes.com/2021/01/09/magazine/trump-coup.html.

early exponent of "birtherism": Adam Serwer, "Birtherism of a Nation," *Atlantic,* May 13, 2020, https://www.theatlatic.com/ideas/archive/2020/05/birtherism-and-trump/610978/.

QAnon: Adrienne LaFrance, "The Prophecies of Q," *Atlantic,* June 2020, https://www.theatlantic.com/magazine/archive/2020/06/qanon-nothing-can-stop-what-is-coming/610567/; Ilana Strauss, "The Dark Reality of Betting Against QAnon," *Atlantic,* January 1, 2021, https://www.theatlantic.com/politics/archive/2021/01/betting-against-qanon-predictit/617396/; Sabrina Tavernise, "'Trump Just Used Us and Our Fear': One Woman's Journey Out of QAnon," *New York Times,* January 30, 2021, https://www.nytimes.com/2021/01/29/us/leaving-qanon-conspiracy.html.

250 *openly embraced it:* E. J. Dickson, "A Timeline of Trump's QAnon Presidency," *Rolling Stone,* October 27, 2020, https://www.rollingstone.com/culture/culture-features/qanon-trump-timeline-conspiracy-theorists-1076279/.

251 *posted his picture:* Hannah Levintova and Dan Friedman, "The Head of Albania's Conservative Party Faces Criminal Charges, and an Ex-Trump Aide Is Involved," *Mother Jones,* June 13, 2019, https://www.motherjones.com/politics/2019/06/the-head-of-albanias-conservative-party-faces-criminal-charges-and-an-ex-trump-aide-is-involved/.

253 *I might be "Anonymous":* "I Am Part of the Resistance Inside the Trump Administration," *New York Times,* September 5, 2018, https://www.nytimes.com/2018/09/05/opinion/trump-white-house-anonymous-resistance.html; Anonymous, *A Warning* (New York: Twelve, 2019); Margaret Hartman, "All the Theories on Who Wrote the Anonymous Anti-Trump Op-Ed," *New York Magazine,* September 6, 2018, https://nymag.com/intelligencer/2018/09/theories-who-wrote-trump-op-ed.html.

device to expel officials: Meredith McGraw, "White House transfers top national security aide after whisper campaign," *Politico,* February 20, 2020, https://www.politico.com/news/2020/02/20/top-national-security-aide-anonymous-book-116325.

257 *trusted the federal government:* "Little Public Support for Reductions in Federal Spending," Pew Research Center, April 11, 2019, https://www.pewresearch.org/politics/2019/04/11/little-public-support-for-reductions-in-federal-spending/.

258 *Steve Bannon:* Philip Rucker and Robert Costa, "Bannon vows a daily fight for 'deconstruction of the administrative state,'" *Washington Post,* February 23, 2017, https://www.washingtonpost.com/politics/top-wh-strategist-vows-a-daily-fight-for-deconstruction-of-the-administrative-state/2017/02/23/03f6b8da-f9ea-11e6-bf01-d47f8cf9b643_story.html.

260 *full transcript:* U.S. Congress, House of Representatives, Permanent Select Committee on Intelligence, joint with the Committee on Oversight and Reform and the Committee on Foreign Affairs, Deposition of Fiona Hill, 116th Cong., 1st sess., 2019, https://docs.house.gov/meetings/IG/IG00/CPRT-116-IG00-D010.pdf.

262 *"blood coming out of her wherever":* Holly Yan, "Donald Trump's 'blood' com-

ment about Megyn Kelly draws outrage," CNN, August 8, 2015, https://www.cnn.com/2015/08/08/politics/donald-trump-cnn-megyn-kelly-comment/index.html.
Women's anger is not: Soraya Chemaly, *Rage Becomes Her: The Power of Women's Anger* (New York: Simon & Schuster, 2019); Rebecca Traister, *Good and Mad: The Revolutionary Power of Women's Anger* (New York: Simon & Schuster, 2019).
female icon status: Ellie Hall, "Fiona Hill Gave a Relatable Answer About Women's Anger During Her Impeachment Testimony to Congress," *BuzzFeed News,* November 21, 2019, https://www.buzzfeednews.com/article/elliehall/fiona-hill-women-anger-impeachment-answer.

13. THE HORRIBLE YEAR

264   *annus horribilis of 2020: Global Trends 2040: A More Contested World* (McLean, VA: U.S. National Intelligence Council, 2021), https://www.dni.gov/files/ODNI/documents/assessments/GlobalTrends_2040.pdf.

267   *ad hoc manner:* Julian Borger, "'Trump thought I was a secretary': Fiona Hill on the president, Putin and populism," *Guardian,* June 12, 2020, https://www.theguardian.com/us-news/2020/jun/12/fiona-hill-trump-putin-populism-interview.
four hundred thousand Americans: "COVID-19 United States Cases by County," Johns Hopkins University and Medicine Coronavirus Resource Center, accessed April 29, 2021, https://coronavirus.jhu.edu/us-map.
close to two hundred thousand: "Coronavirus in the U.S.: Latest Map and Case Count," *New York Times,* updated April 29, 2021, https://www.nytimes.com/interactive/2021/us/covid-cases.html.
Urgent action: Joe Davidson, "GAO report slams Trump administration response to the coronavirus pandemic," *Washington Post,* February 3, 2021, https://www.washingtonpost.com/politics/gao-trump-covid-biden/2021/02/02/38f0a0a8-65a4-11eb-bf81-c618c88ed605_story.html.

268   *long-standing failure:* Ken Alltucker, "Roughly 40% of the USA's coronavirus deaths could have been prevented, a new study says," *USA Today,* February 11, 2021, https://www.usatoday.com/story/news/health/2021/02/11/lancet-commission-donald-trump-covid-19-health-medicare-for-all/4453762001/.
Dr. Anthony Fauci: Donald G. McNeil, Jr., "Fauci on What Working for Trump Was Really Like," *New York Times,* January 24, 2021, https://www.nytimes.com/2021/01/24/health/fauci-trump-covid.html.

269   *dose themselves prophylactically:* Jeffrey Kluger, "Accidental Poisonings Increased After President Trump's Disinfectant Comments," *Time,* May 12, 2020, https://time.com/5835244/accidental-poisonings-trump/.
The Fifth Risk: Michael Lewis, *The Fifth Risk* (New York: W. W. Norton, 2018).

270   *size of the crowd:* Megan Garber, "The First Lie of the Trump Presidency," *Atlan-*

tic, January 13, 2019, https://www.theatlantic.com/politics/archive/2019/01/the-absurdity-of-donald-trumps-lies/579622/.

a slow-motion coup attempt: Fiona Hill, "Yes, It Was a Coup Attempt. Here's Why," *Politico,* January 11, 2021, https://www.politico.com/news/magazine/2021/01/11/capitol-riot-self-coup-trump-fiona-hill-457549.

271   *"4eva":* Aila Slisco, "After Senate Votes to Acquit, Trump Shares Bizarre Video Suggesting He Will Be President '4eva,'" *Newsweek,* February 5, 2020, https://www.newsweek.com/after-senate-votes-acquit-trump-shares-bizarre-video-suggesting-he-will-president-4eva-1485984.

President Niinistö praised: Maegan Vazquez, "Finnish President encourages Trump to keep democracy 'going on,'" CNN, October 2, 2019, https://www.cnn.com/2019/10/02/politics/sauli-niinisto-finland-president-counters-donald-trump/index.html.

272   *take votes:* Jim Rutenberg et al., "77 Days: Trump's Campaign to Subvert the Election," *New York Times,* January 31, 2021, https://www.nytimes.com/2021/01/31/us/trump-election-lie.html.

273   *Praetorian Guard:* Jonathan Stevenson, "Trump's Praetorian Guard," *New York Review of Books,* October 22, 2020, https://www.nybooks.com/articles/2020/10/22/trump-law-order-praetorian-guard/.

her voluminous handbag: Peter Baker et al., "How Trump's Idea for a Photo Op Led to Havoc in a Park," *New York Times,* June 2, 2020, https://www.nytimes.com/2020/06/02/us/politics/trump-walk-lafayette-square.html.

cleared a crowd: Philip Bump, "The lingering questions about the clearing of Lafayette Square," *Washington Post,* June 10, 2021, https://www.washingtonpost.com/politics/2021/06/10/lingering-questions-about-clearing-lafayette-square/.

274   *declare martial law:* Amber Phillips, "Could Trump declare martial law to try to steal the election?," *Washington Post,* December 24, 2020, https://www.washingtonpost.com/politics/2020/12/24/could-trump-declare-martial-law-try-steal-election/.

unprecedented public letter: Ashton Carter et al., "Opinion: All 10 living former defense secretaries: Involving the military in election disputes would cross into dangerous territory," *Washington Post,* January 3, 2020, https://www.washingtonpost.com/opinions/10-former-defense-secretaries-military-peaceful-transfer-of-power/2021/01/03/2a23d52e-4c4d-11eb-a9f4-0e668b9772ba_story.html.

federal court vacancies: John Gramlich, "How Trump compares with other recent presidents in appointing federal judges," Pew Research Center, January 13, 2021, https://www.pewresearch.org/fact-tank/2021/01/13/how-trump-compares-with-other-recent-presidents-in-appointing-federal-judges/.

"his judges": Paul Blumenthal, "Trump Calls Them 'My Judges.' Will They Side with Him in Separation of Powers Fight?," *HuffPost,* October 24, 2019, https://www.huffpost.com/entry/trump-judges-lawsuits_n_5db1d70ee4b03285e87ba2fd.

275   *two thousand local newspapers:* Margaret Sullivan, "These local newspapers say Facebook and Google are killing them. Now they're fighting back," *Washington Post,* February 5, 2021, https://www.washingtonpost.com/lifestyle/media/west-virginia-google-facebook-newspaper-lawsuit/2021/02/03/797631dc-657d-11eb-8468-21bc48f07fe5_story.html.

including his lies: "NYT's Ben Smith on the Future of the Media After Trump," PBS, November 10, 2020, https://www.pbs.org/wnet/amanpour-and-company/video/nyts-ben-smith-on-the-future-of-the-media-after-trump/.

Trump put a loyalist: Josh Dawsey, Lisa Rein, and Jacob Bogage, "Top Republican fundraiser and Trump ally named postmaster general, giving president new influence over Postal Service," *Washington Post,* May 6, 2020, https://www.washingtonpost.com/politics/top-republican-fundraiser-and-trump-ally-to-be-named-postmaster-general-giving-president-new-influence-over-postal-service-officials-say/2020/05/06/25cde93c-8fd4-11ea-8df0-ee33c3f5b0d6_story.html.

his *"enemies list":* Brett Samuels, "Trump ramps up rhetoric on media, calls press 'the enemy of the people,'" *Hill,* April 5, 2019, https://thehill.com/homenews/administration/437610-trump-calls-press-the-enemy-of-the-people.

276   *belatedly acknowledged:* Kate Conger, Mike Isaac, and Sheera Frenkel, "Twitter and Facebook Lock Trump's Accounts After Violence on Capitol Hill," *New York Times,* January 6, 2021, https://www.nytimes.com/2021/01/06/technology/capitol-twitter-facebook-trump.html.

147 Republican representatives: Karen Yourish, Larry Buchanan, and Denise Lu, "The 147 Republicans Who Voted to Overturn Election Results," *New York Times,* last updated January 7, 2021, https://www.nytimes.com/interactive/2021/01/07/us/elections/electoral-college-biden-objectors.html.

cowing them into submission: Jack Brewster, "They Will Get Primaried: Trump, his Allies, Threaten Republicans Who Won't Object to Electoral College," *Forbes,* January 6, 2021, https://www.forbes.com/sites/jackbrewster/2021/01/06/they-will-get-primaried-trump-allies-threaten-republicans-who-wont-object-to-electoral-college/?sh=60dcd00d1855.

"Donald Trump's Republican Party": Quint Forgey, "'I'm going to be in your backyard': Trump sons threaten primaries for GOP lawmakers," *Politico,* January 6, 2021, https://www.politico.com/news/2021/01/06/trump-threat-primaries-gop-lawmakers-455366.

278   *put against the wall:* Hill and Gaddy, *Mr. Putin,* 25–26.

279   *bayed for his blood:* Melissa Macaya et al., "Trump's second impeachment trial: Day 2," CNN, February 10, 2021, https://www.cnn.com/politics/live-news/trump-impeachment-trial-02-10-2021/h_d2f3d6b3e463825e7f13c4a06b2f6451.

executive power and privilege: Ann E. Marimow, "A president 'is not above the law," Trump lawyer asserts in batting back criticism of his impeachment defense," *Washington Post*, January 30, 2020, https://www.washingtonpost.com/local/le gal-issues/a-president-is-not-above-the-law-trump-lawyer-asserts-in-batting-back-criticism-of-his-impeachment-defense/2020/01/30/7b9b06ce-438f-11ea-b5 fc-eefa848cde99_story.html.

refused to help: Donald Ayer, "Why Bill Barr Is So Dangerous," *Atlantic,* June 30, 2019, https://www.theatlantic.com/ideas/archive/2019/06/bill-barrs-dangerous-pursuit-executive-power/592951/; Michael Balsamo, "Disputing Trump, Barr says no widespread election fraud," Associated Press, December 1, 2020, https:// apnews.com/article/barr-no-widespread-election-fraud-b1f1488796c9a98 c4b1a9061a6c7f49d.

refused to attend: Jacey Fortin, "Trump Is Not the First President to Snub an Inauguration," *New York Times,* January 19, 2021, https://www.ny times.com/2021/01/19/us/politics/presidents-who-skipped-inaugurations .html.

280 *Prestwick Airport:* Peter Swindon, "Donald Trump could be planning Turnberry trip as Scots airport told to expect a high-flyer the day before Joe Biden's inau-guration," *Sunday Post,* January 3, 2021, https://www.sundaypost.com/fp/don ald-trump-could-be-planning-turnberry-trip-as-scots-airport-told-to-expect-a-high-flyer-the-day-before-joe-bidens-inauguration/.

14. THE GREAT RECKONING

285 *his inaugural speech:* Joseph R. Biden, Jr., "Inaugural Address," Washington, D.C., January 20, 2021, https://www.whitehouse.gov/briefing-room/speeches-remarks/2021/01/20/inaugural-address-by-president-joseph-r-biden-jr/.

288 *"the rules-based global order":* Michael E. O'Hanlon, *The Art of War in an Age of Peace: U.S. Grand Strategy and Resolute Restraint* (New Haven: Yale University Press, 2021), 180–181.

turnout was also historic: Jacob Fabina, "Despite Pandemic Challenges, 2020 Elec-tion Had Largest Increase in Voting Between Presidential Elections on Record," United States Census Bureau, April 29, 2021, https://www.census.gov/library/ stories/2021/04/record-high-turnout-in-2020-general-election.html.

highest vote tallies: Domenico Montanaro, "President-Elect Joe Biden Hits 80 Million Votes in Year of Record Turnout," NPR, November 25, 2020, https://www. npr.org/2020/11/25/937248659/president-elect-biden-hits-80-million-votes-in-year-of-record-turnout.

the most secure on record: "Joint Statement from Elections Infrastructure Gov-ernment Coordinating Council & the Election Infrastructure Sector Coordinat-ing Executive Committees," *U.S. Department of Homeland Security Cybersecu-rity & Infrastructure Security Agency,* November 12, 2020, https://www.cisa.gov/ news/2020/11/12/joint-statement-elections-infrastructure-government-coordi nating-council-election; *United States of America — General Elections, 3 November 2020: Statement of Preliminary Findings and Conclusions* (Washington: Organization for Security and Co-operation in Europe, 2020), https://www.osce.org/files/f/documents/9/6/469437.pdf.

289 *no suspicion: Foreign Threats to the 2020 US Federal Elections* (McLean, VA: U.S. National Intelligence Council, 2021), https://www.dni.gov/files/ODNI/documents/assessments/ICA-declass-16MAR21.pdf.

ransomware attacks: Ellen Nakashima and Jay Greene, "Hospitals being hit in coordinated, targeted ransomware attack from Russian-speaking criminals," *Washington Post,* October 29, 2020, https://www.washingtonpost.com/national-security/hospitals-being-hit-in-coordinated-targeted-ransomware-attack-from-russian-speaking-criminals/2020/10/28/e6e48c38-196e-11eb-befb-8864259bd2d8_story.html.

penetrate U.S. governmental systems: David E. Sanger, "Russian Hackers Broke into Federal Agencies, U.S. Officials Suspect," *New York Times,* December 13, 2020, https://www.nytimes.com/2020/12/13/us/politics/russian-hackers-us-government-treasury-commerce.html.

deigned to issue: Vladimir Putin, "Поздравление Джозефу Байдену с победой на выборах Президента США" [Congratulations to Joseph Biden on the victory of the U.S. presidential election], press release, Moscow, December 15, 2020, http://kremlin.ru/events/president/news/64660.

Exit polls: "Exit poll results and analysis for the 2020 presidential election," *Washington Post,* updated December 14, 2021, https://www.washingtonpost.com/elections/interactive/2020/exit-polls/presidential-election-exit-polls/.

290 *Joe Biden had won:* Mark Muro et al., "Biden-voting counties equal 70% of America's economy. What does this mean for the nation's political-economic divide?," *The Avenue* (blog), Brookings Institution, November 10, 2020, https://www.brookings.edu/blog/the-avenue/2020/11/09/biden-voting-counties-equal-70-of-americas-economy-what-does-this-mean-for-the-nations-political-economic-divide/.

$15-an-hour minimum wage: Greg Allen, "Floridians Vote to Increase State's Minimum Wage to $15 Per Hour," NPR, November 11, 2020, https://www.npr.org/2020/11/11/933937204/floridians-vote-to-increase-states-minimum-wage-to-15-per-hour.

turnout among Black Americans: Rashawn Ray, "How Black Americans saved Biden and American democracy," *How We Rise* (blog), Brookings Institution, November 24, 2020, https://www.brookings.edu/blog/how-we-rise/2020/11/24/how-black-americans-saved-biden-and-american-democracy/.

fault lines: William A. Galston, "The Bitter Heartland," *American Purpose,* March 31, 2021, https://www.americanpurpose.com/articles/the-bitter-heartland/.

Quinnipiac University poll: "74% of Voters Say Democracy in the U.S. Is Under Threat, Quinnipiac University National Poll Finds; 52% Say President Trump

Should Be Removed from Office," Quinnipiac University Poll, January 11, 2021, https://poll.qu.edu/poll-release?releaseid=3733.

291 *"American carnage"*: Donald J. Trump, "The Inaugural Address," Washington, D.C., January 20, 2017, https://trumpwhitehouse.archives.gov/briefings-statements/the-inaugural-address/.

292 *white Christians' fears*: Robert P. Jones, Daniel Cox, E. J. Dionne, Jr., et al., *How Immigration and Concerns About Cultural Changes Are Shaping the 2016 Election* (Washington: Brookings Institution and Public Religion Research Institute, 2016), https://www.prri.org/wp-content/uploads/2016/06/PRRI-Brookings-2016-Immigration-survey-report.pdf.

idea of American democracy and unity: For an in-depth discussion of the development of these and the impact of Trump's political approach, see David French, *Divided We Fall: America's Secession Threat and How to Restore Our Nation* (New York: St. Martin's, 2020); Jonathan Haidt, *The Righteous Mind: Why Good People Are Divided by Politics and Religion* (New York: Vintage, 2013); Yuval Levin, *A Time to Build* (New York: Basic, 2020); Yuval Levin, *The Fractured Republic: Renewing America's Social Contract in the Age of Individualism* (New York: Basic, 2016); John Sides, Michael Tesler, and Lynn Vavreck, *Identity Crisis: The 2016 Presidential Campaign and the Battle for the Meaning of America* (Princeton: Princeton University Press, 2018); and Darrell West, *Divided Politics, Divided Nation: Hyperconflict in the Trump Era* (Washington: Brookings Institution, 2019).

predominantly white and male: Robert Pape, "Opinion: What an analysis of 377 Americans arrested or charged in the Capitol insurrection tells us," *Washington Post*, April 6, 2021, https://www.washingtonpost.com/opinions/2021/04/06/capitol-insurrection-arrests-cpost-analysis/; Alan Feuer, "Fears of White People Losing Out Permeate Capitol Rioters' Towns, Study Finds," *New York Times*, April 6, 2021, https://www.nytimes.com/2021/04/06/us/politics/capitol-riot-study.html.

had lost assets: Todd C. Frankel, "A majority of the people arrested for Capitol riot had a history of financial trouble," *Washington Post*, February 10, 2021, https://www.washingtonpost.com/business/2021/02/10/capitol-insurrectionists-jenna-ryan-financial-problems/.

296 *bore the brunt*: Alan Reube and Nicole Bateman, *Who are the workers already impacted by the COVID-19 recession?* (Washington: Brookings Institution, 2020), https://www.brookings.edu/research/who-are-the-workers-already-impacted-by-the-covid-19-recession/.

died in higher numbers: Elise Gould and Valerie Wilson, *Black workers face two of the most lethal preexisting conditions for coronavirus — racism and economic inequality* (Washington: Economic Policy Institute, 2020), https://www.epi.org/publication/black-workers-covid/.

out of work: Bureau of Labor Statistics, "The Employment Situation — January

2021," news release no. USDL-21-0158, February 5, 2021, https://www.bls.gov/news.release/archives/empsit_02052021.pdf.

consumer spending by America's affluent: Emily Badger and Alicia Parlapiano, "The Rich Cut Their Spending. That Has Hurt All the Workers Who Count on It," *New York Times,* June 17, 2020, https://www.nytimes.com/2020/06/17/upshot/coronavirus-spending-rich-poor.html.

U.S. meatpacking plants: Abigail Abrams, "House Democrats Launch Investigation of OSHA, Meat Plants over COVID-19 Outbreaks," *Time,* February 1, 2021, https://time.com/5935089/democrats-investigation-meatpacking-coronavirus/.

without benefits: Marcela Escobari, Ian Seyal, and Michael J. Meaney, *Realism about reskilling* (Washington: Brookings Institution, 2019), https://www.brookings.edu/research/realism-about-reskilling/.

eighty-three million adults: Arloc Sherman et al., *New Data on Hardship Underscore Continued Need for Substantial COVID Relief* (Washington: Center on Budget and Policy Priorities, 2020), https://www.cbpp.org/research/poverty-and-inequality/new-data-on-hardship-underscore-continued-need-for-substantial.

299   *aren't expected to do well:* Megan Specia, "Parents, Students and Teachers Give Britain a Failing Grade over Exam Results," *New York Times,* August 14, 2020, https://www.nytimes.com/2020/08/14/world/europe/england-a-level-results.html.

300   *top of a birch tree:* Alexey Malgavko, "Siberian student scales birch tree for internet access as classes move online," Reuters, November 16, 2020, https://www.reuters.com/article/us-health-coronavirus-russia-blogger-idINKBN27W1Y1.

failure rates: Valerie Strauss, "More students than ever got F's in first term of 2020–21 school year — but are A-F grades fair in a pandemic?," *Washington Post,* December 6, 2020, https://www.washingtonpost.com/education/2020/12/06/more-students-than-ever-got-fs-first-term-2020-21-school-year-are-a-f-grades-fair-pandemic/.

301   *as much a personal crisis as a jobs crisis:* Helaine Olen, "The pandemic is devastating a generation of working women," *Washington Post,* February 5, 2021, https://www.washingtonpost.com/opinions/2021/02/05/pandemic-is-devastating-generation-working-women/.

$4.56 trillion: Chuck Collins, "Updates: Billionaire Wealth, U.S. Job Losses and Pandemic Profiteers," Inequality, updated April 15, 2021, https://inequality.org/great-divide/updates-billionaire-pandemic/.

304   *federal reserve banks:* For a defense of an empowered U.S. Federal Reserve, see Robert Hockett and Aaron James, *Money from Nothing: Or, Why We Should Stop Worrying About Debt and Learn to Love the Federal Reserve* (Brooklyn: Melville House, 2020).

"American National Investment Bank": Anthony F. Pipa and Natalie Geismar,

Reimagining rural policy: Organizing federal assistance to maximize rural prosperity (Washington: Brookings Institution, 2020), https://www.brookings.edu/research/reimagining-rural-policy-organizing-federal-assistance-to-maximize-rural-prosperity/.

national wealth fund: Eric Lonergan and Mark Blyth, *Angrynomics* (Newcastle upon Tyne: Agenda, 2020).

15. NO MORE FORGOTTEN PEOPLE

307   *deliberately promoted:* Wilkerson, *Caste.*

White mobs: Olusoga, *Black and British,* 454–466.

308   *address accessibility and affordability:* In early September 2020, two St. Andrews final-year students approached me to throw my hat into the ring for the October 2020 election of a new St. Andrews rector: a high-profile but unpaid position working directly with a student committee to advocate for a set of issues and push the university on reforms. The other two candidates were Leyla Hussein, a well-known Somali British psychotherapist and social activist from London, and Ken Cochran, a St. Andrews–based alumnus. As the campaigns were student generated and led, the platforms overlapped. In the end, the 2020 campaign was won by Leyla Hussein. It was a historic first. Leyla Hussein was only the third woman rector and the first Black rector. She was also the first Black senior figure to be appointed in any position in the more than six-hundred-year history of St. Andrews University.

As a result: David Olusoga, "I was born black and working class. The identities need not be in opposition," *Guardian,* April 13, 2019, https://www.theguardian.com/commentisfree/2019/apr/13/i-was-born-black-and-working-class-the-identities-need-not-be-in-opposition.

Olusoga tweeted: David Olusoga (@DavidOlusoga), "I am biased, because I was brought up not far from where she comes from, and because we are from a similar class backgrounds, but Fiona Hill is absolutely remarkable," Twitter, June 12, 2020, 1:50 p.m., https://twitter.com/DavidOlusoga/status/1271500112821395456.

growing up mixed-race: Dave Simpson, "Fine Young Cannibal Roland Gift: 'I went back to where being pretty didn't matter,'" *Guardian,* December 3, 2020, https://www.theguardian.com/music/2020/dec/03/fine-young-cannibal-roland-gift-i-went-back-to-where-being-pretty-didnt-matter.

310   *moved millions of people:* Lamia Kamal-Chaoui, Edward Leman, and Zhang Rufei, *Urban Trends and Policy in China* (Paris: Organisation for Economic Co-operation and Development, 2009), https://www.oecd.org/china/42607972.pdf.

programs to alleviate poverty: Kamal-Chaoui, Leman, and Rufei, *Urban Trends and Policy,* 8.

311   *new labor force: China in the 2010s: Rebalancing Growth and Strengthening Social*

Safety Nets (Paris: Organisation for Economic Co-operation and Development, 2010), 8–9, https://www.oecd.org/china/44878634.pdf.

312   Dream Hoarders: Richard Reeves, *Dream Hoarders: How the American Middle Class Is Leaving Everyone Else in the Dust, Why That Is a Problem, and What to Do About It* (Washington: Brookings Institution, 2017).

313   *promoting social mobility:* Andre M. Perry, Carl Romer, and Anthony Barr, "In Philadelphia, efforts to increase educational attainment must consider the racial earnings gap," *The Avenue* (blog), Brookings Institution, April 27, 2021, https://www.brookings.edu/blog/the-avenue/2021/04/27/in-philadelphia-efforts-to-increase-educational-attainment-must-consider-the-racial-earnings-gap/.

315   *overcrowded U.S. public schools:* Anthony Abraham Jack, *The Privileged Poor: How Elite Colleges Are Failing Disadvantaged Students* (Cambridge: Harvard University Press, 2019).

316   *being contact-poor:* James H. Fowler and Nicholas A. Christakis, *Connected: How Your Friends' Friends' Friends Affect Everything You Feel, Think, and Do* (New York: Little, Brown, 2011).

        data analysis of social networks: Camille M. Busette, *How We Rise: How social networks in Charlotte impact economic mobility* (Washington: Brookings Institution, 2020), https://www.brookings.edu/essay/how-we-rise-how-social-networks-in-charlotte-impact-economic-mobility/.

317   *County Durham's average annual salary:* https://www.durhaminsight.info/economy-and-employment/. The UK mean in 2002 was £37,000, roughly equivalent to $51,000, while the U.S. average salary for 2020 was $56,310. See "Average household income, UK: financial year ending 2020 (provisional)," Office of National Statistics, July 22, 2020, https://www.ons.gov.uk/peoplepopulationandcommunity/personalandhouseholdfinances/incomeandwealth/bulletins/householddisposableincomeandinequality/financialyearending2020provisional; "May 2020 National Occupational Employment and Wage Estimates: United States," U.S. Bureau of Labor Statistics, accessed April 29, 2021, https://www.bls.gov/oes/current/oes_nat.htm.

320 · *highest recorded state school intake:* Rachel Hall, "Drive for more student diversity paying off, says Oxford University," *Guardian,* May 10, 2021, https://www.theguardian.com/education/2021/may/11/drive-for-more-student-diversity-paying-off-says-oxford-university.

        68 percent in 2019: Sean Coughlan, "State school numbers rise at Cambridge," BBC, September 9, 2019, https://www.bbc.com/news/education-49614294.

        still out of their league: Claire Hann Danny Dorling, "The Oxbridge Access Question Has Not Been Settled," *Times Higher Education,* October 17, 2019, https://www.timeshighereducation.com/opinion/oxbridge-access-question-has-not-been-settled; "Record state school admissions at Oxford as landmark access programme begins," *Oxford University,* September 17, 2020, https://www.ox.ac.

uk/news/2020-09-17-record-state-school-admissions-oxford-landmark-access
-programme-begins.

321 *"We think it's unfair"*: Donna Ferguson, "'You need someone on the inside': the
state school students helping peers into Oxbridge," *Guardian*, November 23, 2020,
https://www.theguardian.com/education/2020/nov/23/you-need-someone-on
-the-inside-the-state-school-students-helping-peers-into-oxbridge.

not in "high-skilled employment": *Skills for Jobs: Lifelong Learning for Opportunity and Growth* (London: Department for Education, 2021), 6, https://assets
.publishing.service.gov.uk/government/uploads/system/uploads/attachment
_data/file/957856/Skills_for_jobs_lifelong_learning_for_opportunity_and
_growth__web_version_.pdf.

went on to university: "Immediate transition to college," National Center for
Education Statistics, accessed May 6, 2021, https://nces.ed.gov/fastfacts/display
.asp?id=51.

initial enrollment rates: "Participation measures in higher education," Gov.uk,
November 26, 2020, https://explore-education-statistics.service.gov.uk/find-stat
istics/participation-measures-in-higher-education/2018-19.

322 *UK unemployment peaked*: Labour Market Statistics, April 2014 (London: Office for National Statistics, 2014), 4, https://webarchive.nationalarchives.gov.uk/
20160105211838/http://www.ons.gov.uk/ons/rel/lms/labour-market-statistics/
april-2014/statistical-bulletin.html.

325 *creating and replicating programs*: Rebecca Winthrop with Adam Barton and Ei-
leen McGivney, *Leapfrogging Inequality: Remaking Education to Help Young People Thrive* (Washington: Brookings Institution, 2018).

16. NO MORE FORGOTTEN PLACES

331 *migration and mobility*: William H. Frey, "Just before COVID-19, American migration hit a 73-year low," *The Avenue* (blog), Brookings Institution, December 15,
2020, https://www.brookings.edu/blog/the-avenue/2020/12/15/just-before-covid
-19-american-migration-hit-a-73-year-low/.

333 *thirty million Americans . . . were uninsured*: "Census: Nearly 30 million U.S. residents uninsured when surveyed in 2019," *American Hospital Survey*, September 17, 2020, https://www.aha.org/news/headline/2020-09-17-census-nearly-30
-million-us-residents-uninsured-when-surveyed-2019.

335 *America's health-care sector*: Ryan Nunn, Jana Parsons, and Jay Shambaugh, *A
dozen facts about the economics of the US health-care system* (Washington: Brookings Institution, 2020), https://www.brookings.edu/research/a-dozen-facts-about
-the-economics-of-the-u-s-health-care-system/.

"left-behind-workers": Gabriel Winant, "Manufacturing Isn't Coming Back. Let's
Improve These Jobs Instead," *New York Times*, March 17, 2021, https://www.nytimes.

com/2021/03/17/opinion/health-care-jobs.html. See also Winant's *The Next Shift: The Fall of Industry and the Rise of Health Care in Rust Belt America* (Cambridge: Harvard University Press, 2021).

336   *Stuart recommended:* Stuart M. Butler, *Achieving an equitable national health system for America* (Washington: Brookings Institution, 2020), https://www. brookings.edu/research/achieving-an-equitable-national-health-system-for-america/.

337   *national development program:* Jeff Stein, "Mitt Romney unveils plan to provide at least $3,000 per child, giving bipartisan support to President Biden's effort," *Washington Post,* February 4, 2021, https://www.washingtonpost.com/us-policy/2021/02/04/romney-child-benefit-stimulus/.
      "transformative placemaking": Jennifer S. Vey and Hanna Love, *Transformative placemaking: A framework to create connected, vibrant, and inclusive communities* (Washington: Brookings Institution, 2019), https://www.brookings.edu/research/transformative-placemaking-a-framework-to-create-connected-vibrant-and-inclusive-communities/.

338   *"Marshall Plan for Middle America":* William Peduto et al., "Opinion: Eight mayors: We need a Marshall Plan for Middle America," *Washington Post,* November 22, 2020, https://www.washingtonpost.com/opinions/2020/11/22/marshall-plan-middle-america-eight-mayors/.

339   *"domestic development corporation":* Pipa and Geismar, *Reimagining rural policy.*
      forty-six million people: Kim Parker et al., *What Unites and Divides Urban, Suburban, and Rural Communities* (Washington: Pew Research Center, 2018), 18, https://www.pewresearch.org/social-trends/2018/05/22/what-unites-and-divides-urban-suburban-and-rural-communities/.

341   *largest donations:* Nicholas Kulish, "Giving Billions Fast, MacKenzie Scott Upends Philanthropy," *New York Times,* December 20, 2020, https://www.nytimes.com/2020/12/20/business/mackenzie-scott-philanthropy.html.
      dropped packets of money: Iliana Magra, "Cash Appeared on Their Streets for Years. Now, Villagers Know Why," *New York Times,* January 14, 2020, https://www.nytimes.com/2020/01/14/world/europe/money-blackhall-colliery.html.

342   *national service-year program:* Richard V. Reeves and Isabel V. Sawhill, *A New Contract with the Middle Class* (Washington: Brookings Institution, 2020), https://www.brookings.edu/wp-content/uploads/2020/10/FMCi-Middle-Class-Contract-DIGITAL-VERSION.pdf.
      funding for national service: Inspired to Serve (Washington: National Commission on Military, National, and Public Service, 2020), https://inspire2serve.gov/reports/final-report.
      and produces reports: Tesia Mamassian, in discussion with the author, November 23, 2020.

343   *twenty-six thousand jobs:* Patricia Cohen, "What the Rebirth of This Old Steel Center Means for Trump," *New York Times,* January 9, 2020, https://www.nytimes.com/2020/01/09/business/economy/trump-pennsylvania-economy.html.

346   *90 percent of UK local taxes:* "Tax and devolution," Institute for Government, accessed April 29, 2021, https://www.instituteforgovernment.org.uk/explainers/tax-and-devolution.

349   *volunteers in* Kynren: Andrew Corry, "Kynren Blog — My Experience," https://corryandrew.wordpress.com/about/.

 bind Ebac to the area: Ebac Ltd., "Secret Millionaire gives away his fortune — company now owned by a foundation to promote manufacturing investment," news release, April 20, 2012, https://www.recognitionpr.co.uk/clients/ebac-ltd/secret-millionaire-gives-away-his-fortune-company-now-owned-by-a-foundation-to-promote-manufacturing-investment/.

350   *"As an employer":* Chris Lloyd, "Ebac millionaire John Elliott puts business in trust to benefit community," *Northern Echo,* April 20, 2012, https://www.thenorthernecho.co.uk/news/9660327.ebac-millionaire-john-elliott-puts-business-trust-benefit-community/.

 turn workers into stakeholders: Yuki Noguchi, "Why Chobani Gave Employees a Financial Stake in Company's Future," NPR, April 28, 2016, https://www.npr.org/sections/thesalt/2016/04/28/476021520/why-chobani-gave-employees-a-financial-stake-in-companys-future.

INDEX

Abe, Shinzō, 210

Affordable Care Act, 181, 268

Alinikoff, Emily, 112–13

Allison, Graham
   Hill and, 116, 117–18, 128–29, 136, 142, 193
   notetaker during/book on Cuban Missile
      Crisis, 129–30
   Russian-Japanese academics project,
      128–29

Alston, Philip, 158–60

American Association for the Advancement
   of Science, 138

"American carnage," 291

Amherst College initiatives for disadvantaged students, 314–15

Anderson, Fiona, 67

Anne, Princess, 40

"Anonymous," 253

Antifa leftists, 242

Appalachian region mayors' article, 338, 339

Apprentice, The, 187, 189, 198

Archbishop of Canterbury and Queen Elizabeth II, 54

Aspen Ideas Festival (2014), 101–2, 107

al-Assad, Bashar, 200, 227

Atlantic, 220

baby boomer generation, 155, 197

bakery workers' strike (1970s UK), 39

Balls, Ed, 100, 101, 102, 103

BAME (Black, Asian and Minority Ethnic),
   308, 309

banks/bank accounts and Hills, 114

Bannon, Steve, 258

Barnes, Christopher, 87

Barra, Mary, 222

Barr, William, 279

Bartle, Angela, 73

BBC News presenters and accent, 100

Beamish, Living Museum of the North,
   346–47

Beatles, 85

Belfer Center for Science and International
   Affairs, 125

Bergen, Charlie, 200

Berlin Wall fall, 97, 115

Bertolaet, Bonnie
   background/Hills and, 313, 315
   Science Club for Girls of Greater Boston,
      313–14, 325

Biden, Hunter, 239, 261–62

Biden, Joe
   inauguration, 279
   Trump wanting "dirt" on, 3, 239, 261–62,
      272
   unity/opportunity and, 285–86, 290
   2020 election/Trump's Big Lie and, 3, 270

Billingham/ICI chemical plant, 191–92

Bird, Mike, 87, 88
Birnbaum, George, 248
"birtherism," 249
Birx, Deborah, 269
Bishop Auckland
  alcohol/drugs and, 43
  as "Bish Vegas," 32–33, 348
  Brexit and, 175–76, 179, 185
  bulldozing past/"reclamation," 33–35
  cars and, 32
  cyber connectivity, 297
  decay/deterioration, 7, 30–35, 96–97
  Doggarts department store, 34, 41
  economy of nineteenth century, 22
  economy of twentieth century/beyond,
      22
  entertainment for children, 34–35
  history, 31–33
  income levels, 317
  job opportunities, 31
  King James I School/Boys' Grammar
      School, 31, 33, 63
  leaving/staying reasons, 329–30
  Newgate Street, 31–32, 349
  Rotary Club/financial aid, 77, 78, 324
  Ruffer buying/Auckland Project, 348–50
  trains and, 33–34
  voting/breaking Red Wall, 176
  white supremacist groups, 309
  See also coal mining
Bishop Auckland General Hospital
      (BAGH), 31, 36, 37
  See also specific individuals
Bishop Barrington Comprehensive School/
      Hill, Fiona
  bullies/incidents and, 52
  free meals and, 50–51
  information on colleges and, 62–63
  libraries/information, 49–50
  research paper, 52–53
  school location, 49, 51
  system/exams and, 50, 51–53
  teacher issues, 50, 52
Bishop of Durham, 31
"Bish Vegas"/ "Viva Bish Vegas," 32–33, 348
Black and British: A Forgotten History (Olu-
      soga), 308

Black Lives Matter movement/protests, 224,
      242, 265–66, 273
"Blair's girls," 102
Blair, Tony
  background, 101
  George W. Bush and, 214
  Hill/Aspen Ideas Festival (2014), 101–2,
      107
  Labour Party and, 103
  as prime minister/administration, 59,
      101, 103
Bloom County (comic strip), 5
Bolton, John, 206, 209, 220, 252
Bragg, Billy (singer), 85
Breathed, Berkeley, 5
Brexit
  Brexiteers' approach/strategies, 171,
      172–73
  consequences, 170, 171
  David Cameron and, 169, 170
  Hill's English family/Bishop Auckland
      and, 175–76, 179, 185
  immigrants and, 173
  labels and, 173–74
  lumping Brexit-Trump, 171, 172–73, 181,
      185, 280
  referendum expectations/outcomes
      (2016), 169, 170–71
  Russian meddling and, 171
  supports/critics views (summary), 169
  Trump in UK during referendum, 171,
      213, 280
  UK's forgotten places and, 170
  See also populism/populists
British Railways, 31
British Steel Corporation, 30
Brokaw, Tom, 86
Brookings Institution/Hill
  beginnings/work, 123
  conference/"tea lady," 130–31
  gender discrimination, 130–31
  gender wage gap, 138, 139, 142–44
  pandemic and, 265
  Putin and, 133
  website curriculum vitae, 246–47
Browder, Bill, 229–30
Brown, Louise, 73

Busette, Camille, 316–17, 332
Bush, George H. W., 178, 227
Bush, George W., 3, 8, 102, 178, 184, 193, 214, 240
Butler, Stuart, 336
BuzzFeed News, 247–48, 249

Callaghan, James, 39
Cameron, David, 169, 170
Campaign for Nuclear Disarmament (CND), 61
Carbon County, Pennsylvania, 346
Carnegie Moscow program, 222
Carroll, Lewis, 31, 241
Caste: The Origins of Our Discontents (Wilkerson), 307
Castor, Steve, 262
Castro, Fidel, 277
Ceausescu, Nicolai, 278
Charles, Prince, 216
Charlotte, North Carolina and upward mobility promotion, 316–17, 332
Charon, Steve, 200
Chayes, Abram ("Abe"), 126–27
Chayes, Antonia Handler, 126–27
Cheltenham Ladies' College, 74
Chobani/Food Incubator, 350
Citizens Advice Bureau, Bishop Auckland, 324, 326
Civil Rights Act (U.S./1964), 105, 157
Clash of Civilizations, The (Huntington), 127
class. *See* discrimination/class (UK)
"clever lasses," 54, 56, 319, 363
climate change/consequences, 177, 199, 216, 264–65, 293
Clinton, Bill, 178, 214
Clinton, Hillary
    emails/Trump and, 183, 184, 233, 234
    myth on Ukraine election interference and, 260
    presidential campaign/election and expectations, 176, 179, 183–84
    QAnon conspiracy/myth and, 249
    Russia/Putin and, 183, 185
    as secretary of state, 183
Close House/private aid, 341–42

coal mining
    anthracite coal, 112–13
    conditions/social life (Roddymoor), 26
    Co-op system (UK), 25, 337
    County Durham history, 23–27
    Durham Miners' Association (DMA), 26, 77–78, 102–3, 111, 122, 324, 327
    dying villages, 23–27
    health issues, 26–27
    international recruitment notices to DMA, 111
    loss of industry/consequences, 20, 22, 23–27, 32–35, 36, 73, 96–97
    miners' strike (1984–1985), 72–73, 177
    strikes, 23, 25, 39, 69, 72–73, 77, 89, 177, 179
    in U.S./Pennsylvania, 111, 112–14, 171
    See also extractive industry; *specific individuals/locations*
Coats, Dan, 232
Cohen, Roberta, 130
Cold War/"war scares" (UK), 60–61, 69, 236, 237–38
college professors/administrators creating opportunities, 359–60
college students creating opportunity, 360, 360–61
Communist Manifesto, The (Marx and Engels), 277
Connected: How Your Friends' Friends' Friends Affect Everything You Feel, Think, and Do, 316
Consett, 30–31
Consett Steel Works closing, 73, 179
conspiracy theories/myths
    authoritarians/populists and, 249
    "birtherism," 249
    patterns with, 244
    Protocols of the Elders of Zion, The, 248, 249
    QAnon, 249–50
    Soros conspiracy, 247–48
    Ukraine interference in U.S. election, 232, 239, 260, 287
    See also coup/Trump's attempt
Cornstein, David, 220, 249
Council on Foreign Relations (CFR), 192

County Durham
   average annual salary, 317–18
   coal mining history, 23–27
   education assistance/opportunities, 17, 52,
      78, 323–24
   See also specific individuals/locations
coups
   communication sources and, 275
   description of historical coups, 270–71
   examples/individuals, 271–72
   Russia and, 277
   "self coup," 271, 272, 273, 276, 278, 285
coup/Trump's attempt
   description, 270–73
   election certification and, 273, 276,
      278–79
   impeachments and, 270
   intimidating election officials/Pence and,
      272–73, 274
   January 6, 2021, rallies/insurrection, 10,
      224, 270, 273
   lies/Big Lie and Trump supporters, 10,
      250, 270, 272, 274, 275–76, 288
   resistance to, 273–74, 276
   testing for limits and, 271–72, 273
COVID-19 pandemic
   child care and, 301
   descriptions, 264
   divisions over, 265, 287, 293, 295–97
   education effects (U.S.), 300
   education effects/socioeconomic bias
      (UK), 297–99, 311, 320
   environmental degradation and, 264
   "essential workers" and, 296, 335–36
   internet connectivity and, 297, 299,
      299–300
   masks/physical distance and, 265, 268
   other natural disasters and, 264, 265
   pandemic warnings and, 264
   poor/low-skilled workers and, 295–97
   populist countries' failure with, 265,
      266
   Russia, UK, U.S. failures with, 265
   unemployment, 296–97, 301–2
   U.S. health system deterioration and,
      267–68

   wealthy people and, 301
   women/single mothers and, 295–96,
      300–301
COVID-19 pandemic/Trump and admin-
      istration
   failures of, 267, 268–70, 335
   GAO report, 267
   inequalities and, 267–68
   Lancet Commission report, 267–68,
      335
   press conferences/misinformation,
      268–69
   "winging it" vs. experts, 268–70
Crabtree, Charles (Charlie)
   information on scholarships/financial
      aid, 61–62, 77
   life/activities, 61
   question on USSR/Russia, 61–62, 237
creating opportunities
   exchanges and, 358, 361
   hosting students, 358
   mentoring, 357, 358, 359, 360
   networks and, 359
   overcoming biases, 357–61
   overview, 357–61
   programs' information/access, 360
   solutions (U.S.), 302–5
   volunteering, 358, 359, 360
   See also equality of opportunity (over-
      view)
critical thinking, 310
Cruz, Ted, 276, 278
Cuban missile crisis, 129–30, 198. *See also*
      Graham Allison
Curry, Edwina, 57

Dalpino, Catharin, 130
Davidson, Mr., 63
Davison, Aidan, 341–42
Day After, The (film), 60
Defcon 3, 192–93
democracy
   authoritarianism and, 266
   Biden and, 286
   crisis in U.S., 9–10
   not leaving people behind and, 356

equality of opportunity (overview) and,
    305–6
Trump's attempted coup and, 285–86
Trump/supporters and, 259
See also creating opportunities
Democratic National Committee (DNC)
    server/emails, 183, 184, 232–33
Department of Homeland Security (DHS)
    creation, 302
Dershowitz, Alan, 279
Detroit Regional Partnership (DRP), 342–43
discrimination and race/racism (UK)
    accents/dialects and, 104
    BAME students/working together, 308
    bias/prejudice and, 307
    Black working-class students and, 307–8
    County Durham and, 71–72
    immigration/Enoch Powell's speech, 71
    Malika's experience, 104–5
    race as amplifier, 308
    race riots, 70, 72
    slavery/slave trade and, 70–71
    See also gender discrimination
discrimination and race/racism (U.S.)
    as caste system/race significance, 18, 104,
        105, 107–9, 306
    civil rights movement/legislation, 105
    Danica's experience, 108
    divides around Boston area, 103–4
    divisive policies/consequences, 307
    generational wealth differences, 157
    institutionalized restrictions, 307
    opportunity gaps and, 308–9
    pitting Blacks against working-class
        whites, 307
    race as negative amplifier, 306
    school desegregation and, 106–7
    segregation, 307
    slavery/slave trade and, 306
    Tom's experience, 106–7
    See also gender discrimination
discrimination/class (UK)
    accent/dialect and, 65, 99–100, 102, 104
    education and, 161–64, 306, 320–21
    geographic origin and, 17–19, 65, 89–90,
        99–101

Hill/examples, 64–65, 99–101, 102
Hill realization of her class, 17–18, 22
Hill unprepared educationally and, 103,
    104, 105, 106–9
Labour Party promoting social mobility
    and, 102–3
Malika's experience, 104–5
middle class described, 18
place in society, 17–19
prevalence/significance, 18, 308
questions asked to establish/conse-
    quences, 17–18, 38, 45, 65
upper class described, 18–19
See also gender discrimination
discrimination/class (U.S.)
    discrimination against Hill (Harvard),
        98, 99–101
    upper middle class, 18
    See also gender discrimination
divisions (U.S.)
    backgrounds of arrested/insurrection
        and, 292
    Biden action to repair, 285–86
    COVID-19 pandemic and, 265, 287, 293,
        295–97
    digital media and, 293–94
    extremists and, 293–94
    identity loss and, 291, 292
    immigrants/immigration and, 265, 291,
        292
    inequalities, 290–92, 295
    polarization/crisis, 13–14, 183, 185
    poverty and, 295
    presidential election (U.S./2020) and,
        288–92
    Quinnipiac University poll (2021),
        290–91
    as security threat, 293–94
    unemployment and, 291
    views on public servants, 293
    See also coup/Trump's attempt; Trump,
        Donald
divisions/solutions (U.S.), 302–5
Dixon, Heather, 48
Dream Hoarders (Reeves), 312
Dr. Who (UK TV series), 40

Durham Miners' Association (DMA), 26, 77–78, 102–3, 111, 122, 324, 327
Durham Miners' Association (DMA) financial aid
    Alfred, Angela, Fiona trip, 77–78
    Crabtree's information, 77
    Fiona Hill and, 77–78, 324

Ebac Foundation/jobs, 349–50
economics course (Harvard/Hill)
    Hill's background knowledge and, 114–16
    need for social protection funds, 115, 118, 325
    Professor Kornai, 114–15
    reforming socialist economies, 114–16
Eden Theatre, Bishop Auckland, 31–32, 34
Educated (Westover), 354
education (UK)
    Cardiff Council, Wales, 162–63
    class discrimination and, 161–64, 306, 320–21
    County Durham, sponsoring education/ extracurricular programs, 17, 52, 323–24
    COVID-19 pandemic effects/socioeconomic bias, 297–99, 311, 320
    disadvantaged students and, 161–64
    disadvantaged students banding together/Team Upside and, 320–21
    improvements/Finland model and, 162–63
    inequalities/reform and, 44, 45, 47–48
    of leaders and, 299
    London, 165–66
    minorities statistics, 163
    opportunity changes (1970s/1980s), 48
    Oxbridge, 58, 63, 66–67, 75, 89, 103, 320
    Parliament's Education Select Committee, 163
    student debt comparison with U.S., 152
    system/sorting by eleven-plus exam, 46–47
    "White British" students, 163
    See also education; *specific schools*
education (U.S.)
    COVID-19 pandemic effects, 300
    inequality/effects, 9, 157

opportunity changes, 46
Science Club for Girls of Greater Boston, 313–14, 325
See also education; *specific schools*
education
    China and, 311
    connections and, 312, 313–14, 316–17
    creating networks/experiences, 317–21
    critical thinking and, 310
    "doubly disadvantaged," 316
    elite and, 312–14, 317, 320–21
    exchange programs, 323, 327–28
    funding and, 311–12
    health discrepancy and, 157
    Hill's funding opportunities, 323–24
    importance (overview), 309–12, 352–55
    K-12 system importance, 311–12, 355
    lack of education/consequences, 310
    lifelong learning, 321–23, 353–54
    minorities/women and, 310, 313–14, 353
    need for systematizing opportunity, 325–28
    opportunity hoarders, 312–14
    poor/disadvantaged students and, 312–16, 352–53
    poverty/university life changes and, 69
    "privileged poor," 315
    removing obstacles and, 309–10, 311–12
    role models and, 354
    seizing opportunities, 323–25
    student debt and, 148, 152–53, 323
    study on upward mobility promotion, 316–17
    university programs, 314–15
    volunteers/mentors and, 326, 360
    See also specific generations; *specific individuals/schools*
Elizabeth II, Queen
    crowning of, 54
    daughter's wedding and, 40
    other U.S. presidents/leaders and, 214
    Trump and, 212–13, 214, 221
    wealth/status, 221
Elliott, John (Ebac Foundation), 349–50
Ellis, Michael, 229
emigration vs. migration, 331
Engels, Friedrich, 277

Entous, Adam, 205–6, 242, 245
equality of opportunity (overview)
    common purpose/difficulties, 307–9
    democracy and, 305–6
    discrimination barriers and, 306–7
    identities and, 309
    at individual level, 305–6
    institutional reform and, 306
    undoing political damage, 306–7
    working together, 306–7
    See also creating opportunities; discrimi-
        nation and race/racism; discrimi-
        nation/class; education; gender
        discrimination; specific areas
Erdoğan, Recep Tayyip, 220, 221, 228
Esper, Mark, 273, 274
Essence of Decision (Allison), 130
Etherley Lane elementary school, 48, 60–61,
    321
Eurasia Foundation, 12–13, 141–42, 247, 339,
    340–41
Euromissile crisis (1977–1987), 60, 197, 237
European Bank for Reconstruction and
    Development (EBRD), 339
European Union
    UK referendum on membership (1973),
        169
    See also Brexit
exchanges and creating opportunities, 358,
    361
executives/CEOs creating opportunity,
    357–58
extractive industries
    cycles in, 20, 24–25
    global economy shifts/effects, 20–23
    oil shocks/effects, 20
    See also coal mining

Facebook, 182, 275, 276, 294
Farage, Nigel, 170, 171, 172, 174, 179
Fauci, Anthony, 268, 269
federal lands under Trump, 223
Fifth Risk, The (Lewis), 269–70
financial crash (1929), 25
Financial Times, 5
Fine Young Cannibals (band), 308
Finkelstein, Arthur, 248

Fisher, Elizabeth (Elizabeth Lacey, Cousin
    Elizabeth), 54, 67
Fisher, Peter, 54
Florrie, Aunt, 41
Floyd, George/murder, 265
Flynn, Michael, 193, 194, 203, 212, 250
Foer, Franklin, 220
Ford Motor Company, 342
Ford, Gerald, 204–5
Foreign Agent Registration Act (FARA),
    246
Forgotten Americans, The (Sawhill), 144–45
Foster, Derek, Lord, 59, 63, 65–66
Fox News, 186, 192–93, 207–8, 209, 210, 211,
    216, 242, 262, 268, 275
Friedman, Milton, 22
Fruman, Igor. See Parnas/Fruman
Further and Higher Education Act
    (UK/1992), 151

Gaddafi, Muammar, 278
Gaddy, Cliff, 192–93
Gaetz, Matt, 259–60
gender discrimination
    appearance/clothes and, 2, 124–25, 260
    childbirth/maternity leave and, 147
    COVID-19 pandemic and, 295–96,
        300–301
    c-word, 245, 253
    Hill and, 3, 54–55, 78, 124, 125–27, 128–34,
        261, 262–63, 353
    inequality and, 124–25
    looking for role models, 56–57
    male harassment (Fiona/Angela), 55–56,
        78
    poverty/class and, 54, 55, 78
    USSR survey/schoolgirls wanting to be
        prostitutes, 128
    working mothers and, 255
    See also Russia/gender
gender wage gap
    documentation on, 137
    effects on children, 144–45
    fixed pay and, 137
    government positions and, 147
    Lilly Ledbetter Fair Pay Act (U.S./2009),
        139–40

gender wage gap (*cont.*)
    maternity leave, 147
    negotiations, 137–38, 141, 144
    over lifetime, 140
    overview, 136–45, 146–47
    pay significance, 140
    "previous pay" and, 141–43
    racial salary gap and, 146
    single mothers, 144, 145, 146
    women voting for Trump and, 136
gender wage gap/Hill
    becoming a citizen and, 140
    Brookings Institution, 138, 139, 142–44
    Eurasia Foundation, 141–42
    Kennedy School, 137, 138, 140–41
    maternity leave and, 147
    NIO, 143–44
    not having information on, 137–38
    PhD and, 136, 140–41
    "previous pay" and, 141, 142–43
General Motors, 222, 342, 345
General Strike (UK/1926), 39
generations
    socioeconomic opportunities and (overview), 148–49
    See also specific generations
Generation X
    defined, 149
    education and, 148–49
    January 6, 2021, insurrection and, 292
    money and, 149
    socioeconomic opportunities and, 148–49
Generation Z
    defined, 150
    demographic shifts and, 155
    education and, 150–52
    socioeconomic opportunities and, 150–52, 166, 306
"Ghost Town" (song), 35
Gift, Roland, 308
Gill, Margot, 88–89, 135–36
Ginsburg, Ruth Bader, 139
Girl Guides (UK), 318–19, 325
Giuliani, Rudy, 239, 272
Goldstein, Amy, 155–56
"Goodbye America" (song), 85

Goodman, Jeff
    education/lifelong education, 321–23, 325
    Hill family and, 63, 321, 325, 331
    moving possibility and, 331
Gorbachev, Mikhail
    arms/nuclear weapons, 85–87, 90, 197, 227, 235, 236
    coup against, 277
    Crabtree and, 61
    George H. W. Bush meeting, 227
    Reagan-Gorbachev summit (1988), 85–87, 90, 197, 227, 235
    as Soviet leader/policies, 95, 98, 120, 172, 224
    Yeltsin replacing, 117
Gore, Al, 184
Gould-Davis, Nigel, 88, 101
government shutdown (U.S.), 258
Grandma Vi
    background/farming and, 40–41, 73, 76
    buses and, 41–42
    Fiona's Oxford interview and, 64, 65
    Goodman and, 63
    husband/death, 40
    money/being economical, 40–42
    visiting Hill family, 34
Grant, Ulysses S., 24
Great Depression/effects, 58, 109, 150, 156, 157, 173, 295
Great Recession/effects, 10, 148, 150, 153, 154, 159, 292, 295, 306, 337, 341, 350
Greenberg, Maurice ("Hank"), 131
"Greenham Common woman," 61
Grenell, Richard
    background, 241, 251–52
    on NSC/Hill, 252–53
    as Trump loyalist, 241
Guardian, 308, 320, 321, 331
Guevara, Che, 277

Hartnett, Mary, 55
Harvard
    campus vs. other parts of town, 93–94
    recruiting low-income/unconventional students, 89

Soros-funded programs, 247
town-gown tensions, 94
Harvard Business Review, 137
Harvard/Hill
  application process information, 86–88
  arrival, 93
  discrimination and, 98, 99–100, 107, 108
  economic course, 114–16
  History Department PhD, 116, 135, 136
  Kennedy Scholarship interview/closet
    incident, 88, 89, 99
  Knox Fellowship/interview, 88–89
  master's program/Russian Research
    Center, 94
  question on UK North-South divide/
    Hill's response, 89–90
  Strengthening Democratic Institutions
    Project, 116, 118
  See also Belfer Center; Kennedy School of
    Government/Hill; *specific indi-*
    viduals
Harvey, Derek, 200, 202, 203, 204
Hawley, Josh, 276, 278
health care (UK)
  care description, 334
  COVID-19 pandemic and, 335–36
  Hill family and, 334, 335
  jobs and, 334–35
  See also specific components
health care (U.S.)
  COVID-19 pandemic and, 335–36
  "deaths of despair," 157–58
  inequality and, 157
  jobs and, 333, 335
  life expectancy, 157
  single-payer system and, 336
  socialized medicine and, 336
  uninsured, 333
Helsinki summit (2018)
  arms control and, 227, 228, 232
  bilateral mutual legal assistance treaty
    (MLAT) and, 229–30, 233
  date/location, 226–27
  discussions, 227, 228–31
  DNC missing server/Hillary Clinton's
    emails, 232–33

Hill not wanting press conference/con-
    sidering ending it, 231, 234
interpreters, 231
Mueller's indictment of Russians and,
    229–30
press conference, 231–33, 234
Russian interference in U.S. election and,
    231, 232–33, 234
Trump monologue at press conference,
    232–33
Trump "winging it"/feelings on, 229–31,
    232–33
Henriksen, John, 99, 103–4
heroin epidemic (UK/1980s and 1990s), 43
Higher Education Act (U.S.), 46
Hill, Alfred/Alf
  background, 110–11
  birth/birthplace, 19, 25
  on Bishop Auckland/Roddymoor, 35
  childhood/poverty, 25, 38, 47, 355
  coal mining/identity, 19, 25, 26, 36–37, 47,
    110, 291
  coal mining in Pennsylvania and, 111,
    113–14, 343
  education, 47
  health issues/death, 26, 334
  helping parents, 27, 28
  hospital (BAGH) work, 18, 19, 26, 36–37,
    38–39, 78, 80, 112, 188, 334, 335
  Keens' visit/life opportunity compari-
    sons, 110–12
  move to Bishop Auckland, 27
  payment for hospital work, 38–39
  retirement/pension, 145
  speaking out/NHS representative, 188
  UN joke, 35, 158
  watching boxing with Fiona, 186–87
  work positions summary, 19
  See also Hill, Fiona/parents and sister;
    Hill, June/Alfred
Hill, Angela
  birth, 38
  Bishop Barrington Comprehensive
    School, 49, 50–51
  childhood, 32, 33, 34–35, 39, 43, 60–61,
    318–19

Hill, Angela (*cont.*)
   concerts/trips with sister, 85, 245
   Etherley Lane elementary school, 60–61
   leaving County Durham/life after, 329,
      330, 331
   part-time jobs, 43
   risk of nuclear strike and, 60–61
   role models and, 56
   social media attacks on Fiona and, 247
   Stirling University, 313
   See also Hill, Fiona/parents and sister
Hill, Billy (uncle), 25
Hillbilly Elegy (Vance), 355–56
Hill, Fiona
   birth and timing/environment, 7, 23, 30,
      38, 46, 94, 334, 355
   childhood, 7, 19–20, 27–28, 32–35, 39–40,
      41, 42–44
   illness, 334
   leaving County Durham/relocating in
      U.S. and, 32, 148, 329
   life/career summary, 3, 7–9
   luck/opportunities (summary), 12, 148,
      353, 355
   New York Times article, 287
   part-time jobs, 42–43, 55–56, 208
   role models and, 56–57
   on stories, 4
   See also specific organizations/schools
Hill, Fiona/early education
   decisions on future education and, 57,
      59–63
   Durham High and, 48–49
   eleven-plus exams, 48
   Etherley Lane elementary school, 48,
      60, 321
   importance of, 8, 44–45
   internships, 326
   opportunity and, 7, 44
   Oxford entrance exam, 63–64
   Oxford/Hertford College interview,
      64–66
   Oxford/Hertford College interview trip-
      ping, 65
   risk of nuclear strike/public service an-
      nouncement and, 60–61

school exchanges, 52, 55, 56, 65, 75, 323
   See also education (UK); *specific schools*
Hill, Fiona/Keen, Ken
   buying a house, 146
   daughter, 2, 146, 147, 195, 245, 255, 297–98,
      306
   finances and, 135, 144, 145–46
   at Harvard, 99, 103–4
   Pennsylvania trip, 113
   quarter incident, 125
   wedding, 109, 135, 145
Hill, Fiona/parents and sister
   bread making and, 39
   child care/June leaving job, 38, 319
   clothing and, 41, 64
   Dorothy ("Red Dot"/June's cousin), 61
   educated relatives/("clever lasses"), 45,
      53–54
   electricity and, 39
   Encyclopedia Britannica, 49–50, 75
   food, 50–51
   health care, 334, 335
   home ownership/consequences, 37–38,
      74, 318, 319–20, 335
   Oxford and, 63
   poverty/multigenerational poverty and,
      4, 8, 12, 38–40, 41, 42–43, 46–47,
      50–51, 146, 355
   television and, 40
   transportation and, 42, 345
   university/college encouragement and,
      53–54
   See also Grandma Vi
Hill, Fiona (UK/May's personal adviser), 212
Hill, Granny
   Alfred possibly leaving and, 111
   allotment, 26, 27–28, 81, 84, 245
   banks and, 114
   box/"death box," 28–29
   death, 30
   Fiona caring for, 27–29
   health issues, 27, 28, 29, 30
   life after husband's death/Bishop Auck-
      land, 29–30
   life after husband's retirement/Roddy-
      moor, 27–29, 37, 80–81, 347

Hill, Jenny (Elizabeth Thompson/"Vital Spark"), 31–32, 327
Hill, Jonathon ("Uncle Jonty"), 26
Hill, June
  birthplace, 19
  education/training, 38, 47, 318
  hospital/medical work and, 19, 36, 37, 38, 78, 80, 147–48, 334, 335
  on Trump, 280
  Vi (mother), 34
  visiting Fiona/America, 2, 297
  volunteer work/on poverty, 159
  See also Hill, Fiona/parents and sister
Hill, June/Alfred
  as comparatively older parents and, 318
  educated relatives/neighbors and, 45, 53–54, 319–20
  education importance for children, 8, 43–44, 45, 61–62, 77, 77–78, 87, 87–88, 318–20
  Fiona helping financially, 145
  home ownership/consequences, 37–38, 74, 318, 319–20, 335
  meeting/marrying, 19, 27
  social support and, 337
Hill, Thompson, 31–32, 78
Hill, William ("Billy") Thompson
  allotment, 26, 27–28, 84, 245
  banks and, 114
  coal mining and, 24–25, 29, 47, 78
  Fiona caring for, 27–29
  health issues/death, 26, 27
  life after retirement (Roddymoor), 27–28, 29, 37, 347
  living conditions/unemployment, 25
  social activities, 26
  swearing and, 245
  World War I and, 24, 28–29
Hitler, Adolf, 242, 249, 250
Holmes, David, 2
Home Alone 2 (film), 198
hosting students to create opportunities, 358
Housing Act (UK/1980), 120
Huntington, Samuel, 127
Hunt, Mr., 74–76
Huntsman, Abby, 208

Huntsman, Jon, 208
Hussein, Leyla, 396n

Immelt, Jeff, 131
impeachments/Trump
  closed-door deposition/Hill, 259–60, 287
  first impeachment, 3, 10, 259–60, 279
  Hill's attention afterwards, 3, 4–5
  Hill's November 2019 testimony/preparation, 1–3
  second impeachment/significance, 10, 270, 280
  warning for U.S. and, 292
indentured servants (UK), 70–71
industry. See coal mining; extractive industries; manufacturing sector; postindustrial challenges
Indyk, Martin, 238
influenza pandemic (1918), 173, 264
Infowars (website), 245, 246, 247
insurrections
  January 6, 2021, rallies/insurrection, 10, 224, 270, 273
  possible future events/outcomes, 14
Intergirl (film), 128
Intermediate-Range Nuclear Forces (INF) Treaty
  Bolton/NSC staff and Russia meetings, 236
  creation/fraying of, 235
  Merkel/others experience, 237–38
  Trump ending/suspending and consequences, 235, 236, 237
International Monetary Fund (IMF), 118
IRA (Provisional Irish Republican Army), 69
Irish Northern Aid Committee (NORAID), 105
Irving, Bill, 73
Israeli-Palestinian relations/negotiations, 238

Jack, Tony, 315–16, 320
Jacobite Rebellion (1715), 280
Janesville (Goldstein), 155–56

January 6, 2021, rallies/insurrection, 10, 224, 270, 273
Jarrow March (1936), 25
Jefferson, Arthur, 31, 34
Jim Thorpe (town), 113, 348
Johnson, Boris
    background/education, 5, 299
    becoming prime minister, 214
    Brexit and, 170, 179
Jones, Alex, 245, 247, 249
Jordan, Jim, 259

Kapital, Das (Marx), 114, 277
Keen, Irma, 109, 110
Keen, Irma/Jim
    children, 110, 145
    children's educational grants, 324
    lifestyle/finances, 145
    meeting, 110
    moves/moving, 110, 330–31
    visiting Hill's parents/Bishop Auckland, 109, 110, 111, 112
Keen, Jim, 109–10, 111–12
Keen, Ken
    background/influences, 145
    Harvard, 99
    MBA/private sector career, 135, 144
    on midwestern accents, 103–4
    See also Hill, Fiona/Keen, Ken
Kellogg, Keith, 193, 206
Kelly, John, 237
Kelly, Megyn, 262
Kennedy, John F., 88
Kennedy Scholarship, 88
Kennedy School of Government/Hill
    academic career and, 135
    Allison and, 116, 117–18, 128–29, 136, 142
    clothes/Zinberg's suit, 125, 126, 127
    gender wage gap, 137, 138, 140–41
    notetaking/misidentification, 129–30
    starting job, 116
    travels overview, 117–18
Khan, Sadiq, 212, 213
Khasbulatov, Ruslan, 278
King James I School/Boys' Grammar School, 31, 33, 63
Kislyak, Sergey, 194

Knox Fellowship, 88–89
Knox, Frank, 88
Koppel, Ted, 128
Kornai, János, 114–15, 118, 324
Kushner, Jared, 184, 200, 201, 202, 208
Kynren: The Story of Us, 348–49

Labour Party
    party elites vs. working-class members, 103
    promoting social mobility, 102–3
Lacey, Elizabeth (Elizabeth Fisher, Cousin Elizabeth), 54, 67
Laurel, Stan, 31, 34
Lavrov, Sergey, 227
Lafayette Square clearing/Trump photo op, 273
Lazorchick, Susan, 112
Ledbetter, Lilly, 139–40
Lee, Peter, 122
Legvold, Robert, 86–87
Lehigh Gorge State Park, Pennsylvania, 113
Lehigh Valley Economic Development Corporation, 343
Lemire, Jonathan, 232
Lenin, Vladimir, 277
Levinson, Molly, 1, 126, 260
Lewis, Michael, 269–70
Lilly Ledbetter Fair Pay Act (U.S./2009), 139–40
Living Museum of the North, Beamish, 346–47
Lockey, Sidney, 53, 78
Losch, August, 52
Luna, Nick, 186

MacArthur Foundation "genius grant," 138–39
McFarland, K. T.
    background, 192, 204–5
    Hill/NSC and, 192–93, 196, 197, 205
    nominated as U.S. ambassador to Singapore, 194
McFaul, Michael, 230
Mack, Connie
    attacks against Hill, 246–47
    background, 246

FARA filing, 246
  Orbán and, 246
"Mackems," 24, 178
MacLeod, Mary Anne/Scottish family, 212, 213, 280
McMahon, Linda, 187
McMaster, H.R./NSC
  background, 194
  departure, 233, 234
  Harvey/Rayburn and, 203
  Hill and, 194, 195, 196, 197, 200, 202, 206
  on Russian interference in elections, 233–34
  as target, 194, 204
  Trump and, 194, 195, 201, 202, 231
Macron, Emmanuel, 210, 217
Magill, Julia
  Cambridge interview dinner and, 66–67
  Cardiff Council position, 162–63
  education/disadvantaged students and, 162–63
Magnitsky, Sergei, 229–30
mail-in ballots, 272
Major, John, 57
Maloney, Suzanne, 130
Mamassian, Tesia, 342
manufacturing sector
  cycles in UK/U.S./Russia, 20
  global economy shifts/effects, 20–23
  oil shocks/effects, 20
Mar, Earl of, 280
Marshall, Dr., 52, 62
Marshall, George C., 338
Marshall Plan
  development plan for rural America, 338, 339–40
  for Europe, 338, 339
Marx, Karl, 114, 277
Mattis, Jim, 209
Matviyenko, Valentina, 127
Maynes, Bill, 141, 142
May, Theresa, Trump and, 211–12, 213, 214
mentoring to create opportunities, 357, 358, 359, 360
Merkel, Angela, 217, 237–38
migration vs. emigration, 331

militias
  plots to kidnap governors, 288
  Putin and, 225
  in U.S., 219, 224, 288
  See also insurrections
Millennials (generation)
  education and, 150, 151–52
  socioeconomic opportunities and 149–51, 166, 306
  as the "unluckiest generation," 150
Milley, Mark, 273
Mironyuk, Svetlana, 132, 134
Montenegro and NATO, 196
Moor, Sarah, 88, 99, 101
Moscow
  divide with rest of country, 96
  as global city, 96
  people wanting to move to/government preventions, 123
Moscow year (1987–1988)/studies (Hill)
  accommodations, 81–82
  alternative/revolutionary music, 84–85
  becoming a "Russia expert" and, 79–80, 324
  building parts falling off/consequences, 83
  car/sinkhole incident, 83–84
  collective farm work, 84
  deficit period (USSR) and, 81
  electric kettle incident, 82
  exploding televisions in Moscow, 81
  food/shortages, 80–81
  hazards overview, 82–84
  HIV test, 79
  Moscow descriptions/family allotments, 80–84, 90
  music/dance, 84–85
  NBC News job, 85–87
  overview/life in Moscow, 79–87
  political background (UK/USSR), 79, 80
  possibly dropping out/parents' financial insecurity and, 80
  power outages, 83
  "public toilets"/incident, 82–83
  Reagan-Gorbachev summit (1988), 85–87
  specialty stores and, 82
  transportation, 83–84, 85

Moscow year (1987–1988)/studies (Hill) (*cont.*)
 U.S. graduate schools/Harvard application process information and, 85, 86–87
 water contamination, 83
Mr. Smith Goes to Washington (film), 110
Mueller, Robert
 indictments of Russians, 185, 229
 investigation (Russia/U.S. 2016 presidential election), 184–85, 229
multigenerational poverty, 8, 12, 355
Muslims and Trump, 212

Nabiullina, Elvira, 132
Napoleon, 57
Napoleon III, 248, 271–72
National Association for the Advancement of Colored People (NAACP), 106
National Coal Board, 72
National Health Service (NHS/UK), 19, 36, 37, 38, 80, 145, 169, 179, 188, 303, 319, 334–35, 336
National Intelligence Council (NIC)
 creation/functions, 143
 Hill and, 143, 147
national intelligence officer (NIO), 143, 147, 193
nationalism growth
 generational differences, 70
 Scottish/Welsh, 70
 white English nationalism, 71–72
National Security Council
 criticism of/as not part of Trump team, 252–54
 pay gap with West Wing/value and, 255
 Trump access and, 251
 turf war, 203
 See also specific individuals
National Security Council/Hill
 atmosphere description (summary), 192
 clothes/sneakers and, 195–97, 205–6, 208
 joining/reasons for joining, 191–93
 naïveté, 191
 notetaking, 205, 206
 pay/pay raise (near departure) and, 254–55

people advising resignation following Helsinki summit, 234–35
Russia expertise and, 192–93, 195–97
as target/threats, 194, 204, 242–47, 249, 252–53
Trump and, 3, 8, 194, 195–97, 199–204, 205, 207, 212
Trump mistaking Hill for secretary, 199–204
Trump-Putin Hamburg meeting and, 231
Ukraine policy and, 261–62
as working mother, 195, 255
See also Helsinki summit
National Union of Mineworkers (NUM), 72, 324
Nautilus Pompilius (band), 85
Nena (singer/band), 60, 237
Netanyahu, Benjamin (Bibi), 248
New Deal/programs (U.S.), 157–58
news communication (summary)
 newspapers shutting down, 275
 sources/"big networks" vs. current situation, 274–75
 See also specific sources
Newsmax, 275
New Yorker, The, 205, 245
New York Times, 268, 287, 299
Nicholas II, Czar, 226
Nielsen, Kirstjen, 253
Nightly News, 86
Niinistö, Sauli
 Helsinki summit and, 227, 228
 in White House/on democracy, 271
1984 (Orwell), 69, 250
"99 Red Balloons" (song), 60, 237
Nixon, Richard M., 204
Nobel, Alfred, 215
Noble-Eddy, Mr., 48
North East railway network, 31
Northern Echo, 350
nuclear weapons
 Cold War/war scares (UK), 60–61, 69, 236, 237–38
 Euromissile crisis (1977–1987), 60, 197, 237
 other countries (besides U.S./Russia) and, 235–36

Reagan-Gorbachev summit (1988), 85–87, 90, 197, 227, 235
Trump and, 197, 198–99, 227, 235
See also specific agreements

Obama, Barack
economic policies and, 154
Hill and, 3, 8, 193
Lilly Ledbetter Fair Pay Act and, 139–40
Nobel Peace Prize, 216
Trump and, 178, 181, 198–99, 249
UK/Buckingham Palace and, 214
Obama, Michelle, 2
Office of the Director of National Intelligence (ODNI) creation, 143, 302
Office of the Parliamentarian, 259
Ofqual (UK), 298–99
oil embargo (1970s), 20
Olusoga, David, 308
OPEC (Organization of Petroleum Exporting Countries), 20
Open Society Foundation (OSF), 246–47
opioid crisis, 157
opportunities
creating, 357–61
disadvantaged students and, 136–37, 161–64
following World War II, 148–49
Hill and (summary), 12, 148, 353, 355
infrastructure of opportunity, 11–12, 13, 36, 46, 55, 59, 97, 120, 123, 136, 148, 151, 166, 176, 302, 305, 309, 311, 316, 320, 323, 325, 328, 332, 334, 337, 339, 340, 347, 348, 350, 357
students from richest families and, 166
summary on, 136–37
time/generation and, 148
work needs and, 11–12
See also equality of opportunity; *specific individuals*
opportunity/place (summary)
as antidote to populism, 350–51
building on local assets, 342–44
development plan for rural America, 338, 339–40
importance, 328
leaving/brain drain and, 330–31, 354

private/individual aid and, 340–42, 347–50
relocating/health care and, 333
relocation support, 332–33
safety networks and, 336–37
starting from scratch and, 330–33
tourists/museums, 346–47
transportation, 344–46
See also equality of opportunity; *specific places/individuals*
Orbán, Viktor
meetings with Trump, 219–20, 228, 250
political campaign and, 248
Soros and, 248, 250
Trump envious of, 220, 221
Trump/White House "first" visit and, 246
Organization of Petroleum Exporting Countries (OPEC), 20
Orwell, George, 26, 69, 250
O'Sullivan, Meghan, 130
Our Kids: The American Dream in Crisis (Putnam), 150–51
Outer Hebrides, Scotland, 213
Oxbridge, 58, 63, 66–67, 75, 89, 103, 320
Oxbridge and feeling "out of my league," 66–67
Oxford
Hill feeling "out of my league," 66
student statistics, 66

Packer, Asa, 346
pandemics
influenza pandemic (1918), 173, 264
See also COVID-19 pandemic
Pape, Robert, 292
Paris Climate Agreement/Accord, 177, 216
Parnas/Fruman
attacking Yovanovitch, 239–40
as businessmen working in Ukraine, 239
Giuliani and, 239
Trump/manipulating Trump, 239, 240, 242, 250
wanting "dirt" on Joe/Hunter Biden, 239
Parnas, Lev. *See* Parnas/Fruman
Pasternak, Boris, 87
Pence, Mike, 273, 276, 278–79
Peterlin, Margaret, 200, 202

Phillips, Mark, 40
Pipa, Tony, 339
Playboy Magazine, 198
plebiscitary democracy, 286–87
Pocono Mountains, Pennsylvania, 113, 346
political parties (U.S.)
 description, 219–20
 extreme views and, 218–19
 Republican Party/Trump takeover, 276,
  280–81
Pompeo, Mike, 230
populism/populists
 background/examples, 277
 corruption/wealth, 221
 "cultural despair" and, 156, 291
 demographic changes and, 154–56
 descriptions, 171, 172
 "forgotten" people/disaffected voters and,
  137, 153, 173, 181
 getting others to do their bidding, 278–79
 grievances and, 166, 181, 216, 224, 276–78
 history/timing of emergence, 173, 180, 185
 immigrants and, 154–55, 173
 kleptocracies and, 221
 labels and, 173–74
 lumping Brexit/Trump, 171, 172–73, 181,
  185, 280
 media use, 350–51
 money and, 286
 nepotism/cronyism, 222
 "people, the" and, 173, 175, 222, 277
 postindustrial divides and, 277
 promises and, 137, 156, 173, 349–51, 355
 racial diversity and, 155
 rise of, 153–56, 173
 security interests and, 251, 253, 263
 self-obsession and, 277
 socioeconomic inequality, 153–54
 supporters' lack of education and, 310
 susceptibility to influence and, 238
 Tea Party movement (U.S.), 154, 156
 unequal areas of generational/racial
  diversity, 155–56
 See also Brexit; Putin, Vladimir; Trump,
  Donald; *specific individuals*
Port Clinton, Ohio, 150–51
Porte Étroite, La (Gide), 74

Portsmouth Peace Treaty, 216
postindustrial challenges
 comparing UK, U.S., USSR, 93–98,
  117–20, 266
 Rust Belts, 7, 97, 123, 172, 264–65, 266, 296
 See also populism/populists; *specific
  components; specific locations*
poverty (UK)
 education and, 160, 161–62
 poverty level statistics, 39
 removal of safety nets and, 159–60
 UN representative visiting/reporting,
  159–60
 See also specific individuals/locations
poverty (U.S.)
 education and, 160
 overview, 156–58
 statistics on, 156–57
 UN representative visiting/reporting, 160
PPE studies/degree, 65–66, 98–99, 101
president (U.S.)
 changes over time, 218
 See also specific individuals
presidential election (U.S./2016)
 outcome/patterns, 183–84, 238, 294, 310
 Trump as candidate description, 10
 See also specific individuals
presidential election (U.S./2020)
 divides/patterns, 288–92
 turnout/statistics, 288
 See also coup/Trump's attempt; *specific
  individuals*
Presley, Elvis, 32–33
professionals creating opportunity, 358–59
Protocols of the Elders of Zion, The, 248, 249
Proud Boys, 224
Provisional Irish Republican Army (IRA),
 69
public servants
 criticism/treatment of, 257–58, 293
 government shutdown and, 258
 Trump depiction of, 258
Putin, Vladimir
 background, 182, 223–24, 225
 Biden as president and, 289
 blaming others, 225
 Brookings Institution/Hill and, 133

coming into power, 10–11, 173
curtailing political freedoms, 137
disinformation/weaponizing and, 247
diversion tactic/pointing out U.S. racial issues, 268
divisions/exploiting and, 225
Farage and, 172
Hill's books on, 4, 101, 133, 192–93
Hill sitting beside at meetings/reasons, 133–34
Hill's knowledge on, 192–93
militias and, 224
nostalgia/national heroes and, 224
"people, the" (*narod*) and, 172, 224–25
Soviet memorials, 224
strategies, 171–72, 173, 222, 225, 247, 268, 294
term limits and, 278, 279, 287
unity and, 225–26
wealth of, 221
Western stereotypes of Russia and, 132–33
worries about execution/getting others to do your work, 278
See also Helsinki summit; populism/populists; Russia; Trump, Donald/Putin
Putnam, Bob, 150–51

QAnon, 249–50
Queen of Hearts/"Off with their heads," 241–42

race/racism. *See* discrimination and race/racism
racial salary gap
gender wage gap and, 146
See also discrimination and race/racism
railway deterioration (UK), 31
Rashawn, Ray, 146
Raskin, Jamie, 259, 260
Rayburn, Joel
Hill and, 200, 202, 203, 204
NSC/Middle East and, 200, 203
Trump and, 200, 202
Reagan, Nancy, 86
"Reaganomics," 23

Reagan, Ronald
government policies/economy, 22–23, 117, 118, 149, 154, 181, 236, 306–7
McFarland and, 205
Queen Elizabeth and, 214
Reagan-Gorbachev summit (1988), 85–87, 90, 197, 227, 235
Soviet Union/Cold War, 98
Trump and, 198
Received Pronunciation (RP), 100, 104
recommendations
divisions/solutions (U.S.), 302–5
See also creating opportunities; *specific components*
Red Cross (UK), 319
Reeves, Richard, 312
referendums (UK)
description, 169–70
voter turnout and, 170
See also Brexit
Republican Party/Trump takeover, 276, 280–81
retired people creating opportunity, 358
RIA Novosti, 132, 134
Richardson, Louise
background, 160–61
views on poor students/ability to learn, 161
Rivlin, Alice
background, 138–39
gender wage gap and, 138–39, 142
Road to a Free Economy, The (Kornai), 115
Roberts, John, 210–11
Robertson, George/Lord Robertson, 80
Roddymoor
and coal mining, 19, 26
comparisons to Moscow, 80, 81
descriptions, 19, 26, 30, 35, 80, 81
See also specific individuals
Roosevelt, Franklin Delano, 157
Roosevelt, Teddy, 216
Rosenstein, Rod, 184
Ruffer, Jonathan
buying Bishop Auckland/Auckland Project, 347–50
paintings and, 348

Russia
    alcoholism/drug addiction and, 120, 157
    coups/political violence (summary),
        277–78
    COVID-19 pandemic and, 265, 300
    cyberattacks against U.S. (2020), 289
    democracy to autocracy change, 11
    example/cautionary tale for U.S., 10, 12
    health care and, 119–20, 333
    Hill's experience with "moonshine"
        (*samogon*), 120
    lack of communications/reforms, 119
    oligarchs, 221
    "pogrom" word, 225
    political connections and, 221
    postindustrial challenges/comparisons
        with UK (1990s), 117–20, 266
    reform programs/ "shock therapy" and
        consequences, 117–20
    remote cities/cities in Siberia and, 122–23,
        124, 266, 300
    Rust Belts of, 9, 266
    St. Petersburg Metro terrorist attack,
        195–96
    Siberian temperatures, 122
    state housing/stock, 120–21
    towns establishment/destruction, 121–24
    See also Moscow; *specific components/*
        individuals; USSR
Russia/gender discrimination
    Hill and, 128–29, 130–31, 133–35
    misogyny/sexism, 127–28
    prostitute misidentification, 128–29
    women in media/finance (early 2000s)
        and, 132
    women losing jobs (1990s), 119
Russia/Trump and election interference
    consequences, 184, 231, 263, 294
    proxies, 182–83
    Russians meeting with Trump relatives,
        184
    tactics, 182–83
    Trump's reaction/consequences, 233, 234
    Ukraine interference myth and, 232, 239,
        260, 287
    See also Mueller, Robert
Russo-Japanese war, 216

Rust Belts, 7, 97, 123, 172, 264–65, 266, 296
Rutskoi, Alexander, 278–79

St. Andrews
    advantage/privilege and, 72
    extracurricular experiences/résumés and,
        76–77
    rector position election and, 396n
    as "second choice," 75
    working-class students and (besides Hill),
        73, 76–77
St. Andrews American Foundation, 159–60
St. Andrews/Hill
    changing geographic place and, 73
    class and, 74–79, 98
    concerts/transportation, 85
    financial help, 77–78, 323–24
    financial insecurity/part-time work,
        76–79
    Gide's *La Porte Étroite* essay/incident,
        74–76
    golfer harassment incident, 78
    June, Angela, Fiona's weekend trip, 67–68
    reading/making up for limitations, 75
    rector position election and, 396n
    roommates
        Fiona Anderson, 67
        Malika, 104–5
    Russian language studies, 77, 79–87
    selecting, 62–63, 68
    sports/exercise and, 77
    Sullivan, Mr., and, 68
    UK political events during, 69–73
    university as life change, 69
    See also Moscow year/studies (Hill)
salaries
    County Durham average annual salary,
        317–18
    UK/U.S. comparison, 297n
    wages restrictions/effects (hospital and
        council workers, UK), 39
    See also gender wage gap
Salman, King of Saudi Arabia, 210
Sanders, Bernie, 183
Sawhill, Isabel ("Belle"), 144–45
Scaramucci, Anthony, 209
Scargill, Arthur, 72, 73

Science Club for Girls of Greater Boston, 313–14, 325
Scott, MacKenzie
  background, 341
  philanthropy and, 341, 347–48, 350
seal colony, Eden River Estuary, 76
September 11, 2001, terrorist attacks/effects, 256, 302
Sergei Magnitsky Act, 230
Shanahan, Patrick, 228
Shriver, Maria, 86
Silent Generation, 150
Silva, Jennifer, 155–56
slavery/slave trade, 70–71, 306
solutions. *See* creating opportunities; *specific components*
Sondland, Gordon
  background, 251
  Hill and, 261, 262
  Trump/manipulating Trump, 251, 252, 261–62
Soros conspiracy myth, 247–48
Soros, George
  anti-Semitism and, 248–49
  Open Society Foundation (OSF), 246–47
  Trump and, 242
"Soros Mole" label and Hill, 243, 245
Specials (band), 35
spring break volunteering, 360
Starks, Danica, 108
START agreement, 227
Star Trek (TV series), 40
Star Wars (film), 33, 34
Stein, Jill, 183
science, technology, engineering, and mathematics (STEM), 51, 313, 314, 325
Stent, Angela
  Aspen Ideas Festival/Blair, 101–2
  background/family background, 101, 102
  gender discrimination, 135
  Hill and, 101
Stern, Fritz, 156
Stewart, Jimmy, 110
Stockton and Darlington Railway, 31
Stone, Roger, 184, 245, 246, 247, 248, 249
Stuart, James Edward, 280
Stuart, James Francis Edward, 280

student debt, 148, 151–53, 323
Sturgeon, Nicola, 280
subsidies/tax breaks problems, 343–44
Sullivan, Mr., 68

tariffs and Trump, 173, 177, 187, 188, 189, 198, 227, 256
tax breaks/subsidies problems, 343–44
Taylor, Miles, 253
Tea Party movement (U.S.), 154, 156
Tebbit, Norman/wife, 42, 70
Teesdale Mercury, 326
Ten Pound Poms scheme, 111
Tereshkova, Valentina, 278, 279
Thatcher, Margaret
  background/family, 58–59, 100
  Carlton Club, London and, 57
  coal miners' strike (1984–1985), 72–73
  Conservative Party annual conference/IRA attack, 69–70
  consolidation/centralization of government, 346
  criticism/activism against, 35, 58–59
  cutting NHS budget, 80
  description, 57–58
  gossip about, 57–58
  government policies/economy, 7, 22–23, 30–31, 42, 58, 79, 80, 89, 95–96, 117, 118, 149, 158, 236, 291, 306–7, 319, 346
  as Iron Lady, 57
  not promoting other women, 57
  postwar safety nets/"nanny state" and, 58, 158, 181
  Soviet Union/Cold War, 98
  state housing and, 120
  unemployment and, 23, 30–31, 58
  voice lessons, 100
Thorpe, Jim, 113–14
Threads (film), 60
Tillerson, Rex
  background, 197, 231
  Russia and, 196–97, 201, 231
Tobytown, Maryland, 344–45
Today (TV show), 86
transportation
  breakthroughs following World War II and, 21

transportation (*cont.*)
  Great Lakes/coastal areas (U.S.), 21
  Hill family and, 42, 345
  Moscow, 83–84, 85
  places lacking/jobs and, 344–45
  river systems (UK), 21, 24
Travellers (UK), 32, 37, 72, 104, 162, 163, 374n
Trenin, Dmitri, 222
"Troubles, the"
  in 1984, 69–70
  Boston (U.S.) and, 105
  Conservative Party annual conference/
    IRA attack, 69–70
Trudeau, Justin, 241
Trump, Donald
  acting officials and, 241–42
  administration/walking on eggshells and,
    203
  apologies and, 202
  Apprentice, The, 187, 189, 198
  arms control/negotiator and, 197, 198–99,
    227
  authoritarianism/authoritarians and,
    219–26, 228, 232, 233
  background, 178, 179, 180, 183, 185, 277
  bankruptcies, 180
  "birtherism" conspiracy/Obama, 249
  border wall, 173
  boxing/wrestling and, 187
  bragging about shooting someone/no
    consequences, 219
  branding U.S./MAGA articles, 190
  building/construction and, 178
  as businessman, 179, 180
  campaign/white working class and,
    176–77, 179–80
  comeback plot and, 280–81, 285
  comparisons to Thatcher, 181
  Confederate-era statues/names, 224
  crediting himself/blaming others, 172,
    177–78, 181, 189, 225, 233
  cronyism, 223
  democracy and, 286–87, 288
  disinformation/weaponizing and, 247
  divisions/exploiting, 225, 226, 285, 286,
    291–92
  dynasty desires, 214, 279–80

  ego/self-obsession, 176, 178, 189–90,
    208–11, 215–17, 233, 235, 250–51, 268,
    279
  as eighties man, 197–99, 238
  election/campaign and use of any infor-
    mation, 184–85
  "elite" and, 180, 258
  environment and, 177, 216, 223
  family business methods/U.S. and,
    185–88, 190, 205, 208, 214
  flattery/attention and consequences,
    208–14
  "forgotten" people/places and, 172,
    176–77, 181
  golf/golf courses, Scotland, 171, 213, 216,
    228, 279, 280
  Hill's friends/relatives and, 179, 185
  "his judges," 274
  image/the look and, 208
  immigrants and, 173
  inaugural address, 291
  inheritance, 179
  insults against/consequences, 240–42
  labels and, 173–74
  leaving White House, 279
  lifestyle, 179–80
  loyalists and, 241, 252–53, 259, 267, 269,
    274, 275
  media attacks by, 234, 271, 275
  media ending accounts and, 276, 279
  media use/lies, 174, 186, 209, 224, 234,
    242, 262, 270, 271, 272, 274, 275–76,
    279, 350–51
  meetings details and, 229
  militias and, 224
  misogyny/women's appearance and,
    205–6, 207, 242, 253, 262
  on Mueller investigation, 184
  "nasty list"/enemies list, 209, 211, 213, 241,
    242–43, 269, 275
  Nobel Peace Prize and, 215–16
  "nonplayers" and, 207, 242, 255
  nostalgia/national heroes and, 224
  notetaking views, 205
  nuclear weapons interest, 227
  "Old Pretender"/"young pretenders"
    and, 281

"people, the" and, 176, 190, 224–25, 258, 277
presidency overview, 285
presidential election (2016) and, 176
privatization and, 223
promises/jobs and, 136, 177–78, 180–81, 285, 355
protests against, UK, 213–14
Reagan/Thatcher and, 198–99
"shows" during presidency, 187–89, 215, 268, 286
steel/aluminum workers "show" at White House, 187–89
steel/coal and, 177–78, 187–89
supporters dismissing flaws/problems, 179–80
susceptibility to influence/manipulation, 228, 238, 240, 250–51
on taxes, 223
Tea Party movement and, 154
traits/supporters' views of traits, 179–80
turnover in administration, 241–42
UK state visit/his family and, 211–14, 215
U.S. reputation/status decline with, 218, 223, 235, 258–59, 287–88
"winging it" vs. briefing material, 227–28, 229–31, 232–33, 237–38, 268–70
working mothers and, 255–56
worldview, 172–73, 184
See also coup/Trump's attempt; Helsinki summit; National Security Council/Hill; populism/populists; specific aspects
Trump, Donald, Jr., 184, 212, 252, 276, 281
Trump, Donald/Putin
authoritarianism and, 219, 223
comparisons, 221–23, 224–26
Hamburg meeting/interpreter's notes, 231
Putin flattering Trump, 210
St. Petersburg Metro terrorist attack and, 195–96, 197
supporters' similarities, 224
Syria, 200–201
See also Helsinki summit; populism/populists
Trump, Eric/Lara, 281

Trump, Ivanka
on father, 176
father praising, 215
Hill and, 196, 202, 203
Lafayette Square event and, 273
position/Trump meetings and, 200, 201, 208, 255
wardrobe/fashion and, 196, 207
women's empowerment and, 255–56
as "young pretender," 281
Tsipras, Alexis, 210–11, 241
Twitter, 5, 174, 182, 186, 209, 212, 243, 247, 275, 276, 279, 294, 295

Ukraine
Hill and, 3, 261–62
myth on U.S. election interference, 232, 239, 260, 287
Trump wanting "dirt" on Bidens and, 3, 239, 261–62
See also specific individuals
Ulukaya, Hamdi (Chobani), 350
Ungar, Sam, 1, 259, 261
United Kingdom (overview)
diversity and, 164–65
following World Wars/safety nets, 303
London diversity, 164–65
postindustrial challenges/comparing UK, U.S., USSR, 8–9, 94–98
postindustrial challenges/Russia comparison, 117–24
towns establishment/destruction, 121–22
See also specific components; specific individuals/locations
United Nations
Alfred Hill's joke, 35, 158
visiting UK, 158
visiting U.S., 158
United States (overview)
China's rising power and, 293, 310–11
crisis of opportunity, 13–14
inequality/reforming, 9–10, 13
postindustrial challenges/comparing UK, U.S., USSR, 8–9, 10, 94–98
See also specific components; specific individuals/locations

United States
 Agency for International Development,
  340
 future populists and, 287
 Postal Service, 223
 reputation/status decline with Trump,
  218, 223, 235, 258–59, 287–88
University of East Anglia Russian course
  (Norwich, England), 77
USSR
 centrally planned economy/interlinks,
  94–95
 decline/collapse of, 12, 94, 95
 disinformation/weaponizing and, 247
 "dry year"/alcohol ban, 120
 economical inflexibility, 95
 establishing/destroying cities, 122
 health care, 119
 oil and gas production, 81, 94
 perestroika, 128
 postindustrial challenges/comparing UK,
  U.S., USSR, 94–98
 private/individual aid and, 340
 survey/schoolgirls wanting to be prosti-
  tutes, 128
 See also Russia

Valdai Discussion Club, 132
Vance, J. D., 354–55
volunteering to create opportunities, 358,
  359, 360
Voting Rights Act (U.S./1965), 105

Wagon Works, Shildon, 31, 347
"Waiting for the Great Leap Forwards"
  (song), 85
Walmart, 343
Wang, Joe, 208, 229
Washington Consensus, 118
Washington Post, 2, 204
Watson, Marjorie, 88–89
Wear Valley, County Durham, 344, 345
Weber, Alfred, 52
Wellington, Duke of, 57
We're Still Here (Silva), 155–56
Westerhout, Madeleine, 202

Westover, Tara, 354, 355
"White British," 163–64, 317
white supremacists, 219, 307, 309
"White teenagers" (UK), 164
Wikipedia page, Hill, 245
Wilkerson, Isabel, 307
Williamson, Gavin, 299
wind power, 216
Winter of Discontent (1978–1979), 39
Witton Castle, 42, 208
Witton Park ironworks, 52–53
Wolosky, Lee, 1, 259, 261
Women's March (January 2017), 206
Women Who Work (Ivanka Trump), 255
Woodward, Bob/Trump tapes, 219, 226
World Bank, 118, 123, 338, 340, 341
World War II Blitz, 191–92

Xi Jinping, 220, 221

Yeltsin, Boris
 descriptions, 287
 political violence and, 278, 287
 presidency/administration, 127, 172, 221,
  224, 228
 reform programs/ "shock therapy," 117–20
Yom Kippur War, 20
Yovanovitch, Marie (Masha)
 background, 240
 calls/conspiracy theories about, 239
 demonization of public service and, 193
 as "Obama holdover," 239
 Parnas/Fruman attacks on, 240–41
 Trump firing/threats, 238, 241, 251
 as Ukraine ambassador, 238
Yudaeva, Ksenia, 132

Zakharova, Maria, 132
Zelensky, Volodymyr, 3, 241, 274, 297
Zinberg, Dorothy
 academic background, 125–26
 appearances/Hill, 126
 background, 138
 gender wage gap and, 138, 142
Zorkin, Valery, 279
Zurbarán, Francisco de, 348